Deviant Behavior

A Social Learning Approach
Second Edition

Ronald L. Akers

University of Iowa

Wadsworth Publishing Company, Inc., Belmont, California

Sociology Editor: Stephen D. Rutter

Production Editor: Catherine Aydelott

Printed in the United States of America

1 2 3 4 5 6 7 8 9 10–81 80 79 78 77

Library of Congress Cataloging in Publication Data

Akers, Ronald L
   Deviant behavior.

   Bibliography: p.
   Includes indexes.
   1. Deviant behavior. 2. Socialization. I. Title.
HM291.A42   1977   301.6′2   76-54851
ISBN 0-534-00515-2

*To my wife, Caroline; my children, Ronnie, Tami, and Levi;
and my parents, Charles and Thelma*

Contents

v

Tables

Preface to the First Edition

This book is about several types of disapproved behavior which have aroused major social concern and efforts to "do something about" them: drug use and addiction; homosexuality; prostitution; white-collar, professional, organized, and violent crimes; suicide; and mental illness. Social stigma is attached to those who have or are believed to have engaged in such behavior. Laws have been passed and formal organizations have been erected to control these types of behavior through the application of criminal penalties or through prevention and treatment programs. *Deviant behavior* is the more or less neutral term sociologists have come to use for behavior that has been the subject of such attention.

Part one, an overview of the main problems and theories of deviance, examines the central questions about deviant behavior and the ways in which sociologists have answered them. Part two introduces a *social learning theory* of deviant behavior, which the remainder of the book then applies to the principal forms of deviant behavior. The theory integrates the "differential association" explanation of sociologist Edwin H. Sutherland with the behavioral learning theories of B. F. Skinner and other psychologists. Briefly the theory says that a person learns to commit deviant acts through interaction with his (primarily social) environment. In this social setting, consequences are attached to his behavior, which *reinforce* (reward) or fail to punish deviant acts to a greater extent than they reinforce conforming behavior, and his association with others furnishes him with *definitions* that make the deviant behavior seem more desirable or justified than alternative conforming behavior.

Part three discusses drug use from the vantage point of this social learning approach. The various types of drugs and their effects are outlined, the amount and characteristics of opiate and hallucinogenic drug use are described, and observations on public policy, the law, treatment, and control are made, but the focus is on the social learning process by which persons progress into opiate addiction and the use of hallucinogenic drugs such as marihuana and LSD.

Each subsequent part discusses one type or a limited number of related types of deviant behavior and considers a social learning explanation of each form of behavior. The degree of thoroughness reflects in part how much is known about the behavior under discussion. For instance, a fairly complete and tightly reasoned process of becoming homosexual is spelled out, but the typical process of moving into prostitution is less completely explained.

In addition to offering an explanation of each type of deviance, I review the literature on its extent and variation, historical trends, other theories, controversies, and other relevant aspects of the problem. Which topics are emphasized, again, depends largely on the stage of knowledge about the form of deviance. For example, there is much information on group rates of suicide, and therefore an entire chapter (18) discusses variations in suicide rates. On the other hand, virtually nothing is said about rates of homosexual behavior because virtually nothing is known about them.

Because the book is written from an original perspective and offers explanations of deviant behavior which have not appeared in this form anywhere else, I like to think that the book contributes to the professional literature on deviant behavior. I believe that sociologists and other social scientists will find much that is of interest to them. But this is not primarily a theoretical monograph addressed only to my colleagues. Rather it is intended for use in sociology courses in social disorganization, deviant behavior, social problems, and criminology or in similar courses in psychology, education, and social work. With this in mind, I have attempted to touch on several areas that are well known to the professional but must be included to introduce the subject to the student. All the principal theoretical perspectives in the field are discussed, and with the exception of delinquency, all the major kinds of deviance are included. The topics are tied together by the consistent application of a single theoretical perspective, but each chapter can be understood on its own. The instructor will find that most material ordinarily presented in textbooks is covered here. In addition the instructor's manual will assist him in constructing objective and essay examinations on the book, preparing student projects and assignments, and selecting relevant classroom films.

I have written with the student in mind. I have tried not to compromise a complex issue or argument by oversimplifying it, but I try to state it simply. I do not talk down to the student, but I have attempted to avoid the overuse of specialized terms. I hope that the interested, motivated student will find the book challenging without being incomprehensible, understandable without being intellectually condescending. Some parts will be more easily understood by the student who has some background in sociology, and other parts by the student who has some background in psychology. However, the book should be intelligible to the reader with a minimal background in either.

Part of the book is based on my previously published work. Portions of chapter 2 are taken verbatim from "Problems in the Sociology of Deviance: Social Definitions and Behavior," *Social Forces* 46 (June 1968): 456–65. Permission from *Social Forces* (University of North Carolina Press) is gratefully acknowledged. The theory presented in chapter 4 is based on the one developed in collaboration with Robert L. Burgess, which appeared in "A Differential Association—Reinforcement Theory of Criminal Behavior," *Social Problems* 14 (Fall 1966): 128–47. Parts of chapter 6 are based on a paper written with Burgess and Weldon Johnson, which appeared as "Opiate Use, Addiction, and Relapse," *Social Problems* 15 (Spring 1968): 459–69.

My debt to Robert Burgess is only suggested by citing these collaborative efforts. It was primarily the challenge and stimulation of exchanging ideas with him that moved me to take seriously the relevance of behavioral psychology for sociology. In many respects he has been my tutor as well as my collaborator. Otto Larsen saw the possibilities in what Burgess and I were doing at an early date and was the first to suggest that we should write a book on deviant behavior using the perspective we were developing. The encouragement and support of Travis Hirschi and Rodney Stark, advisory editors for Wadsworth, were instrumental to the process and completion of the writing. Donald R. Cressey and Gerald Slatin also read the entire manuscript and Paul Friday read portions of it. I want to thank them for their excellent reviews; the book has benefited greatly from their valuable comments and constructive criticisms. I owe special thanks to Travis Hirschi, who read and thoroughly reacted to every version and revision of the manuscript from the first to the last. Whatever integrity of content and facility of style the book possesses are much the result of his tireless attention to what I wrote and how I wrote it. Beulah Reddaway and others under her direction typed several of the early drafts. Robert Mutchnick assisted me with the indexing. I am glad for the tradition which allows me to thank these people while absolving them of any responsibility for any defects and shortcomings in the book.

Finally, I am indeed happy to have the chance to record publicly my appreciation for the good-natured, if sometimes bewildered, patience with which my wife, Caroline, and my children tolerated the presence of a semi-recluse around the house during the months I worked on the manuscript. Without their faith and affection not a word would have been written.

Preface

Although it has been only four years since the first edition of *Deviant Behavior* was published, there have been significant developments in the sociology of deviance. In this revision, therefore, I have been concerned with reporting relevant new research and data and bringing the references up to date. Two other major objectives were to pay more attention to organized social definitions and reactions to deviant behavior, and to present the social learning approach to better illustrate it and its relationship to structural theories.

Pursuit of these goals resulted in concentrating the major revision in what are now the first four parts of the book: central problems and perspectives in the sociology of deviance, deviant drug use, drinking and alcohol behavior, and sexual deviance. Although I have revised all of the first edition, I have changed the last three parts on criminal behavior, suicide, and mental illness the least.

The developments in the field which have attracted the most attention are the theoretical debates; new empirical evidence; and reformulations revolving around labeling, consensus, and conflict theories, especially the more radical and Marxian versions of conflict theory. I have reviewed these in chapters 2 and 3.

Since the publication of the first edition the public has had front-page illustrations of some of the corporate crimes discussed in the chapter on white-collar crime. These high-level crimes by governmental officials, usually referred to as the Watergate crimes, and the illegal acts in various governmental agencies are instances of deviant behavior which have far-reaching effect in American society. Therefore, in chapter 18 I have added an analysis of the Watergate crimes as a type of political crime. Also, I have reviewed new findings on the extent, variation, and correlates of deviant behavior which have been reported since the first edition (especially chapters 7 and 8 on drug use, 10 and 11 on drinking, and 13, 15, and 16 on sexual behavior).

As in the first edition, the major aim of the book is the description and theoretical explanation of deviant behavior. But this edition gives much greater attention to social definitions and to forms of organized societal response to deviance: law enforcement, treatment, and prevention. Three new chapters deal solely with these issues: chapter 9 on public policy on drugs, chapter 13 on sexual norms, and chapter 17 on the control and treatment of sexual deviance. Also, my revision and expansion of the section on the aversive conditioning of alcoholism resulted in a new section in chapter 12 on alcohol control and treatment of alcoholism. The general issues of definitions and variations in suicidal behavior in chapter 22 now include discussion of suicide prevention clinics.

The social learning approach of the first edition remains the unifying theme for this edition. I have not modified my use of the theory to account for each of the types of deviant behavior because I have not altered my theoretical stance toward deviance. Therefore I have not changed the explanations, although I have revised the discussion in appropriate places to take into account new research which either confirms or challenges the social learning perspective (for example, opiate addiction in chapter 7). I have also combined what were separate chapters on Sutherland's original differential association theory and social learning theory into a single chapter (4). In the process, I have reduced the detailed discussion of differential association. I have better illustrated the social learning process in deviance by giving concrete examples from the various kinds of deviance described and analyzed in the book. These were formerly not presented until the last chapter.

While the other theoretical approaches were each critically analyzed in the first edition, the social learning approach of the first edition was presented without critique, and I did not give the connections between social learning and the other theories much more than a couple of paragraphs until the last chapter. That resulted in the impression that there was nothing to criticize about social learning, and the relationships among the theories were not made clear in the beginning. I have added a section in chapter 4 on critiques of and empirical evidence on social learning as an explanation of deviant behavior. I am obviously not the one to present a highly critical appraisal of my own approach, but I have tried to give the reader an idea of some of the criticisms of and objections to the approach. From some chapters of the first edition, including the last, I have written a separate chapter (5) to emphasize the complementary relationships between social learning and the structural theories. Most of what was the last chapter in the first edition has now been moved to earlier chapters in this edition. The concluding and summarizing chapter has been dropped.

The overall organization of the book remains the same. Part one reviews the central issues and theories in the sociology of deviance, including the social learning theory which is then applied to the principal forms of deviance examined in the remainder of the book. Each of the subsequent six parts then examines a particular type of deviance. As before, my objective has been to contribute something to the literature on deviant behavior, while keeping the student reader in mind.

I would like to acknowledge some of the people who helped with this edition: Paul Friday of Western Michigan University, who made valuable evaluations of the first and second editions, knows how much I appreciate his efforts to make both the original and revised editions theoretically sound and integrated; nonetheless I welcome the chance to acknowledge publicly my debt to him. I am also grateful to Mary Booth, Grossmont College; Morris A. Forslund, University of Wyoming; James E. Gallagher, University of Maine at Orono; Clarence Schultz, Southwest Texas State University; and Jon Turner, Grossmont College, each of whom read and evaluated every portion of the revision. This edition owes much to their insightful and learned comments and suggestions. I appreciate very much the fine job of indexing done by Marcia Radosevich and Lonn Lanza-Kaduce. My thanks to these people does not, of course, place any responsibility on them for any inadequacies or failures in the revision, for which I alone am accountable.

I also take this opportunity to thank again those who helped with the first edition. I especially want to thank my wife, Caroline, and my children for their patience and support during all those times when my work on the book meant they simply did without a husband and dad.

Part One	*Central Problems and Perspectives in the Sociology of Deviance*

Chapter Four

*A Social Learning Perspective on
Deviant Behavior   39*

1

Basic Concepts and Issues:
Deviant Behavior and Social Control

Billy M., a seventeen-year-old who lives in the black ghetto of New York, has been using drugs off and on since he was thirteen. For the past year he has been addicted to heroin, which he buys from the local connection and sometimes mixes with a little cocaine when he can get it. He now spends about $40 a day on his habit. Taking money from his mother's purse, snitching at the corner store, and bumming money from friends stopped bringing in enough long ago, so Billy now burglarizes houses, spends many hours shoplifting, and tries to accumulate enough money to buy more drugs than he needs so that he can "deal" the rest to others. He spent some time in the juvenile detention center and once stayed six months in a "training school" for delinquent boys, but he has not yet been arrested on a drug or theft charge. If he is, he will be tried by an adult court and will be subject to imprisonment.

Joe L. is a thirty-six-year-old father of three children; he has been married for fifteen years and provides well for his wife and family. He is buying a nice home in the suburbs, he owns a decent old car and is buying a new one, and he belongs to a number of social clubs. Joe is a middle-level executive in the accounting department of a large merchandising firm. For the past three years he has embezzled company funds to supplement his salary, which is inadequate to cover all the payments and dues. He does not take much at a time, but since he started he has taken almost $18,000. He knows he has no way of replacing the money, and it is just a matter of time until he is caught.

Marilyn C. is twenty-two. As a teenager in a small town she had little chance to date boys, and the dates she had were not very satisfying. She could not forget her mother's warnings about the terrible things boys try to do to girls. When she was twenty she moved to the city, got a job, and became friendly with a woman who lived down the hall in the apartment house. She found herself growing more than just fond of the woman, and once when she was spending the night with her friend, what started as gentle caresses ended in passionate kissing and mutual masturbation.

Since then she has engaged in sexual relations with a number of women and spends more and more of her evenings in a "gay" bar. She has dated men and has even had coitus with a couple of them, but these relationships were not as satisfactory as her affairs with women. She is not sure that she is completely homosexual, and it bothers her that she is doing something she knows others abhor. But as time passes she adjusts to the idea and finds herself enjoying homosexual relationships more.

Colman C. is a fifty-five-year-old senior executive of a multinational corporation. In the last presidential election in the United States he illegally contributed $150,000 of corporate funds to the Republican candidate and $35,000 to the Democratic candidate. He has also bribed officials and businessmen in foreign countries to obtain important governmental and private contracts for his company. In at least one foreign country his company used its influence and money to help "friendly" candidates for government offices. He was called to testify before a senate investigation committee and legal action is pending against him and others high in his company's corporate structure. He pointed out to the senators and believes strongly that nothing he has done in other countries violates American law. While he admits that the campaign contributions were technically illegal, he does not consider them wrong. Everything he did was in the interest of maintaining stable business relations and a good climate for his business around the world.

Ron H. is a thirty-year-old construction worker who has been unemployed for most of the last three years. Last year his chronic complaints about a "bad back" and his wife's behavior with men at the cocktail lounge where she is a waitress got worse. He turned down one job offer and left another job after a week because he "just didn't feel good." Seven months ago he had another violent fight with his wife before she went to work, accusing her of sleeping with many of her customers. He knew she was because a mark on her forehead, visible only to him, appeared every time she did it. He followed her to work, slapped her around, broke some chairs, and fought with the bartender and a customer. He was arrested, but upon petition of his wife (who said she "couldn't take his crazy behavior anymore") he was found mentally incompetent by the county lunacy board and was committed to the state mental hospital, where he has been for the last three months, diagnosed by the psychiatrist as a "paranoid schizophrenic" with "secondary psychophysiological symptomatology."

Similar profiles[1] could be drawn for the alcoholic, the speed freak, the marihuana smoker, the professional thief, the Mafia boss, the murderer, the prostitute, and the homosexual. These people illustrate the subject of this book, deviant behavior—that is, they have all behaved in ways considered unacceptable by many in society or by a few who are in a position to judge them.

---

[1] The profiles used as examples are not individual cases of living persons; rather, they are hypothetical, composite illustrations.

However, we are not concerned with what is unique in individual cases such as these. Rather, we wish to locate general patterns among the many separate cases and facts about deviance. Indeed, if one wants, as social scientists do, to explain deviant behavior, he must try to see the broader structures and processes. The social scientist must formulate the explanation carefully, must locate and use information (data) responsibly, must verify the explanation, and must know what other objective observers have to say about the problem. The knowledge gained in this way is indispensable to whatever action one believes is needed. It matters little whether one wants to curtail deviance, to increase it, or to change public policy related to it; the starting point is systematic knowledge gained through competent research and careful analysis.

Why is Billy an addict? Why does Colman break the law? Why are there so many Billies and so few Joes in the lower-class slums of big cities? How did society decide that Marilyn's choice of partners for sexual intercourse should be outlawed? How does society react to Ron, and why is his treatment different from the treatment accorded Billy? These and similar questions have concerned citizens and social scientists for a long time. The sociologist organizes his efforts to answer these questions around the study of three interrelated phases of one process: (1) the establishment of social *norms* of right, correct, or expected behavior; (2) deviation from or violation of those expectations by groups and individuals in society; and (3) the *reactions* of other groups, individuals, and control agencies to such deviation. The second part of this process, *deviant behavior*, has commanded the most attention from social scientists and receives the most attention in this book. However, we do not lose sight of the first and third problems, which together comprise *social control*.

Social Control

Social norms are group-supported definitions of expected behavior in specified situations. Normative expectations—definitions of right and wrong, standards of conduct, and rules and regulations—evolve out of social interaction. These in turn form the basis for ordering interaction, something like the rules of a game or the script of a drama. When these expectations are not met too frequently, or when conformity to them becomes completely unpredictable, then orderly interaction begins to break down. Whether or not the nonconformity and disruption of order are desirable is also a question of normative definitions. If one has a stake in the established normative system, nonconformity is a serious problem. But one who is alienated from that system may see widespread or conspicuous nonconformity as a desirable mechanism whereby valuable social change can be effected.

Every society and group has a set of social norms, some applying to everyone in the system, some to almost everyone, and others only to persons in particular age, sex, class, ethnic, or religious categories. Some norms apply to a wide range of situations; others govern specific situations. In a heterogeneous society different systems of normative standards exist side by side, and one may automatically violate the expectations of one group simply by conforming to those of another. This means that to talk meaningfully about deviant behavior one must specify within what system and from whose norms the deviation occurs (Cohen 1966:12–15). The picture is complicated by the fact that the normative system contains what could be called real and ideal, operative and idealistic, or minimum and maximum expectations. That is, most people in a social system are aware of and can recite what one should do or say in a given situation, but they are also aware that there are more realistic standards and limits within which behavior is still acceptable, even though it does not come up to the ideal.

Social control refers to the formal and informal ways society has developed to help ensure conformity to the norms. Social *sanctions* are central to social control. Sanctions are positive (meant to be rewarding) or negative (meant to be punishing) reactions to behavior. (They may also be applied to the possession of certain physical characteristics.) Conforming behavior is met with positive sanctions, and nonconforming behavior is met with negative sanctions. The sanctioning varies from mild to extreme expressions of approval or disapproval: a pat on the back, a smile, a nod of assurance, a word of praise, monetary reward, public recognition, awards; or ridicule, denial of affection, stripping of status, physical and capital punishment.

When sanctions are applied directly in response to a person's behavior we say that *external control* has been exerted. Over time sanctioning behavior may lead to the development of *self-control*. By being subjected to social sanctions in conjunction with verbal and behavioral examples beginning in childhood, the individual learns from his parents, peers, and others what are considered the right and wrong things to say and do in a variety of contexts. As he matures he learns the cultural expectations (rights and obligations) which go along with the age, sex, marital, occupational, and other social roles he takes on throughout his life. He comes to conform to the rules on his own and applies sanctions to himself just as others would. Even when he is alone he behaves as if others were present to apply sanctions. Or when others are present he behaves as if they have applied sanctions, even though they have not and do not. The process whereby a person takes as his own the ideas of right and wrong shared by others is *socialization*.

After the initial period of socialization most people conform by controlling their own behavior without further directly applied sanctions. Every social system relies to a considerable degree on socialization to develop self-control among the population. But control continues to be exerted through the application of direct external sanctions. Therefore, when someone violates the rules, even after he has undergone the relevant socialization, there is some chance that external sanctions will follow. The prime mechanism in controlling behavior then is the external application of sanctions. Rewarding proper and punishing improper behavior not only corrects the person's conduct at a given time but also acquaints him with what is expected and helps teach him to direct his own behavior.

Deviant Behavior

Behavior may be socially approved, tolerated, or disapproved, and these social judgments provide the criteria by which we determine what is conforming or deviant. Thus the nature of the act—deviant or conforming—is a matter of social definition. The sociologist defines deviant behavior by observing the operation of social control in a social system. Observation of social control in societies around the world and through time has revealed that although all social systems have definitions which select some actions and stamp them as deviant, there is great variation in which behavior is singled out. Behavior that is considered right or a matter of moral obligation in one society may be considered wrong or of no consequence in another society (Edgerton 1976). Within the same society, behavior that is considered wrong at one time may be considered right at another time. In American society, for instance, the social definitions of both smoking marihuana and smoking tobacco have changed over time. Once severely condemned by almost all groups and strongly controlled by law, marihuana use is becoming increasingly acceptable to and tolerated by broad segments of society. Cigarette smoking was once considered evil. Cigarette sales to adults were banned in fourteen states and sales to minors banned in all states. By World War II cigarette smoking had become not only acceptable but socially desirable for adults. In the last decade, cigarette smoking has again undergone redefinition. It is unpopular now, this time in consideration of our health. Cigarette smoking is being increasingly regulated and is coming to be considered deviant, although not criminal (Nuehring and Markle 1974).

In defining deviance, the sociologist starts with the assumption that there are no absolute categories of inherently deviant behavior and that all human behavior is natural. No behavior is intrinsically unnatural or deviant, but only so in relation to social definitions which can vary by time and place. This assumption has sometimes been interpreted as a denial that consensus can form around any norm. However, the idea that no behavior is inherently deviant does not mean that we should deny the regularities and patterns within a society or across cultures (Lemert 1972; Goode 1975). Indeed, there are some actions defined as and still considered to be deviant by most societies (Edgerton 1976). For example, research reveals that there is strong agreement within American society across class, sex, race, age, and other group lines and considerable consensus across societies on both the criminality and relative seriousness of theft and personal violence (Wellford 1975; Rossi et al. 1974; Thomas et al. 1976; Pease et al. 1975). Other research shows that even though views of some acts as deviant do vary by situational factors, there is considerable stability in the relative disapproval of some acts from one situation to another (Orcutt 1975). Some actions, such as unprovoked and capricious violence against innocent victims and indiscriminate sexual behavior, seem always and everywhere to be considered deviant.

Note, however, there has not been complete consensus for any of these acts, and all have been tolerated by subgroups within societies. Moreover, ideas vary about what actually constitutes the "wrong" behavior (capricious violence or promiscuous sexual behavior, for example). Murder may be condemned by almost everyone as criminal, but whether a particular instance of taking a life is defined as murder varies considerably. It depends, for instance, upon whether or not the victim is a member of an out-group defined as the enemy, or whether or not the victim "deserves" death. One group's terrorist acts of murder against innocent persons are another's justifiable tactics of freedom fighting. Finally, it should be remembered that even when there is agreement that something is wrong, there may be strong disagreement over what to do about it (for example, capital punishment or imprisonment).

Thus, the notion that deviance is not in the quality of the act does not mean that there will always be disagreement about it. It does not mean that there are never real harmful consequences of some acts which make most people in most societies consider them wrong most of the time. It means only that there is no necessary relationship between the nature of the act itself and whether people see it as good or bad, right or wrong. Lack of consensus on some norms does not mean that there is no consensus on any norms. At the same time, consensus that some behavior is deviant means only that there is normative agreement among members of society; it says nothing about the intrinsic qualities of the behavior itself or of the people who engage in it. Ultimately it is how the behavior and people are regarded by society which leads the sociologist to regard them as deviant.

In the most general sense, then, the sociologist defines deviant behavior as that which deviates from or violates one or a set of social norms, whatever these may be (Cohen 1959:462). Deviance in this very general sense includes a great many acts, most of which are mildly punished, or just disapprovingly tolerated even when they occur in public with many witnesses. Examples are the loud-mouthed bore at a party, violations of manners and etiquette, and so on.

One Sunday morning at the Methodist church in a college town, a young man suddenly stood up while the minister was speaking and loudly booed him. Whatever the motivation (he did it to meet a challenge by his sociology professor), the boo elicited only turned heads, subdued murmurs, looks of disapproval, and some laughter. The minister said with a chuckle that sometimes he felt like booing himself, and moved on to another topic. No one scolded the student who booed, there was no organized response to him, and no one attempted to sanction him during or after services. Few can deny that while booing is acceptable public behavior at a sporting event, it violates the social expectations regarding how one behaves in church. Many would also consider the professor's challenge to do so to be a violation of the norms governing his teaching role. But in the cases of the student and the professor, their deviance does not elicit broad social concern and ordinarily does not result in organized societal reaction. Actions which could be called deviant in this very general sense are not included in the meaning of deviant behavior used in this book. Rather, the term is used here in a much more restricted sense.

One may deviate by doing more than is expected, by being more upstanding and more moral or by going further in the approved direction than is necessary to stay within the bounds of conformity. The father who is extremely devoted to his wife and family, the soldier who is valiant above and beyond the call of duty, the child who never gives her parents any trouble may be deviating from the norms applying to their roles. But this type of deviation is more likely to be rewarded or applauded than to be punished. Negative reactions, if any, are likely to be envy or jealousy. Deviation in an approved direction is not included in our conception of deviance here and is usually not considered subject matter for the study of deviant behavior.

We consider here only behavior which deviates in a disapproved direction. More specifically, attention is directed primarily to instances of *disapproved behavior considered serious enough to warrant major societal efforts to control them, using strong negative sanctions or treatment-corrective techniques.*[2] This does not imply that there is complete consensus on the undesirability of all kinds of deviant behavior included here. Each continues to generate controversy over its definition as a serious deviation warranting some effort to control it. Rather, this conception implies that we examine only behavior that departs from norms held by large or socially, economically, and politically powerful segments of American society.

Organized Social Reaction to Deviance in American Society

To gain some idea of what behavior exceeds the tolerance limits in a social system, we can observe how it is defined and related to by those who support this normative system. We can see that major concern about certain kinds of deviance has been expressed by large or powerful elements of society when: laws are passed; programs are initiated; money, time and personnel are allocated; and organizations are created to combat or control the occurrence of specified behavior or to punish, treat, or "cure" those who engage in it. All of the major kinds of behavior that are examined in this

---

[2]See the discussion of sociological definitions of deviant behavior in Gibbons and Jones 1975:42–51 and Sagarin 1975:1–62.

book meet this criterion. Surveys of public definition and reaction provide additional evidence for the legitimacy of considering most of them deviant in American society (Rooney and Gibbons 1966; Simmons 1965).

Much of what we call *deviant behavior* is also criminal in the legal sense, either directly or indirectly. Homicide, suicide, embezzlement, underage drinking, assault, activities of organized criminals, and so on are directly forbidden by law. Alcoholism and heavy drinking are not illegal, but being drunk in public may be illegal (although several states no longer treat public drunkenness as a criminal offense and now allow detoxification and treatment as alternatives to imprisonment). Drug addiction is not itself illegal, but frequent use of or addiction to drugs almost guarantees that the laws against illegal possession of drugs will be violated. Marihuana smoking is not illegal itself, and possession of small amounts of marihuana for personal use has now been effectively decriminalized in several states. But using marihuana is still widely considered deviant and a person who possesses it in sufficient quantities is still subject to criminal penalties. Moreover, deviant behavior which is not directly illegal, such as drug addiction, is more likely to result in criminal prosecution than are some kinds of specifically illegal acts (such as adultery).

Thus, we will study the varieties of deviant behavior here with some attention to organized public-governmental or private reactions to them. These reactions tend to take on one or both of two major forms: (1) *law enforcement*, making and enforcing laws to control, regulate, deter, or prevent the occurrence of the deviant behavior; and (2) prevention or *treatment*, which involves setting up programs to change the social conditions that are believed to cause deviant behavior, and rehabilitating people defined as wayward deviants into conforming society. Law enforcement is always a matter of public policy; treatment is often in the hands of private specialists and professionals. The criminal justice system is coercive; treatment is often offered on a totally voluntary basis to people who define themselves as deviants needing change.

However, the distinction between law enforcement and treatment should not be drawn too severely. Treatment often is mandated by public policy either directly through existing institutions or through the formation of governmentally operated facilities. It can also operate through support of private efforts by grants of public monies. When what is called "treatment" is coercively applied to unwilling, nonvoluntary "patients," then it becomes indistinguishable from legal penalty (for example, the commitment of those judged mentally incompetent, or the forced enrollment of an alcoholic in a treatment program as part of the conditions of probation set by a judge). One aspect of our interest in the sociology of deviance, then, is the description and understanding of law enforcement and treatment directed toward those acts and people defined as deviant.

2

Perspectives on Social Definitions and Reactions

In chapter 1 we saw that the sociology of deviance is concerned with the whole process of norms→deviation→reactions – that is, the sociologist wants to examine and to explain not only norm violation but also norm making and enforcing. Thus two central problems need to be studied: (1) *social definitions* (and reactions) – how and why certain kinds of behavior and people become defined and reacted to as deviant; and (2) *deviant behavior* – how and why some people come to engage in actions or acquire the characteristics defined as deviant.

Accounting for Social Definitions: Consensus and Conflict

In the broadest sense, the explanation of social definitions is an explanation of why groups and societies have the values and norms they do. Why is some conduct considered deviant and some not considered deviant? In a narrower sense, questions such as these can be raised: By what process did some members of American society come to define Billy's addiction (to use the profiles in the previous chapter) as unworthy behavior? Was there ever a time when taking money from someone who has freely entrusted it to you, as Joe did, was not a crime? How and when did it become a crime? How is it decided and who decides that an action is deviant and that the resources of the public and state will be brought to bear against it? Accounting for social definitions involves proposing answers to these kinds of questions.

There are two basic approaches to answering these questions: One is the assumption that social control reflects some broad normative *consensus* in society. Other explanations suggest group *conflict* (Chambliss and Seidman 1971:17, 40–52; Hills 1971:3–4).

Consensus Model

The consensus model was dominant in sociology until two decades ago and is represented mainly by the writings of late nineteenth and early twentieth century sociologists and legal scholars (Sumner 1906; Ross 1901; Pound 1942; Ehrlich 1936). In this view there is society-wide normative consensus and public policy reflects this consensus. The traditional view of it is exemplified in the work of the nineteenth-century sociologist, William Graham Sumner. Sumner (1906) saw prevailing "folkways and mores" in society — unorganized, intuitive standards of right and wrong which have gradually developed over a long period of time and to which all segments of society subscribe. Legislation *expresses* these mores — it does not readily *change* them. Many conflict theorists continue to criticize this consensus model as the major sociological view today. In fact, it is no longer a major current perspective on social definitions. However, one version of consensus theory has some present-day adherents. It is the theory that certain kinds of behavior are defined as deviant because if left uncontrolled they would disrupt orderly society. Because therefore it is in everyone's interest to control these kinds of behavior, there is considerable agreement throughout society on norms regulating behavior in a way that is *functional* for the whole society (Davis 1966:324–50; Wellford 1975).

Conflict Model

The dominant sociological view today is one version or another of a *conflict* approach. Rather than seeing an overall unity or consensus in society, conflict theories start with the heterogeneity, diversity, and lack of uniformity in modern society. Various groups in society support values and interests that may be conflicting or incompatible with those of other groups so that the pursuit of an interest by one group hampers or interferes with the pursuit of other values by another group. This means that one group is considered deviant by another group, but it does not mean that the rival groups are internally disorganized. Also, it does not mean that overall social organization is weakened: "In the conflict model . . . we find that societies and social organizations are shaped by diversity, coercion, and change. . . . In other words, society is held together by force and constraint and is characterized by ubiquitous conflicts that result in continuous change" (Quinney 1970:9–10).

The more powerful the group supporting a normative stance is, the more likely it is that this position will become established and that the group will not be defined as deviant by others (Vold 1958; Chambliss 1969; 1975; Chambliss and Seidman 1971; Quinney 1970; Turk 1969).

Characterizing the two models in such an unqualified way is somewhat misleading, however, because the difference is mainly one of emphasis. The earlier theorists who stressed that law is the formal enactment of widely held norms and is aimed toward overall societal purposes also recognized that law is often the enactment of only the norms and interests of specific groups (Ball and Simpson 1962; Sumner 1906:39, 55, 169, 209). Similarly those who take a basically conflict approach may also note that some laws are based on general consensual norms (Chambliss 1969).

In one sense all conflict approaches are intellectual descendants of the thoughts of Karl Marx, the nineteenth-century philosopher who formulated the basic tenets of communism. Marx's communism was both a critical theory of capitalist society as ruled by the bourgeois class, and the philosophical basis for the "classless" communist society which is supposed to overrule it. Until recently, however, conflict theory has gone beyond class conflict to interest-group conflict of all kinds and has had more similarity to political–interest-group theory, or a *pluralistic* model of society. In this model, society is comprised of working arrangements, balancing of forces, and contending groups "in a shifting but dynamic equilibrium of opposing group interests and efforts" (Vold 1958:204). The *pluralistic conflict* approach proposes that there are many different groups with varying amounts of power, which are successful on certain issues and not on others, and none of which is all-powerful. Powerless groups may not have much impact on any issue but there are a variety of power centers rather than a monolithic, all-powerful elite group (Rose 1967; Quinney 1970:32–43). Several conflict theorists, however, have now gone back to the Marxist *power-elite* conception of a two-class society with a ruling class controlling the legal, political, economic, and other systems to promote its own interest. A major example of this theoretical development in the sociology of deviance is found in the work of Richard Quinney.

Quinney (1970) has been a major spokesman for a conflict perspective on group interests and power in the formulation, interpretation, and administration of law from an essentially pluralistic viewpoint. But his latest writings have rejected this view, and his theory is now a self-proclaimed Marxian model of class domination. Although he recognizes some diversity of interest and some relatively unimportant conflict among its members, Quinney argues that a ruling class has achieved complete control of society and uses the legal system and other mechanisms of defining and apprehending deviants only to its own interests. The real conflict, then, is between the ruling class and all the others who are either victims of repression or lackeys of the power elite. This ruling class is said to be characteristic of capitalistic societies, especially the United States. The principal interest for the ruling class is the existing repressive capitalist order. The only answer to this repression is to establish a "socialist" system (Quinney 1974a; 1974b; 1975).

Much of what Quinney and others present as a Marxian model of the formation of social definitions and control of deviance is primarily repetition of Marxist ideology presented as self-evident truth and a call to change the system. As such, the model is not empirically testable and should be compared to rival social-political ideologies such as liberalism, democratic socialism, and other rival visions of utopia. Because it *judges* the system, it cannot legitimately be compared with sociological theories which attempt to *explain* the system as it is. For such a comparison to be valid, the power-elite model would have to be compared empirically with alternative theories, where basic contentions are presented as hypotheses to be tested.

For instance, one could test the notion that there is a cohesive ruling class in America which determines the content and operation of the law to promote its own interest. Some data have been collected showing a concentration of wealth in American society, and Quinney (1974a) has assembled data on the composition of national commissions on crime and violence that have overlapping membership of wealthy, prominent, and powerful people. These data do not show, however, that there is a single ruling elite (as contrasted with the pluralist model of several elites and power centers) who directs the law and against whom the law is never applied. Several of the men listed by Quinney as in the power elite, for instance, have subsequently been convicted for offenses related to Watergate. Also, the data do not demonstrate that what is defined as deviant and the actions taken against deviant behavior serve only the interest of that elite.

Testing the idea that a repressive, self-serving power elite is mainly found in capitalistic societies requires some detailed cross-cultural and historical comparisons with real (not idealized versions of) noncapitalistic societies. Such cross-cultural comparisons are sometimes dismissed as superfluous (Wolfe 1973). It is difficult to see how such studies would support the idea that in democratic systems such as the United States there is a power elite with tighter and more repressive control than the rulers have in systems such as the Soviet Union, for example. Whatever the merits of Marxist philosophy, societies modeled on it have, in fact, developed privileged elites and have been invariably totalitarian and repressive.

Mintz et al. (1976) have commented on the "problems of proof in elite research," and this discussion is only suggestive of the sort of research that would have to be done and what might be concluded from it. There are several studies which allow testing the relative empirical validity of a general pluralistic conflict model and the consensus model. We now turn to a consideration of them.

Empirical Validity of Consensus and Conflict

First, there are studies of groups and interests involved in legislation, administration, and court decision making in both the historical and contemporary formation of public policy. These studies have covered the formation of policy on theft, vagrancy, alcohol, prostitution, drugs, smoking and other issues of public policy on the definition and control of deviant behavior. The preponderance of evidence from these studies supports the conflict model. The interests that become involved in policy formation may be those of dominant social classes, geographical regions, labor, business, farm, religious, professional and other organized pressure groups, and even governmental agencies themselves. (See the review of research and reprinted studies in Akers and Hawkins 1975:41–108.)

Second, there are studies of public opinion and normative sentiment regarding various forms of behavior. These gauge opinion on whether acts are desirable or undesirable but also measure how seriously deviant some acts are judged. There is a very strong consensus in American society, cutting across class, age, sex, educational, racial, and regional divisions on the deviance and seriousness ranking of those acts which have traditionally been part of the criminal law such as murder, assault, rape, robbery, and theft. Virtually everyone rates violent personal crimes as the most serious ones. Moreover, there is an amazing cross-cultural similarity in the level of seriousness at which these acts are ranked. There is less agreement within and across societies on the desirability of and need for outlawing such things as drugs, abortion, and dissent from government policy (Newman 1974; Thomas et al. 1976; Wellford 1975; Pease et al. 1975). These findings support a consensus model regarding some behavior and norms such as violent and personal crimes, and a conflict model regarding others.

The third type of relevant study is of the application of law against those identified as deviant. The conflict model would predict that the less powerful people would more likely be arrested, prosecuted, convicted, and given more severe penalties for the same offense than the more powerful. In concrete terms this means conflict theorists propose that the law is not applied on the basis of behavior and other relevant legal factors; instead, the police, courts, and the rest of the criminal justice system discriminate on the basis of race, class, sex, age, and other social characteristics of suspects and defendants (Chambliss and Seidman 1971).

Racial and class discrimination by the criminal justice system has been observed for some time, but good research on the issue is fairly recent. Several studies have now been done on the issue for both juvenile and adult populations. Some studies show discrimination (Hall and Simkus 1975; Petersen and Friday 1975) — that the social characteristics of offenders do affect judgments about the offenders. Nevertheless, judgments about offenders are also strongly affected by the seriousness of the deviant acts of which they are accused or convicted. Moreover, the relationships of factors such as race and class to police decisions to arrest, to court decisions regarding guilt and sentencing, and to length of time in prison tend to reduce greatly when legal variables such as seriousness of offense and prior criminal record are controlled. Those variables which remain important are not directly indicators of race or class, but rather include such situational behavior as the demeanor of the suspect and the wishes of the complainants or victims. (See the reviews of many of these studies in Hindelang 1969; Hagan 1973; Wellford 1975; Akers and Hawkins 1975:109–46; and Gibbons 1976:38–43.)

Almost all of this research has been done since 1960, and it may be that at one time discrimination in the system was so rampant and obvious that no research beyond casual observation was needed to uncover it. With the advent of the civil rights movement and Supreme Court decisions supporting civil liberties, the control agents may have become so sensitive to discrimination that they changed, doing everything possible to avoid decisions on other than strictly legal grounds. It could be then that by the time careful research was done, the system had been changed. Whatever the reason, while instances of discrimination are still observed, on the whole now people charged with the same offense (particularly if it is a serious offense) and with the same criminal background are treated in the criminal justice system much the same whatever their race, class, sex, or age.

My judgment of the empirical evidence is that there is little support at this time for a narrow power-elite conception of the way social definitions are constructed and applied. Also, a modified pluralistic conflict theory fits reality more closely than a model which sees most or all laws coming from and operating in the interests of a broad normative consensus in society. In a politically organized society, the establishment of official policy defining deviance and the appropriate reaction to it is accomplished through the same political process by which any public policy is formed. But in a democratic society where the people have collective power and majority rule and consent of the governed are central values, that political process is not one of monolithic control by a ruling class.

Public Policy through Pluralistic Conflict

The political process in democratic society does include the activity of competing interest groups attempting to register their desires and values on and through the legislature and government. In this conflict, those groups with more power, that is, that are better organized, have more resources, or greater numbers, will be the winners. Therefore, to a great extent the law incorporates and the official enforcement machinery carries out the norms and dictates of the dominant and politically successful elements in society. To play a part in the formulation and administration of public policy, the interest groups need not act directly as pressure groups; they can influence indirectly as reference groups. Public officials may make decisions based on a moral or political perspective derived from reference groups — the social groups with which they identify and to which they refer for their view of the world. A reform legislator, a crusading prosecutor, a conscientious policeman, and an upright judge who act according to the interest or value systems with which they identify and who carry out policy congruent with that system need no—indeed would probably resent and resist—direct pressure from the groups in whose interests they act.

Admitting the importance of power and conflict, however, does not deny consensus and the broad public interest in the mixture of influences on the law. Clearly, public policy derives from both the norms for which there is widespread support and the norms supported primarily by certain social, political, and economic groups in society. Therefore, the explanation which best accounts for social definitions of deviancy uses both the functional-consensus and pluralistic-conflict arguments. Society has norms for which there is wide support and majority agreement, although not a total consensus, that prevails among virtually all subgroups in society. This sort of evidence suggests that at least some norms serve societal functions, but there are alternate ways of serving the same function, and the solution is often arrived at through conflict. Although the politically dominant subgroups of society can make public policy to a great extent reflect their interest, the law also reflects the past, current, and changing functions of the whole society. Important as they are, group pressures form only a part of the total political process. Not all legislation and public decisions are entirely the outgrowth of the compromises and victories of identifiable group interests; at least a core of public policy grows out of and supports widely held values and protects the whole society.

That core of consensual values is most clearly seen in the almost universal condemnation in modern society of personal violence, destruction of property, fraud, and other forms of predatory crimes against unwilling victims. These values are embodied in the criminal legal codes, and the criminal law is designed to protect the lives and property of everyone. There also tends to be little conflict on the need for legal regulation of commerce, public health and safety, and the flow of traffic on public roads. The laws designed to protect the environment, control pollution, limit the depletion of natural resources, and deal with other ecological problems clearly are to the benefit of the whole society. Nevertheless, in each of these areas there remains considerable disagreement over the most effective and proper means of handling the problem or over what are the proper sanctions for violation of the law. While there is little dispute that murder is wrong and a serious offense, for instance, there is disagreement on whether or not capital punishment is the best way for society to punish it. Moreover, in a modern, heterogeneous society, the normative consensus that does exist seems not to go much beyond those just mentioned. What constitutes deviant sexual behavior, the undesirability of certain forms of drug taking, the morality of abortion, and other "moral" issues are common examples of areas where there is not much agreement either on what should be defined as deviant or on how severely it should be punished. For example, at this writing, a bill to outlaw all exchange of sexual favors for money *and* a bill to legalize prostitution are both being considered in the *same* legislative session in Iowa.

The extent to which policy relating to a specific form of deviance represents the outcome of group conflict is a question that ultimately must be answered through research on the formulation of that policy. However, the more restricted the population to which the policy refers and the less visible the outcome, the more the policy is likely to be subjected to direct pressure from interest groups. The closer the law comes to reflecting widespread moral sentiment, the more difficult it is to attribute its existence to the influence of specified groups (Akers 1968b). Of course, a group or coalition may and often does attempt to sway public sentiments, to increase the amount of agreement that a given act is abhorrent and should not go unpunished. By the same token, a group that champions a cause that is consistent with existing mores and folkways has an increased chance of success. Finally, note that much current policy, which now reflects the moral concerns of nearly all segments of society, at one time was the subject of heated controversy among narrower interests.

Similar statements could be made about the less formal process of establishing extralegal definitions of deviant behavior and the application of sanctions to its occurrence by more informal social audiences than those connected with the formulation and implementation of the law.

Summary

The central problems in the sociology of deviance are: (1) How and why do certain kinds of behavior and people become defined and reacted to as deviant? Answering this question includes the study of (a) the establishment of rules, definitions, norms, and laws, the infraction of which constitutes deviant behavior, and (b) reaction to people who have or are believed to have violated the norms. (2) How and why do some people come to engage in actions or acquire the characteristics defined as deviant?

The first question has been addressed in this chapter mainly by analyzing the consensus and conflict models of the formation of prevailing social definitions of deviance and the operation of the control system. The conflict perspective includes both a pluralistic and a power-elite version. Studies of the enactment of public policy, the operation of the criminal justice system, and public opinion lend more support to a pluralistic conflict model. That is, considerable agreement is found on a core of social norms. Beyond those consensual values, groups conflict over differing interests. Differences in group power largely determine which interests become paramount.

The second question has to do with the cause of deviant behavior. In the next chapter the major structural theories of deviant behavior will be presented.

3

Structural Perspectives on Deviant Behavior

Structure and Process in
Accounting for Deviant Behavior

Attempts to explain deviant behavior have been addressed to two interrelated problems: (a) accounting for group and structural variations in rates of deviancy and (b) describing and explaining the process by which individuals come to commit deviant acts. The first problem is the one of trying to make sense of the differences in the location and amount of deviant behavior in various groups, such as those defined by social class, age, sex, race, religion, and ethnic status. The second problem means asking how a person *typically* (not just in a specific case) moves from nonaddict to addict, from drinker to chronic drunk, from straight to gay, or from obedience to violation of the law.

Cressey (1960) calls the two problems *epidemiology* and *individual conduct* respectively. Others discuss the first problem as sociological and the second as psychological (Cohen 1959:461; 1966:41–47). We will most often refer to them as *structural* and *processual*; explanations of group rates are structural and accounts of movement into deviance are processual. But whatever terms one uses, the twin problems of explaining the differential location of deviance and deviants in the social structure and how individuals come to behave deviantly are the central concerns of theories of deviance.

No theory is exclusively structural or processual, because in the final analysis all theories propose answers to the same question: Why do some people commit deviant acts and others do not? Whether a theory is structural or processual then depends on *emphasis*. The major thrust of structural theories is the contention that more people in certain groups or classes will engage in deviancy than those in other groups. This contention carries with it implicit or explicit assumptions or propositions about the processes by which these structural conditions produce higher probabilities of deviant behavior. The burden of processual theories is carried by the assertion that the individual commits deviancy because he has encountered a particular life history. But this also says something about the deviancy-producing groups, structures, and circumstances the individual must encounter to increase the probability of his becoming or remaining deviant.

An extension and reformulation of Sutherland's (1947) "differential association theory," the major processual theory of deviant behavior, will be presented in the following chapters and will serve as the basic framework for the rest of the book.[1] The other major perspectives in the field will be reviewed in the remainder of this chapter. They are primarily structural in emphasis — that is, they are concerned mainly with the kinds of structures and environments that produce certain kinds and rates of deviance. The *social disorganization-anomie theories* and the *conflict theory,* presented first, clearly carry this emphasis. The theories presented next, *labeling* and *social control theories,* are more mixed; they lean toward deviance-producing structures but also have a noticeable concern with individual selection into deviancy. The important contribution of each is to deviant etiology, but the conflict and labeling perspectives also have something to say about social definitions.

Social Disorganization and Anomie

A social system is described as organized if there is internal consensus on consistent norms and values and strong ties among the members and if social interaction proceeds in an orderly way. To the extent that relationships fail to develop or are disrupted, normative consensus is lacking, or order breaks down, the system is described as disorganized or anomic. The basic proposition of this approach is that when disorganization and anomie occur, deviant behavior is also likely to occur. Thus, the more disorganized the group, community, or society is, the higher its rate of deviant behavior will be.

A number of conditions have been taken as instances of disorganization or anomie.[2] One set of social conditions often described as disorganized and conducive to deviant behavior is that prevailing in the lower-class slums

---

[1] There are other processual theories relating to specific types of deviant behavior such as embezzlement (Cressey 1953), drug addiction (Lindesmith 1947; Alksne et al. 1967), marihuana and other drug use (Becker 1953; Carey 1968); check forgery (Lemert 1953), and mental illness (Scheff 1966).

[2] All of the following have been included at one time or another: lack of social cohesion (integration, solidarity, unity); breakdown in personal and social controls; disequilibrium, disruption, malalignment, or incompatibilities among the elements of a social system; conflict among norms or groups; normlessness, and so on. There is voluminous literature on this perspective. See Merton 1938; 1957; Rose 1954: Chap. 1; Cohen 1955; 1959; 1965; 1966; Cloward and Ohlin 1959; 1961; Clinard 1964; Shaw and McKay 1942; Faris 1955; Lander 1954; Elliott and Merrill 1961; McGee 1962; Turner 1954; Dynes et al. 1964.

of large cities. These urban areas are said to be disorganized because they are characterized by conflict, decay, lack of neighborhood cohesion, incomplete and broken families, weak conventional controls, and shifting populations of heterogeneous racial and ethnic groups. The disorganization of these areas is believed to be the reason why they have long experienced high rates of deviance of all kinds—crime, delinquency, drug addiction, alcoholism, mental illness, and prostitution.

However, this emphasis on the anomic situation of the lower-class urban dweller has been superseded by another theme in the disorganization-anomie tradition often referred to as *strain theory*. In strair. theory the form of anomie which produces deviant behavior results from the malintegration of cultural *ends* and societal *means*.

As originally formulated by Merton (1938), this means-ends theory pictures American society as permeated by an emphasis on success goals, values, aspirations, and standards of the predominant middle class. Everyone (especially males) is socialized to aspire toward high achievement and success, but there is less emphasis and socialization in the approved, conventional educational and occupational means of achievement. Moreover, although the success ethic applies to all levels of the class structure (and is embodied in the educational system to which all class levels are exposed), those at the bottom have an unequal opportunity to avail themselves of the legitimate means to achieve the goals. Therefore, because they continue to aspire to success, they will turn in disproportionate numbers to whatever effective illegitimate means are available.

The gap between the cultural ends and the means which a group's location in the social structure makes available is experienced at the individual level, ordinarily at least by the time of adolescence, as a discrepancy between his aspirations (what he hopes to achieve in life) and his expectations (what he more realistically believes is possible for him). In Cohen's (1955) version of the theory, this discrepancy is caused by the fact that lower-class boys must live up to middle-class status criteria. The conventional standards are adopted by authoritative adults (principally teachers in the schools) and are applied to students from all class backgrounds. But the lower-class boys cannot meet these standards. The status frustration causes a reaction against the standards themselves,[3] and a collective solution is arrived at by the construction of anticonventional standards and norms of conduct the boys can meet. By participation in the "delinquent subculture," which Cohen (1955) describes as "negativistic," "malicious," and "nonutilitarian," the lower-class youth can gain status by living up to standards which are the direct opposite of conventional standards.

---

[3]Stinchcombe (1964) makes use of this notion in the form of "expressive alieration" or "rebellion" against authority. He differs from Cohen, however, in arguing that the discrepancy between present aspirations and future prospects is greater for middle-class youth facing future downward mobility than for lower-class youth.

Cloward and Ohlin (1961) note that the deviant adaptations to the means-ends discrepancy depend not only on youths' relation to the structure of legitimate opportunities but also on their relation to the illegitimate opportunity structure. Just because groups are deprived of conventional occupational opportunities does not mean that deviant ones are automatically available. Whether or not lower-class adolescents have access to criminal opportunities depends on the social organization of their neighborhood and the presence of successful adult criminals. In some areas of the city they do not have even criminal alternatives and adopt a nonutilitarian, "conflict" (gang fighting) subculture. In areas organized around criminal adults and values a more utilitarian, "criminal" subculture evolves. For those who are "double failures" (in the conventional sense as well as in both the conflict and criminal subcultures) there is a "retreatist" drug culture.

The high rate of deviance in the lower class is not attributed to a breakdown in norms and social control in the lower class. Rather, the lower class is seen as the major focal point of anomie-induced strain which the society as a whole experiences. The strain is produced by the disjuncture between society's cultural standards, which incorporate the dream of equality and success for all, and the actual inequality in the distribution of educational and occupational opportunities for the realization of that dream. The strain may be felt by persons at any level, but the inequity is most severe for the members of the lower class, the disadvantaged, and minority groups.

A major emphasis in anomie theory has been the development of *deviant subcultures.* Thus far the major formulations of strain theory have been applied to delinquency, and we have referred only to delinquent subcultures, with adolescent male gangs as the prime participants (Cohen 1955; Cloward and Ohlin 1961; Spergel 1964; Downes 1966). However, anomie theory has been applied to a whole range of deviant behavior, and the concept of subculture has a long tradition in sociology not confined to anomie theory (Arnold 1970).

Evaluation of Social Disorganization-Anomie

1. The disorganization-anomie approach places heavy emphasis on the predominance of deviancy among the lower-class population — the same population supposedly characterized as the most disorganized and the most deprived of opportunities. Recent research has cast doubt on this supposition. Certain kinds of deviant behavior are concentrated in the lower class, but a considerable amount of delinquency and "white-collar crime" occur in the middle classes and in advantaged groups (Nye 1958; Akers 1964; Vaz 1967; Sutherland 1949; Geis 1968). Disorganization-anomie cannot, without modification, explain deviant behavior among groups that are not deprived of conventional opportunities or are not disorganized.

2. Even if one is willing to grant that the probability of deviancy is higher among disorganized segments of the population, there remains the problem of explaining why even here everyone does not violate the law and conventional morality. Why, even under conditions that can be described as the most disorganized, does the majority of the population remain conforming?

3. Although deviance may be defined differently from disorganization, often the only evidence adduced to describe a part of the city or a segment of the population as disorganized is the fact of high rates of deviance.[4] This circular reasoning problem has been avoided in studies which have found that delinquent behavior is related to anomie, measured by the discrepancy between aspirations and expected achievement among adolescent boys. The results of that research do not strongly support all aspects of anomie theory (Reiss and Rhodes 1963). Nonetheless, the evidence is that boys at all class levels have similar initial aspirations; lower-class boys and nonwhite boys perceive that their legitimate opportunities are narrower; delinquent and gang boys (at all class levels) are apt to feel closed off from conventional opportunities and are more aware of illegal opportunities. Moreover, the school experience for lower-class boys is often filled with failure and status strain, which leads them to drop out or to engage in delinquency (Short and Strodtbeck 1965; Empey and Lubeck 1971; Elliott 1966). Finally, recent research has shown that there is a fairly strong relationship between perceived opportunity and delinquency for female as well as male adolescents and for both black and white youths (Datesman et al. 1975).

4. In general this approach seems not to give due credit to different value positions. What is seen as disorganization from one position may be seen as organization or reorganization from another. What seems to be normlessness may simply be different norms. It may be that deviant behavior among the lower class results from social disorganization, but it may also be that some lower-class neighborhoods are simply organized around unconventional values (Kobrin 1951). The delinquent behavior of lower-class youth may represent adaptations to the deprivation of the means to live up to middle-class standards. But it could also be that lower-class youth do not relate at all to those standards. Rather, they may automatically violate them simply by trying to achieve status in a separate lower-class subculture (Miller 1958). What seems like disorganization may be highly organized systems of competing or conflicting norms or subcultures, which may contribute through diversity to the overall organization of society. This is the major point of the conflict theorists, to whom we now turn.

---

[4]Cohen (1966) seemingly avoids this circular reasoning problem by arguing that disorganization, rather than the cause, may be one outcome of deviant behavior. Anomie causes deviant behavior, which in turn may produce disorganization in a social system. Thus Cohen's formulation is something to the effect that anomie → deviant behavior → disorganization. The usual form of the argument is disorganization → deviant behavior. However, insofar as Cohen means by *anomie* what others refer to as *disorganization* he does not avoid the tautological error.

Conflict Approach

Conflict theory attempts to answer both of the central questions about deviance in essentially the same way. The power-elite theorists have yet to offer a theory of why deviant behavior occurs, but the pluralists view both the definition of deviant behavior (particularly legal definitions) and the occurrence of what is defined as deviant behavior as the result of group conflict. That is, the interests, values, and goals of the stronger groups survive the struggle and become the more or less official definers of deviance. (See the discussion of social definitions in the previous chapter.) The whole process of law making, law breaking, and law enforcement becomes a direct reflection of conflict between social, economic, and political interest groups and collectivities. Those who produce legislative and political victories win control over the police power and dominate the policies that decide who is likely to be involved in violation of the law. The conflict continues through the judicial proceedings of prosecution and trial and in the treatment of violators by those who wish to enforce the law. Essentially the same process is seen to operate on a less formal but no less real basis in the production and enforcement of other than legal definitions of conformity and deviance. The most powerful groups control the societal control mechanisms so that their norms and values are used as the criteria for behavior. Deviant behavior is the ordinary, learned, expected, and normal behavior of individuals caught up in cultural and group conflict (Vold 1958:203–13).

Deviant behavior may result from direct group clashes or simply from acting according to one's own group norms and thus automatically violating those of another group. A number of instances have been suggested in which cultural and group conflict produce illegal and deviant behavior in one or both of these ways. Foreign immigrants and rural migrants to urban areas within this country may bring with them a set of conduct norms and values different from those already in residence. Religious, ethnic, racial, and other minority groups may conflict with and adhere to a different set of behavioral guidelines than those of the dominant conventional society (Sellin 1938; Sutherland 1947).

Many crimes are incidental to clashes between the established system and persons who are attempting to induce change in the social order. Fighters in the struggle to change the racial caste system and to combat what is defined as oppression clash with upholders of the established order. Both sides believe they are right, and violence and property damage are inflicted by both sides. Workers in the civil rights movement engage in civil disobedience and break the law, not because they are anomic or disorganized but because they espouse the cause of a group which defines the laws as the evil instruments of an oppressive system. Blacks were lynched, churches were bombed, and other personal violence was inflicted on whites and blacks by the white racists (including sheriffs and police) in support of a segregated system they believed to be right and just.

The laws and conventional standards are frequently violated by political reform, protest, and radical groups. The violation may be nonviolent disruption and symbolic acts or simply violation by noncompliance, such as that engaged in by conscientious objectors, tax protestors, draft card burners, and draft resisters. But if the protest is pushed to the point of questioning the validity of the entire system (as it has been by black power groups, radical white groups, and others), the outcome is revolt, rebellion, or revolution. Indeed, the behavior of the newer, more violent, radicals (more often of the Left than of the Right these days), such as bombing buildings, fighting with police, killing, and "trashing" property, is justified by an explicitly revolutionary ideology. As these groups clash with the police and other groups, a number of offenses against the existing criminal law may occur—murder, personal violence, sabotage, seizure and destruction of property, theft, and burglary. As supporters of the established legal system, the police and other authorities may also violate the law in attempts to control the protesting groups. The same kind of violence and law violation occurred on both sides during the severe labor-management conflict of the 1920s and 1930s.

In all of these instances, who is deviant or criminal depends on which side is most successful. If the revolution is successful, the former rulers become the criminals; if it is not, the rebels are the criminals. The white supremist who previously enforced the law against and branded as criminal the blacks who violated the Jim Crow and trespass laws is today the one who is more likely to be the criminal for violating the civil rights of blacks.

Most of the instances cited carry implications of appeal to what the violators consider "higher values" and morality than those supported by the enforcers. The reformists and protestors announce their deviancy publicly and disavow the norms they violate. But conflict theorists also perceive elements of group conflict even in the behavior of the type of deviant who tries to hide his deviancy and acknowledges the legitimacy of the norms he is breaking (Merton and Nisbet 1966:808–11). Although unorganized and relatively powerless, they may still be perceived as a threat by the majority (Lofland 1969:15). For instance, conflict theorists often present juvenile delinquent and criminal gangs as minority groups out of sympathy with the norms of and conflicting with the dominant majority. Vold (1958:220–42) emphasizes that organized crime is simply one type of business system, organized for profit, which is in conflict with (and which establishes shifting accommodations with) legitimate society.

Evaluation of the Conflict Approach

1. By insisting that we go beyond seeing conflict as simply one path to disorganization and become sensitive to the heterogeneity of modern society, this approach has made a valuable contribution to understanding the way crisscrossing and balancing cleavages and group compromises and solutions to conflict contribute to societal organization. However, stopping with

this conflict image of society is in turn incomplete. Granted that American society is heterogeneous, there is still more to society than the working arrangements of a congeries of conflicting groups and interests. Society is also held together by the smaller or larger number of widely held, often weakly articulated but also often explicitly stated values, common assumptions, and images of the world. This is a chief factor in providing what continuity and unity exists in a diversified society. Only by stretching the issue somewhat can we call those who violate these broad values and norms simply representatives of some group interest at variance with the dominant view.

Also, as even some conflict theorists themselves recognize, not all conflict contributes to unity; some conflict in fact disrupts organization. The limiting case is when the system is divided into two warring camps, each denying the right of the other to exist. At this stage we can no longer talk about conflicting groups in the same system; rather, we have two separate and fighting systems (Coser 1956:93).

2. However, before this stage is reached conflict theory can account for some variations in deviance between groups, but this perspective is much less applicable to deviation within groups. It does not provide answers to the processual question of how a person becomes deviant. How or why does a person come to deviate from certain norms of his own group, norms he ostensibly holds to and is fighting for, whether they are the widespread normative prescriptions and proscriptions just mentioned or those of a more restricted subculture?

3. Granted that the laws result in part from group conflict, does it follow that most crime is simply the result of continuing that conflict beyond the legislature? Surely we can say that most murder, theft, burglary, rape, and arson are not simply behavior incidental to group conflict. What about other kinds of deviant behavior? Homosexuals and drug addicts are in conflict with organized society, but insofar as they represent values of groups or subcultures at odds with society, the groups themselves were formed as a result of and are organized around deviant actions of their members and societal reaction to them. Thus the group membership is just as likely to result from the deviance as the deviancy is to result from group membership. Moreover, is it valid to say that all homosexuals and drug addicts positively valuate their behavior? What about the alcoholic, the mentally ill, the suicide? What group values do they support?

What this implies is that the conflict approach seems more appropriate to the analysis of the behavior of groups and individuals involved in *ideological and political confrontations.* It is less appropriate to the analysis of the behavior of those involved in many types of common-law crimes, usual deviations, and vices.

4. The conflict school rightly emphasizes that one cannot assume widespread consensus in public opinion about what is right and desirable from which misled or "unadjusted" individuals deviate. This perspective leads

us to ask and suggests why certain values and norms become dominant and others do not. For this reason the conflict approach is *potent as an explanation of the formation and enforcement of the norms themselves; it is less powerful as an explanation of deviant behavior.*

Perhaps in recognition of this fact, the more recent expressions of the conflict theory of deviance emphasize the group-power–conflict dimension in making the law and enforcing it, and modify the conflict approach when applying it to deviant behavior. Either that or they simply ignore the question of why people violate norms. For instance, Turk (1966; 1969) dismisses the explanation of criminal behavior as the main sociological task; instead, he insists that it is most important to explain how or why certain persons are assigned the social status of criminal. He uses the conflict approach to account for the operation of the criminal justice system. (See also Chambliss and Seidman 1971.) Quinney (1970; 1975) relies heavily on power and conflict as key concepts in explaining the formulation and application of criminal definitions, but when he explains the behavior of those defined as criminal, he relies on self-concept, differential association, learning, commitment, and other variables not included in group conflict.

The Marxian, power-elite versions of conflict theory (see the discussion in chapter 2 on pp. 15–16) ignore or provide only sketchy answers to the question of why some people, including some of those in power, violate legal and other norms. "Radical" theorists severely criticize the reactionary implications and assumptions of other theories of deviant behavior, but they have not proposed a coherent alternative conflict theory of deviant behavior (Quinney 1974a; Liazo 1972; Taylor et al. 1973; Reasons 1975; Spitzer 1975).

The Labeling Perspective

The labeling perspective is similar to the conflict approach in emphasizing the formation and application of social definitions. Indeed, the two approaches have become so closely identified in arguing that social reactions to deviance are unequally applied against the less powerful groups that some sociologists see conflict and labeling theorists as almost interchangeable (Hagan 1973; Wellford 1975). The labeling perspective revolves primarily around the premise that deviance is not a personal quality or created by the deviant's acts; rather, it is created by group definitions and reactions. Some people attach a deviant label to certain acts and people, and it is this label that makes them deviant. This refrain is repeated time and again (Becker 1963:9; Erikson 1964:10–11; Kitsuse 1964:88). Thus, the labeling perspective is notable for insisting that we shift our attention from exclusive concern with the deviant to include a major concern with the process of applying deviant labels.

The important questions then are not about why some people come to engage in deviant behavior, but: Who applies the deviant label to what and to whom? Whose rules should prevail and be enforced? Under what circumstances is the deviant label successfully and unsuccessfully applied? How does a community decide what forms of conduct should be singled out? What forms of behavior do people in the social system consider deviant? How do they interpret such behavior? What are their reactions to individuals who manifest such behavior? The labeling theorists' answers to these questions revolve around differences in power. Actions are labeled as deviant depending upon whether or not they are in harmony with the values of the more powerful groups. The less powerful groups and individuals are more likely to be selected as deviant for violating social norms even if they are not more likely to have actually violated them. Whether or not people are branded with a stigmatized label then results more from who they are than what they have done (Becker 1963).

Although questions about deviant behavior itself would seem to be of secondary importance in the labeling approach, it has in fact been and continues to be very interested in deviants and deviant behavior. Indeed, the unique feature of the labeling perspective is its central contention that the labeling reaction may contribute to the causation of deviant behavior. As Becker (1963) says, this approach views deviance as essentially an interactive process between those who commit or are believed to have committed deviant behavior and others in society who define and react to the acts and people as deviant. Some rule violators do not think they have been dealt with unjustly. They accept the legitimacy of the norms they have broken, and they accept the right of others to enforce the norms. Societal reaction to their deviance may keep them from engaging in further deviant behavior—that is, it may have the intended consequence of deterring norm violation. But the key point in the labeling perspective is that the disgrace of a person who is labeled as deviant often furthers rather than discourages his deviant behavior (Tannenbaum 1938; Becker 1963; Schur 1965). By a process that one writer has called "role engulfment" (Schur 1971) the *stigmatization* of the deviant causes him to view himself as irrevocably deviant. Thus the application of deviant labels may operate as a self-fulfilling prophecy influencing the one labeled as deviant to continue to be deviant. This may force him into various forms of *secondary deviance.*

Secondary deviance, a concept first introduced by Edwin M. Lemert to illuminate the role of social reaction in the cause of deviant behavior, is an important concept in the labeling approach. "Secondary deviation refers to a special class of socially defined responses which people make to *problems created by the societal reaction* to their deviance" (Lemert 1967:40–41, italics added). Thus, when deviants engage in behavior in which they would not have otherwise participated (had they not been labeled as deviants), and when they develop social roles and patterns they would not have developed except for the application of social control measures, secondary deviance is produced. Societal reaction may motivate an individual to participate in deviant subcultures. Therefore, rather than reducing deviant behavior, social control often helps build new deviant social forms. For example, a deviant subculture with a full-blown deviant ideology can form; complete with a set of values from which they judge and condemn their condemners, and receive others branded as deviant by society. Whether or not one becomes part of a deviant group, the fact that he has been apprehended and labeled may be a major, if not the most important, element leading to the subsequent construction of a deviant identity and pursuit of a deviant role or career (Becker 1963; Lofland 1969; Matza 1969).

Social control can also create deviance by prohibiting something for which there continues to be demand, such as gambling, drugs, or prostitution. This prohibition creates the necessity of constructing a black market to supply the demand. Organized crime is then attracted to this black market, where because of the demand for the market, prices are inflated and the profits are large enough to make it worth the risk of legal penalty. Also, in the demand of drug addicts for their drug supply, for example, the demand does not lessen with the unavailability of the supply; people may turn to illegal activities to get the money needed to pay the artificially inflated prices. Many of these prohibited activities are "crimes without victims" (Schur 1965). With no complaining victim, it is difficult both to know the laws are broken and to enforce them. Police officers sometimes illegally deceive or entrap victimless criminals in order to apprehend them. Also, the extremely lucrative trade in prohibited goods and services makes a lot of money available for the corruption of law enforcement officials (Hawkins and Tiedeman 1975:338–63).

The social control system is also able to affect both the rate and form of deviance in which deviants are identified primarily on the basis of "invented" or imputed and unseen characteristics. For instance, the systems set up to control such things as witchcraft and religious heresy in Renaissance England and Europe and in colonial America and "politically subversive" thoughts in the Soviet Union appear largely to have defined and determined the very behavior they were meant to control (Erikson 1966; Currie 1968; Connor 1972). The rate and variation of other forms of deviance involving overt, clearly definable acts, such as theft and violence, are much more likely to reflect social forces other than the actions of social control agents.

The labeling perspective captured the imagination of both academic sociologists and correctional practitioners in the 1960s and continues as a major if not the dominant approach in the 1970s. Practitioners commonly assume that they are as likely to have negative as beneficial effects on the deviants with whom they deal. Because of this, a "diversion" movement has developed in the past decade to keep as many apprehended offenders as possible out of the criminal and juvenile justice systems. It is based largely on the assumptions of labeling theory. The idea is that diverting people from the system will avoid the deviance-amplifying effect that official labeling is believed to have, and that it is better for the formal control system just to tolerate the deviant conduct of and not to punish many offenders, especially young ones. One proponent has called this solution "radical nonintervention" (Schur 1973). Others have called for the "decriminalization" of victimless behavior and other legal reforms to reduce problems of corruption in law enforcement and the influence of organized crime (Morris and Hawkins 1969).

Evaluation, Critiques, and Revisions of the Labeling Perspective

1. It is redundant to insist that deviance is socially defined. This has been a basic part of the sociology of deviant behavior for at least four decades. There are few who would quibble with the basic contention that the deviant nature of acts is not in the acts or the person committing them but rather in group definition and reactions. It is true that in the effort to untangle the causes of deviance, researchers and theorists sometimes become overly concerned with the conditions and characteristics of the deviants themselves, to the neglect of questions about the norms and enforcers. Most energy has been devoted to behavioral questions, but that in no way implies that sociologists contend that there is something inherently evil or deviant about the behavior itself.

2. The labeling approach does rightly emphasize, although neither wholly originally nor uniquely, the importance of studying social definitions and the process by which acts and people get labeled as deviant. But when labeling theorists have attempted to answer questions about social definitions, they say little more than what conflict theorists have been saying for some time—that is, the norms and values of the dominant groups in society will prevail. The dominant groups will successfully apply their ideas of who are deviant, will become the official definers of deviance, and will resist being defined as deviant themselves. The labeling approach agrees with conflict theory that in the official control system, more people from minority groups and the lower class are labeled and punished as deviant than are middle- and upper-class people.

As we have seen, however, the empirical evidence does not support this labeling-conflict view of the criminal justice system as being grossly discriminating and more interested in who a person is than in what kind of offense he has committed. (See the discussion pp. 17–18.) The evidence has been collected mainly on the actions of the formal control agents, however, and there are virtually no data on how much attention the average person (not in an official position) pays to the personal character (age, race, sex, class) of the person rather than to that person's behavior after he or she is labeled as deviant. However, there have been studies of decisions made by people outside the official criminal justice system, such as store owners who apply laws to shoplifters caught in their stores by calling the police. These studies show that even at this more informal level, labeling decisions are based mainly on such things as the value and quality of goods stolen rather than on the age, race, sex, or class of the shoplifter (Cohen and Stark 1974; Hindelang 1974a).

3. Although theorists of the labeling school sometimes come close to saying that the actual behavior of deviants is unimportant, *the central contribution of the labeling perspective is its conception of the impact of labeling on behavior, namely that the labeling often leads to further deviance.* One sometimes gets the impression from reading the literature on labeling that people mind their own business until bad society comes along and slaps a stigmatized label on them. Thus forced into the role of deviant, the individual has little choice but to *be* deviant. It is, as Gouldner (1968) and Bordua (1967) note, an "underdog" ideology. To present the argument in this way is an exaggeration, of course, but such an image can be easily gained from an overemphasis on the causal impact of labeling on deviance. The more reasonable version of this image is the main contribution of the labeling school to the sociology of deviance. Because of this image, we are now more alert to the importance that norm enforcement and public policy may have in the furtherance of deviancy.

When carried too far, however, this insight serves as a blinder. The earliest critiques of labeling by Gibbs (1966), Bordua (1967), and Akers (1968a) took exception to the image of the deviant being forced into a deviant identity and role by a stigmatized label, and found the labeling theory deficient in a number of ways. These critics have been joined in more recent years by a growing chorus of objections to many aspects of labeling theory.

Akers (1968a) argued that while labeling can increase the probability that certain stigmatized persons will commit future deviancy and promote deviant behavior that might not have occurred otherwise, the label does not create the behavior *in the first place.* People can and do commit deviant acts because of the particular contingencies and circumstances in their lives, quite apart from or in combination with the labels others apply to them. The labeling process is not completely arbitrary and unrelated to the behavior of those detected and labeled. Errors are made, labels are falsely applied, and criteria extraneous to behavior are used, but we do not react, for instance, to people as homosexuals unless they exhibit behavior we believe to be indicative of homosexuality. The courts do not stigmatize with the label of criminal until they legally determine that criminal acts have been committed. Therefore, while secondary deviation may occur, the deviant behavior itself is prior to and forms the basis for the label; in this sense the behavior creates the label. It is reasonable to assume, then, that the deviant behavior could continue without or in spite of, not because of, the public label. The theoretical problem Akers (1968a) identified is that of specifying the ways and under what conditions an interactive process involving both behavior (deviant) and definitions (labelers) will take place. What determines when a behavior pattern not previously specifically stigmatized will become defined as deviant, and when labeling increases or decreases the probability of further involvement in that pattern? (At least two recent critics of labeling have attempted to specify the variables involved in answering this question. See Thorsell and Klemke 1972; Tittle 1975).

Bordua (1967:153) offered a similar critique, arguing that by assuming the deviant to be an "essentially empty organism" the labeling theorists present a picture of "all societal response and no deviant stimulus."[5] Others have since pointed out that people do not simply acquiesce passively to the application of a deviant label. Rather than accepting it and letting it define their identities, they take an active role in fighting back, rejecting, denying, and otherwise negotiating the identity they want (Rogers and Buffalo 1974; Levitin 1975). Other critics have found fault with labeling theory for a number of reasons. In spite of its claims to be interested in the labeling process, the proponents of the labeling perspective have been more concerned with the deviant than with social control. It has not shown labeling to be either a necessary or sufficient condition for a deviant identity. The labeling approach has tended to emphasize the appreciation of the exotic and bizarre but powerless deviant and deprecation of the lower-level, also relatively powerless, control agents such as police officers while ignoring the deviance (corporate crime, governmental corruption, and so on) of the most powerful groups (Davis 1972; Liazo 1972; Hirschi 1973; Hagan 1973; Taylor et al. 1973).

4. Perhaps the most damaging criticism of labeling theory is a result of the attempts to test empirically the central idea that the label often leads to negative self-concept and a stabilized deviant career. Most of the studies have been unable to find support for this contention. The experience of being labeled and punished as a deviant appears to be much less significant in promoting further deviance than the labeling approach leads one to believe. Official labeling deters deviance much more frequently than labeling theory leads one to believe. This conclusion is supported by studies of official processing of delinquents, deterrence of criminal behavior, the hospitalization of mental patients, the labeling of school children by teachers, the labeling of sexual behavior, and the labeling of other forms of deviant behavior.[6]

5. Some labeling theorists have recognized much of the mounting criticism against the labeling perspective and have agreed that many of the points are valid. They have tended to forsake both formulations that see negative labeling producing deviance automatically, and the extreme ethical subjectivism and relativism of earlier labeling theory. The revisions tend to retreat from the central notion of the impact of labeling as deviance-causing and to re-emphasize understanding the labeling process itself

---

[5]These criticisms do not apply to the writings of Lemert (1967; 1972; 1974), who consistently maintains the primary-secondary deviance distinction. Other labeling theorists do not consistently maintain this distinction, but there are places where they too sometimes recognize that deviance may exist before the label (Becker 1963:19–20; Kitsuse 1964).

[6]There are now a number of these studies. See the reviews of research in Thorsell and Klemke 1972; Mahoney 1974; Tittle 1975; Gove 1975.

(Kitsuse 1972; Lemert 1974; Goode 1975; Hawkins and Tiedemen 1975). It remains to be seen whether, even with these responses to criticisms and revisions, labeling theory will be able to maintain through the 1970s the dominance it had in the sociology of deviance in the 1960s.

Social Control Theories

The basic assumption of control theories is that crime, delinquency, and other forms of deviance are not so much caused by forces motivating people to violate norms as they are simply not prevented (Nye 1958:3–9). Thus, whereas other theories start with the question of why some men do not conform (that is, why some are deviant), control theories ask, Why does anyone conform (that is, why don't we all violate rules)?

> In control theories, [this] question has never been adequately answered. The question remains, Why *do* men obey the rules of society? Deviance is taken for granted; conformity must be explained (Hirschi 1969:10).

The answer given is that we conform because social control has been effective. Whenever internal or external controls break down or weaken, deviance is likely to result; when controls are strong, deviance is restrained (Reiss 1951). Early control theorists assumed that man will naturally push against the rules of society and break through them unless his instincts and impulses are controlled. One is motivated to conform by social control; he needs no motivation to deviate. Later control theorists, however, borrow and attempt to incorporate motivating factors from other theories (Reckless 1967:469–83), simply refer to other theories (Hirschi 1969:34–34), or appeal to situational factors (Briar and Piliavin 1965:36–38).

Control theories remain little interested in describing the impetus to deviance. They tend to take for granted that the impetus applies to everyone, and they concentrate on tracing the features of the control system which keep almost everyone in line and the fractures in social control which allow some to deviate.

> The question "Why do they do it?" is simply not the question the theory is designed to answer. The question is "Why don't we do it?" There is much evidence that we would if we dared (Hirschi 1969:34).

However, control theories vary in the extent to which motivation to deviate is considered with forces toward conformity. Hirschi, after examining his data, concludes that the "natural motivation" assumption needs to be modified and that inducements such as approval of deviant peers may need to be added (1969:239–31).

Containment

In one variant of control theory, containment theory, the individual can be "pushed" toward deviance by internal impulses and drives (discontent, hostility, aggressiveness, and so on) or "pressured" and "pulled" in that direction by a "bad" environment (poverty, deprivation, bad companions, poor opportunities, subcultures, and so forth). Individual and social controls, which are called inner and outer containment respectively, act as countervailing forces "containing" or controlling those prone to deviance. If neither the inner nor outer buffers can handle these impulses, the individual becomes deviant. Evidently one or both can do the job. A weak individual can be contained by strong outer controls. If the outer containment (supervision and discipline, cohesion of the group, moral front, and so on) is weak, one can still be kept from norm violation by the inner buffers of ego strength or a "good self-concept." This "self-concept," which renders one more or less vulnerable or responsive to a deviant environment, plays the biggest part in the theory. For instance, it has been used to explain the fact that only some boys in a high-delinquency area are delinquent. A "good" or "insulated" self-concept enables the conforming boy to withstand that which leads others of his peers into delinquency, whereas a "bad" or "vulnerable" self-concept lets him succumb (Reckless 1967:444–83; 1961; 1970).

Social Bonding

The other major version of control theory, which might be called social bonds to conformity or commitment to conformity, also makes use of a self factor. But whereas containment theory sees the deviant as one who has failed to acquire a deviancy-resisting concept of himself (or one who has acquired a deviancy-susceptible image), bonding theory sees him as having broken away from prior ties to conventional groups and institutions. The assumption is that "delinquent acts result when an individual's bond to society is weak or broken" (Hirschi 1969:16). The lack or loss of conventional ties and identity, overcoming one's stake in or commitment to conformity (Toby 1957; Briar and Piliavin 1965; Becker 1960) sets one free ("drift," Matza 1964), and makes him a candidate for deviant acts, roles, and identities.

The elements of this bond, according to Hirschi (1969:16–30), are attachment to others, commitment to conforming pursuits (calculated investment in "conventional lines of actions" which would be risked by deviant actions), involvement in conventional activities, and belief in the moral validity of the group's or society's norms. The stronger these bonds with the activities and beliefs of parents, conventional adults, school teachers, and peers are, the more the individual's behavior will be controlled in the direction of conformity. The weaker they are, the more likely he is to violate the rules. The bonds are viewed as highly intercorrelated; the weakening of one is probably accompanied by the loosening of another (Hirschi 1969:27–30).

Evaluation of Social Control Theories

1. Reckless and his associates and students have conducted research into the self-concept of adolescents in high-delinquency areas (Reckless et al. 1956; 1957; Scarpitti et al. 1960; Dinitz et al. 1962). The findings have been interpreted by Reckless as supportive of the entire containment theory, but they are really relevant only to part of it—that is, outer deviant influences controlled by inner containment. The findings do not touch on the situations of externally induced deviance versus outer containment, internally induced deviance versus outer containment, or internally induced deviance versus inner containment. Moreover, a number of methodological shortcomings and problems of interpretation have been noted about the self-concept research (Tangri and Schwartz 1967; Jensen 1970).

There is some evidence that delinquents do not share a conventional morality from which they must break in order to drift into misdeeds (Hindelang 1970). And Hirschi's own research shows that attachment to conventional religion is not a deterrent to delinquency (Hirschi and Stark 1969). Other research by Hirschi (1969), however, supports the major propositions of his theory, although the strongest relationship found by Hirschi is between delinquency and association with delinquent friends, a finding not anticipated by the theory. Similarly, other research finds that attachment to peers leads to conforming to conventional behavior only when the peers are themselves conventional; attachment to delinquent peers increases the likelihood of delinquency (Linden and Hackler 1973; Conger 1976). Jensen (1969) found that certain conventional (if false) beliefs about the police are a deterrent to delinquency, and perceptions of high probability of formal punishment deter some other types of deviance (Waldo and Chiricos 1972; Burkett and Jensen 1975; Tittle and Rowe 1973). These findings are consistent with control theory. Hindelang (1973) did not support control theory regarding attachment to peers and parents, but did support the theory in other respects for both males and females (Hirschi's study included only males). Most other data support most of the propositions about attachment, identification, and commitment to conformity. And on the whole, social bonding control theory stands up reasonably well in the face of empirical evidence (Hindelang 1973; 1974b).

2. Social control is exerted through *sanctions* or laws, both in direct external control and in training for self-control. But recognition of this is only implicit in control theory as currently formulated; little is said directly about sanctions. However, it would seem reasonable that control theories could easily be restated to replace their present implicit treatment of sanctions

with explicit statements about the structure and operation of social rewards and punishments to control behavior. Toby (1974:95) explicitly states the importance of rewards and punishment in social control.

Social bonding control theory sees the family as a bastion of conventionality. The amount of supervision of children's activities, the quality of parent-child relationships, the mutual rejection or acceptance and communication within the family, and the strength of the person's identification with his parents are all stressed (Hirschi 1969; Nye 1958; Briar and Piliavin 1965). Although these are pictured as indicative of the individual's commitment to his family, they may also be seen as indicative of the extent to which the family group is able to sanction his behavior effectively in the direction of conformity.

Bonding theory also refers to the person's perceptions and attachment to the conventional values and legal system in its concern with the conception of oneself as a person who will get into trouble with the police and its concern with beliefs about the law and the police (Hirschi 1969; Briar and Piliavin 1965; Matza 1964). These are not direct references to the specific, deliberate efforts of the formal control system to deter deviance. However, they are clearly relevant to the deviance-preventing effects of formal and legal sanctions.

Thus the direct role of sanctions in the socialization process — the molding of the individual's commitment to conformity and development of self-control — could be made part of control theory. Also, control theory could include the type and effectiveness of informally applied sanctions by parents and peers as well as the formal application of sanctions by the legal and correctional system to control violation of norms. When this is done, control theory becomes especially compatible with the social learning theory presented in chapter 4.

Summary

The principal structural theories of deviant behavior include social disorganization-anomie, conflict, labeling, and social control. These have been examined in this chapter. The major processual theory has been differential association. Differential association and a reformulation of it, which will comprise the central social learning perspective from which deviance will be viewed throughout the rest of the book, are the subjects to which we now turn.

4

A Social Learning Perspective on Deviant Behavior

The theories reviewed in chapter 3 are primarily structural and have dominated sociological thinking about deviance. We turn now to the presentation of a social learning theory as an explanation of the process of engaging in deviant behavior. This theory is an integration of Edwin H. Sutherland's processual theory of behaving in violation of social and legal norms and the broader principles of modern learning theory.

Sutherland's Theory

Sutherland's "differential association" theory of criminal and delinquent behavior was first stated in the third edition (1939) of his criminology textbook, *Principles of Criminology*, although the second edition (1934) contained some preliminary ideas on the theory. The 1939 version of the theory indicated clearly that Sutherland was interested in both process and structure because the first part referred to differential association as a process, and the latter part of the theory referred to conflict and disorganization as two structural situations that determine the patterns of association and hence criminal behavior. When Sutherland revised his theory in the fourth edition (1947), he dropped the structural elements of the theory and expanded and clarified the rest of it to produce a purely processual theory. Sutherland did not thereby reject the need for structural explanations. Indeed, he continued his interest in group rates of criminality by incorporating conflict and disorganization into "differential social organization" to explain why people have the associations they do have and thus to account for variations in group rates of crime. He saw this as a separate theory from (but consistent with) his revised processual theory of differential association.

Donald R. Cressey, who has revised the Sutherland text from its fifth through all subsequent editions, has deliberately left the theory as Sutherland presented it in 1947. This is the version to which the majority of adherents and critics alike refer and that has been the object of repeated efforts to test and revise through the years. The theory as presented by Sutherland is in the form of nine declarative statements (Sutherland and Cressey 1970:75–77):

1. Criminal behavior is learned.

2. Criminal behavior is learned in interaction with other persons in a process of communication.

3. The principal part of the learning of criminal behavior occurs within intimate personal groups.

4. When criminal behavior is learned, the learning includes (a) techniques of committing the crime, which are sometimes very complicated, sometimes very simple; and (b) the specific direction of motives, drives, rationalizations, and attitudes.

5. The specific direction of motives and drives is learned from definitions of the legal codes as favorable or unfavorable.

6. A person becomes delinquent because of an excess of definitions favorable to violation of law over definitions unfavorable to violation of law.

7. Differential associations may vary in frequency, duration, priority, and intensity.

8. The process of learning criminal behavior by association with criminal and anti-criminal patterns involves all of the mechanisms that are involved in any other learning.

9. While criminal behavior is an expression of general needs and values, it is not explained by those general needs and values since noncriminal behavior is an expression of the same needs and values.

Although the entire set of statements collectively make up the theory of differential association, the sixth statement was referred to by Sutherland as the "principle of differential association" and is seen as the heart of the theory; it is that *one commits criminal acts because his accepted "definitions" of the law as something to violate are in "excess" of his accepted definitions of the law as something that can, must, or should be obeyed.* Thus, it is not a simple theory of associating with "bad companions"; rather it is concerned with contact with criminal "patterns" and "definitions" (normative evaluations) *balanced against* contact with conforming definitions, whether this contact comes from association with those who commit crime or with those who are law-abiding (Cressey 1960:49).

To summarize, the differential association theory as Sutherland finally presented it states that one learns criminal behavior in a process of symbolic interaction with others, mainly those in his primary groups, who present him with both criminal and anti-criminal patterns, techniques, motivations, and definitional stances toward the legal norms. The balance of criminal and anti-criminal definitions determines whether one will be conforming or deviant with respect to a given legal code. If the balance of definitions is favorable to law, the outcome is conformity; if violation definitions are in excess, criminal behavior is the result. This balance is based on the frequency, duration, priority, and intensity with which one is exposed to lawful or criminal definitions. If one is exposed to law-violating definitions and at the same time is relatively isolated from law-abiding definitions, or if he is exposed to the former first, more frequently, for a longer time, and with greater intensity than to the latter, he will deviate from the law.

From the impressive body of literature that has grown up around differential association theory, it is clear that the theory has had a major impact on thinking about crime and deviance.[1] DeFleur and Quinney (1966) demonstrate that the theory as stated by Sutherland is internally consistent and capable of producing testable deductions if the concepts are properly measured. Furthermore, the empirical evidence on differential association is basically favorable. Nevertheless, many researchers report difficulty in measuring some concepts, and the theory as Sutherland stated it does not specify what the learning process is or what "all of the mechanisms that are involved in any other learning" are. Revisions have been attempted, therefore, to handle these problems (Glaser 1956). However, until Burgess and Akers (1966b) none was a full reformulation of the theory, nor made explicit the nature of the underlying learning process involved in differential association, as Cressey recognized was needed (Cressey 1960:54).

A Social Learning Theory: Differential Association-Reinforcement

In an effort to provide the more accurate specification of the learning process called for by Cressey, I collaborated with Robert L. Burgess to reformulate differential association theory, a reformulation that we called "differential association-reinforcement" (Burgess and Akers 1966b). We took our cue from C. Ray Jeffery (1965) who had argued earlier that the large and growing body of knowledge about learning in experimental behavioral science had direct implication for differential association theory and should be used in its modification. The set of principles we used is variously called

---

[1]See the review by Cressey 1960; Sutherland and Cressey 1974; and Burgess and Akers 1966b.

Skinnerian (after B. F. Skinner), operant conditioning, reinforcement, or simply behavior theory.[2] By whatever name, these are very general and powerful behavior principles of precise learning mechanisms which have been worked out and verified in laboratory settings and which can be extended, applied to, and tested in more complex social situations. We contended then that by integrating Sutherland's differential association theory into this more general set of learning principles, we could provide the revision needed to make the theory more testable and to indicate more clearly the learning processes.

Our revision was a statement-by-statement reformulation of Sutherland's theory, but it was not intended as an alternative theory. Rather, of necessity some ideas not intrinsic to differential association were introduced and additions were made to the original propositions. The reformulation was a new broader theory which integrated differential association with differential reinforcement; one could not arrive at it starting with reinforcement theory and ignoring differential association or by starting with differential association and ignoring reinforcement theory—hence the name of differential association-reinforcement. I now usually refer to the theory as a *social learning* theory, but the earlier designation as differential association-reinforcement is still appropriate. Although Burgess and I retained Sutherland's references to criminal and delinquent behavior in our reformulation, it was our intention that it apply to any form of deviant behavior. The remainder of this chapter presents the theory as extended to deviant behavior in general, and this social learning theory provides the unifying framework within which each form of deviance is examined throughout the book.[3]

By dropping the last statement and combining the first and eighth statements in Sutherland's theory, the Burgess-Akers reformulation reduced the theory to seven statements consistent with the principles of modern behavior:[4]

1. Deviant behavior is learned according to the principles of operant conditioning.

2. Deviant behavior is learned both in nonsocial situations that are reinforcing or discriminating, and through that social interaction in

---

[2]See Skinner 1953; 1959. In the process of using and analyzing operant conditioning theory, Burgess and I were led to codify a concise list of operant principles, which should serve as a quick summary of the major items in operant conditioning theory (Burgess and Akers 1966a). In addition, you may want to examine some of the research and writing in Skinnerian theory. See, for instance, Bijou and Baer 1961; Staats 1964; Honig 1966. A number of introductory psychology textbooks explain operant theory; a good one is Whaley and Malott 1969. For other learning literature see Ullmann and Krasner 1964; 1969; Eysenck 1964; Bandura and Walters 1963; Bandura 1969; Staats 1975.

[3]What follows is an introductory overview of the theory as I see it now. For the technical rationale and discussion of the literature, concepts, and research see Burgess and Akers 1966b.

[4]See footnote 2 for citations to some of the literature on this set of learning principles.

which the behavior of other persons is reinforcing or discriminating for such behavior.

3. The principal part of the learning of deviant behavior occurs in those groups which comprise or control the individual's major source of reinforcements.

4. The learning of deviant behavior, including specific techniques, attitudes and avoidance procedures, is a function of the effective and available reinforcers and the existing reinforcement contingencies.

5. The specific class of behavior learned and its frequency of occurrence are a function of the effective and available reinforcers, and the deviant or nondeviant direction of the norms, rules, and definitions which in the past have accompanied the reinforcement.

6. The probability that a person will commit deviant behavior is increased in the presence of normative statements, definitions, and verbalizations which, in the process of differential reinforcement of such behavior over conforming behavior, have acquired discriminative value.

7. The strength of deviant behavior is a direct function of the amount, frequency, and probability of its reinforcement. The modalities of association with deviant patterns are important insofar as they affect the source, amount, and scheduling of reinforcement.[5]

These seven statements contain terms which need definition and present only a bare outline of a theory. The following discussion is to clarify terms, the basic propositions of the theory, and the way in which the theory will be applied throughout the remaining chapters of this book.

Operant Behavior

The set of behavior principles referred to in the statement 1 actually includes propositions about respondent as well as operant behavior. *Operant behavior* is mediated primarily by the central nervous system, and involves the large striated muscles, as contrasted with *respondent behavior,* which is controlled primarily by the autonomic nervous system and involves the smooth muscles. Operants are voluntary; respondents are reflex or involuntary responses. Respondents are contingent upon antecedent or eliciting stimuli. Operants, on the other hand, are capable of being influenced by

---

[5]See Burgess and Akers 1966b. In the original Burgess-Akers statement the words *criminal behavior* were used where the words *deviant behavior* appear here. Also, statements 5, 6, and 7 are worded somewhat differently here than they were in the 1966 statement.

stimulus events which follow them. Thus, respondents are unaffected by the outcome or change they produce in the individual's environment. Your hand will always withdraw from a hot stove (unless physically restrained or unless the reflex is operantly, and bravely, superseded) and will not be affected by changes moving your hand causes. Depriving someone of food will inevitably produce hunger pangs, and showing him food will make his mouth water (although he may for any number of reasons voluntarily refuse to eat the food). A puff of air or movement of an object which threatens to intrude into the eye makes the eyelid flutter or close.

Actually, the distinction between autonomic reflexes as entirely unresponsive to instrumental conditioning, and operant behavior is being questioned more in behavior theory. It is possible through so-called biofeedback to exert some voluntary, central nervous system control over such autonomic processes as blood pressure and pulse rate (Staats 1975:538–42). Moreover, the same stimulus can have a dual function of eliciting a respondent behavior and at the same time influencing an operant (Staats 1975:37–38).

Reflexes respond automatically to heat, food, and intrusions as *unconditioned stimuli*. But they can be conditioned to be elicited by other *conditioned stimuli* in the same way that Pavlov conditioned his dog to salivate at the sound of a bell. Through Pavlovian or "classical" conditioning, the hand can be made to jerk back as from a hot stove at the sound of a bell, the mouth to water as at the sight of edibles with the sound of a buzzer, and the eyelids to blink at the touch of a hand. But the response itself is still elicited by a prior stimulus.

The form and rate with which operant behavior occurs, however, depends on *instrumental conditioning*. That is, the behavior is acquired or conditioned by the effects, outcomes, or *consequences* it has on the person's environment. Operants are not automatic responses to eliciting stimuli; instead, they are capable of developing a functional relationship with stimulus events. They are developed, maintained, and strengthened (or conversely are repressed or fail to develop), depending on the feedback received or produced from the environment. In this sense the stimulus following or *contingent* on an operant controls it; the preceding stimulus controls a respondent.

Any behavioral episode may be a complex combination or chain of both operant and respondent behavior. But social behavior (including deviant behavior) is predominantly operant. Therefore, the principles of behavior theory of most interest to us are those which detail the way environmental consequences react on and affect behavior. Differential association-reinforcement theory is only incidentally concerned with responses which are entirely unconditioned reflex reactions to internal or external eliciting stimuli. The theory does not attempt to explain why one has reflex actions. But at various places in the following chapters we use processes of respondent conditioning in conjunction with operant conditioning in our analysis (see, for example, the chapter on sexual behavior).

The theory does not explain how or why behavior based solely on some physiological condition or inherited attribute occurs. Why one is physically deformed, extremely ugly, brain damaged, or handicapped is not within the purview of the theory. Why the handicapped, deformed, or ugly person attempts to avoid the company of others, to conceal his deviant characteristics, or to engage in activities designed to mitigate, lessen, or deflect the stigma others attach to him *is* explainable by the theory.

The theory is also incapable of accounting for why anyone or anything is socially defined as undesirable. It is capable of accounting for the reactions of the one who is so stigmatized to the sanctions others apply to him. The theory does not say how or why the culture, structure, and social patterning of society sets up and implements certain sets and schedules of reactions to given behavior and characteristics. It does say what the impact of these reactions will be on the individual and what the impact of his counterreactions will be on others.

With these background comments in mind, let us turn now to a brief review of operant learning, to which the first proposition of the theory refers. The basic process is this: *stimuli following or contingent upon an operant determine the probability of its future occurrence.* The two major parts of this process are *reinforcement* and *punishment*.

Reinforcement

Technically reinforcement is the process whereby a response-contingent stimulus has the effect of strengthening the response (increasing the rate or probability of recurrence). In less technical terms, sometimes our behavior is met by reactions from others (or has some other consequences attached to it) which influence us to do the same thing again under similar circumstances. Two kinds of consequences of behavior affect behavior in this way.

First, we may be motivated to continue the behavior because we have been rewarded for doing so. That is, our actions are followed by pleasant, pleasing, desirable, or enjoyable events. When these strengthen behavior, *positive reinforcement* has occurred. The pleasant consequences may be any of the positive social sanctions listed in the first chapter. They may be social approval or status; they may be symbols of approval such as a grade or a medal. The reward may be money. The positive reinforcer may be the effect from something physically consumed, such as food, drink, or drugs. Whatever it is, it is defined as a positive reinforcer because it is added to rather than taken away from the environment.

The second type of reinforcement, *negative reinforcement*, is based on taking something away from the environment. That is, one may engage in some activity which enables him to remove or avoid unpleasant or painful stimuli, and this too will reinforce that activity. Behavior produced or maintained in this way is usually labeled *escape-avoidance behavior* because it allows one to avoid aversive events. In negative reinforcement we repeat an act, not because we have been or expect to be rewarded for it, but because it forestalls, mitigates, or removes something that otherwise would be punishing.

Positive and negative reinforcement have the same behavioral effect; both increase the rate of behavior. But in positive reinforcement this effect is produced by the addition and in negative reinforcement by the removal or avoidance of some stimulus event. In the laboratory a person can be conditioned to press a button at an increased rate by rewarding him for doing so (positive reinforcement). But he can also be made to press at a rapid rate by giving him an electric shock which can be shut off only by pressing the button (negative reinforcement). In the first example his behavior has been reinforced by adding rewards; in the second his behavior has been reinforced by removing the electric shock. The child who puts up his bicycle every evening because in the past he has been spanked when he did not has had his behavior negatively reinforced; the one who does so because in the past he has been given a treat has had his behavior positively reinforced.

Punishment

When the events following behavior have the effect of repressing or weakening it (technically decreasing the rate at which it is emitted), we say that *punishment* has occurred. As with reinforcement, punishment may be brought about by either the addition or subtraction of stimulus events. When the decrease in behavior is brought on by adding punishers as consequences of behavior it is defined as *positive punishment*. Removing a privilege or reward is *negative punishment*. The criminal who ceases to steal or cuts down after having been convicted and given harsh sentences in the past has been positively punished. The motorist who reduces his fast driving after having had his license and money (in fines) taken away has been negatively punished.

In the common-sense meanings it may seem a contradiction in terms to call receiving punishment "positive" or to say it is "negative" to escape punishment. But the terms are not used here as judgments of good and bad; they are used simply in the sense of plus and minus. The following table shows the way in which reinforcement and punishment are positive and negative:

Stimulus	Behavior increases— reinforcement	Behavior decreases— punishment
+	Positive Reinforcement (reward received)	Positive Punishment (punisher received)
−	Negative Reinforcement (punisher removed or avoided)	Negative Punishment (reward removed or lost)

Social and Nonsocial Reinforcement

What is likely or not likely to be reinforcing or punishing for what and for whom is not part of operant learning principle. Such predictions about the probable reinforcing or punishing relationship that a stimulus has with a class of behavior can be made from experimentation and observation. Predictions can also be made from existing knowledge about biological, psychological, and sociocultural variables. It is through these observations that substantive kinds and sources of reinforcement and punishment are incorporated into social learning.

At the physiological level, satisfaction of hunger, thirst, and sex drives tends to be reinforcing for all humans (as well as other organisms) who are in a state of deprivation of food, water, or sex. Also, approving responses, recognition, status, and acceptance from significant others are universal social reinforcers for humans. Within a society there are commonly valued rewards which have acquired such generalized value—money is the most obvious example—that they tend to reinforce any behavior that achieves them. Also there is commonly valued behavior that is likely to produce positive social sanctions from others in that society. But within the society numerous subcultures may vary from the larger society in the kinds of behavior valued and the stimuli which are reinforcing for the participants. Ultimately, of course, each individual has a unique conditioning history. But a knowledge of group history, social structure, and cultural values enables us to make some predictions about what are likely to be available and effective reinforcers for members of specific groups. Through observation of individuals who are exposed to a given set of recurring stimuli, we can say something about what typically will happen when other individuals are exposed to the same stimuli. Finally, by observing an individual's behavior we can determine what specific parts of his behavior are under the control of what specific stimuli.

Unconditioned or intrinsically rewarding physiological stimuli mentioned above may be defined as nonsocial and are involved in shaping and maintaining behavior. Behavioral adaptations must be made to the physical environment. Also, the individual can and does acquire behavior more or less on his own without contact, directly or indirectly, with any of the other reinforcers listed above, and we can describe that learning also as nonsocial. However, most of the learning relevant to deviant behavior is the result of social interactions or exchange in which the words, responses, presence, and behavior of other persons make reinforcers available, and provide the setting for reinforcement or are the behavior reinforcers. Many of the social rewards are highly symbolic and intangible and are reinforcing because they fulfill ideological, religious, political, or other goals. Even the more tangible rewards such as money and material goods gain their reinforcing value from the prestige and approval value they have acquired in society. One may be reinforced by these rewards for some particular pattern of behavior in a nonsocial context in the narrow sense that other people are not present at the time and do not respond directly to his behavior. But this is still social reinforcement in the sense that one finds the acquisition of these things reinforcing mainly because of their social desirability. Without social acceptance as a generalized medium of exchange for socially defined rewards, money would be so much paper and metal with no function as a reinforcing stimulus. One may reinforce or punish his own behavior even when alone. But this *self-reinforcement* is still social in that one takes the role of others as if they were present, responding to his own behavior as learned previously from others. In a well-fed society, the reinforcement coming from the consumption of food is mainly the conditioned reinforcement from association with the social setting in which food is customarily consumed. Moreover, symbolic rewards sometimes override nonsocial reinforcers — for instance, when one goes on a hunger strike to make a political point.

We recognize that learning can occur in connection with nonsocial rewards and punishment, but it is the power and centrality of the direct and symbolic social rewards in society which lead to labeling this theory *social learning*. The theory further proposes that the groups and individuals that comprise or control the major sources of the individual's reinforcement will have the greatest influence on his behavior. Usually these are primary groups, which Sutherland emphasized, but they can also be secondary or reference groups. They may be imaginary groups, persons, and situations portrayed through the books and the mass media. They may also be the more formal bureaucratic organizations like an individual's school or job, including agencies of social control and law enforcement.

Imitation

In addition to their role in directly reinforcing behavior, these groups influence behavior by providing models for *imitation*. Sutherland's theory has often been erroneously construed as only a restatement of the simplistic imitation theory of the nineteenth-century French sociologist Gabriel Tarde. Sutherland recognized that imitating others is one way of learning, but that learning is "not restricted to the process of imitation" (Sutherland and Cressey 1970:77).

Imitation is engaging in behavior after observation of similar behavior. Two conceptions of imitation are current in modern learning theory. First, imitation is seen as a special learning process on the same level as instrumental and classical conditioning. The individual is not himself rewarded for certain actions immediately, but he observes a model's behavior being rewarded and as a result of this *vicarious reinforcement* emulates the actions of the model. Or an entire new behavioral pattern may be acquired simply through modeling, without trial and error or external reinforcement for it.

Others have disputed this conception of imitation and see imitation as derived from direct operant conditioning. In this second conception, imitating behavior is itself a learned ability acquired through direct reinforcement. Also, a seemingly spontaneous behavioral episode following observation of another person's behavior is merely the chaining together at a given time of a series of previously disconnected acts which are already part of the imitator's behavioral repertoire (Bandura 1969:118–203; Burgess et al. 1970; Staats 1975:161–200; Parton 1974).

Whether imitation is a special learning process or part of the general class of instrumental processes, it is clear that modeling or imitating is an important part of social learning, and can be expected to be important in learning deviant behavior. It is especially important in the acquisition of novel behavior as contrasted with the maintenance of behavioral patterns once established.

Differential Reinforcement

The specific process by which deviant behavior becomes dominant over conforming behavior in specified situations is *differential reinforcement.* In the simplest terms, differential reinforcement means that given two alternative acts, both of which produce and are reinforced by the same or similar consequences, the one which does so in the greatest amount, more frequently, and with higher probability will be maintained. In a sense the one that has been more successful in obtaining the desired payoffs will become dominant. Differential reinforcement operates when both acts are similar and both are rewarded, but one is more highly rewarded. But differential learning of this kind is most dramatic and effective when the alternatives are incompatible and one is rewarded while the other is unrewarded. One can be continued strongly and the other discontinued even more quickly and effectively if while the first is rewarded the other is punished, even mildly.

Amount of reinforcement simply refers to the measurable quantities of the reinforcer—food, tokens, money, approval, and so on. Frequency and probability of reinforcement are based on *schedules of reinforcement,* of which there are basically two types, *continuous* and *intermittent.*[6]

On a continuous schedule each response is followed immediately by a reinforcing stimulus. For example, a child who is given a penny or a piece of candy immediately each time he spells a word correctly would have his spelling behavior on a continuous reinforcement schedule. Any schedule of reinforcement which is discontinuous, which departs from this continuous

---

[6]These and the following comments refer only to reinforcement, but the concepts of amount, frequency, probability, and schedules also apply to punishment.

pattern, is an intermittent schedule. Reinforcement can be intermittent in time — that is, there is an interval or lapse of time (either a fixed or variable length of time) between the act and its reinforcement. The man who must work a week before getting paid and the one who must work an entire month before getting paid are both on intermittent schedules, but the one who is paid every week has a higher *frequency* of reinforcement. Another type of intermittent schedule is based on the ratio of responses to reinforcement — the number of acts or the number of times one must repeat an act to achieve some reward. The burglar who breaks into three houses before he finds something worth stealing and then has to burglarize ten more before he scores again has a lower *probability* of reinforcement for burglary than the thief who is reasonably sure of making a score in at least every other house he breaks into. Continuous schedules are rare in society; nearly all patterning of social reinforcement is intermittent. The varied time intervals between performances and reward (or punishment) and the uncertainties connected with receiving social rewards give behavior much of its variety, complexity, and stability.

We know, of course, that the same behavior can be rewarded at one time and place and punished at another time and place. Whether others react to one's actions in such a way that they are reinforced depends on what is considered good, desirable, approved, necessary, important, or what have you, and this depends on the values of those with whom one customarily interacts. For this reason the frequency, duration, priority, and intensity of differential association with deviant and nondeviant cultural and behavioral patterns have an impact on reinforcement. They should affect whether deviant or conforming behavior is rewarded and, if so, in what amount, how frequently, and with what probability.

Definitions Favorable to Deviant Behavior and Discriminative Stimuli

In the original differential association theory Sutherland pointed to two things that are learned which are conducive to law violation: (1) learning techniques which make one able to commit crime and (2) learning definitions which motivate him or make him willing to violate the law. Both techniques and definitions are retained in the reformulated theory, differential association-reinforcement.

Obviously the necessary techniques to carry out deviant behavior must be learned before one can commit deviant acts; inability to perform them precludes commission. Many of the techniques, either simple or complex, are not novel to most of us. Rather, the required component parts or the complete skill is acquired in essentially conforming or neutral contexts to which many of us have been exposed—driving a car, shooting a gun, fighting with fists, signing checks, sexual intercourse, and so on. Other skills are specific to given deviant acts—safe cracking, counterfeiting, pocket picking, jimmying and picking doors and locks, bringing off a con game, administering narcotics, and so forth—and most of us would not be able to perform them or at least would be initially very inept.

Definitions are normative meanings which are given to behavior—that is, they define an action as right or not right. Sutherland's conception was that the individual is exposed, through interaction with other people, to definitions that approve certain acts prohibited by law and to definitions that condemn the acts. If the approval definitions of the behavior are in excess, the person would be willing to commit the act and violate the law.

These definitions have been incorporated into the reformulated differential association-reinforcement theory by viewing them as verbal behavior (overt and subvocal), which can be reinforced, and by viewing them as included in the class of stimuli called *discriminative stimuli*. Discriminative stimuli are stimuli which become associated with reinforcement. In addition to the reinforcers, other stimuli are ordinarily present when behavior is reinforced—the physical surroundings, one's own feelings, others' behavior, one's own and others' spoken words, and so on. Those that customarily accompany reinforcement (or punishment) come to be associated with it; they set the stage or provide the *cues* for the reinforcement. In a sense discriminative stimuli signal the actor that when they are present he can expect reinforcement. In social interaction the place, the people, and what they say all act as cues which allow one to recognize situations in which certain behavior is appropriate and is likely to be rewarded or is not appropriate and is apt not to be rewarded. Through differential reinforcement we learn that some behavior is appropriate, approved, and likely to be rewarded in some situations and not in others.

The child who remains quiet and inactive while his parents are with other adults and are attempting to carry on a conversation will be rewarded and perhaps told later, "I was so proud of you." But the same child who behaves the same way on the playground with other children will soon be excluded from the group; if he wants the attention and approval of his playmates he must join in. After this happens a few times he learns that he will be positively reinforced for quietness when adults are around but not when adults are absent and other children are around. The presence of adults is discriminative for behaving quietly, whereas the presence of children is discriminative for playing. Discriminative stimuli thereby increase the probability that the behavior will recur beyond that provided by the reinforcing stimuli, although discriminative stimuli have no independent reinforcing value themselves. To the extent that the stimuli in one situation are similar to those of another in which the person has been reinforced for some behavior, he will behave similarly in both situations.

Among the most important of stimuli which can become discriminative in social interaction are verbal symbols. Social reinforcers typically consist of or are delivered through words, and verbal interaction often accompanies nonverbal reinforcement ("I love you," "That's nice"). A significant portion of these verbal stimuli are comprised of normative definitions which evaluate the behavior in question as good or bad, right or wrong, justified or unjustified. When social sanctions are applied to behavior something evaluative will probably be said ("Lying is not right," "Good little boys don't do that"). After a while these evaluative definitions associated with the reward and punishment of behavior become discriminative for the behavior.

Basically two classes of verbal discriminative stimuli are operative in deviant behavior. First, there are those which place the behavior in a positive light, *defining it as desirable* or permissible. These would be associated with *positive reinforcement* through the reactions of others who share a subculture. Within the subculture the behavior seems appropriate, and one who conforms automatically violates the notions of appropriate behavior held by other groups in society. Thus it would be analogous to learning conforming behavior defined as desirable in American society, but which would be deviant in another society.

These positive verbalizations may be the "higher values" conception of some groups in conflict with the established order. Some deviant groups, such as homosexuals, may develop full-blown ideologies which define their behavior as contributing a positive good to the world. But although the existence of such groups can be established and such verbalizations can be identified, the type of definition which probably occurs more frequently is the second type.

This second type is comprised of definitions which are discriminative for deviant behavior by virtue of the fact that they *neutralize definitions of the behavior as undesirable.* They make the behavior, which others condemn and which the person himself may initially define as bad, seem all right, justified, excusable, necessary, the lesser of two evils, or not "really" deviant after all. This type of definition was first used by Cressey (1953) in analyzing deviance. He referred to "verbalizations," "rationalizations," and "vocabularies of adjustment and motives."[7] Taking their lead from Cressey, Sykes and Matza (1957) laid out several "techniques of neutralization" used by delinquents to counter antidelinquent definitions and make delinquencies seem all right. These techniques function to make the delinquent acts seem justified and deflect social and self-disapproval. These neutralizing definitions are peculiar extensions of "defenses to crime" contained in the general conforming culture and incorporated into the criminal law and include "denial of responsibility," "denial of injury," "denial of the victim,"

---

[7] All of these owe much to Mills' (1940) "vocabulary of motives," which includes a way of talking about behavior and a way of making sense of both acceptable and unacceptable behavior.

and "condemnation of the condemners." Others have used terms such as "accounts" (Lyman and Scott 1970:111–43) and "disclaimers" (Hewitt and Stokes 1975).

Such definitions have probably originated primarily through the process of *negative reinforcement*. That is, they serve to defend against or to avoid the punishment that comes from social disapproval of the activity by oneself and others. Behavior has escaped or avoided punishment in the presence of these definitions and is punished in their absence.

For example, the child who has become accustomed to being punished for running over his little sister with his bicycle accidently runs into her one time, and his parent, seeing that his bike went out of control, does not punish him, saying something like, "It was an accident, it wasn't your fault." On another occasion he runs into his sister intentionally and avoids a spanking by telling his dad, "It was an accident." This does not have to happen many times before he learns that if behavior is defined as his fault he is likely to be punished, but if it is defined as an accident, he will probably escape punishment.

Some neutralizing definitions become incorporated into deviant subcultures (along with the positive definitions noted above). For persons participating in those subcultures then the neutralizations are reinforced in two ways: they are positively reinforced by gaining approval in the subculture and negatively reinforced by providing a defense against the blandishments of those outside the subculture. Examples of such neutralizations which have become part of subcultural ideologies include those employed by professional thieves: "Everybody has his racket," "Everyone has larceny in his heart," "The thief is at least honest about his crookedness, the square john is hypocritical about his"; those used in the homosexual subculture: "I can't help myself, I was born this way"; and those used in prostitution: "Every wife is really a prostitute exchanging sexual favors for room and board," "Prostitution protects other women from attack by kooks."

However, most neutralizing definitions discriminative for deviant behavior are probably learned from carriers of conventional culture, including social control and treatment agencies themselves. For nearly every norm we have a norm of evasion—that is, there are accepted exceptions to or ways of getting around the moral imperatives in the norms and the reproach expected from violating the norms. Thus "Thou shalt not kill" is nearly always accompanied by implicit or explicit exceptions (except in time of war if the victim is the enemy, in self-defense, in the line of duty, to protect life and limb, and so on). The moral injunctions against physical aggression are suspended if the victim can be defined as the initial aggressor and therefore deserves to be attacked. Premarital and extramarital sexual behavior can go without negative social sanctions because, "After all they loved one another and established a 'meaningful' relationship," "Temptations that great couldn't be resisted by anyone," "With a wife like that what would you do?" Some rationalizations, such as *nonresponsibility*, can be generalized to a wide range of disapproved behavior. "I couldn't help myself," "It wasn't my fault," "I am not responsible," "It was an accident," "He started it," "I was drunk and didn't know what I was doing," "I was so mad I just blew my top."

These types of definitions are often expressed as excuses for one's own and others' deviancy, and punishment which would otherwise follow is withheld or is considerably mitigated. The individual then learns the excuses himself, either directly or through imitation, and uses them to lessen self-reproach and disapproval from others. They would therefore seem to be important in cases where initial moral abhorence or obstacles to deviant acts must first be overcome by the individual before he can commit them.

This hypothesizes that an excess of one set of definitions over another in the sense of a cumulative ratio is not crucial for deviance, as Sutherland would have it. Rather, the deviant outcome is determined by differential reinforcement for and the relative discriminative stimulus value of one set of verbalizations over another. That is, the using of the definitions is an operant behavior which can be reinforced, but the definitions may in turn serve as discriminative stimuli for other behavior, provided that they accompany (at least occasionally) reinforcement of the behavior. Of course, deviant actions may be reinforced and may recur without being accompanied by definitions. However, insofar as that reinforcement is customarily accompanied by such definitions, it is more likely that the behavior will recur in situations to which the definitions can be applied. The variations in one's differential association with individuals and groups are important then, and not only with regard to the kind of deviant or antideviant definitions to which he is exposed; they also influence the amount, frequency, and probability of reinforcement for deviant or nondeviant behavior and verbalizations and hence increase the probability that the definitions will become discriminative for deviance.

Critique of and Research on the Social Learning Theory of Deviant Behavior

The social learning theory of deviant behavior has been cited in both the professional and pedogogical literature in the sociology of deviance and criminology.[8] Attention is not, however, the equivalent of acceptance or

---

[8]The Burgess and Akers article on differential association-reinforcement has "attracted attention from sociologists and criminologists, being quoted, referenced, and reprinted" (Adams 1973:489). Cressey (Sutherland and Cressey 1974) cites the theory as one of the more promising theoretical developments, and many textbooks now include a discussion of it along with other major theories in the discipline (Mauss 1975; Quinney 1975; Fox 1976).

validity. The theory should not and has not been taken as is; it has been subjected to both critical and empirical examination. One criticism of the basic learning principles on which the theory is based is that they are tautological. That is, unless one is careful with the way terms are defined and propositions are stated, the principles become true by definition and therefore not capable of being tested empirically. For instance, to say that behavior is strengthened because it is reinforced is a circular, untestable statement when the very strengthening of the behavior is taken as evidence that the behavior has been reinforced. Burgess and I offered a resolution of this problem, namely carefully separating definitions and propositions in behavior theory (Burgess and Akers 1966a).

The theory continues to be criticized for this shortcoming, however, and our resolution may not be satisfactory. The tautology problem is seldom encountered in the laboratory testing of the basic principles since there is always clear separation of the manipulation of reinforcement contingencies by the experimenter and the changes in the behavior of the subject(s). Tautology is not much of a problem as the theory is applied here since locating substantive sources and kinds of stimuli reinforcing specific forms of behavior avoids circularity. For instance, the proposition that one uses marihuana because he has been differentially reinforced for such behavior in that he finds its effects pleasurable, is rewarded by approval from and acceptance by his drug-using friends, and is not inhibited from using it by informal sanctions of parents or by fear of legal sanctions is nontautological and testable.

Social learning theory (differential association-reinforcement) has also been criticized for incorrectly and incompletely incorporating operant conditioning principles and not adequately dealing with the importance of nonsocial reinforcement (Adams 1973). On the other hand, the very inclusion of nonsocial reinforcement and the integration of behavioral concepts with Sutherland's theory have been strongly criticized (Taylor et al. 1973:131–33). The issue seems mainly semantic and is resolved simply by making plain what one means by "social."

"Social" reinforcement is conceived of here broadly as involving not just the direct reactions of others present while an act is performed, but also the whole range of tangible and intangible rewards valued in society and its subgroups. Nonsocial contingencies are more narrowly confined to un- conditioned physiological and physical stimuli. This conception of social reinforcement neither violates the spirit of Sutherland's theory nor is in- consistent with basic learning theory, which is uninterested in the sub- stantive nature of stimuli.

The learning principles have received empirical support from systematic experimental studies with both infrahuman and human subjects in labora- tory settings. Recent studies outside the laboratory in more natural settings and the application of learning principles in behavior modification projects have provided further confidence in the basic notions about classical and instrumental conditioning, schedules of reinforcement, generalization, discrimination, and so on.[9]

Although the "excess" of definitions has not been successfully studied, most of the central ideas in Sutherland's differential association theory have also received empirical support. While not all research directed toward testing the theory has supported it, on balance, the empirical evidence accumulated thus far supports the importance in deviant behavior of associations in primary groups such as family and peers. The evidence supports the importance of the priority, intensity, duration, and frequency of these associations, and of normative definitions and perceptions (Cressey 1953; Reiss and Rhodes 1964; Ball 1957; Short 1957; 1958; 1960; Voss 1964; 1969; Matthews 1968; Ball 1968; Krohn 1974; Jensen 1972; Burkett and Jensen 1975).

Thus, both specific differential association theory and the general behavior theory with which it is integrated to produce the social learning approach have received considerable empirical validation. However, the social learning theory presented here has yet to receive much direct empirical testing. Research done on the deterrence of criminal behavior through legal sanctions and threat of punishment is relevant and tends to be consistent with social learning. This research generally tends to support the proposition that the certainty (whether objective or perceived) of penalties has some deterrent effect on criminal behavior, while severity of punishment seems not to have much effect (Waldo and Chiricos 1972; Tittle and Logan 1973; Silberman 1976). The deterrence research does not provide a full test of learning theory, however, because the reinforcement for criminal behavior that the threat of legal penalties must offset and other reinforcement contingencies surrounding the behavior are not measured in that research. Also, deterrence researchers seldom refer to modern learning theory and do not present their findings as tests of it.

Anderson's (1973) findings provide more direct support for social learning. She found that both formal and informal sanctions have an effect on marihuana use. Those most likely to use marihuana were those who did not perceive a legal risk, whose parents did not actively disapprove, and who had friends who both used and approved of marihuana. Conger's (1976) findings on delinquent behavior and attachment to peers and parents also provide support for a social learning theory of deviant behavior. His findings are consistent with the principle of differential reinforcement in that delinquent behavior is most likely when positive peer reinforcement for delinquent acts is combined with low reinforcement for conventional behavior through "low stakes in conformity." Also, Conger found a high

---

[9]See references in footnote 2; see also McGinnies and Ferster 1971 and research reported in *Journal of Experimental Analysis of Behavior* and *Journal of Applied Behavior Analysis.*

correlation between the specific delinquent acts of friends and a person's own delinquent acts. This finding lends support to the proposition that delinquency is learned not only through direct reinforcement from delinquent friends but also through observation and imitation of their behavior.

Neither Anderson nor Conger set out to collect primary data to test a social learning theory of deviant behavior. Both used sets of data already collected for other purposes and tested the theory by examining the extent to which the data were or were not consistent with it. This is essentially the technique used here, and a considerable amount of other empirical grounding of the theory will be presented in later chapters. Judged by the data, there is support for the theory but further research is needed to collect data expressly for the purpose of testing this theory. Therefore, the rejection or acceptance of the social learning approach should be based on its utility in explaining the full range of deviant behavior examined in this book and on research by others, not just on what is said in the immediate context of this chapter.

Summary of the Theory and How It Will Be Used

After examining in the next chapter the issue of the relationship between social learning and social structure, each of the following chapters is devoted to a detailed examination of a particular form of deviant behavior — drug use, alcoholism, sexual deviance, criminal behavior, suicide, and mental illness. These are the major types of deviance that most clearly fit the definition presented in chapter 1 and have most often occupied the attention of social scientists interested in deviant behavior. The social learning theory is used to explain the process of coming to engage in *each* of these kinds of deviant behavior. This theoretical perspective is the thread that runs throughout the book, tying the chapters together. A summary of the theory is: The primary learning mechanism in social behavior is operant (instrumental) conditioning, in which behavior is shaped by the stimuli that follow or are consequences of the behavior. Behavior is strengthened through reward (positive reinforcement) and avoidance of punishment (negative reinforcement) or weakened (punished) by adversive stimuli (positive punishment) and lack of reward (negative punishment). Whether deviant or conforming behavior occurs and persists depends on the past and present rewards or punishment for the behavior, and the rewards and punishment attached to alternative behavior (differential reinforcement). In addition, a person learns to evaluate definitions of the acts as good or bad. These definitions are themselves verbal behavior (vocal and subvocal) which can be directly reinforced and also function as discriminative (cue) stimuli for other behavior. The more a person defines his behavior as a positive good or at least justified, the more likely he is to engage in it. A person will participate in deviant activity then to the extent that it has been differentially reinforced over conforming behavior and defined as more desirable than, or at least as justified as, conforming alternatives. While all of the mechanisms of learning are recognized, the emphasis will be on differential reinforcement and definitions favorable to deviant behavior. The theory is applied to deviant behavior in the following ways:

1. The sources, content, and impact of differential reinforcement, positive and negative reinforcement and punishment, conditioning, imitation, and other behavioral processes will be identified on the basis of available research findings and reasonable inferences from them.

Positive reinforcement is identified in the descriptions of most types of deviant behavior. For instance, the preaddictive use of opiates in a drug subculture and the use of hallucinogenic drugs are rewarded by the recognition and approval of drug-using peers. Moderate drinking by adolescents is socially reinforced in some families and peer groups, and excessive drinking is positively reinforced in some drinking groups. Social rewards are also attached to playing a homosexual role in the homosexual community. Prostitution is economically more rewarding than conventional jobs for some women, and the prostitute builds reinforcing relationships with others in the life. Occupational crimes are financially rewarding, and having the good opinion of and acceptance by coworkers and supervisors also influences the participation of some executives in corporate crimes. The professional thief finds crime remunerative and is also reinforced for his criminal activity by the prestige and acceptance with fellow thieves. Suicidal behavior and mental illness can be reinforced by increased social attention following self-injurious behavior or "psychotic" episodes. In addition to social reinforcement, taking drugs is conditioned by the reinforcement of the effects of the drugs; drinking may continue because of the positive effects and good taste of the alcoholic beverage; and deviant sexual behavior may be chosen because of the greater sexual pleasure derived from it than from conventional sexual behavior. The effects of these activities may be intrinsically pleasurable, but they are also conditioned to be so by their association with social reinforcement.

Negative reinforcement is identified in opiate addiction; one motivation of the addict is to avoid or escape the sickness which accompanies abstinence, and drug-taking may become his general response to other unpleasant conditions. In addition to the positive support received from some groups for heavy drinking, many alcoholics drink large quantities of alcohol in order to deal with anxiety and problems. Negative reinforcement is intertwined with positive inducements in other forms of deviance. For example, in some cases suicidal behavior is an attempt to resolve unbearable problems; the prostitute remains in the business partly because she fears what her pimp would do if she left; embezzlement is the white-collar worker's resolution of a problem.

2. The sources and nature of the definitions (the verbalizations and rationalizations discussed above) and other discriminative stimuli conducive to the deviant behavior will be located and described.

Positive definitions are favorable to deviance because they evaluate the behavior positively and tend to be learned by participating in deviant subcultures. Illustrations are the "cool" view of opiate use and the personal and intellectual benefits attributed to hallucinogenic drugs in drug subcultures, the glorification of homosexual behavior in the homosexual community, and the "prostitution helps keep the sex freaks from your daughters" ideology in prostitution.

The subcultures also offer definitions that characterize the behavior as not necessarily desirable but as excusable, justified, not really bad, or not the fault of the individual. These *neutralizing or justifying definitions* are more plentiful than positive definitions. They are found both in subcultures and in the general culture. For example, both the subcultural addict and the physician addict neutralize their initially unfavorable definition of opiates (because they are addictive) by saying, "I can control it." The physician addict also justifies his use of opiates as necessary to combat his ailments and to allow him to be effective despite fatigue from overwork. Initially negative definitions of homosexual behavior are overcome and homosexual acts justified as "not really queer." Later the homosexual rationalizes his continued homosexual behavior by thinking, "This is just the way I am." Both the prostitute and professional thief may justify their behavior by condemning the immorality and hypocrisy of the "straight" world: "Others are doing much the same thing, but they don't get caught and aren't honest enough to admit it." Corporate executives who violate restraint of trade laws try to rationalize their actions with the belief that such action is not really criminal or harmful to society. The embezzler also defines his theft as not really stealing, as only borrowing or at least as justified in his case. The person who lashes out with savage violence and seriously injures or kills others may account for his actions by saying, "They deserved it," or "I just couldn't help myself; I blew my stack and didn't know what I was doing." A person may justify his suicide attempt by blaming others or by believing it is the only way out of suffering a tragic loss or critical illness.

3. As the above should make clear, in examining both the definitions and the reinforcing processes the primary aim in each case will be to locate the patterns of *differential association* which provide the individual with the group contexts and sources of *social reinforcement*. However, nonsocial, physical, and physiological stimuli will be recognized and incorporated into the explanation where appropriate.

4. *Differential reinforcement and definitions* will be identified. However, the analysis focuses on the positive and negative reinforcers for the deviant behavior. Less attention will be paid to comparison of these with the punishing consequences of the behavior and the counteracting reinforcement and punishment of conforming alternatives. For example, this comparison will

be made in showing the differential reinforcement of professional crime. Sometimes it is a major part of the analysis, for instance, in the relative pleasure derived by homosexuals from homosexual and heterosexual alternatives. But even when it is not stated explicitly, the understood requirement is that deviant behavior results from greater reinforcement *on balance over* the probability of punishment and the contingencies on other behavior.

Similarly, more space will be devoted to showing the kinds of positive and neutralizing definitions favorable to deviance than to showing the anti-deviant definitions over which they have ascended. However, the guiding principle throughout is that the definitions favorable to deviance are conducive to deviance because on balance they have been reinforced more and have acquired greater discriminative value than unfavorable definitions. This is explicitly stated in discussing definitions that overcome original inhibiting definitions — overcoming initial distaste for drugs, neutralizing abhorrence of homosexuality, and overcoming learned definitions of embezzlement as criminal. Even so, the principle holds even where it is left implicit.

5. The usual result of the analysis is to spell out a *typical process* or processes through which the person progresses from conforming to deviant behavior — a "natural history" of becoming a homosexual, an addict, an alcoholic, and so on. For each type of deviance a typical learning history is outlined which shows how a person first engages in the behavior and then progresses to more habitual or stable patterns, even when some phases of that process are not themselves deviant — for example, moderate drinking.

6. The emphasis throughout is on *learning to do* something that is defined by others as deviant. Obviously, however, deviant behavior can also result from *learning failures.* Failure to learn the proper conforming responses either may be defined directly as deviant — that is, behavioral deficits such as in mentally retarded people — or may allow the development of other deviant behavior.

7. Each type of deviance considered is *carefully defined,* and where appropriate, controversial issues in the conceptual definitions are examined.

8. Insofar as they are known, the *amount,* variations in *group rates,* historical trends, and other relevant descriptive aspects of the deviant behavior are presented. In some cases the connection between the group rates and the behavior process leading to deviance is shown.

9. Finally, in some chapters observations on public policy, the law, treatment, and control are presented.

5

Behaviorism, Social Learning, and Structural Perspectives

Behaviorism and Social Learning

The revision of differential association outlined in chapter 4 is based on behavioral reinforcement principles. However, some readers will recognize that some concepts and ideas used here come from other behaviorally oriented theories and are not part of orthodox Skinnerian behaviorism. Also the reader who is familiar with differential association theory will recognize that its "symbolic interactionism" is retained here to some extent. Thus a brief comment is appropriate on how this social learning perspective relates to behaviorism, before we examine the question of how it relates to the structural perspectives presented in chapter 3.

Symbolic interactionism, based on the early writings of Cooley (1902) and Mead (1934), is the predominant social psychological orientation in sociology. Briefly, symbolic interactionism stresses the exchange of meanings communicated in face-to-face interaction through verbal and gestural symbols. Especially emphasized is the impact this interaction has on the individual's self-concept and image of himself.

Operant conditioning theory, as formulated by Skinner (1953) and those who work in the Skinnerian tradition, is based on a strongly behavioristic epistemology. Behaviorism rejects all "mentalistic" constructs — propositions about what people are thinking — and internal stimuli. Only directly observable, overt behavior and external environmental stimuli can be studied scientifically. Hence, the only propositions worthy of consideration are those about the relationship between overt behavioral responses and observable stimuli. There is no reference to behavior resulting from or mediated by internal mental or emotional events. Behaviorism recognizes two major forms this relationship can take: (1) a stimulus elicits a reflex response, and through pairing other stimuli can come to elicit the same response (respondent conditioning; classical conditioning; Pavlovian conditioning); (2) a behavior, by operating on the environment, produces a stimulus or is followed by a stimulus which feeds back upon the behavior and conditions its future occurrence (operant conditioning; instrumental conditioning). In earlier times behaviorism was based entirely on the first kind of stimulus-response relationship (Watson 1930). Modern behavioral learning theory, even though it may be referred to as operant theory, now includes both, but at least since Skinner it has emphasized the second kind of stimulus-response relationship. The insistence that only overt events can be studied has remained, and laboratory experimentation (with animals and humans) has remained the primary research strategy. Experimental behaviorism is now a major part of psychology (see Hill 1963).[1]

In reformulating differential association by integrating it with these general learning principles we relied primarily on the substance and to some extent the behavioristic style of work in the Skinnerian tradition (Burgess and Akers 1966b).[2] Operant behavior recognizes the importance of verbal behavior in human interaction as both response and stimulus. However, the concept of verbalization in this social learning theory is taken more from the meaning of *definition* in the original Sutherland theory than from the way in which verbal behavior is treated in modern behavior theory. As long as the definitions are seen as only overt verbal responses or as audible, verbal discriminative stimuli, they are congruent with, although not emphasized by, operant theory. But insofar as it is implied that one may apply these definitions to his own behavior in a sort of conversation with himself or to protect his self-concept, it is congruent primarily with the symbolic interactionism contained in the original differential association. Moreover, the idea that one cognitively engages in self-reinforcement guided by the norms he has internalized and other covert events is not given much place in behavioristic theory. Such postulated "mentalistic" processes are denounced by orthodox operant conditioning theory.

However, not all reinforcement learning theories are as strictly behavioristic as Skinnerian operant theory. Learning psychology has a long tradition of reinforcement theories with cognitive overtones, which have developed somewhat independently and somewhat in interaction with operant theory. These differ from strict behaviorism in utilizing notions about cognitive and symbolic processes such as self-reinforcement, anticipation of reinforcement, and vicarious reinforcement. The social learning theories of Rotter (1954) and Bandura (Bandura and Walters 1963; Bandura

---

[1] Even clinical psychology, which for so long has been in conflict with experimental psychology, has developed treatment procedures based on behavioral learning theory. The clinical application has tended to be referred to in general as *behavior therapy* or *behavior modification*. Some of this is classical conditioning, some is strictly Skinnerian, and some is a combination of these, with some reliance on notions about intrapsychic processes. See Eysenck 1964; Ullmann and Krasner 1964; Bandura 1969.

[2] Operant theory has been used by others in sociology. Homans (1961; 1969) was one of the first sociologists to use Skinnerian theory. Kunkel (1975) has also related sociological interest in social problems and in social structure to operant theory. The major work using operant principles to analyze general concepts and problems of long-standing interest to sociologists is by Burgess and Bushell (1969).

1969) and Staats (1975) are prime illustrations of this type of reinforcement theory. The sociopsychological model of Ullmann and Krasner (1969), although it is closer to operant theory, incorporates ideas about social labeling, role-playing, and social structure not found in behavioral theory. Both Rachman and Teasdale (1970:97–118) and Bandura (1969:38–45, 564–623) maintain that internal, cognitive processes operate in behavioral conditioning, including respondent conditioning. Bandura, for instance, says that there are

> [i]nnumerable studies demonstrating that, under many conditions, self-described covert events have much greater predictive power and regulatory influence over behavior than the externally manipulated variables. . . . One cannot account satisfactorily for human behavior while remaining entirely outside the organism, because overt behavior is often governed by self-generated stimulation that is relatively independent of environmental stimulus events. . . . In naturalistic situations a brief external stimulus often initiates a long chain of cognitive activities that is largely determined by mediational associative linkages (1969:38–39).

Staats (1975:48) noted that "enough evidence is available to indicate that the same principles that hold for external stimuli and responses appear to be applicable to internal, covert behavioral process." However, Bandura (1969:45) pointed out that "internal symbolic control" is just one element in learning. An overemphasis on internal, mental processes can lead to almost mystical constructions about what is going on in people's heads.

The social learning theory as developed and used here more closely resembles the reinforcement theories of Rotter, Bandura, Staats, Ullmann and Krasner (1969) and others than it resembles psychological formulations of a "purer" Skinnerian behaviorism.[3] Social learning then is "soft" behaviorism. Much attention is paid in the following pages to behavior and its relationship to external environmental stimuli. But there is no effort to avoid whatever connotations of cognition there are in the emphasis on definitions as rationalizations of and vocabularies of motives.

The Relationship of Social
Learning to Structural Perspectives

Each view on deviance reviewed in chapter 3 has something to recommend it. Although exceptions were made to each, some support was given to each. Also, while these views do not present an entirely unified perspective on deviance, there are few irreconcilable differences and there is a good

---

[3]For an overview of reinforcement theory with special emphasis on social learning theory and its application to a range of areas, see McLaughlin 1971. For a comprehensive presentation of "social behaviorism," see Staats 1975.

deal of overlapping among them. Both the conflict and labeling approaches emphasize the power differences between the definers and the deviants. Stress on the failure of socialization and social control is common to the disorganization-anomie and control theories: all share an emphasis on the structural conditions conducive to deviance. With some effort these approaches could probably be successfully integrated, but that job is left undone here. Rather, I want to indicate briefly the way in which these structural perspectives are congruent with social learning theory.

The basic premise of the social learning approach is that both conforming and deviant behavior are learned in the same way; the substance and direction of the learning is different, but the general process is the same for both conforming and deviant behavior. This theory is not that one becomes deviant because he is a certain kind of person, he inherited the tendency, or that the deviance is merely a manifestation of an intrapsychic trauma or disturbance he has undergone. Rather, the theory is that he has simply learned to respond to his environment and his human makeup in ways that others (and perhaps he too) define as deviant.

This learning proposition has been widely accepted in sociology and is quite consistent with the structural approaches to deviance. None of these approaches denies that normal learning processes are involved in the acquisition of deviant behavior. All would agree that the individual's behavior is shaped by the situations he has experienced in his life history. In fact, as has been shown, the burden of these structural theories is to show what kinds of situations and structures lead to deviant behavior.

But none of them adequately specifies the *process* by which social structure shapes individual behavior. The structural theories refer to the structure of learning environments likely to produce deviant behavior—breakdowns in social control, growing up in disorganized areas of the city, participation in deviant groups and subcultures or in groups in conflict with the established order, deprivation of legitimate opportunities, exposure to anomic conditions, or being labeled deviant—but they do not specify *how* they do produce deviant behavior. However, the learning perspective *does* specify the process by which social structure produces individual behavior. Thus social learning is complementary to, not competing with, the structural theories. The deviancy-producing environments have an impact on individual conduct through the operation of learning mechanisms.

The connection between social structure and the mechanisms of learning which shape individual conduct can be viewed in this way: the general culture and structure of society and the particular groups, subcultures, and social situations in which the individual participates provide learning environments in which the norms define what is approved and disapproved and the reactions of others (for example, in applying social sanctions) attach different reinforcing or punishing consequences to his behavior. In a sense, then, social structure is an arrangement of sets and schedules of reinforcement contingencies.

We will show that some groups and segments of society have higher rates of some kinds of deviant behavior than other groups. For every form of deviance on which we have information, the level of deviance varies systematically by such factors as age, sex, religion, ethnic classifications, race, occupation, socioeconomic status, and place of residence. These social characteristics indicate the individual's location in the structure of society, the particular groups of which he is likely to be a member, with whom he interacts, and how others are apt to respond to him and his behavior. Therefore, they reflect which behavioral and normative patterns the person will be exposed to and which of his behavior is likely to be approved and rewarded or disapproved and punished.

The connection between variations in group rates and the reinforcement and definitions of individual behavior is implicit in all the chapters, but it is stated most clearly in the chapters on drinking, suicide, and mental illness. However, in the social learning analysis for each behavior it is shown that the person who engages in deviant behavior has been differentially associated with those who provide definitions favorable to and reinforcement for his behavior. For some kinds of behavior this occurs in subcultures—for example some types of drug use, homosexuality, prostitution, professional crime—and for other kinds it occurs outside specific subcultures in family, peer, work, and friendship groups—for instance, drinking, occupational crime, suicide, mental illness. In each case whether one commits the deviant acts or remains conforming is largely determined by his interaction with others, whom he imitates and who directly reinforce his actions. Each person must also contend with the consequences (mainly punishment) which the formal and legal control agents attach to his behavior, but these consequences are often remote and uncertain and they therefore have less impact than the person's immediate primary groups.

Control

From this point of view, then, *control theory* is the theory that is most compatible with social learning. The central idea in control theory is that conformity is maintained when conventional social controls are strong and deviant behavior results when the controls are weak. "Effective social control" can be easily interpreted to mean that the social sanctions successfully reinforce conventional behavior and extinguish deviant behavior by rewarding conformity and punishing nonconformity. The structure of social control in society arranges contingencies of reinforcement in such a way that most people are kept in line most of the time. Conforming behavior is successively shaped over time (socialization) and becomes largely self-controlled; we learn to define most deviant acts unfavorably and to apply sanctions to our own behavior. Moreover, we remain liable to at least intermittent reinforcement for conformity and punishment for deviance. The loosening of attachment to conventional groups means that the individual is no longer effectively controlled by the rewards and punishment of those groups. Neutralizing definitions facilitate the breaking of these ties by countering antideviant definitions. The person may then behave deviantly because he has become isolated from those who would continue to approve and reinforce his conforming behavior and to punish his nonconforming acts.

Ordinarily this is where control theory stops; the stage is set for deviant behavior by the failure of conventional controls. But control theory can be extended a step beyond this. Deviance may result only from the ineffective operation of conventional controls, but the person may also gravitate to other groups or may encounter situations in which the controls operate positively to reinforce his deviant behavior. Thus the person whose ties with conformity have been broken may remain just a candidate for deviance; whether he becomes deviant depends on further social or other rewards. Social control is still functioning when the individual's behavior comes under the influence of the sanctions of deviant subcultures or other groups, only the direction of that control is deviant by the standards of the conventional groups with which he has broken.

Control theory has been most often and most successfully used to account for juvenile delinquency. Delinquency is discussed in the presentation of general perspectives on deviance, and one form of delinquency, underage drinking, is analyzed. Although no chapter is devoted to delinquency as a separate form of deviant behavior, we can demonstrate that delinquency can be accounted for by a social learning analysis and that such an analysis is consistent with control theory. Lack of attachment to conventionality means that the youngster is isolated from (or is unable to obtain) sufficient reward for conformity in the family, school, and conforming peer groups. His delinquency is not prevented, and he may develop ties with delinquent peers who facilitate the lessened effect of conventional controls by exposing him to neutralizing definitions, by negatively sanctioning his efforts at conformity, and by positively reinforcing his delinquent behavior.

Group sanctions that reward other kinds of deviant behavior are referred to in several places, but the analyses of drinking and sexual behavior provide the clearest illustrations of the way social controls set up the conditions for learning deviance. It is shown, for example, that social controls tend to shape drinking behavior in certain groups. In groups with prescriptive norms most people do drink moderately, and in groups with proscriptive norms most do not drink at all. However, when individuals loosen ties with a proscriptive group they become isolated from the drinking-prevention control of that group and tend disproportionately to become heavy drinkers. It will also be shown that the alcoholic's somewhat excessive drinking may not be sufficiently controlled by a group with relatively moderate norms until it gets so out of hand that he is no longer welcome in that group. His break with the more moderate group opens the way for his move to other groups which tolerate and reward his heavier drinking. Similarly, we will see that

conventional controls may insufficiently train some people in sexual conformity and may set the stage for learning sexual behavior in deviant contexts.

The other theories can also be interpreted as making statements consistent with social learning about the structural conditions that promote or
hinder deviant behavior.

Disorganization-Anomie

First, *anomie*, the malintegration of cultural ends and means or differential opportunity, sets up conditions for differential reinforcement. The
cultural ends may be viewed as general rewards which are sought by most
people and which are able to reinforce whatever behavior serves as effective
means to them. When the individual is in a life situation in which illegitimate behavior (delinquency, prostitution, crime behavior) is more likely to
produce those rewards in greater amounts than the conventional educational,
economic, political, and other activities, the illegitimate behavior will be
differentially reinforced over the conventional behavior. Second, the "normlessness," or lack of clear and consistent norms, which characterizes disorganized groups may be experienced as stressful by the individual; actions
which reduce or resolve the strain for him will be negatively reinforced, and
these may be defined as deviant (for example, excessive drinking). The deviant adaptation to anomie, whether it produces greater rewards or is reinforced by alleviation of stress, is more likely to be tried if the person is exposed to subcultures that have successful deviant models and favorable
definitions.

Conflict

The proposition in *conflict theory* that deviant behavior is simply the
actions of members of groups which have lost the battle for power or the
groups which are motivated to violate the law because they are in ideological
conflict with the established order applies most clearly to political crime and
seems not directly applicable to most kinds of deviance discussed here.
However, the basic idea that there is normative conflict in society and that
behaving as a conforming member of one group may automatically make one
deviant with respect to another group is clearly consistent with the social
learning approach. Within one group a person is provided with positive
definitions and is reinforced for behavior which would be negatively defined
and punished in another. Participation in a drug or criminal subculture, for
instance, means that one learns behavior which is unacceptable outside the
subculture.

Labeling

We have seen that negative labeling by official agencies does not enhance deviance as often as labeling theory would predict. However, to the extent that labeling someone deviant and treating him differently sometimes makes him more deviant it may be viewed as a social learning process. First, the apprehension and official labeling of someone may reduce his chances to pursue conventional alternatives to achieve the same rewards he has obtained by deviant means. This in turn may increase the chance that he will become more deeply involved in groups which add reinforcement and rationalizations for his deviant behavior. Second, being publicly branded a deviant may support the disapproval of the person by his neighbors, relatives, and others in the community, who then fail to respond in a rewarding way to his efforts to "reform," as shown, for example, in the discussion of relapse in opiate addiction. Third, the conditions under which the person is punished or "treated" as a result of his legal or official assignment to deviant status may be conducive to learning new or maintaining old patterns of deviant behavior. Incarceration in prison may enable the criminal to learn additional criminal behavior. The structure of rewards and punishment in the mental hospital ward often reinforces "sick" behavior.

The labeling perspective also points to the unintended deviance-inducing consequences of certain public policy. The illegality of some goods and services, such as drugs and gambling, set up the monopolistic tariffs which increase the rewards to those who are willing to risk supplying the demand, such as organized criminal syndicates. The high price of illegal drugs means that many addicts cannot support their habits through conventional income-producing activities, and hence commission of property crimes is reinforced because it is a means to drugs.

Summary

Social learning is a general processual approach which will be applied to the major forms of deviance in American society analyzed in this book. It is a "soft" behaviorism, compatible with the principal structural theories of deviant behavior. Therefore, it holds some promise as an integrating orientation in the sociology of deviance.

Part Two

Deviant Drug Use

6

Types and Effects of Drugs

We live in a drug-saturated society. The different kinds of drugs available in this country number in the hundreds, the number of drug takers are counted in the millions, and the doses taken per year number in the billions. Some of these drugs are difficult to obtain, whereas others are as handy as the over-the-counter shelves of the corner pharmacy. Some drugs put you to sleep; others wake you up. If you are underactive, depressed, too relaxed, lethargic, too tired, or not aggressive enough, there are drugs available to bring you out of it. There are also drugs for the person who is too active, overanxious, overaggressive, or tension-ridden. There are pills, capsules, or liquids for losing or gaining weight, for alleviating pain, or for just feeling good.

Most drug use in this country is legitimate use of legitimate substances. However, some use is not legitimate in one way or another, and this is what will concern us in this chapter. It keeps the discussion of deviant drug taking in perspective if we remember that it occurs within the larger context of a drug-oriented society. Sometimes the results of drug taking are beneficial; at other times they are disastrous. But at all times drugs are part of the modern, urbanized, industrial society in which we live.

Some drugs, such as opium, cannabis, alcohol, and various "witches' brews" (Cohen 1969:63–67), have been used by mankind for thousands of years. Others, such as LSD, tranquilizers, antibiotics, synthetic opiates, amphetamines, and barbiturates, have become known more recently. New forms, derivatives, and usages of ancient drugs continue to be developed; new synthetics continue to be compounded; new pharmacological qualities have been discovered in natural herbs and plants; and novel uses of household items and solvents, such as paint thinner, glue, and cleaning fluid have been encountered. The anticipation of a drug-free society is about as likely to be fulfilled as was the dream of a totally dry society in the early days of prohibition.

It will also help to keep the discussion in perspective if we remember that the way society views drug use changes through time, and at any given time there are conflicting definitions of what is legitimate drug usage. One can find defenders of every drug and drug practice that is condemned. Opiates have been celebrated and condemned; marihuana has its proponents and detractors; LSD has been declared the curse of mankind and the best hope of salvation through self-knowledge. There is currently conflict about the extent of harm caused (see the closing section of this chapter), if any, about the propriety of attaching criminal sanctions to their use, and about the proper regulation, if any, that should be applied. A good deal of nonsense, half-truths, falsehoods, and distortions have been uttered on all sides. At the same time, a careful and objective body of knowledge about drugs and their use has been accumulated, and it helps provide a better understanding of the problem.

Basic Definitions:
Drug Use, Habituation, and Addiction

Drug use refers to both legitimate and illegitimate use of any of the range of natural and synthetic substances. However, in this chapter it usually refers to *deviant* drug-oriented or drug-seeking behavior. Thus it will be used synonymously with such terms as *drug abuse*, a term that is increasingly used in the literature to mean both the misuse of legal drugs and the use of illicit drugs.

There are basically three phases of drug-using behavior: (1) *initial* (prehabitual) use; (2) *habituation*, and (3) *relapse* (preceded, of course, by a period of abstinence). *Initial* use is experimental, occasional, and irregular ingestion of drugs by someone who does not have a prior history of sustained use. *Habituation* is defined here as the regular use of a drug continued over time. The term is used in the neutral sense that one can make a habit of doing or using anything — regularly brushing his teeth, wearing a particular style of dress, eating at certain times, having a glass of water with meals, or kissing his wife. One can acquire the habit of using many different kinds of drugs and substances, and the quality of the observable behavior, other things being equal, does not differ radically from one to the other.

The habitual use of some substances seems to be more readily acquired, and once acquired, the habit is seemingly more compulsive and harder to quit than with other drugs. Generally the less enjoyment the habit holds, the fewer the unpleasant consequences of quitting are, and the harsher the outcome of continuation is, the more readily one is able to give up the drug. Although they are partly a product of the "habit-forming" properties of the drug itself, these consequences also depend on other factors. The usual setting in which drugs are taken, reliability of supply, vagaries of personal background, and societal definitions are all important in determining how compulsive habituation to drugs is.

Some differences in the effects of drugs are relatively independent of these other factors. *Tolerance* to a drug means that the body becomes progressively immune to the toxic effects of the drug; hence there must be an increase in the dosage to achieve the same results. Physiological *dependence* refers to the actual tissue and cellular changes that take place in the process of adaptation to the substances introduced into the body by the drug. Dependence means that the body must have periodic dosages of the drug to function normally and to maintain physiological homeostasis. The absence of the drug upsets the drug-adapted bodily equilibrium, and malfunctioning and sickness set in. The production of physiological dependence plays a central role in habituation to certain drugs.

It is known at this time that these effects invariably accompany the administration of opiates after a short time and sometimes accompany the use of some depressants, such as barbiturates, tranquilizers, and alcohol. It has not been conclusively demonstrated that they occur with any other drugs. When habituation involves these physiological qualities, the term *addiction* is applied. Habituation is the general concept referring to all drug habits; addiction is a subtype of habituation with distinguishable properties.

Relapse is the return to use or habituation of a drug after one who has had the habit stops taking the drug for a period of time significantly longer than the customary or average period between administrations while he was habituated. Thus the marihuana smoker who regularly smokes two or three cigarettes a week cannot be said to have given up the habit and then relapsed if he does not smoke again until the next week. Because it involves a definite period of abstinence sickness, complete withdrawal and relapse are more easily identified in cases of addiction than in other kinds of habits; hence relapse is usually discussed in connection with opiate use. But relapse to opiates after undergoing the symptoms of withdrawal and shedding oneself of the physiological dependence is just one subtype of relapse. The same behavior sequence occurs when the marihuana, tobacco, or coffee habitué stops for a while and then resumes his habit.

Types and Effects of Drugs

One way of classifying drugs is presented in table 6–1. The drugs listed under each heading do not exhaust the possibilities; only the major ones are listed. For each drug named in the table's semitechnical terminology there is one or more corresponding slang or argot term. Some of the street names will be mentioned in subsequent discussion but are omitted from the table.

The two groups listed in the table which are the major drugs in deviant use are the opiates and the hallucinogens. They are the most commonly

Table 6–1
Types of drugs[a]

1. Opiates	2. Hallucinogens
A. Opium	A. Indian hemp
pure opium	marihuana (marijuana,
laudanum	mariguana)
paregoric	bhang
B. Opium derivatives	ganja
codeine	hashish
morphine	charas
narcotine	THC (tetrahydrocannibol)
papaverine	B. Other natural hallucinogens
thebaine	morning glory seeds
C. Morphine derivatives	nutmeg
diluadid	peyote
heroin	psilocybe mushroom
D. Synthetic opiates	others – epena, jimson weed,
meperidine (Demerol and	fly agaric (central agent
Nesentil)	probably belladonna)
methadone (Dolophine)	C. Chemicals – modifications or
isomethadone	derivatives
percodan	LSD (lysergic acid diethylamide)
	DMT (dimethyltryptamine)
	mescaline (peyote)
	psilocybin (mushroom)
	psilocin (mushroom)
	STP (dimethoxy-
	methylamphetamine)

3. Depressants, Sedatives, and Tranquilizers	4. Stimulants
A. Barbiturates	A. Amphetamines
amobarbital (Amytal)	amphetamine (Benzedrine)
butabarbital	dextroamphetamine (Dexedrine)
pentobarbital (Nembutal)	B. Nonamine stimulants
phenobarbital (Luminal)	cocaine
secobarbital (Seconal)	
B. Tranquilizers	
chlordiazepoxide (Librium)	
chlorpromazine	
diazepam (Valium)	
meprobamate (Miltown)	
C. Other: bromides – chloral-hydrate	

5. Solvents and Deliriants

aerosol sprays	cleaning fluids	gasoline
airplane glues	ether	paint thinners

[a] The table and the attendant discussion are drawn from a number of sources. The listing and discussion of opiates, depressants, stimulants, and solvents are drawn mainly from O'Donnell and Ball 1966; Ausubel 1958:9–10; Blum 1967b:29–37; DeRopp 1961:135–66; Time-Life editors 1965:106–12; Lindesmith 1968:243–47; Cohen 1969:69–104, 132–33. The listing and discussion of marihuana, LSD, and other hallucinogens are drawn primarily from Barron et al. 1964; Cohen 1969:11–67; Solomon 1966; Taylor 1966; LaGuardia Committee 1966; Lindesmith 1967: 222–26; Weil et al. 1968; Blum 1967b:24–29; Grinspoon 1969; Hollister 1971; Dishotsky et al. 1971.

abused, and most law enforcement effort is aimed at suppressing their use. The other agents listed are a part of the drug problem, however, and although most of our attention is directed to opiates and hallucinogens, the other drugs—depressants, stimulants, and solvents—deserve some comment.

How Do Drugs Affect the Nervous System?

Although still not fully understood, the process by which drugs affect the central nervous system appears to be as follows: The basic unit of the nervous system is called the *neuron.* There are billions of neurons in the human system. Each neuron is composed of receptors (dendrites) at one end connected to transmitters at the other end by an axon. *Neurohormones* (norepinephrine, serotonin, and acetyl-choline) are produced by the neurons and released into the micro-scopic space (synapse) between neurons. Sensory information, then, is passed along through the system by moving from the receptor end of the cell to the transmitter end out into and through the neuro-hormones in the synaptic space to the receptor end of the next cell. The process can be diagrammed as:

```
                        Synapse
                      *   *   *
        Neuron                        Neuron
(dendrites—axon—transmitters) *  * (dendrites—axon—transmitters)
    1        2          3     *  *  *    5        6          7
                      Neurohormones
                           4
```

The dendrites (1) stimulated by chemical action produce an electrical impulse which moves along the axon (2) to the transmitters (3). The transmitters release the electrical charge into the neuro-hormones (4), which convert the electrical charge to a chemical ac-tion. This in turn stimulates the dendrites in the next cell (5). The dendrites produce an electrical impulse which moves along the axon (6) to the transmitters (7), and the process is repeated.

When drugs are ingested, they enter the blood stream and are carried to the central nervous system where they interfere with the electrochemical process we just described: They affect the production of neurohormones in the synaptic spaces. Certain drugs like alcohol, opiates, marihuana, and depressants inhibit the neurohormones, contributing to the lowered level of activity associated with taking (at sufficient dosage levels) these drugs. Other drugs such as cocaine and amphetamines stimulate the production of an excess of neuro-hormones. This increases the electrochemical activity of the neuro-hormones, which produces the excitation associated with taking these drugs (Bettinger 1972; Girdano and Girdano 1973).

Depressants

Barbiturates (of which there are twenty-five varieties) include pheno-barbital, secobarbital, butabarbital, and pentobarbital.[1] They are regularly prescribed in medical practice as sedative, hypnotic, or sleep-inducing medication to fight insomnia and to encourage relaxation. Used in thera-peutic quantities barbiturates are safe and nonaddicting. Nonetheless, overdosages are lethal and are easily produced by simply taking a much larger number of pills than the prescribed dosage. Even prescribed dosages can produce ill effects such as coma and even death when taken in com-bination with alcohol. Taking overdoses of barbiturates is a common form of suicide (mainly among women), and barbiturates are implicated in acci-dental deaths and poisonings of those who unwittingly take too many pills to sleep after a night of heavy drinking. Some traffic accidents are also attributable to loss of control while under the influence of barbiturates.

Moreover, not only do many people develop a tolerance and become habituated to barbiturates but this type of drug can produce true physical dependence, complete with severe withdrawal symptoms. One may not only form the habit of relying on sleeping pills to get to sleep; since they can be addicting, chronic abuse may also mean that one comes to rely on the drugs just to keep from getting sick. It should be reiterated that this happens only when *large dosages* are taken; it does not occur with small prescription-level dosages. While on the drug the barbiturate addict suffers extreme drowsiness, disorientation, depression, and speech, motor, and judgment impairment. Withdrawal from barbiturates is likely to be more severe than withdrawal from opiates. Within hours after cessation of drug taking the barbiturate addict becomes overly agitated. This agitation increases until hallucinations and delirium and perhaps epilepticlike convulsions develop. The person may even become comatose or die (Lauie 1967:44).

Barbiturates are involved in the illicit supply-demand market, where they are known by several names: "barbs," "nimbies," or "seccys" (taken from brand names); "yellow jackets," "red devils," "blue heavens" (after the color of the pills and capsules); or "goofballs" (after the effects). Bar-biturates seem to be used more in rotation or combination with alcohol or amphetamines and other drugs rather than alone to the exclusion of other drugs.

Tranquilizers (Miltown, Equanil, Librium, and others) are nonbar-bituric depressants which were developed primarily as medicinal adjuncts to psychotherapy with mental patients. The larger dosages are still used in this way, while smaller dosages are prescribed by physicians for general use as sedatives and "nerve" medicine. Some drugs find their way from the pharmacy or family medicine chest into the hands of drug experimenters.

---

[1] If we count bromides, chloral hydrate, and other sedatives and hypnotics similar in effect to barbiturates, there are over forty varieties.

They are used as "downers" to help bring one down from a bum trip on hallucinogens or stimulants (barbiturates too are used for this purpose). As yet tranquilizers are not much implicated in the illicit drug traffic.

As new drugs are discovered or compounded from known substances, however, the potential for illicit use of them is always present. A recent example of this is *methaqualone* which was first placed on the legal prescription market as a nonbarbituric sedative under various trade names like Quaalude, Sopor, and Optimil. Much of the supply was diverted to the black market where it was called "sopers" and was popular because it was believed to be nonaddictive and a safe downer. But it was soon discovered that the margin between a safe prescription-level dosage and an unsafe overdose is very small. And, as with any depressant, it is especially dangerous when combined with alcohol. It has become apparent to drug users that this is not a safe drug. Its illicit use appears to have subsided, although there are no good figures on the extent of its usage (Chambers et al. 1974).

Stimulants

Amphetamines have exactly opposite effects of the barbiturates. The barbiturates are "down" drugs; the amphetamines are "up" drugs. That is, they have an antidepressant and stimulant effect on the central nervous system which increases wakefulness and alertness and masks the symptoms of fatigue. Tolerance develops rapidly and larger dosages are needed for the same effect, but *physiological dependence does not develop*. Overdosages cause delusions, hallucinations, dizziness, and sometimes death.

In addition to medical use, at least three other patterns of amphetamine use are discernible. First, *Benzedrine* has long been used by truck drivers, writers, and others to keep awake and alert for long periods of time without sleep. Benzedrine (bennies), *Dexedrine* (dexies), and other "pep pills" are used by college students for alertness during finals week, the writing of term papers, and other times of sleepless, cram studying. Second, amphetemines are used in experimentation with other drugs, mainly as part of the college and college-related (that is, hippies and high school students in college towns) drug scene. Sometimes they are taken in addition to hallucinogens; at other times they are taken in addition to or in combination with barbiturates and opiates. Third, any of these patterns may lead to habituation. Ill effects are manifest in their most extreme form only with habitual usage. The amphetamine most often implicated in habituation and the most severe problems of abuse is *Methedrine* ("meth," "crystal," or most commonly, "speed").

Staying high on any amphetamine for long periods of time leads to chronic insomnia interspersed with periods of deep exhaustion and fatigue (since the drug only gives the feeling of nonfatigue and does not really relieve it). The user becomes overly nervous and agitated; he is skittish and ill at ease all the time, and he is unable to sit still for even a short time.

All the amphetamines are part of the illicit drug traffic, and habitual high-level use of any will have this result. A few years ago methedrine was the one most implicated in the production of "speed freaks" or "meth monsters"—those who display all these symptoms in extreme form. Also, it seems that speed was more likely than the other amphetamines to be used in connection or in combination with opiates, particularly heroin. There is no chemical link between the two, and they are not cross-tolerant; one is a stimulant and the other is a depressant. But there are similarities in style of administration and supply source (Carey 1968:44).

Cocaine comes from the South American cocoa plant, the leaves of which are chewed by natives to battle fatigue and the effects of high altitude. The effects of cocaine are similar to those of the amphetamines, although the substances are chemically unrelated. Tolerance develops but *physical dependence does not*. Cocaine too is injected intravenously and is often mixed with heroin or morphine in "speedballs." Cocaine is less readily available and is much more expensive than are the amphetamines, but it is still taken (by sniffing or snorting) by sizable numbers. It is used by lower-class slum dwellers and has also come into increased use among more affluent groups including well-to-do actors and entertainers.

Solvents and Deliriants

In recent years a number of common household solvents have been sniffed, ingested, and even injected into the veins by youngsters seeking new substances on which to get high. They are not regularly part of the drug-users' supply, and since they are easily available otherwise, they do not form part of the illegal drug traffic. The most frequent practice of this type has been glue sniffing—placing ordinary airplane glue in a bag or sock and inhaling the fumes. Inhalation of the fumes or other forms of ingestion produces drowsiness, dizziness, slurred speech, and if taken in sufficient quantity, delirium and unconsciousness. One does not develop dependence on these substances, but they are extremely toxic and even moderately long exposure can produce irreparable damage to the liver, kidneys, bone marrow, and brain.

Opiates

All natural opiates are products of *opium*, which is the purified juice of the green, unripened seed of the white opium poppy, grown principally in the Middle East and Southeast Asia. Opium has been used since antiquity as a panacea for illness and has long been a basic pain killer. Mixed with other substances it can be eaten, and dried further it can be smoked.

"Eating" and smoking opium were the common practices of confirmed addicts until the first part of the twentieth century (see Sonnedecker 1958; Eldridge 1962:4–7; Kolb 1958). *Laudanum* is opium tinctured with alcohol. During the nineteenth and early twentieth centuries its use constituted a sizable portion of the opium consumption. *Paregoric* is a camphorated tincture of opium; it too was a common drugstore item in the nineteenth century, and it can still be purchased in limited quantity in pharmacies today, sometimes without a prescription. Opium solutions were also often the active ingredients in nineteenth century patent medicines.

Pure opium and soluble opium eventually gave way to *morphine* and *heroin* as drugs of choice by addicts. Morphine is a refined alkaloid derived directly from opium; it is several times more potent than pure opium. *Codeine* and other opiates (narcotine, papaverine) are also natural derivatives of opium. Morphine was first extracted in 1804, and because it too satisfied the opium appetite it was regarded as a cure for opium addiction. Morphine came into wider use during and after the Civil War. The hypodermic needle was invented shortly before the Civil War, and morphine injections became the standard treatment for pain from wounds and disease on both sides of the conflict. Because it was still believed that one acquired the opium appetite by eating opium, injections were not believed to be habit forming, although many physicians knew by that time that morphine taken orally produced a more avid appetite than opium (Lindesmith and Gagnon 1964:163; Lindesmith 1967:129–30; Clausen 1966:201; Kolb 1958:31–32). Morphine subsequently became the preferred drug of female addicts and was used almost as frequently as opium by men. By the twentieth century it was the most commonly used opiate by both men and women. Earlier it was sniffed or mixed with other things and eaten, but injections eventually became the preferred method of administration.

Heroin is by far the most potent of the opiates. It cannot be extracted directly from pure opium but must be derived from morphine. Heroin was first refined from morphine in 1898, and because it took smaller dosages than morphine to achieve the same effect, heroin was also hailed for a while as a cure for the morphine or opium habit (Lindesmith and Gagnon 1964). After the turn of the century heroin became known on the streets and was sniffed in powdered form, a practice (called "snorting") still engaged in by some novices. Injection of water-dissolved heroin became and remains the common method of addicts. However, American soldiers in Vietnam resurrected the practice of smoking opium and heroin (often mixed in tobacco cigarette) and also practiced snorting in the belief that only injections, not smoking or snorting, is addicting. For the past two decades heroin has been the most commonly ingested of all illegally used opiates, although morphine continued as the drug of choice for women and physician addicts until recently. Since heroin is no longer used in medical practice, all heroin in the United States is illegal and must be smuggled in.

Meperdine (Demerol) and *methadone* (Dolophine) are modern synthetic drugs which have the same effect as natural opiates but which are not derived from opium. They were synthesized in a search for nonopiate analgesics. It quickly became apparent that Demerol and Dolophine were just as addicting as opiates, but when it was learned that withdrawal symptoms were somewhat less severe with them than with morphine or heroin, they were pressed into service in the treatment of addicts. Switching addiction to one of the synthetics and then gradually lowering the dosage to the point where withdrawal would produce only mild reaction became the standard treatment procedure at some hospitals for addicts.

Opiates are the "hard" narcotics; they form the standard against which the addicting properties of other drugs are judged. Although they vary in potency, they are all pain-killing drugs, and any will serve to contract and maintain addiction. There are many forms, all of which have been snuffed, eaten, injected subcutaneously ("skin popped"), and injected intravenously ("mainlined"). The variety of opiates, the myriad ways they can be taken, and their cross-tolerance are summed up effectively by William Burroughs:

> When I say addict I mean an addict to *junk.* . . . I have used junk in many forms: morphine, heroin, dilaudid, eukodal, pantapon, diocodid, diosane, opium, demerol, dolophine, palfium. I have smoked junk, eaten it, sniffed it, injected it in vein-skin-muscle, inserted it in rectal suppositories. The needle is not important. Whether you sniff it smoke it eat it or shove it up your ass the result is the same: addiction (Burroughs 1961:209).

The effects of opiates.   The natural opiates and their synthetic analogs are first of all analgesics (pain fighters) and depressants. They help to reduce the effects of pain, they increase insensitivity to pain, and they lower body activity. First dosages may result in nausea, vomiting, itching, and other unpleasant effects, but they may also produce pleasant feelings, contentment, or *euphoria.* The drug is also reported to give an initial "kick," or exhilaration, followed by the ease and nonworry of euphoria. Tolerance and dependence develop rapidly and almost invariably with opiate use.

When the confirmed addict is under the influence of the drug he tends to be subdued, nonaggressive, and withdrawn. There is no organic deterioration directly attributable to the toxic effects of opiates; however, an overdose can cause a comatose condition or death. In recent years there have been reports of a dramatic increase in the number of "OD" (overdose) deaths—especially among young users.

Moreover, long-term addiction can be debilitating. Loss of appetite, emaciation, susceptibility to infectious disease, accident proneness, chronic constipation, and infection from the needle, cuts, and burns all plague the addict. The long-time street addict is often haggard, thin, run-down, and generally in poor health. However, the addict who has a more certain supply of good drugs at reasonable expense and who watches his diet can maintain a habit, hold down a job, and keep in fairly good shape, although not in as good a condition as when he is not addicted. This principle has been applied in methadone maintenance treatment programs. The addict is admitted to the program as an outpatient. He is supplied with a daily dosage of methadone at no or nominal cost to satisfy his habit and negate the necessity of procuring illegal heroin. Although this program does nothing with addiction but maintain it, it does allow the addict to keep a job and to spend his money on things other than drugs. Thus he does not have to resort to crime to support an extremely expensive heroin habit. The extravagant claims which have been made for the success of these programs and the claims that methadone blocks the effects of heroin without producing a high are unsubstantiated, however. (See the discussion of methadone maintenance programs in chapter 9.)

Withdrawal.   Itchy, running nose and watering eyes, restlessness, nervousness, and nausea are among the early symptoms of opiate withdrawal. The eye pupils, "pinned" or constricted while on the drug, become dilated. Head pains, stomach cramps, muscular pains in the back, legs, and arms develop. One sweats profusely, vomits, gets the "dry heaves," diarrhea, alternate hot and cold chills, goose flesh ("cold turkey"), and jerks his arms and legs ("kicking the habit").

The distress is always present with opiate withdrawal, which at its worst can be a terrible physical ordeal. But withdrawal may be quite mild. The severity of withdrawal depends on the strength and purity of the drugs the addict has been using and how long he has been addicted, the setting and situation (in a jail cell, at home, in a hospital room, and so on), who is present at the time, and the expectations the addict brings to the experience.

Hallucinogens

These drugs have been called psychotomimetic, psychotropic, psychedelic, consciousness-expanding, mind-altering, and other names, depending on whether they were being condemned or praised, but they are most often referred to here as hallucinogenic drugs or simply hallucinogens (Barron et al. 1964).

The flowering and top parts of the female Indian hemp (*Cannabis sativa*) contain the most cannabinol, the basic ingredient in marihuana, bhang, ganja, and hashish or charas. All of these substances contain the same active ingredient, but they differ in potency and quality in much the same way that the alcohol content and quality of beer, wines, and liquor differ.

Charas-hashish, for instance, is some five to eight times more potent than bhang or ordinary marihuana (Grinspoon 1969:3). The *marihuana* (marijuana) used in the Western Hemisphere, mainly Mexico and the United States, is the cut and dried top parts of low to average quality or uncultivated female hemp plant. In this part of the world it is almost invariably hand-rolled and smoked in cigarette form, although it or hashish may also be smoked in a pipe. In the 1920s and 1930s marihuana was known as "reefers," "muggles," "tea," "gauge," "Mary Jane," and other terms. Today, the most common names are "pot" and "grass," although these were used earlier, and some of the early terms are still occasionally heard. The hemp of roughly the same low potency as marihuana has been known for centuries in India as *bhang*, where it is smoked and also prepared as tea (Taylor 1966:37–38; Lindesmith 1967:224; Goode 1970:14–15).

Ganja (ganga) is also the top of female hemp, but is harvested from a cultivated and higher grade plant than marihuana or bhang. From these plants comes the most potent natural cannabis — charas — which is

> the pure, unadulterated resin from the tops of the finest female plants of Indian hemp, usually those grown from ganja. But in charas the resin is always extracted. It is known to us only by the name of *hashish*, and from it medicine derived the drug known as *cannabis indica* (Taylor 1966:39).

Ganja-quality marihuana is also grown in the Western Hemisphere and is available in this country. "Hash" (hashish), although much more expensive than marihuana, is also used in the United States, and psychedelic shops and suppliers furnish hash pipes as well as cigarette papers and roach holders (devices for holding the butt of the marihuana cigarette so that it may be smoked to the end without burning one's fingers).

Tetrahydrocannabinol (THC) has long been recognized as the active agent in the cannabis resin, but not until 1965 was a successful synthesis accomplished (Weil et al. 1968:1234).

LSD (LSD–25) is a lysergic acid first synthesized from ergot, a wheat and rye fungus, in 1943. *Psilocybin* and *psilocin* are derived from Latin American mushrooms and in the early and mid-1950s were used with LSD by groups experimenting with consciousness-expansion. *Mescaline*, the active agent in the buttons of the peyote cactus, was also used in these experimentations. The mushroom drugs are relatively rare today in the United States, but Indian religious groups still chew the peyote buttons (as their ancestors did), and mescaline enjoys a brisk trade in the black market (Barron et al. 1964:3–6).

Effects of hallucinogens.   None of the hallucinogenic substances produces dependence and the addictive type of habituation. They vary greatly in potency and specific effects, but all are capable of producing changes in sensory perceptions. They affect the central nervous system and in sufficient quantity can produce "mind-altering" hallucinations. But reports of the hallucinogenic experience range from descriptions of dramatic effects to reports of no effects. The actual effects depend not only on the potency and size of the dosage taken but also on the social and physical setting, the individual's expectations, and other variables. The more potent hallucinogens, such as LSD, may produce complex alterations in perceptions of taste, odors, color, light, visual objects, and sounds. Crossing or confusion of the senses may occur, so that one "smells" color or "sees" music (Barron et al. 1964: 7–9). These and other more complicated visual and auditory hallucinations can be interpreted as either a welcome expansion of one's sensory universe or as a frightening psychosis, depending on from whom one learns his definition of the experience (Blum 1967b:27–28; Becker 1967). Although it has often been charged with chromosomal and genetic damage, there is no reliable evidence that LSD in dosages usually taken causes chromosome damage, cancer, or genetic mutation in humans (Dishotsky et al. 1971).

The effects of the low-grade marihuana usually consumed in this country are probably best described as intoxication, light-headedness, dizziness, or a high. These effects are somewhat akin to but qualitatively different from those of alcohol, and there is no morning-after hangover (Lindesmith 1967:222–23; Ausubel 1958:95–96; Solomon 1966:320–21). The overall effect of marihuana is depressant rather than stimulant, resulting in drowsiness, dreaminess, and heaviness. Such reactions as vomiting, nausea, and sickness may occur in naive users. More dramatic reactions are likely to occur with high doses of THC. Smoking the less potent marihuana cigarettes causes an initial increased pulse and respiration rate, but pupil size and reflexes are unaffected. Driving a car and other tasks are not significantly affected (Weil et al. 1968:1235, 1239–40; Grinspoon 1969:9; Hollister 1971).

Recently, however, marihuana has been charged with much more dramatic and disastrous effects than any of these. In addition to the many unsubstantiated but at one time popular stories of marihuana-induced psychosis, violence, and crime, claims have surfaced that marihuana severely damages the user's health. There have been reports that smoking marihuana even in relatively moderate amounts irredeemably damages the brain, lowers bodily resistance to cancer and infection, raises the risks of genetic defects and hereditary diseases, leads to sterility and impotence in men, causes lung damage, and produces an "amotivational syndrome" that reduces the desire to work and achieve. Although lung damage is associated with frequent deep inhalation of smoke, whether from tobacco or marihuana, none of these other allegations of health impairment from moderate marihuana usage have been substantiated by careful research. But what about heavy use of marihuana over a long period of time? Does that lead to noticeably reduced health? There has been only one recent study of a control group of non-users compared with a group of users who had smoked heavily over a period of years. The study was done in Jamaica where smoking ganja has been a cultural tradition among working-class males. The group of smokers had used marihuana before the age of twenty, smoked at least eight "spliffs" (joints) *a day*, and had been doing so for an average of seventeen and one-half years. The study revealed no significant differences between the physical or mental health of the users and non-users and no evidence of the amotivational syndrome in the users (Brecher and Editors 1975). In short, there is little hard evidence that marihuana consumption produces harmful physical or psychiatric effects (Secretary of Health, Education, and Welfare 1972; 1975).

Summary

The two major categories of drugs used deviantly are *opiates* (for example, heroin) and *hallucinogens* (for example, marihuana and LSD). In addition, depressants, stimulants, and solvents are sometimes implicated in deviant patterns of use. Any of these drugs may be used habitually, but physiological dependence does not develop with hallucinogens and stimulants. Physical dependence is produced by opiate use and is sometimes produced by depressants.

7

Opiate Drug Use

Extent of Use and
Characteristics of Opiate Users

Estimates based on official law enforcement reports, populations of hospital and treatment programs, cases of serum hepatitis (caused from use of infected needles), and similar sources indicate that at least since the late 1960s the number of habitual opiate users in the United States has not been under 100,000 (Ball and Chambers 1970). The estimates of the maximum number of opiate addicts range up to 1,000,000, but the true figure is probably closer to 200,000. The number of people with some experience with illegal opiates is greater than this, of course, because it would include all those currently or formerly experimenting with opiates, occasional users, and even one-time-only users.

There has not been a study of a representative sample of the entire population to gauge the overall rate of use and addiction, but there have been surveys of national samples within certain age categories. One study of a sample of U.S. males aged twenty to thirty found that 6 percent reported use of heroin sometime in their lives and 2 percent reported current heroin use (O'Donnell et al. 1976). A study of returning Vietnam war veterans found that over 40 percent had tried some opiate during their duty in Vietnam. Twenty percent considered themselves addicted (almost all smoked or sniffed opium rather than injected heroin), and 11 percent had used opiates in the twenty-four hours previous to the time of discharge. After return to civilian life in the United States, less than 10 percent of the men continued to use narcotics of some kind. Indeed, only one in three of those who were using drugs at the time of discharge continued to be addicted to opiates (Robins 1973). A national sample of high school seniors found that 2.7 percent of the males and 2.3 percent of the females reported taking heroin at least once, and .2 percent of the total sample reported using heroin frequently enough (twenty or more times in the past month) to be considered addicts

(Johnston 1975; see the similar figures in Johnston 1973). Since these samples encompass populations who have experienced the highest rates of addiction (namely adolescent and young adult males), the percentages of use and addiction in the total population are less.

The rate of narcotics use and addiction before the Harrison Act in 1914 restricted it was apparently considerably greater than it has been since then. Before 1914 there were no restrictive laws, and one could purchase opiates at moderate prices directly from suppliers, pharmacies, and physicians. Doctors prescribed opiates for many illnesses, and many patent medicines contained a high percentage of opiates. Society was more tolerant of opiates: opiate addiction was considered perhaps unfortunate, but neither its use nor addiction was considered evil or cause for social ostracism and criminal sanctions (Sonnedecker 1958:16–21; Lindesmith and Gagnon 1964:165–66). It is not surprising that the proportion of the population using opiates was nearly twice what it is now. Some estimates place the total of opiate addicts before 1914 at more than 1,000,000 users (Eldridge 1962:7; Ausubel 1958:62; Nyswander 1963:31); other estimates place the number of addicts at a low of slightly more than 100,000 and a high of more than 250,000 (see Lindesmith 1967:110–11; Isbell 1963:159).

The number of opiate users declined steadily to a low point during World War II. There was a marked increase after the war that peaked in the early 1950s, but use declined again to another low point in the early 1960s (Ball and Cottrell 1965:471–72). After that opiate use increased (O'Donnell et al. 1976; Richman 1974).

Because the Harrison Act and the enforcement policies of the Federal Bureau of Narcotics and its state counterparts affected which segments of the population had access to opiates, the characteristics of users and addicts changed. At one time opiate use was linked mainly to medical practice and self-medication. Users and addicts were mostly white, were fairly evenly distributed among the social classes (with a tendency toward concentration in the middle and upper classes), were middle-aged, were as likely or more likely to be rural dwellers than urban dwellers, were more likely to be women, and were likely to use some opiate other than heroin. With the change in policy the major source of supply became illegal channels and the major drug of use became heroin. Use and addiction became concentrated among urban, lower-class, nonwhite, and delinquent or criminal males (Lindesmith and Gagnon 1964:163–67; Lindesmith 1967:130–32). The former pattern of use continues on a diminished scale, however, and is confined mainly to the South (Ball 1965:203–11; Bates 1966).

Sex, Age, and Location of Opiate Users

Studies of opiate users in the latter part of the nineteenth century and the early part of the twentieth century found about two-thirds to be female and the average age of addicts to be between forty and fifty years of age.

Since then women have tended less and men have tended more to become addicted (about 85 percent of opiate addicts now are men), and the average age at first addiction and the average present age of addicts have decreased (Winick 1965:7–9; Ausubel 1958:63; Ball and Cottrell 1965:471; Blum 1967a:48).

The drop in age among opiate users was noticeable from 1940 to 1950, and it continued into the 1950s. The dramatic postwar increase of opiate use and addiction among adolescents seemed "to be petering out" in the late fifties, although not soon enough to stem the overall decade-long decrease in the average age of addicts. In 1940 the average age was over 41; by 1950 it had dropped to 35, and by 1960 to 32 (Bates 1966:66). By the middle of the 1960s the average age at first addiction began to come back up, reflecting the decline of heroin use among adolescents, including delinquent gang boys, after the peak years of the early 1950s (Klein and Phillips 1968). And by the 1970s the average age of addicts in treatment had declined to 25—nearly three-fourths of the heroin addicts had begun use before age 21 (Chambers 1974; O'Donnell et al. 1976).

Until the late 1930s the highest rates of addiction were in the South, and addicts tended to be from small towns. This has changed so that now over half of the opiate addicts in the United States reside in New York City, and about nine out of ten are from cities with popuations of 50,000 or more. Most addicts today are male, young, and from the large cities of the North. The rate of new cases of opiate addiction appears to have peaked and may be declining in the largest cities; however, the incidence rate for smaller cities has increased. That is, although urban populations continue to have the highest proportions of opiate users and addicts, the smaller cities are adding new cases of addiction at a faster pace. Indeed, spread of heroin use in the United States has taken on a pattern that resembles the spread of technological innovations and diseases. For each, the incidence rate begins and reaches a peak first in the very largest cities on the two coasts. It then becomes highest for the next largest category of cities moving inland and peaks. The process is repeated for even smaller cities, and eventually limits itself when it reaches a saturation point (Hunt 1974).

Racial and Social Characteristics of Opiate Users

In earlier periods the percentages of whites and blacks in studies of addict populations were equivalent to the percentages in the general population. The proportion of the general population that is black has stayed at 11 percent. But the proportion of blacks in the known population of addicts admitted for treatment increased drastically around 1950 from about 10 percent to more than 30 percent, where it remained into the 1960s (Bates 1966:62–63). By the early 1970s blacks made up more than four in ten of those admitted to hospitals or other drug treatment programs (Chambers 1974) and constituted an even higher portion of the untreated cases of opiate use and addiction (O'Donnell et al. 1976:37; Johnston 1973:195). In certain places, there are proportionately more minority than non-minority group members found among addicts—for instance, Puerto Ricans in New York City and Mexican-Americans in California (Blum 1967a:48).

At least since the 1950s, addicts have been concentrated in the slums among members of minority ethnic groups and among those on the bottom of the socioeconomic scales of education, employment, and income (Chein et al. 1964:45–74; Winick 1965:10–16; O'Donnell and Ball 1966:9–10; Ball and Chambers 1970). While this description remains largely accurate today, heroin use has spread out of the slums into middle-class and upper-class neighborhoods (*Newsweek*, July 5, 1971:27–32; Hollister 1971) and the difference between proportions of black and white users has diminished (O'Donnell et al. 1976:vii). In fact, since the late 1960s we seem to have embarked on a heroin "epidemic" reminiscent of that of the early 1950s, this time a significant portion of that upsurge is from outside the slums. We can see that white, middle-class status is less predictive of insulation from heroin addiction. It is likely, however, that if the pattern of the drug epidemic of two decades ago repeats, this epidemic will also abate probably sometime in the 1970s. There are mixed signs now that while it has not ended, the current epidemic may already have peaked, and that the rate of heroin addiction is no longer rising (O'Donnell et al. 1976; Richman 1974; Hunt 1974).

Aside from recent changes in the social characteristics of opiate addicts, one outstanding exception to the foregoing characterization of opiate users is physicians and others in the health professions who become addicted. With the exception of jazz musicians during the 1950s, physicians have the highest rate of opiate use and addiction of any occupational group (Winick 1959). Estimates of the rate of addiction among physicians range from eight to one hundred times that of the general population. Medical and paramedical professions (with the exception of pharmacists) have had consistently high rates for a long time and for all Western countries. Contrasted with the average street addict, who is a young, unmarried slum dweller using heroin, the typical physician addict is older, he started his habit later in life, he is married, he continues to practice his profession for some time after addiction, and he uses Demerol, Dolophine, or morphine (Blum 1967a:49; Modlin and Montes 1964; Putnam and Ellinwood 1966; Winick 1964).

Opiate Use, Addiction, and Relapse: A Social Learning Analysis[1]

Preaddiction Use of Opiates

At least three types of social contexts function as environments or learning paths in which opiate-directed behavior is acquired. The major one

---

[1]This section is based on Akers et al. (1968).

today is *subcultural.*[2] Another, formerly important in this country, is essentially a *conventional* introduction to opiates for the alleviation of real or imagined ills, either through self-medication or under medical supervision.[3] There is also an *occupational* avenue to drugs by which physicians, nurses, and other health professionals are recruited to opiate use. Each of these patterns provides the crucial variables for drug use: *availability* of the drug, *ability* to administer it properly, patterns of *definitions* which define use as desirable or appropriate, and *differential reinforcement.*

The subcultural pattern

Social reinforcement.   Opiate users in the U.S. disproportionately reside in the slum areas of big cities. People in these areas are likely to be deprived of opportunities to obtain a wide range of social and material rewards. This absence of conventional reinforcers may lead to failure to acquire conventional behavior; and this in turn becomes the basis for failure to obtain approval and status in the larger society. At the same time, deviant activities of various kinds, including drug use, are rewarded.

This does not mean that a majority of people in these areas will become addicts, users, or even tolerant of drugs. Even in the slum neighborhoods of very high use only a minority are really involved (Burnham and Burnham 1970). But there is a "sufficient number to provide a philosophy — or at least a set of rationalizations to the growing youngsters whose family background and personality make them potential recruits to delinquency" (Blum 1967a:50). Here a person is likely to be exposed to drugs; addicts visibly reside here, peddlers and pushers ply their trade, providing availability and connections. The apparent widespread use in some neighborhoods provides a receptive climate for others to try it. In short, conditions are set for the emergence of a specifically drug-oriented subculture which is tolerant of drugs and provides social reinforcers such as approval, recognition, and prestige for experimentation with drugs (Chein et al. 1964:78–108; Clausen 1966:210–12; Clinard 1968:323–30; Finestone 1957; 1964; Sutter 1969; 1970). The carriers of this subculture develop characteristic ways of life, have a world view with special attitudes and definitions of use and addiction, and share a drug-oriented jargon.

It is not enough to live in a slum environment. Exposure to subcultural definitions and differential association with other users who provide reinforcement are critical. The first drug experience is not usually pushed aggressively on a person by proselyting friends or pushers giving away free

---

[2]There are several subcultures covered under this. For the most part reference is to the addict subculture found in the urban slums, but other more or less deviant and more specialized subcultures found among career criminals, prostitutes, jazz musicians, Orientals in earlier times, and beatniks would also be included. A subculture of heroin use was also transplanted and nurtured in the military in Vietnam.

[3]These first two correspond roughly to Lindesmith's "nontherapeutic" and "therapeutic" patterns of recruitment to opiates (1967:128–34).

samples to recruit more customers. Rather, introduction usually occurs in intimate group settings with friends who support experimentation with a range of drugs. This first experience is typically not solely for the sake of trying the drug but for gaining acceptance, identification, and status in the group. It nearly always takes place in the company of peers on the street, a rooftop, at a dance or party, in a car, or at school (Lindesmith 1967:133–34; Blum 1967a:50 and 52; Chein et al. 1964:149–52; Ball 1967:408–13; Kobrin and Finestone 1968:117–30; Alksne et al. 1967:224–25). Thus these friendship groups make drugs available and provide social reinforcement for learning the techniques and definitions of drug taking.

> Heroin use started in an unsupervised street setting, while the subjects were still teenagers. The youthful initiate usually had smoked marijuana with neighbourhood friends before using opiates. In the case of both marijuana smoking and heroin use the adolescent peer-group exercised a dominant influence (Ball 1967:412).

Preaddiction use of opiates then tends to be casual, recreational, and supported primarily by the social reinforcement of friends.

First Exposure to Heroin Is Usually in a Small Group of Peers

I was at a party. Everybody was having a good time. I wanted to be one of the crowd. I thought, if it didn't hurt them it wouldn't hurt me. That started the ball rolling. They were sniffing it that time. Two or three pulled out a few caps; said, 'Here, if you want to, try.' I accepted. They weren't trying to addict me; they just gave it to me (Chein et al. 1964:151).

And two of my friends, you know, they were brothers; one of them was twelve and the other was thirteen, like they shoot up and all. . . . Since I had seen them doing it I knew what it was already, more or less. I went and took it and then I knew what it felt like and I liked it. Then from there on I kept on using it (Larner and Tefferteller 1964:33).

I never thought in my wildest dreams that I would ever be hooked on something like heroin. . . . But when I met Herb and went over to his place, everybody there was shooting up all the time, I felt kinda left out, so I used to tease Herb about giving me some. I decided I was really hooked when I shut off for six days . . . and couldn't sleep (*Newsweek*, July 5, 1971:27).

The probability that a person will try drugs and continue to use them in this initial phase is increased by the presence of *definitions* favorable for drug use. We turn now to a closer examination of these definitions conducive to drug use.

Definitions conducive to opiate use.   Many who are exposed to deviant subcultures define drug use in positive terms from the beginning, or at least they are exposed to attitudes favorable to or tolerant of use. In these cases there are few moral obstacles to overcome, just as most people encounter few negative definitions in coming to the point of driving an automobile, drinking soft drinks, trying liquor, or smoking a cigarette for the first time. These activities might even have been defined as desirable either in themselves or as ways of gaining acceptance from others.

The initiate into the drug subculture learns *both positive and negative definitions* toward drugs in the same way. He may be initially morally neutral, may be ignorant of the probable consequences of drug use, or may give it no thought (Ball 1967:412). For many, the first exposure is to positive definitions — "Try marihuana, it does good things to you," "Be cool, try heroin," "It is really a good high," and so on. However, even in a tolerant subculture persons are familiar with definitions of drug use as illegal, dangerous, or stupid, and they know the tyranny the drug can have over a person's life if he becomes addicted (Clausen 1966:214). If a person associates with those who define drugs in this way and he does not neutralize them, he is not likely to try drugs. Nearly all the nonusers in Chein's study reported that their friends had negative feelings about drugs. Most users said they did not know what their friends thought about drugs or that their friends had favorable attitudes. Most of the nonusers learned the negative definitions — "deterrent information" — from their friends or their own observations of addicts. These negative definitions included the notions that drugs are bad for one's health, are dangerous to life, or are too costly and force one to perform immoral or illegal acts. Those who are relatively isolated from these definitions are more likely to try drugs (Chein et al. 1964:153–56).

As Kobrin and Finestone point out, conventional definitions of drugs are also known among street-corner boys (1968:125–26). Perhaps the most prevalent negative definition of this type is that although status can be gained through drug use, it is bad to get a habit or become "strung out." Even in a subculture receptive to experimentation with drugs, addiction is often frowned upon (Chein et al. 1964:170–73). "Junkie" is not a desirable status. The "righteous dope fiend" who is also a successful pimp or hustler may have prestige in the slum street world, but the "garbage junkie" does not. It is recognized that heroin can become a tyrant and can cause the fiend to fall and lose his cool (Sutter 1970). While experimentation with a range of drugs is supported, the status of drug addict was neither desirable nor acceptable to either addicts or non-addicts. Much effort was exercised to conceal the fact of addiction, which was commonly recognized as indicative of personal weakness and failure (Spergel 1966:243).

This type of prohibitive definition can be neutralized, however, by rationalizing that one can control drug intake at the occasional stage without getting hooked, that it happens to others but will not happen to him. This is a common rationalization among beginning users, and many then are surprised when they become addicted (Lindesmith 1968:74–76). The beginning user often

> does not realize he is getting the habit at all. He says there is no need to get a habit if you are careful and observe a few rules, like shooting every other day. Actually, he does not observe these rules, but every extra shot is regarded as exceptional. I have talked to many addicts and they all say they were surprised when they discovered they actually had the first habit (Burroughs 1963:80).

Another form this "it-won't-happen-to-me" definition takes is in what Feldman (1970) calls the ideology of the slum "stand-up cat." Taking heroin without getting hooked may be seen as another way to meet and beat a challenge.

> His challenge is to triumph in a situation where previous heroes have failed. Using heroin, controlling its addictive effects, and eventually stopping becomes the test of toughness, of danger, and of chancing what for others has been the inevitability of fate. . . . Foremost in the adolescent's belief is a *firm conviction that he is too strong, too tough, and too much of a stand-up cat ever to be defeated by a chemical* (Feldman 1970:92, italics added).

Reinforcing effects of the drug.   Whether or not the first use and occasional use thereafter are defined as nonaddictive, the discriminative stimuli provided by the positive or neutralizing definitions and the social reinforcement from friends operate alone in determining whether one will try drugs the first time. After that first time, another important element enters the picture—*the effects of the drug*. If initial drug effects are pleasant or desirable, if the person likes what the drug does to or for him, it is likely that drug use will be positively reinforced. If the initial experience is aversive, it is not likely that the person will continue using the drug unless the drug effects can be reinterpreted as or conditioned to become positive.

Ausubel claims that the euphoric effects, the pleasant dreamy feelings, the "high" or the "kick" produced by initial administration of opiates generates and sustains further use (1958:26–30, 33). The reinforcing impact of the "flash" should not be underestimated. There is little doubt that experiencing a pleasurable sensation induces further use. In Chein's study over two-thirds of those who experienced initially positive reactions to heroin continued use, whereas only about two-fifths whose first experience elicited unfavorable reactions continued taking the drug (Chein et al. 1964:158). However, Lindesmith, among others, notes that first ingestion of opiates, far from creating anything that can objectively be called euphoric, may produce very unpleasant effects such as nausea, fear, and dizziness. The addict learns to enjoy these effects, but the uninitiated may not enjoy them at all (Lindesmith 1968:23–28; 1966:96–97). For instance, one study found that only about 10 percent of subjects naive to opiates liked what they felt when given morphine (Blum 1967a:42). Two-thirds of the addicts in another study reported positive effects upon first using heroin, but these positive effects were typically the euphoria which followed the nausea and vomiting that also usually accompanied first use (Waldorf 1973:34–35).

The effects do not depend entirely on the intrinsic pharmacological properties of opiates; they also depend on the social setting in which they are taken. The probability that one will experience the uplift, the buoyancy, the kick, or other positively reinforcing outcomes is increased if he has learned to expect such results. The first few times the drugs are usually taken in the company of supportive other people who encourage the user and enhance the pleasure.

Thus even if the intrinsic drug effects are aversive, one can be conditioned to enjoy them. When an unpleasant consequence is presented as necessary for reinforcement, it may become a discriminative stimulus, signaling that reinforcement is just ahead, or it may become a reinforcer itself (Ayllon and Azrin 1966). The initially unpleasant or neutral effects can become redefined as desirable attributes of the drug by pairing them with gaining the social approval, attention, and recognition of significant others. If this conditioning does not take place, taking the drug will continue to be punishing and use will discontinue.

Subcultural use: summary.   In initial and preaddiction use in the subcultural pattern, the social rewards from other users combine with the reinforcing effects of the opiate itself. This offsets the punishing consequences associated with opiate use. Whatever the source of reinforcement, initial and continued use in this early stage is sustained primarily by *positive reinforcement.* A person uses drugs to gain recognition, approval, and acceptance into a peer group; he learns by imitation and direct tutelage the proper method of taking drugs and how to recognize the effects; and he comes to enjoy the effects of the drug itself. He may continue this pattern, may "joy pop," "chippy shot," or sniff only occasionally for a while, then discontinue and never become addicted. The odds are against such an outcome, however. The positive reinforcement of this phase will probably sustain use long enough for the individual to develop tolerance and dependence. Once this happens the stage is set for addiction, in which negative reinforcement is more important.

Of course both positive and negative reinforcement are involved at all stages. One may initially use heroin to avoid the disapproval of his subcultural peers as well as to gain their approval. He may use drugs as a nonadaptive avoidance of personal problems. As he becomes addicted he becomes more and more incorporated into the hard-core addict subculture; eventually almost all his associates are other addicts and suppliers. The positive support addicts give one another and whatever positive effects the drugs continue to have are combined with the negative contingencies in the maintenance of the habit. But in general, trying drugs initially is a function of positive consequences of such behavior, whereas addiction is sustained basically through negative reinforcement.

The differential association with and reinforcement from others in a deviant subculture are not the only conditions which can encourage opiate use. There are at least two other patterns of use and addiction — here called the conventional and the occupational.

The conventional pattern

As we have seen, there was a general cultural tolerance of opiate use in this country in the nineteenth century. The majority of users at that time came to use opiates essentially in a conventional way — for the alleviation of illness — and use and addiction reflected differences in risks of health and ability to secure drugs. These conventional users therefore were more likely to be middle-aged, middle-class women using paregoric, laudanum, and morphine. These were the kinds of opiates to which access was fairly routine; they were taken as other drugs were and required no special learning to administer. Public attitudes defined taking opiates in the same moral category as ingestion of any medicine to maintain health and well-being.

Although this style of drug use was at least marginally socially acceptable, it was not a prerequisite to acceptance into a group and was not socially reinforced. Although many began to enjoy the drug effects, it would seem that first, occasional, and addictive use were sustained principally by negative reinforcement. During the initial phases the maintenance of health and the alleviation of pain provided the negative reinforcement; after addiction it was provided by alleviation of withdrawal pains, whether or not the original illness continued. Given the cultural context of the time, this pattern of use can only be described as conventional, not deviant. This earlier pattern has drastically declined since the passage of restrictive legislation, but it still persists today as a style of use quite distinguishable from the subcultural pattern. (For a review of many aspects of this type of addict see O'Donnell 1969.)

This pattern is "typified by the *middle-aged southern white* who uses morphine or paregoric and obtains his drugs through legal or quasi-legal means" (Ball 1965:203). The southern white addicts began taking drugs through medical channels, do not use heroin, are older than subcultural addicts, and live in small towns or rural areas (Ball 1965; Bates 1966:65–66).

An illegal market once flourished in the southern regions, and a subculture of users mutually benefiting one another as sources of information and supply emerged. It differed from the subculture emerging in the northern cities, being carried mainly by older men in rural areas. As controls tightened the subculture became less able to provide availability. If a person were to remain an addict he had to resort to medical channels for his supply. Thereafter, participation in the subculture carried with it the possibility of arrest and made it more difficult for the person and his physician to continue to define him as an ill person in need of drugs. The southern white subculture therefore declined and has virtually disappeared (O'Donnell 1967:73–84).

People all over the country still come to drugs as medical patients, however. The availability, administration, and definition of the drug ingestion as acceptable are all taken care of in this medical context, much as it was in the nineteenth century. Some persons move from this nondeviant use to securing drugs after the medical purposes are no longer present; some are administered drugs long enough to develop tolerance and dependence, but few go on to become addicted. Those who do may later become participants in an addict subculture, but initially they become users without contact with the urban drug subculture.

The occupational pattern

Physicians who become addicts resemble the conventional addict. They are typically white, older, and come from high socioeconomic backgrounds. Physician drug users know only indirectly of the addict subculture; they do not know its jargon, nor are they familiar with the exotic and spiritual definitions of drug use. Availability for the health practitioner presents no special problems. He may not freely expropriate opiates for his own use, but there are fairly safe ways of doing so. Congruent with availability, physicians use and become addicted, not to heroin to which they have no legal access, but to morphine, in earlier times, and to Demerol and Dolophine in recent years (Putnam and Ellinwood 1966; Modlin and Montes 1964; Pescor 1966; Winick 1964). The physician learns about the analgesic effects of opiates and how properly to administer them as part of his professional education.

He knows that if he has pain, morphine will relieve it. He knows that if he cannot sleep, morphine will bring sleep. He knows that if he has been indiscrete, morphine will relieve his alcoholic hangover. He knows that if he is nervous and jumpy before an operation, morphine will steady him so that he can carry out his task. He knows that if he is weary, morphine will perk him up (Pescor 1966:164–65).

Physicians' rationalization of their own opiate use.   The physician also knows, as part of his training, that opiates are addicting, and he shares the public view of the addict as a deviant. Therefore, in the process of coming to use drugs he applies a set of definitions—verbalizations consonant with drug use. Each does not dream up his own definitions; rather, he applies a set he learns from the conventional culture and from his specialized training —drug use is all right if it is for medication. The usual justification given by physician addicts is the need to take drugs to keep going in service to mankind under the handicap of overwork, chronic fatigue, various kinds of physical disease, insomnia, alcoholism, and personal and professional problems (Modlin and Montes 1964; Winick 1964:268–273).

Also, the physician who starts taking opiates, like the subculture initiate, believes that he will not become addicted. The physician's belief is based on his confidence in his knowledge of drugs and his ability to take them in a way that will not lead to addiction. He learns that only certain kinds of people get "hooked," and he is not one of them. As Modlin and Montes report:

We were particularly impressed with the patients' [physician addicts] magical belief in the nonaddictive properties of Demerol. They believed that (1) "It won't hurt me," and (2) "I can stop any time I want to" (Modlin and Montes 1964:360).

Winick reports that about a third of his physician-addict interviewees were "surprised at becoming addicted," typically stating that "I thought I'd toy with it because I knew enough about it to inhibit its reaction and control its use"; "I thought I was above getting addicted." Winick concludes:

Their professional familiarity with the effect of drugs appears to have provided a rationale for their semi-magical belief that the drugs would somehow have a different effect on them than they had on non-physicians. . . . The majority of these physicians believed that they were too smart to become "hooked" (Winick 1964:270).

The relief of the various complaints in a negative sense and whatever pleasure the drugs provide in a positive sense provides the reinforcement

for use; accompanied by these kinds of justifications they provide the motivation for first and subsequent use long enough to develop tolerance and
dependence. The self-medicating physician may then go on to become the
physician addict.

Opiate Addiction

By whatever path—subcultural, conventional, or occupational—a person
comes to opiates, if he ingests them long enough (sometimes within a
month) he will develop physiological dependence and will suffer withdrawal pains if he stops. But although dependence is necessary, it is not
sufficient for one to begin addictive use—habitual, daily usage over a period of time. Almost forty years ago Lindesmith interviewed addicts and
identified the key element in the process of becoming addicted to opiates.
Before a person becomes addicted he must first undergo a withdrawal experience, learn to associate the distress with abstinence from the drug, and
then take an *active* part in the alleviation of the distress by taking more
opiate. Thereafter, habitual use is sustained by taking the drug to avoid the
distress of withdrawal. Anyone who gets to this point is hooked and will
continue regular use of opiates (Lindesmith 1968:69–156; see also Lindesmith 1938).

> Addiction occurs only when opiates are used to alleviate with-
> drawal distress, after this distress has been properly understood
> or interpreted. . . . If the individual fails to conceive of his distress
> as withdrawal distress brought about by the absence of opiates, he
> does not become addicted, but if he does [form this conception]
> addiction is quickly and permanently established through further
> use of the drug (Lindesmith 1968:191).

Patients can be given dosages long enough to cause dependence, but
they can experience withdrawal without connecting it to lack of the drug.
Therefore they do not take more opiates to alleviate the distress and do not
become addicted. This is probably one explanation of why the conventional
pattern at one time accounted for the largest number of addicts, but today
accounts for relatively few addicts. In earlier times it was relatively easy for
the patient to secure further injections. Today, even if a patient realizes that
his pains are not due to the ailment but to a lack of the pain-relieving drug
he has been receiving, he is not likely to have an opportunity to take an
active part, either directly or by persuading the physician or nurse to give
him further injections, to alleviate the withdrawal distress.

The physiological dependence is the same whether a person is the
passive recipient of drugs as a patient or takes drugs on his own. But the

distinction between *passive* and *active* participation in alleviation of withdrawal once dependence has developed is crucial for addiction. This central notion in Lindesmith's theory is consistent with a learning perspective.
If a person does nothing—is the passive recipient of alleviating drugs—
then the outcome, reduction of an aversive condition, is not contingent on
his behavior, and the behavior will not be reinforced. On the other hand,
if he engages in the voluntary behavior of self-ingestion, he has done something which is capable of being reinforced by the outcome it brings about.
And each time his actions have this outcome the response is strengthened
further. For obvious reasons there have been no studies of experimentally
induced addiction in humans. But laboratory studies of experimental addiction in rats and other animals confirm Lindesmith's central contention and
specify further the ways in which addiction can be explained by learning
principles.

In one series of experiments Nichols produced physiological dependence
to morphine in rats by injecting them with morphine. He then split the
rats into experimental and control groups, and the drugs were stopped to
allow withdrawal to set in. Withdrawal in the control group was alleviated
by further injections, whereas the rats in the experimental group were
allowed to drink a morphine-water solution to alleviate their own withdrawal symptoms. The amount of morphine was the same, but the control
group passively received relief, and the animals in the experimental group
actively effected their own relief of withdrawal distress. When the drugs
were stopped again and withdrawal set in, both groups were given the opportunity to drink either plain water or the morphine solution. The rats
that had been taking morphine themselves chose the morphine and voluntarily increased intake. Those that had been injected all along chose the
plain water even though they were undergoing the same withdrawal as the
other rats (Nichols 1965; see also Nichols et al. 1956; Nichols and Davis
1959).

The Nichols' experiments demonstrated that addiction is behavior
learned through a process of *negative reinforcement* wherein behavior is
sustained by the removal or reduction of some aversive stimulus.

If a response is reinforced by the termination of a noxious
stimulus, the procedure is called "escape training," and the response is called the "instrumental act of escape," or "escape response." A rat which learns to press a bar to turn off an electric
shock is performing an instrumental act of escape which it learns as
a result of escape training.

The disagreeable, distressing, and noxious stimuli of withdrawal symptoms may be terminated by an intake of morphine.
Any response, therefore, which results in a morphine-intake will be
reinforced by termination of the withdrawal distress and tend to
be repeated (Nichols and Davis 1959:259–60).

Experiments by Weeks (1964) lend further clarification. Weeks set up a voluntary self-injection routine for rats in whom he had produced dependence to opiates. Then he manipulated amounts and schedules of reinforcement. When he increased the number of responses (bar pressing) needed for one injection, the animals compensated with higher response rates. The animals rapidly pressed the bar the required number of times until the injection of morphine was delivered, then stopped responding "until time for another shot." The high level of responding followed by a period of quietude after the injection is analogous to the behavior of the subcultural addict whose drug supply is uncertain. He often has to do quite a lot for his shot—secure money, perhaps through stealing; locate his connection or supply; get his equipment, perhaps secreted someplace; prepare his heroin by cooking it with water in a spoon or bottle cap; get the heroin properly strained into the syringe; and so on—and do it all in a short time before or while he is sick. The subcultural addict sometimes appears to be engaged in a continuous, almost frantic, search for a fix; he will do whatever is necessary as many times as needed to get his drug, after which his activity level is reduced until the approach of the time for his next shot (see Larner and Tefferteller 1964; Burroughs 1963; Hughes 1961; Elbin 1961; Time-Life editors 1965). Many subcultural addicts have been conditioned on this kind of low-probability schedule of reinforcement (a high number of responses needed to secure a reinforcer). The one with a reliable supply, such as the physician or conventional addict, is on a high-probability schedule and does not evince this frantic response pattern.

One way in which addiction in humans differs from that in animals is that animal addiction appears to be more strictly *escape* (removing an already aversive condition), whereas humans are capable of *avoidance* (anticipating and therefore avoiding or delaying aversive conditions). The extent to which a human addict can plan ahead for his drug needs is, of course, subject to the reliability of his supply, but if possible he does secure drugs ahead of time and takes a shot before the withdrawal sickness begins. Weeks' rats apparently did not anticipate the onset of withdrawal and made no move to press the bar for an injection until the sickness actually began to set in (Weeks 1964:21). The tendency for the drug-oriented behavior to dominate the life of an addict is also understandable in light of the fact that escape-avoidance training has been used to condition animals to engage in one action, almost to the exclusion of other responses (Verhave 1966:8–9; for further explanation see Akers et al. 1968:465–66).

The change from initial use to addiction has important implications in the life of the physician and conventional user, but this move from recreational and occasional use to addiction has the greatest impact on the life of the subcultural user. Once addicted, he becomes more and more incorporated into the "junkie" life. His associates become almost exclusively other addicts, and his life begins to revolve nearly entirely around drugs. Because he uses much more and must have drugs at regular intervals, he can no longer depend on friends and occasional contacts for his supply. Legal sources are shut off for him, and he must therefore turn to criminal suppliers. Since drugs from this source are very expensive, he needs more money for his habit. He will not automatically turn to money-making crimes or to pushing drugs to support his habit, but he often does (O'Donnell 1966). The probability that he will is increased by the exposure to criminal patterns he has by now had and by his rationalization that the need to keep from getting sick with withdrawal justifies his crime. His increased contact with illegal drug sources and his commission of other crimes makes him more vulnerable to arrest and incarceration. He becomes visible and known to the police and becomes caught up in a cycle of frantic activity to secure drugs, carried out under the threat of arrest while on the street.

Needless to say, if he had stable employment before, he is likely to lose it after addiction. He may steal from his family and friends and becomes increasingly alienated from them. When all the money goes for drugs, just paying the rent and eating are difficult. He is redefined by family, friends, and authorities as a dirty, untrustworthy junkie. In short, drug use for the subcultural addict is no longer the "hip," "cool," "no sweat" experience it was when he was just playing around with drugs.

Recent evidence reported by McAuliffe and Gordon (1974) questions this explanation of the general process of addiction, which argued, based on notions first proposed by Lindesmith, that while positive effects of the opiate and the social support of other users in the drug subculture contribute to addiction to opiates, it is sustained mainly through the negative reinforcement of avoiding the withdrawal symptoms. McAuliffe and Gordon's survey of sixty male and four female addicts in Baltimore led them to conclude that even for chronic addicts, "desire for euphoria appears to be a major factor in the explanation of their behavior" (McAuliffe and Gordon 1974:797). McAuliffe and Gordon include in the concept of euphoria both the initial "impact effect" of the flash or rush when the opiates are injected and the "continuing impact" of the prolonged sense of contentment as the drug spreads through the addict's body. "Weekenders" experience the euphoria less frequently than the "hard-core" addicts who seek opiate euphoria every day.

McAuliffe and Gordon report that almost all addicts report "getting high" some of the time and four out of ten do so at least once a day. Moreover, the frequency with which euphoric effects were reported increased with larger dosages and when the amount of opiate was more than the addict felt was needed to feel normal. Nine out of ten of the addicts expressed a desire to get high at least once a day. All used more drugs than needed to avoid withdrawal sickness. The average excess or "deluxe ratio" used was two and one-half times as much opiate as needed to avoid withdrawal sickness. For both weekenders and hard-core addicts, getting high was a more important reason for taking drugs than it was security from the pains of withdrawal.

Addicts *need* a drug that prevents withdrawal sickness, but they *crave* a drug that makes them high. . . . A combination-of-effects explanation appears to summarize the data better than one based on withdrawal alone. . . . According to our theory, . . . addiction starts to gain strength at the very beginning of opiate use and continues to grow incrementally with each of the many positive reinforcements experienced during the "honeymoon" period. With the onset of physical dependence, euphoria and withdrawal sickness combine in various proportions to yield a complex schedule of reinforcement for the typical long-term addict (McAuliffe and Gordon 1974:811, 812, 829, italics in original).

McAuliffe and Gordon agree with the learning explanation offered here that both positive and negative reinforcement are important in addiction, but they place more emphasis on intermittent positive reinforcement from the pleasurable effects of the drug. Their findings seem to support this position. The levels of dosage taken above that needed to alleviate or avoid the pain of withdrawal are high enough to argue that euphoria is more prominent in continuing addiction than previous learning theories of addiction have asserted. But do their findings show that the positive euphoric effects are more important than the avoidance of withdrawal distress in addiction? There are certain findings in the McAuliffe and Gordon research which cast doubt on the proposition that they are. Also, there are remaining questions to be answered before the relative importance of positive and negative reinforcement processes in addiction can be more accurately determined.

First, even among participants in a subculture that extolls the heroin high, as studied in the McAuliffe and Gordon research, when given a choice, less than half would choose a drug for euphoria only, rather than one which would keep them from being sick all day. Second, only one addict reported getting high each time he injected heroin, and over half the addicts in the study reported getting high less than fifteen out of the past thirty days. Third, the researchers did not ask the addicts how often they use opiates to feel better or keep from getting sick compared to how often they take them just to get high. Fourth, the question of whether euphoria is experienced relatively more or less frequently after addiction than during the preaddiction phase is not addressed in the research. Fifth, would use of drugs continue even if there were no pleasure from them, but their discontinuance were to cause sickness?

Relapse to Opiates

An outstanding feature of opiate addiction is the frequency with which those who successfully withdraw from dependence on the drug start all over and become addicted again. The relapse rate should not be exaggerated, however. The belief that addicts are almost never really "cured" is erroneous; addicts are not inevitably consigned to a lifetime of dependence on the drug. Most addicts do manage to get off and stay off the drug for periods of time, and many accomplish complete abstinence for the rest of their lives, even after a long period of addiction (Winick 1965).

The research on relapse to opiates presents a mixed picture, with varying rates of relapse found, from a low of 8 percent relapse to a high of nearly 90 percent relapse, depending on the population studied. The extent to which one finds a high rate of relapse also depends on the criterion by which the addict is judged to relapse. If the criterion is any relapse of any duration after withdrawal, the rate is higher; if the criterion is the total amount of time addicted compared with the amount of time abstinent during some follow-up period, the rate is lower (O'Donnell 1965). For instance, one study found that although 73 percent of the men and 62 percent of the women relapsed to drug use at least once after release from treatment, 38 percent and 79 percent, respectively, were completely abstinent some of the time during the same period (O'Donnell 1964:954).

Nevertheless, the evidence is clear that the risk of returning to drugs after withdrawal is high. Even Nichols' experimentally addicted rats relapsed when given the chance (Nichols et al. 1956:790). The drug user may fall into a recurring cycle of addiction, abstinence, relapse, and readdiction. The addict may be forced to undergo withdrawal in a jail or to undergo gradual withdrawal in a hospital, and the same day he is released he will go back to mainlining; in fact, he may have had a supply of drugs cached for that very purpose. Some voluntarily commit themselves to "dry up" or "get resistance down" only in order to have a brief return to the high enjoyed before they became addicted or to reduce their habit back down to a level they can financially support.

This problem of relapse is perhaps the most difficult part of opiate-taking behavior to explain. Why, after he no longer needs to avoid withdrawal distress and after he has experienced firsthand the problems of being an addict, does he relapse? One can understand how someone who has never been addicted can proceed into it; he has not yet learned what addiction can mean. One can also understand that addiction can be sustained because the person, however much he wants to stop, is kept going by the need to avoid the pain and, for some, the horrors of withdrawal. But why, after he no longer needs the drug to get away from this and after he has experienced what addiction can do, does he so often go back to it? We offer a tentative answer.

First, the former addict may go back to the same or similar circumstances in which he started in the first place, and he may simply repeat the process in relapse which he underwent in initial use. But this is not all; it is clear that the experience of addiction itself conditions the individual to be even more receptive to opiate use than he was before that experience. Just what about the experience produces the increased receptivity is not entirely clear. It may be that after learning what effects the drug can have he wants to re-capture those effects. As one says:

> Why does an addict go back to drugs? . . . A drug addict knows the feeling of drugs, knows the great sedative it can be, and how wild and complacent it can make a person (Larner and Tefferteller 1964: 59).

Certainly knowledge of what the drug can do is part of it. The surrounding environment, situations, and circumstances when the addict experiences symptoms of withdrawal until relieved by further injections can become discriminative stimuli which elicit feelings of withdrawal even though those feelings have no physiological basis; they nonetheless induce the addict to take a shot. Returning to these circumstances after having shed physiological dependence may again call forth feelings resembling the withdrawal syn-drome (Wikler 1965:85–100). But probably the most important element added by the experience of addiction is the changed reactions of others to the former addict and the application of changed definitions of his actions.

The reception given the ex-addict who is attempting to remain drug-free may account in part for the differences in relapse rates among subcultural, conventional, and physician addicts. In the relapse studies reviewed by O'Donnell, the lowest rate of relapse was found in a study of physician addicts (8 percent); the next lowest relapse rate was found in a study of a conventional upper-middle-class group (33 percent). Six of the seven highest relapse rates were found in studies of addicts in New York City, the city with the largest number of subcultural addicts (O'Donnell 1964:232).

One thing the street addict learns is "once a junkie, always a junkie." He returns to his old associates and encounters the same definitions. Other addicts continue to treat him as a fellow addict and expect him to take up drug use again. He is likely labeled an addict and a criminal by the police. His preaddiction friends and family have seen former attempts to abstain fail; they remain suspicious and do not accept him back as a nonaddict. They continue to react toward him as they acted when he was addicted, and they fail to reward his attempts to remain drug-free, thus playing out a self-fulfilling prophecy (Ray 1964). The physician or middle-class addict, on the other hand, in addition to having undergone withdrawal under more favorable conditions, probably returns to a very different set of circum-stances. He is more likely to be received by family and associates as one who has undergone a period of sickness and needs help in recuperation. They have been accustomed to interacting with him in terms other than his addiction, and they receive him back in much the same light. In short, those with whom he interacts are supportive of and are more likely to rein-force his nonaddict role than are those with whom the subcultural addict associates.

That the probability of relapse is associated with differences in the social environment to which the person returns is shown in recent research. De Fleur and associates (1969), for instance, found that all ex-addicts in their study who were more involved in a subculture of criminal activities, were occupationally unstable, and were less educated relapsed within three years, whereas only about one-third of the steadily employed, better educated, and noncriminal did so. Waldorf (1970) found that among a group of New York addicts only 27 percent had voluntarily abstained (that is, while not incarcerated) for two or more years, but that the likelihood of a relatively long period of abstinence increased with the length of time since first addicted, age, education, and steady employment. Moreover, during the time they were abstinent, 69 percent of those who managed to stay off drugs for at least three months "did not associate with other addicts or users," and 70 percent "were not treated like addicts by others" (Waldorf 1970:233).

A second problem in relapse is the way in which taking the drug to ease withdrawal pains becomes associated with other stimuli; as he avoids the pain of withdrawal with drugs, the addict comes to cope with other pains and deprivations by taking opiates. Hence, taking drugs becomes a general response to a range of problems; he can escape the unpleasantness of a bad job, interpersonal problems, the negative reactions of others, failure to live up to expectations of achievement, and other difficulties. Drug taking is an escape or retreatist adaptation to life's difficulties, but as a consequence of, not the cause of, addiction as some have argued.[4] Complete withdrawal cures the addict of the problem of abstinence symptoms, but it does not cure whatever other problems he may have had. When he encounters them again he is likely to respond in the manner to which he has become accustomed — taking a fix.

Also, opiates not only relieve pain; ingesting an opiate drug can partially substitute for food and sex. Drug taking then may develop as the addict's main response to pain, hunger, and sexual deprivations. As Nichols observes:

> The drives that lead to many activities of the nonaddict lead to only one activity of the addict and all are reduced by one simple action: the injection of an opiate (1965:86).

After withdrawal, the ex-addict still feels pain, gets hungry, and feels sex deprivation, and he may revert to his old habit of responding by taking drugs.

The third important variable in relapse is time. The time variable is salient for two reasons: (1) As we have seen, the human addict is likely to

---

[4]The same point is made by Lindesmith and Gagnon (1964:177–85). For the retreatist argument see Merton 1957:153–55 and Cloward and Ohlin 1960:178–86.

avoid rather than merely escape withdrawal symptoms. While addicted he often anticipates his need of another shot and takes the drug regularly enough that he does not actually experience withdrawal for long periods of time. He becomes conditioned to respond in anticipation, but actual absence, of the withdrawal distress. And even after he has withdrawn and failure to take the drug will not result in an aversive outcome, he continues to behave as an addict. If he continues long enough to behave as an addict even after it is no longer necessary, it will, of course, become necessary again. (2) It should be remembered that initial drug use is in part a function of the positively reinforcing effects of the drug itself. It is not until later that the negative aspects become predominant. This period of time between initial drug use and the disruption of life concomitant with addiction is a fairly long one. The addict who has taken the cure is essentially in the same position with regard to drug effects as the novice. If anything, he is more likely to enjoy initial drug effects, and these are right now, immediate; the problems, even though he is now familiar with them, lie in the more distant future. The longer the time lapse between a response and its consequence, the less control those consequences exert over behavior. The immediate, more pleasant outcomes of drug taking have greater impact on use than the more distant unpleasant outcomes.

Summary

Initial Phase

The process of beginning and completing the initial phase of drug use leading to drug addiction can be summarized as follows. The person may follow one of at least three learning routes—subcultural, conventional, or occupational. Although these differ in detail, all involve the following common process: (1) The person must first find the drug available or learn how to obtain it. Availability is also a factor in addiction, of course, but the addict will be quite ingenious in ferreting out a supply, whereas the drug must be more readily available for the novice. (2) Before the novice will take advantage of the availability of the drug, he must learn and apply appropriate definitions to opiate use which define it either in (a) *positive* terms—that is, as a cool, exciting, or desirable experience to undergo, or (b) in *rationalizing* or neutralizing terms—that is, not really dangerous, necessary to gain other ends, justified, or excusable. Steps (1) and (2) will bring the person to the point of trying or experimenting with drugs, but he will not continue use long enough to develop tolerance and dependence until he takes further steps. (3) He must further learn to administer the drug properly for optimal effect, and (4) he must find the effects intrinsically rewarding or learn to define the effects, whatever they are, as desirable and/or (5) obtain other social rewards upon taking the drug so that aversive consequences are offset.[5]

Addiction

The person will not become addicted until (1) he experiences his first withdrawal symptoms, (2) recognizes them as due to lack of the drug, and (3) then takes an *active* part in ingesting opiates to relieve the symptoms.

Positive reinforcement is the principal process in the *initial phase* of drug use. Addiction is conditioned primarily through a process of *negative re-inforcement* combined with intermittent positive reinforcement. Trying drugs and continuing use in the preaddiction phase of subcultural use is maintained through *positive* and mainly *social* rewards. Conventional and physician users start for less social reasons. For all, however, addiction is conditioned by the *negative* and mainly *physiological* reinforcement of avoiding or terminating the distress of withdrawal. For the subcultural addict, at least, this appears to be combined with the sought-after euphoric effects of the drug and the social reinforcement of the subcultural participation.

Relapse

Relapse to opiates is facilitated by a return to an environment similar to one the addict experienced during addiction, especially one in which the reactions of others fail to accept the former addict and fail to reward his efforts to play a nonaddict role. Relapse may also result from the fact that taking of drugs to avoid or escape withdrawal may become a generalized response to unpleasant events which remains even after physical dependence on opiates is relieved. In addition, the former addict is subject to having his renewed drug taking positively reinforced just as is the novice. The reinforcing effects are immediate, whereas the unpleasant consequences of addiction lie in the future and have much less impact on his present drug behavior.

---

[5] Steps 3, 4, and 5 do not apply to medical patients who under a physician's supervision continue to have drugs administered, sometimes to the point of dependence, for the alleviation of illness or pain.

8

Hallucinogenic Drug Use

Extent and Characteristics
of Marihuana and LSD Use

Marihuana was practically unknown in the United States before the 1930s. Until that time its use was confined chiefly to lower-class Mexican-Americans in the Southwest. Marihuana smoking began to spread into the slums of the big cities and became part of the drug subculture in the 1930s. After World War II marihuana use spread rapidly among the youth of the lower-class areas of the cities, reaching a peak about 1949–50 and continuing at a high rate until the mid-1950s. The practice began to decline somewhat toward the end of the fifties (Ausubel 1958:93–94; Lindesmith 1967:237–39). LSD was unknown until 1943, and its use was confined mainly to psychiatric therapy, to some "elite" artists and literary users, and to professional experimenters until about 1960 (Blum 1967b:25). Subsequently marihuana primarily and LSD secondarily have come into greatly increased use by middle-class and upper-middle class white adolescents and young adults.

Going beyond this general description to pin down just how many and who are taking these drugs remains a difficult undertaking. Nevertheless, some evidence for widespread and remarkable increase in taking LSD and smoking marihuana among young, middle-class whites can be marshaled from scattered sources. In California from 1960 to 1968 arrests for marihuana possession increased more than tenfold, an increase concentrated among the young and white (Carey 1968:44–46; Goode 1970:268–70). That many arrested persons do not come from the background traditionally associated with drug law violations is shown by the fact that since 1961 there has been a marked increase in the proportion of marihuana arrests of persons with no previous criminal record and a marked decrease in the proportion with major prison-arrest records (Grupp 1971).

The increase and growing concentration of use among adolescent and young adults (ages eighteen to thirty), mainly white, who tend to be open to experimentation with other mood-changing drugs was apparent by the mid-1960s (Blum 1967b:24–25). The college and university campuses became and remained focal points for the use of marihuana and other hallucinogens. Attempts to determine the extent of this type of drug use have therefore tended to emphasize college and college-aged populations. Starting about 1965 a number of surveys have been conducted, most of them relatively small-scale and unrepresentative, on various campuses. Subsequently, however, there have been a number of studies of representative samples of college populations, high school students, and the general population. Some of the findings on marihuana use reported from these studies are shown in tables 8–1, 8–2, and 8–3.

Table 8–1
Percentages of marihuana use from some surveys among college and young adult populations, 1965–75

Location and type of sample	Year	Percent have ever used	Percent currently using	Source
Various colleges	1965–66	10% or less		Blum 1967b
New York, college	1967	23		Rand et al. 1970
West Coast, colleges	1967	10–33		Blum and associates 1970b
National, college	1967	5		Gallup poll
Washington state, college	1968	13	5%	DeFleur and Garrett 1970
National, college	1969	22		Gallup poll
National, college	1970	42	21	Gallup poll
National, college	1971	51		Gallup poll
National, college	1974	55		Gallup poll
National, males, 20 to 30 years old	1975	55	38	O'Donnell et al. 1976

Table 8–2
Percentages of marihuana use from some surveys among general adult populations, 1969–74

Location of sample	Year	Percent have ever used	Percent currently using	Source
National	1969	4%		Gallup poll
National	1972	11		Gallup poll
National	1974	18	8%	Drug Abuse Council
Oregon	1974	19	9	Drug Abuse Council
California	1974	28	9	Drug Abuse Council
Iowa	1974	8	3	Resource Planning, Inc.

Table 8-3
Percentages of marihuana use from some surveys among senior and junior high school students, 1967–75

Location of sample	Year	Percent have ever used			Percent currently using			Source
		Male	Female	Total	Male	Female	Total	
California high schools	1967	16%	4%	10%				Mauss 1969
California high schools	1968–69	13–41	7–37					Blum and associates 1970b
National senior males	1969			21			12.8%[a]	Johnston 1973
Selected junior and senior high schools	1971–73							Josephson 1974
age 12–17	1971	11	8	9.5	4		4	
	1973	13	8	10.5	7	1	0	
age 12–13	1971			3			1	
	1973			3				
age 16–17	1971			14			9	
	1973			18			8	
National	1974							Drug Abuse Council
age 12–13				5				
age 16–17				23			10	
National seniors	1975			47.9			27[b]	Johnston 1975

[a]Used more than two times.
[b]Used within past month.

By looking at the tables, one can see that the various studies over the past decade have documented increases in marihuana use. The increase was most dramatic for college and university students beginning in the late 1960s; now more than half the young adults in this country have used marihuana and perhaps a third use it regularly. Significant increases have also occurred among high school (but apparently not junior high) youngsters and among the general adult population. By the time of high school graduation more than four out of ten students will have had some experience with marihuana. About two out of five in the general adult population over eighteen report at least one experience with marihuana. The upward trend in marihuana use has been matched to some extent by increases in the reported illicit use of LSD and other hallucinogens, amphetamines, barbiturates, and other drugs. For instance, in 1967 Gallup polls and other studies indicated that less than 5 percent of the college students had experienced LSD (Rand et al. 1970). In some studies, by 1969 the percentage of college students using LSD had doubled (Blum and associates 1970b:31–47), and by 1972 it had increased by four times in the Gallup poll. In 1969 in a national sample of high school senior males 6 percent reported some use of psychedelics, and by 1975 the percentage had increased to over eighteen (Johnston 1973; 1975). In 1975 more than one-third of the high school seniors had used some illicit drug other than marihuana and half of those had used some drug within the past month, not counting use of marihuana (Johnston 1975). In the young adult male population beyond high school age, 20 percent had used some psychedelic drug at some time and 7 percent currently use psychedelics.

Although blacks are still more likely to use marihuana, cocaine, and hard narcotics than whites, the disparity is less now than before, and the difference in total drug use between whites and nonwhites is not significant. Whites are more likely now than other racial groups to use psychedelics, amphetamines, and barbiturates. Also, marihuana and other hallucinogenic drug use tends to increase with education (O'Donnell et al. 1976:37–38; Johnston 1973:192–201).

Multiple-Drug Use: Does Marihuana Lead to Hard Drugs?

The best answer seems to be no. The evidence is now clear that there is a very high intercorrelation of use among the different types of drugs. The use of any one drug substance (including tobacco and alcohol) increases the probability that one will also use some other drug substance; use of any illicit drug increases the chances of using other illicit drugs. Among those who use substances illicitly, the pattern is most apt to be one of multi-drug usage rather than specialization by type of drug. This multiple-drug use pattern is usually arranged progressively or hierarchically with heroin at the top and alcohol (and tobacco) at the bottom. The more illicit or stronger the drug used, the more likely that other drugs have been and are being used. While heroin users are almost certain to have used other drugs such as marihuana or amphetamines, the reverse is not true—most marihuana or amphetamine users have not used heroin (Johnston 1973:17, 52–69). For instance, in one study (O'Donnell et al. 1976), *all* of those using any type of illicit drug have also used alcohol; 90 percent of those using any other illicit drug also use marihuana; and 90 percent of the heroin and cocaine users have indulged in every other kind of drug (tobacco, alcohol, marihuana, barbiturates, amphetamines, and hallucinogens).

Thus, while it is true that almost all heroin users have previously (or subsequently) smoked marihuana, it is equally true that almost all heroin users have also used many other substances, including tobacco and alcohol. Some drug use nearly always precedes heroin use (starting with heroin and progressing to other substances is rare), so in this sense they all could be said to lead to heroin for some people. However, only a small proportion of the users of any of the other drugs take up the harder drugs. For instance, only 6 percent of the alcohol drinkers, 7 percent of the tobacco smokers, 11 percent of the marihuana users, and 25 percent of the users of psychedelics also use heroin. The proportion of marihuana smokers who go on to hard narcotics is somewhat higher than the proportion of alcohol and tobacco users and somewhat less than the psychedelic drug users who proceed to hard drugs (O'Donnell et al. 1976). But nowhere is the percentage enough to say that once a person uses one of the non-opiates, he has a great likelihood of moving on to opiates.

There is nothing inherent in the pharmacological properties of marihuana or other drugs that induces the users to seek out and use heroin or other opiates. The evidence we have shows that marihuana use is neither a necessary nor sufficient condition for heroin use. The chance that the two will be linked depends on the social setting. If marihuana is initially used in a subcultural setting in which heroin is also used and available, the individual is more likely to progress to heroin. Among users in other social settings in which heroin is not available and its use is frowned upon, there is virtually no connection between marihuana and opiate use (Goode 1969; Pet and Ball 1968; Ball et al. 1968).

Learning to Use Hallucinogenic Drugs

As with opiates, there are several learning paths to the use of hallucinogens. One way is through subcultures conducive to opiate use, such as the slum drug subculture and other subcultural settings like the beatniks and jazz musicians of the 1950s. In the 1960s another major subcultural style of drug use, that of the hippies, developed and provided a new set of definitions favorable to drug use. The term *psychedelic* took on "consciousness-expanding" connotations and spread as a favorable adjective for dress, music, and art styles. Combined with antiestablishment attitudes, dress, and behavior, the use of psychedelic drugs became a major characteristic of the hippie movement. The drug experience was defined as desirable and became symbolic of dropping out of a hypocritical, corrupt, and repressive system. Once this definition of LSD and marihuana became prevalent, it generalized to other drugs: "speed," barbiturates, and even heroin.

The hippie groups were usually college-age and college-oriented young people, and thrived close to certain colleges and universities. College students contributed to and took up both the dissatisfaction with the system (particularly dissent against the Vietnam war) and the drug-using patterns of the hippie subculture (Suchman 1968). Marihuana and other hallucinogenic drug use is still related to integration in the student subculture (Thomas et al. 1975), adherence to "counterculture" values, and political alienation (Johnston 1973:181; O'Donnell et al. 1976:117). However, the alienated college student is no longer the only one who uses drugs. Smoking marihuana has become an integral part of college life and has spread to college-age youth in the military. Marihuana is smoked in an offhand, casual way that would shock the old-time head (see the description of "tea-pads" in Solomon 1966:293). Before, during, or after sports events, dates, public gatherings, parties, music festivals, class, or work will do; there is no special place, time, or occasion for marihuana smoking. The acceptable places and occasions are as varied as those for drinking alcohol. Even many who do not smoke marihuana share the casual, tolerant definitions of marihuana with the users. As the figures in table 8–3 show, the college students' younger brothers and sisters in senior and junior high school have taken up drug use. It is patterned basically after the college style, and there is some evidence that college-oriented high school boys from middle-class families are more likely to smoke marihuana than their peers who are not college bound (Mauss 1969; for contrary evidence see Johnston 1973:196–97).

Although it has become incorporated into a general adolescent and college subculture, this avenue to drugs cannot be described as subcultural in the same sense as the slum and hippie subcultures. Rather, an essentially *conventional* path to drugs, which bears all the earmarks of conventional socialization into alcohol use, appears to be emerging. This drug pattern, of course, is not and never has been entirely confined to college and high school youth. Older adults are also involved. But before, they came to hallucinogenic drugs as leaders or followers in the psychedelic movement, in the future, they will more often simply be adults who continue the social use of marihuana learned during their high school and college years (Akers 1970). This does not mean that all who use marihuana in their student days will continue afterwards. Indeed, just as movement into the student subculture is related to marihuana use, moving out of that subculture and making commitments to marriage, children, jobs, and other roles that are not typical of college students is associated with stopping marihuana use (Henley and Adams 1973; Brown et al. 1974).

Although one may become a habitual user of hallucinogenic drugs, these drugs are not addictive. The real head is probably just as immersed in his psychedelic drugs as the addict is in his heroin, but the movement from recreational to addictive use of opiates is marked by the rather dramatic symptoms of physiological dependence. Habitual use of marihuana, LSD, or other hallucinogens, on the other hand, is more a gradual continuation, on a more frequent and regular basis, of the beginning stages of use. Therefore, the entire process from initial through habitual use of hallucinogens can be accounted for by the same social learning explanation applied to preaddiction use of opiates. Use of a hallucinogen is a function of *social definitions of it as desirable or all right, imitation of other drug users, and the differential reinforcement over abstinence through the positive reinforcement from drug-using associates and the positive effects of the drug itself.* There have been no direct tests of this social learning theory of hallucinogenic drug use. However, research from the 1950s on offers findings consistent with the theory.

According to Becker's study of marihuana use in the early 1950s, initial and subsequent use of marihuana occurs in association with friends who are users and who initially supply the person with the drug and the definitions favorable to its use. A person becomes willing to try marihuana by learning to overcome his initial negative feelings about it. He will not continue beyond this point, however, unless he learns (1) to use the drug properly, (2) to perceive its effects, and (3) to enjoy those effects. Through observation, imitation, and direct instruction in marihuana-using groups, the individual learns the technique to obtain and recognize the "high" effects. If the initial reactions are unpleasant, he must learn to redefine them as pleasurable to continue use (Becker 1963:41–58).

Becker's proposition that the marihuana high is learned has experimental support (Weil et al. 1968), although the social characteristics of pot smokers have changed. The initiate into marihuana smoking today is more likely to approach his first experiences with neutral or positive expectations than was the novice at the time of Becker's study. The "conventional" anti-marihuana stereotypes are less likely to be held by today's non-user, and rationalizations favorable to marihuana use no longer have to be learned from direct participation in marihuana-using groups. However, if an individual continues to believe in the negative definitions of marihuana and associates with others who share this view, he will be deterred from trying the drug. Moreover, the smoker today still typically undergoes the process of learning the proper technique, perceiving the effects, and enjoying them—

primarily through imitation of friends and direct teaching by small groups of friends, who make marihuana available and provide the rationalizations for its use (Goode 1970).

Studies of marihuana use in this country (most of them since the late 1960s) find that association with users is the best predictor of use (see Kandel 1974 for a review of these studies). Users are not only more likely to have current users among their friends, but the frequency and quantity of use and attitudes favorable to its use are related to having current users as friends (O'Donnell et al. 1976:60–75). Counting marihuana users among one's friends does not mean that the friendships were formed as a result of the interest in marihuana; rather the association with users occurs prior to first use of marihuana and smoking marihuana is learned as a result of that association (Krohn 1974).

> Marijuana users report having many more marijuana-using friends than do non-users of marijuana. Moreover, marijuana use increases in direct proportion to the reported number of friends who use marijuana. . . . Marijuana use by one's friends may not only be an important variable in explaining adolescent drug use, *it may be the critical variable.* In a stepwise multiple regression analysis of factors associated with drug use, reported "drug use by close friends" was the *single most important discriminating variable* (Kandel 1974:208, italics added).

As for the reasons marihuana is *not* smoked, it is deterred by the perception of the high risk of apprehension and official sanction (Waldo and Chiricos 1972; Anderson 1973). Parents also influence use (both negatively by disapproving of it and positively by providing drug-using examples). However, these and other sources of punishment and reinforcement are less important than the models and reinforcements provided by using or non-using friends (Kandel 1974; Krohn 1974; Burkett and Jensen 1975; Tec 1974).

Friends Provide First Opportunities to Use Marihuana

I tried it when I was fourteen because some of my friends used it. Most of the people I know who take it are just explorers. Last time I took it was four months ago. . . . I don't think I'll blow grass much anymore except maybe at a party or something. On my first trip I just messed around. That's all I ever did.

I went down to California to see some of my friends who were going to school there. We threw this wild party at his place one night. . . . Then they decided they'd break a stash of pot. . . . We

sat around smoking pot and everybody getting high. I didn't wanna turn down the offer and spoil the evening and I was also curious to see what it's like to smoke pot anyhow, so I went ahead and took in some myself.

I was at my girlfriend's apartment and her boyfriend and this friend of his came over. They were both art majors at this university and we got to talking about pot. . . . Then they asked me if I wanted to try some. I was scared at first but my friends said it doesn't harm you and so I said I'd try it.

(From interviews conducted by the author's students.)

Those who want to become regular smokers cannot depend completely on the friendship network as a supply source. At this point they run a greater risk of discovery by non-users and police. Some find the risks and trouble too great, and they go back to the pattern of occasional use with friends. The initiation and progression into regular use of LSD follows the same pattern, but the person usually has some experience with marihuana before he takes LSD (Carey 1968). LSD is also typically introduced to the user in a group setting. Those who hold positive definitions of LSD (see personal, social, or artistic benefits in it) take it; those who view it negatively refuse it. Those whose initiation occurs in an informal group, who experience pleasant reactions to the drug, and who continue to associate with other users are the ones most likely to move into regular LSD use (Blum and associates 1964).

Summary

Hallucinogenic drugs are taken in a variety of subcultural and conventional settings. Whatever the setting, the progression into use is essentially a learning process that resembles the preaddiction use of opiates. Before a person will try a hallucinogenic drug he must (1) find the drug available or learn how to obtain it and (2) learn and apply either positive or neutralizing definitions to its use. He will not continue beyond the experimental experiences unless he (3) learns to take the drug properly for optimal effect, (4) either finds its effects intrinsically rewarding or learns to define them as desirable, and/or (5) obtains other social rewards contingent upon taking the drug. Initial availability, appropriate definitions, and social reinforcement are typically obtained through association with drug-using friends. The person will not progress to regular, habitual use unless a stable supply can be secured and all the other factors remain operative, so that rewards for use are frequent and great enough to offset both the adverse consequences of use and the rewards for non-use.

9

Public Policy on Drugs:
Law Enforcement and Treatment

The aims of public policy (and private efforts coordinated with it) are and have been to control deviant drug use and to lessen its consequences. The formulae devised for accomplishing these goals have included various mixtures of tolerance, harshly punitive legal enforcement, and treatment of drug users. Sometimes the policy has focused on stopping or containing the supply and sometimes it has focused on stopping or changing the users. Public policy has varied both through time and by type of drug and has reflected and influenced public opinion on the drug problem and what to do about it. The current mixture of law enforcement and treatment responses to deviant drug use can be better understood when seen in historical perspective.

Controlling Deviant Drug Use through Law Enforcement

Addiction to opiates was not considered a law enforcement problem in the nineteenth century. As noted in chapter 6, there was a good deal of sympathy for and tolerance of those with opiate habits. By the beginning of the twentieth century, however, there was growing recognition that the international smuggling and profiteering from the opium trade must be stopped. The United States government signed a multilateral agreement to control the opium trade. As an outgrowth of that agreement, similar pieces of legislation regulating internal opium traffic were passed in several countries. The 1914 Harrison Act was the U.S. version of that internal legislation. Because it was intended to be a regulatory law, little publicity about a "drug problem" and apparently little political maneuvering by organized interest groups accompanied its passage. And even though it was a regulatory law, it represented the first major federal legislation to foster the criminalization of drug addiction.[1]

The Federal Bureau of Narcotics

Responsibility for enforcing the law was subsequently lodged in the same federal bureau that was set up to enforce the nationwide liquor prohibition beginning in 1918. The law was stiffened with stronger penalties in 1922. By 1930 a separate narcotic law enforcement agency, the Federal Bureau of Narcotics (FBN), was formed within the Treasury Department to enforce federal drug laws. In 1968 the FBN was moved to the Department of Justice as part of the Bureau of Narcotics and Dangerous Drugs (BNDD). Later the Office of Drug Abuse Law Enforcement was created and in 1973 was merged with the BNDD to form the Drug Enforcement Administration (DEA), which is the federal narcotic control agency today.

The FBN not only vigorously enforced the law but was a political pressure group that promoted antidrug legislation and punitive enforcement policies. It was a chief instrument in the development of a public policy of criminalizing drug users. This policy prevailed for the next four decades. The personnel of the agency interpreted and enforced the law so that it became extremely difficult for physicians to treat addict patients or prescribe drugs for them, because addicts were considered to be the concern of law enforcement alone. The agency promoted state legislation and played an active part in the enactment of federal statutes. These statutes had increasingly punitive criminal sanctions against the possession and sale of opiates and other drugs.

Major federal legislation was enacted in each decade from the 1930s to the 1960s. Each decade saw the increase of the law enforcement jurisdiction over drugs, a harsher stand toward users and dealers, and lengthened the maximum prison terms for violators. Indeed, the 1956 Narcotic Control Act provided for a possible death penalty for people convicted of selling drugs to minors under eighteen. State laws followed suit and some even made addiction itself a criminal offense (but in 1962 in the case of *Robinson* v. *California*, the U.S. Supreme Court declared such statutes unconstitutional because they outlawed a condition, not an act). Other state and local enforcement agencies were strongly influenced by the enforcement strategy adopted by the Federal Bureau of Narcotics, and it was not long before the strict pattern of harassment of street addicts, frequent arrests of low-level sellers, but infrequent arrests of high-level dope smugglers and wholesalers was established

---

[1]The discussion here centers around the attempts through law to control illicit drugs. In addition to these laws, of course, there has been a series of federal-state efforts, beginning with the Pure Food and Drug Act of 1906, to regulate the purity, safety, and effectiveness of prescription and legal drugs.

throughout the United States. In short, the federal and other narcotic enforcement agencies fostered the emerging public definition of the addict as a depraved criminal. Then, as other drugs like marihuana came into use, the criminalized conception of the opiate user was extended to them (Lindesmith 1967; Lindesmith 1968:239–41; Simrell 1970; King 1974).

> . . . Emphasis in the field of narcotic abuse from 1914 . . . was on rigorous enforcement of the existing federal laws with increasing penalties and less opportunity for probation or parole; additional legislation to tighten controls and to extend similar controls to synthetic narcotics and marihuana; encouragement of state legislation . . . and cooperation with state and local enforcement agencies (Simrell 1970:27).

How Marihuana Became a "Dangerous" Drug

Perhaps the clearest illustration of the FBN role as a political interest group is in Becker's study of the part it played in securing legal control of marihuana (1963:135–46). According to Becker, the FBN used its own reports and those of other governmental agencies to appeal for a marihuana act and prepared information for release to interested organizations, newspapers, and popular magazines. The message conveyed in all these outlets was the same: Marihuana is extremely dangerous — it erodes the motivation and will of users and makes them susceptible to crime and acts of depravity. The popular press picked up the stories of atrocities and heinous crimes committed by people supposedly under the influence of marihuana (Solomon 1966:286–90; Grinspoon 1969). The media presented virtually no information in favor of marihuana, and many myths were promoted as fact.

The bill that eventually became the Marihuana Tax Act of 1937 was originally drafted by FBN personnel and counsel, and Bureau lobbyists testified during the hearings. The bill taxed marihuana so heavily that in effect it banned possession of marihuana. At this point conflicting political interests which the Bureau had not anticipated came to light. The interests of certain groups — medical, pharmaceutical, industrial, and scientific — was anticipated, and possession of it by qualified people in these groups was allowed.[2] But the interests of hempseed oil manufacturers and the birdseed industry had not been foreseen, and representatives of these groups raised objections to the bill; the wording was changed to their satisfaction. No organized group in favor of marihuana opposed the bill, and it passed. A lobbyist from the American Medical Association did question the need for the bill

---

[2]The exemption appears in retrospect to have been merely a matter of form, however. Not until 1968 were scientific researchers able to obtain quantities of marihuana for research without the fear of legal sanctions against them.

and asked for evidence of the harmfulness of marihuana, but it seems that the legislators ignored his testimony (Dickson 1968:152).

The passage of the Marihuana Tax Act, then, illustrates the way in which organized interest groups, including an enforcement agency, can shape public policy on drugs. What would have happened to the bill if the manufacture, sale, and use of marihuana had achieved a place in American society comparable to that of the tobacco industry? Instead, marihuana was classified with opiates and "narcotics" in the federal and state laws regulating drugs, and possession of it carried penalties like those for opiates. Thus the assumption that marihuana is a dangerous narcotic became the guiding principle of drug laws and their enforcement in the United States. We will now turn to the effects of this attitude.

Results of the Law Enforcement Policy

Law enforcement policy has had some of the intended results. The overall level of opiate use declined steadily from the time of the first drug laws until after World War II. Although there have been periods of increase since then, the rate of addiction has not returned to that of the time before the antidrug policy. The law enforcement approach, however, has not prevented the spread of nonopiate drug use, and there have been a number of negative consequences of this approach. For instance, questionable police practices have developed in enforcing drug laws.

Enforcement of laws prohibiting injury to persons or property is aided by the willingness of victims and witnesses to come forward to testify. But enforcement of laws against the victimless offenses like the sale or possession of drugs cannot rely on these sources of information and help in prosecution. Because the parties involved are either willing partners in a commercial transaction or are mainly victimizing themselves, there are no complaining victims. Few people in the drug subculture are motivated to call the police or act as witnesses. Therefore, enforcement must rely on undercover agents who secure evidence and testify in court as witnesses against the seller, or on the information and evidence supplied by informers.

This means that law enforcement agents are sometimes involved in *entrapment* (an illegal act in which a law agent induces someone to commit a crime so the agent can make an arrest) of users into drug selling. The informers are most often themselves addicts and in known violation of the law, yet in order to gain enough evidence to make an arrest of a seller, the narcotics agent must ignore the addict's violations and often even maintain his addiction. This is accomplished either directly by paying the addict off with drugs or indirectly with financial support. Securing evidence by making "buys" of drugs from dealers sometimes results in creating a drug problem where one did not exist before.

The Funny and Not-So-Funny Case of the
Rocky Mountain Connection

In 1971 Idaho's first narcotics enforcement bureau was set up to do something about the small but worrisome drug problem in the state. The bureau's efforts were not very effective and were sometimes ludicrous.

The new bureau had had about $500,000 available as "buy" money and informer pay and a substantial budget for other operating expenses. Word got out that there were some big purchasers of drugs around, and the supplies came into the state to meet the new demand. Some informers, set up by agents to make a "deal," often just took the money and ran. Others hired to get evidence on drug deals began dealing themselves. Agents posed as members of organized criminal syndicates. To make it convincing, they offered to buy guns. The result was a crime wave of gun burglaries. One paid informer claimed to know the structure of the drug network in the entire state. He produced a totally imaginary scheme so involved and comical that it placed a local Pocatello official at the top of the drug market. One complicated, weeks-long undercover operation culminated in the agents making a large buy usable as evidence against the seller, who turned out to be another agent attempting to trap a buyer.

After three years, all of this produced many arrests for possession of marihuana, a few arrests for possession of heroin, and not one arrest of a big dealer. These arrests were purchased by illegal techniques and what one judge in the state described as "totalitarian methods." A great many of the cases were dismissed by the courts. The sometimes funny and sometimes not-so-funny actions of the bureau resulted in little control and seem instead to have produced a drug market where there was practically none before (*Newsweek*, January 27, 1975).

Because buyer, seller, and user are all motivated to dispose of drug evidence to avoid conviction, the police are often pushed to making surprise raids and illegal searches and seizures. Tactics of night-time raids and forced entering to nail drug offenders with the evidence intact are not confined to the distant past. For example, in 1973 federal agents forcefully entered a house in Illinois where, they had good reason to believe, there was a large cache of narcotics. After breaking into the house, they pulled a man out of bed and put a gun to his head and forced him to beg for his life in front of his wife, toward whom the agents made insulting remarks and threatened sexual assault. Because these techniques did not pressure the occupants into confessing where the drugs were hidden, the agents systematically dismantled the place, destroying furniture and making a total wreck of the interior of the house. In spite of these efforts, no drugs were found and the man and woman still insisted they were innocent. The puzzled agents soon learned why they had failed: They had the wrong house! The one they were supposed to have raided was several houses down the block (*Newsweek,* June 9, 1975). How frequently these intolerable tactics, which are *always illegal* (even if the correct house is raided), are used by federal and local narcotic agents is unknown.

As the demand remains for such drugs as heroin and marihuana, the legal ban on their production, distribution, and sale artificially inflates their prices. Whatever control of the drug problem has resulted from the high price of illicit drugs, it has produced a number of socially undesirable side effects. We have seen that the need to pay the high price for heroin often leads addicts to engage in prostitution, burglary, car theft, shoplifting, and other crimes (Chambers 1974; Waldorf 1973:14–15; Stephens and Ellis 1975). The high prices also make profits great enough to offset the risks of apprehension involved in smuggling and distributing the drugs. Indeed, supplying and dealing in the drug black market has been one of the most profitable enterprises of organized crime (see chapter 20). The money to be made has also attracted many unorganized and amateur criminals into the trade, especially into the smuggling and distribution of marihuana but also into the market for Mexican brown heroin. It has now taken up the slack created by the curtailment of the Turkey-to-France-to-U.S. supply of white heroin. The vast amounts of money suppliers and dealers make in the illicit market have been used to corrupt law enforcement officials. Narcotics agents also sometimes get directly involved in the smuggling business themselves or steal drugs from the evidence room and sell directly to dealers.

The law enforcement approach continues as a major orientation of national and state drug policies and in many ways remains the basic policy regarding "hard narcotics" in the United States. However, recent changes emphasize rehabilitation in addition to law enforcement, a less punitive definition of addiction, and a decriminalization of nonopiate drugs, particularly marihuana.

Recent Changes in the Law Enforcement Policy

The balance of political power and public sentiment began to shift somewhat in the direction of a less punitive and more "treatment" approach in the 1960s. A small band of sociologists and medical researchers had objected to the unsubstantiated claims about the horrors of marihuana from the 1940s on, but they were largely ignored for two decades. In the 1950s and early 1960s social scientists and lawyers also began to point out some of the negative consequences for society that are fostered by a strict law enforcement policy. They argued that alternative approaches should be tried (Lindesmith 1967). These voices were gradually heeded, and by the mid-1960s there were noticeable changes. Federal and state policy became less restrictive of medical practice in the area of addiction and more relaxed about unofficial attempts to treat addicts.

Although concern over the emergence of the illicit use of LSD and other drugs such as amphetamines was high enough to produce the 1965 Drug Abuse Control Act, these drugs were defined in the law as "dangerous drugs," not narcotics as they would have been earlier. Use of them carried lower penalties than for narcotics law violations. There were attempts to repeat the same scare tactics which had been used earlier with marihuana. The popular media picked up the horror stories, but they also questioned them, exposed hoaxes, and gave coverage to alternative views in a way that was unthinkable only a few years earlier. In 1966 the first federal drug legislation containing the term *rehabilitation* in its title was enacted — the Narcotic Addict Rehabilitation Act (NARA). Although the Act did retain law enforcement concerns and provided for compulsory treatment (civil commitment), it did represent a modification of the policy of almost total reliance on law enforcement. The liberalizing trend continued through the 1970 federal legislation which shifted greater attention to dealers and drug smuggling and de-emphasized control of the user.

This trend has continued at both the federal and state levels, but there is still strong sentiment supporting a strict law enforcement approach, especially toward dealers and sellers. There is also a growing dissatisfaction with drug treatment programs as a solution to the problem. An outstanding example of this strict approach is the 1973 Emergency Dangerous Drug Act enacted in New York, one of the states which had been leading the movement toward more drug treatment programs. This law moved drug offenses into a more serious felony classification; lengthened the prison terms for all drug violations; imposed mandatory sentences for possession of certain quantities of drugs, even for first offenders; prohibited the use of probation and suspended sentences; restricted parole; and placed severe restrictions on plea bargaining and admitting guilt to a lesser charge. This law is under close scrutiny, and a major evaluation project is underway to gauge the effectiveness of the law in dealing with the problems of drugs and drug-related crimes. Preliminary reports indicate the new drug law has not significantly increased the risk of punishment for drug offenders. Nevertheless several other states are considering similar laws. We can expect a resurgence of harsh, punitive drug control measures in some states in the next few years, especially if the final evaluation of the New York experience is positive.

Perhaps the most dramatic liberalization of drug policy and opinion has occurred with marihuana. Throughout the 1960s relatively harsh maximum penalties were attached to marihuana possession for either sale or use. However, because the defendants were not the "criminal" type anymore, the law became more leniently enforced as courts became reluctant to mete out the full punishment allowed by federal and state laws. Thus, although arrests for marihuana violations continued to increase, conviction rates declined and judges increasingly dismissed, suspended sentence, or granted probation in marihuana cases (Grupp and Lucas 1970). Opposition to marihuana laws grew in the 1960s and accelerated in the 1970s as groups such as LEMAR (Legalize Marihuana) and NORML (National Organization to Reform Marihuana Laws) pressured to change the law, to decriminalize and eventually to legalize marihuana (Kaplan 1971; Goode 1970:265–97). Powerful official and unofficial voices spoke for liberalization of the laws. A national commission (1972) recommended that criminal penalties be removed from possession of marihuana for personal use in private. After studying the issue Consumers Union recommended decriminalization of marihuana (*Consumer Reports*, April 1975). In 1973 the American Bar Association called for total removal of penalties for possession of small amounts of marihuana intended for personal use.

Public opinion came to favor liberalization of marihuana laws. In a 1969 Gallup poll, 80 percent of American adults thought that the marihuana laws should remain as they are or be made more harsh. A Drug Abuse Council survey showed that by 1974 only 40 percent thought that the marihuana laws should be more harsh. Thirteen percent believed the law should remain as is. The majority of adults under thirty-five supported making possession of small amounts of marihuana (either for sale or use) entirely legal or subject only to a civil fine.

Following the change in actual court practices, and both reflecting and influencing this loosening of public opinion, the laws themselves were changed. As recently as 1970, the Controlled Substances Act maintained the federal classification of marihuana as a narcotic (violations carrying the same penalties as heroin violations), but just one year later the classification was amended to separate marihuana from opiates and other hard drugs. Several states lowered marihuana violations from felony to misdemeanor (which reduces the maximum penalty to less than a year and increases the chances for probation). In 1973 Oregon became the first state to totally decriminalize the private use of pot; possession of small amounts, a civil "violation," is subject only to citation (equivalent to a traffic citation) without arrest. By 1975 the Alaska legislature decriminalized marihuana possession at about the same time that the Alaska Supreme Court declared legal the use of marihuana in the privacy of one's home. Effective decriminalization of possession for use (but not of possession for sale) followed in Maine, Colorado, and other states. By the fall of 1976, six more states similarly modified their marihuana laws and several others were considering the same action. There also is some support for a reduction in federal penalties for marihuana violations. If a backlash does not occur, possession of marihuana for use or sale of small amounts will be effectively decriminalized if not totally legalized in most parts of the United States by the end of this decade.

Marihuana use can be expected to increase for some time to come, even without these changes in the law. But the changes will accelerate the increases. Interestingly, the increase will occur among essentially conventional groups as the stigma attached is gradually reduced. Therefore, the proportion of marihuana users who go on to heroin will be smaller than it is now, but enough will move beyond marihuana into other drug use (including heroin) that the spread of marihuana will be accompanied by an increase in narcotic use. A further decriminalization of heroin use will also eventually result in some increase in addiction. If the legal changes are delayed until regular marihuana use has spread to a high proportion of the population and peaked, the effect will, of course, be less dramatic than if the changes occur quickly, before a saturation point has been reached.

Drug Treatment Programs

The most common alternative to the law enforcement approach in the control of deviant drug use is one version or another of the idea that the drug user is sick or troubled, more a victim than an offender, and in need of treatment to help him get off drugs or control his use of them. This conception is most frequently applied to opiate addicts but it has at one time or another been applied to abusers of all types of drugs. Taking this stand toward drug abuse inspires a more sympathetic and less punitive orientation toward drug users. The central approach is to help people lead drug-free lives, not to punish drug users for transgressions. If enough can be "cured" of their drug dependence, then the level of use will be reduced, the black markets will dry up, and crime and other drug-related social problems will be alleviated. Therefore, treatment programs of one kind or another as replacements for or additions to law enforcement programs have been recommended and instituted since the beginning of the public definition of drug use as a social problem.

The specific treatment techniques used singly or in combination have included abrupt or "cold turkey" withdrawal, drug-assisted gradual withdrawal and detoxification, individual counseling and therapy, maintenance of addiction, and group therapy. These techniques have been incorporated into a great variety of programs and treatment settings, each of which has enjoyed some moment in history as the best hope for solving drug problems for individuals and society. The major efforts fall into three general categories: (1) *compulsory treatment* programs in government-operated hospitals or prisons (or under probation or parole supervision in the community); (2) residential and semiresidential *therapeutic communities* or self-help groups in the community, as well as nonresidential programs that attempt to approximate the therapeutic community mood (these began mainly under private auspices but eventually came to include government-financed or operated programs); and (3) *methadone maintenance* programs.

Compulsory Treatment
and Civil Commitments

Since the 1920s efforts have been directed at forcing addicts (and secondarily other drug users) to undergo treatment in prisons, in hospitals, and in the community. They have moved from abrupt and gradual withdrawal to group therapy, individual counseling, ex-addict counseling, approximation of therapeutic communities or other treatments that have at one time or another been popular. Whatever the treatment procedure and whether institutional or community, compulsory treatment of addiction is closely tied to a law enforcement orientation and has a history of failure (Petersen 1974).

In 1935 the first federal narcotics hospital was opened in Lexington, Kentucky as a U.S. Public Health Service hospital; three years later the second one was opened in Fort Worth, Texas. For about the next thirty years, these two establishments constituted the total federal treatment program for addicts. (Both were closed as narcotics hospitals and placed under the jurisdiction of the federal prison system in 1974.) They resembled medium security prisons more than hospitals. The patients had been convicted of federal drug charges and sentenced to the facility instead of serving time in prison. It was possible for addicts to commit themselves to the narcotics hospitals and eventually these voluntary patients outnumbered the convicts. However, many of the voluntary patients committed themselves only after given the choice by the court of that or prison. The technique for both types of patients was to begin dosages of opiates (usually morphine when the facilities first started but later the synthetics methadone or meperidine) sufficient to stave off withdrawal distress. The dosage would then be reduced gradually (over a period of weeks in some cases to a period of several months in others) until the drug could be stopped entirely without withdrawal stress. Thus, the patients were effectively detoxified and taken off their physiological dependence on opiates. The relapse rate was extremely high for both voluntary and involuntary commitments (see the discussion of relapse in chapter 6).

This technique constituted the major difference between being sentenced to a regular federal or state prison or to one of the narcotics hospitals; in prison the treatment typically involved abrupt "cold turkey" withdrawal. The relapse rates were as high as or higher than those for the narcotic hospital populations. In the 1960s prisons began to incorporate counseling and other programs, and detoxification programs were introduced in some local institutions. Under the NARA, drug treatment programs were instituted in federal prisons (1968). They used these techniques with similar disappointing results.

In the early 1960s California and New York began "civil commitment" programs as alternatives to imprisonment for drug offenders. These were meant to be hospitals in which addicts or others with severe drug problems would be committed by a process resembling the civil commitment of persons to mental hospitals. The standard treatment included detoxification if needed and group therapy sessions. There would be no criminal conviction, only the judgment that a person should be involuntarily committed for treatment. The commitment was for a minimum of six months in the institution followed by three years under the supervision of a parole officer in the community. During that time the person was to submit to periodic and unannounced urinalysis to check for opiates in his system. Also, just as one may voluntarily commit oneself to a state insane asylum and just as addicts could commit themselves to the federal hospitals, the civil commitment programs in California and New York allowed self-admissions. In the beginning the difference was that one could not leave when he wished but had to stay the same minimum time and undergo the same parole supervision after release as the involuntary commitments. Later, voluntary patients had no required minimum stay and two instead of three years of aftercare supervision. The result of these state civil commitment programs was about equal to that of the federal narcotics hospitals and prisons: high relapse rates.

Therapeutic Communities

Synanon was formed in California two decades ago by a small group of addicts led by an ex-alcoholic who was convinced that the self-help, group support techniques used by Alcoholic Anonymous would work with addicts. To be accepted into the group, one has to undergo a hazing session that challenges his motivation to change, his desperation for help, and his commitment to getting off drugs. Once accepted by the others, he has to give up all drugs (except coffee and cigarettes) and undergo "cold turkey" withdrawal. The chief method of maintaining the abstinence from drugs is through regular intensive group confrontation session—"synanons." Members of the group attack their rationalizations and excuses for using drugs in the first place. The technique is especially scornful of the addict who blames society or other people for becoming a junkie. It belittles the addict's complaints about how bad he is hooked and how sick he gets without drugs, and it promotes disparaging stories about drug experiences. It attempts to make the person feel he is worthless and without hope until he gets off and stays off drugs. There are no physicians, no professional counselors, and no court referrals—only junkies confronting other junkies (Yablonsky 1962).

The Synanon approach appeared at a time when there was little else available but the official, compulsory programs. It promised an end to the dismal failure record of attempts to treat drug addiction. The members of

Synanon claimed to have found a highly effective method and pointed to the drug-free days accumulated by people who previously had relapsed into drugs. It caught the fancy of some social scientists, and after initially bad experiences in its community, Synanon began to get favorable press coverage. Synanon expanded to other locations and other programs modeled after Synanon began. This approach gained momentum throughout the 1960s as the whole idea of confrontation groups, T-groups, and sensitivity groups gained faddish currency. Daytop Lodge and Daytop Village, Phoenix House, Conquest House, Reality House, Odyssey House and other names were attached to the programs imitating the Synanon group approach in one way or another. Although the reliance on ex-addicts and self-help continued, many of these programs secured federal and state grants and hired a professional staff.

There were several other modifications of the approach, including a broadening of the treatment methods used. Some programs retained the group sessions but the participants did not live with each other. The movement also inspired a whole array of drop-in centers, hot lines, and rap centers, designed especially for adolescents and offering peer-group talk and counsel on drug problems. The intensive "family feeling" of the group was important and all tried to maintain it and to develop a therapeutic antidrug community among those accepted into the program. They also almost uniformly echoed Synanon's claims to great success.

The truth of these claims, unfortunately, has never been adequately demonstrated. Synanon has deliberately not kept records or released data on what happens to the addicts after they leave. (Their argument is that if the record showed anything but a perfect score, then those who do not make it have a ready-made rationalization—they are simply among the small group who fail. For the Synanon program to be effective, recruits must believe that everyone who leaves is a cured addict.) Therefore, there is no objective evidence that Synanon does any better than any other approach in treating drug problems. The programs fashioned after Synanon have kept records (although usually not very good ones) and follow-up studies have been done on several of them. The conclusions from these studies agree that despite demonstrable success with some particular individual cases, the programs do not offer effective treatment for most or even many addicts or other drug abusers (Glasscote et al. 1972; 35–42; Waldorf 1973:94–115; Lukoff 1974).

These studies show that the overall success rate of those who finish the programs (roughly 25 to 30 percent) is better than the success rate of those coming out of the compulsory programs. But they also show that this comparison is not entirely persuasive. Although some of the institutional programs included volunteers, all patients in the therapeutic community programs studied are voluntary, and hence can be expected on the average to have a higher motivation to change than those in the compulsory programs. Furthermore, Synanon, Daytop Lodge, Reality House, and the others all exercise strict screening to admit only those cases that appear most committed to change or most amenable to treatment. Therefore, they have a better risk group to begin with than do the compulsory programs, which are not able to be selective. Also, a very high proportion (75–80 percent) of even this very select group drop out quickly from the program (and these do not get counted as failures of the program), leaving a tiny residue of people who have a pretty good chance of success in any program (or even on their own). Finally, the success cases tend mainly to be those who stay within the program as staff or obtain employment in some other drug program—the professional ex-addicts (see Waldorf 1973:25–27). Those who leave the drug treatment milieu and acquire regular (that is, not drug treatment) occupations in the open community are much less likely to remain off of drugs (Lukoff 1974). In short, for certain drug addicts and under certain conditions the programs offered by these therapeutic communities offer some hope and help, but they appear unable to do what they were originally established to do. They all have similar problems. Although not as much in style as they once were, these programs remain a major component of drug treatment efforts in this country. Many state correctional systems have now incorporated some of their philosophy and techniques into government halfway houses for drug offenders.

Methadone Maintenance

Those who had become addicted before the Harrison Act of 1914, when opiates were more freely and legally available, did not magically become nonaddicted after the sources of opiates became more restricted. Several clinics operated and staffed by private physicians were set up in various parts of the country. Treatment consisted of gradual withdrawal and detoxification if possible, but if necessary opiates would be prescribed for an indefinite period of time to maintain the patient's habit. But this prescription—merely keeping the patient comfortable at his customary habit —was declared illegal by federal enforcement agents. A few physicians were arrested and convicted and the clinics were all closed down by 1922.

Later court decisions upheld the right of physicians to prescribe (in responsible medical practice) for addiction as they saw best for their patients. However, few physicians wanted to risk trouble with the law just for addicts whom many considered to be criminal anyway, and law enforcement agents pursued a policy which in fact made almost any medical practice with addicts illegal (Lindesmith 1967; O'Donnell and Ball 1966). British statutes were essentially the same as the American law, but British legal authorities left addiction alone and considered it basically a medical problem to be handled by physicians. Eventually, addicts were required to register themselves as addicts with the government, but private physicians could prescribe heroin or other opiates and pursue whatever treatment they thought best.

By the mid-1950s several American drug experts (Schur 1965; Linde-smith 1967) were pointing to the British system as a good model for the U.S. The extremely small numbers of addicts in all of Great Britain, the absence of a drug black market, deviant drug subculture, drug arrests, and any rela-tionship between addiction and crime were listed as results of the enlight-ened British system, which kept addiction a medical rather than criminal problem. Law enforcement personnel strenuously objected to adopting the British system here. Moreover, some social scientists observed that the dif-ference between the nature of the American drug problem and the British drug problem existed before, during, and after the differences in the policies of the respective countries developed (Ausubel 1960). Therefore, one could just as easily argue that the relatively benign British policy resulted from the small British drug problem as one could argue that the small drug problem resulted from the benign policy.

We have subsequently learned that neither the benign policy nor the small numbers of British addicts lasted much longer. The addiction rate is still much smaller than in the United States, but beginning in the middle of the 1960s the number of known British addicts began to increase dra-matically; within a decade the number of registered addicts increased four-fold. Britain still does not have the strong organized criminal element in the drug traffic, but a noticeable "gray" market in drugs has developed. An addict subculture has become visible (imported, some say, by Canadian and American addicts who invaded Britain to take advantage of its lenient system). Thus, British policy changed, to enact tougher law enforcement and to restrict the physician's freedom to prescribe opiates. It established government-controlled addiction treatment centers (prescribing both heroin and methadone) as the only ones able to treat and prescribe for addiction (Brantingham 1973; Hawks 1974; Bean 1971; Judson 1974).

The New York Academy of Medicine issued a statement in 1955 calling for the establishment of twenty-four-hour "service clinics" for addicts. But the first modern application of the maintenance approach in this country was in 1965 when a program to maintain addicts on methadone was started in New York. It was not exactly legal at the time, but narcotics authorities had a tolerant attitude and allowed it to proceed. By the later 1960s metha-done maintenance not only had acquired federal approval but enthusiastic support. Programs were established all across the country with federal (and some state) funding. By the mid-1970s over 300 such programs were in opera-tion, ministering to about 75,000 addicts. Methadone maintenance is now the major approach to opiate addiction in the United States. This phe-nomenal growth is attributable less to demonstrated success through the years than to the other features of methadone maintenance.

The maintenance approach is appealing in a number of ways. It came into its own at a time when there was dissatisfaction with law enforcement and the drug-free programs had failed to live up to their early promises. The first programs were based on the theory that addiction is not a social disease but a metabolic disease which must be treated by periodic ingestion of opiates just as diabetes must be controlled by periodic injections of insulin. Further, it was claimed that methadone blockaded the euphoric effects of heroin and produced no such effects itself. The notion that the addict is sick, then, was carried beyond the implication that he should not be punished; he is sick in the strict medical sense and therefore should be treated with strictly medical techniques, namely drugs. Therefore, methadone seemed to offer a quick, cheap, politically acceptable solution to the addiction problem. If addiction is a disease, then there must be a miracle drug to cure it, and methadone seemed to be that drug. Unfortunately, neither the metabolic disease theory nor the blockade theory have proven to be correct (Lennard et al. 1972; Epstein 1974). Methadone is itself an opiate; it serves the same physiological function as heroin in alleviating withdrawal distress and if injected produces much the same effects. Thus, methadone does not block heroin effects; it merely substitutes for heroin in the maintenance of addiction.

The positive features of an addiction maintenance program, however, do not depend on the validity of the blockade theory. Unlike other programs, drug maintenance clinics do not attempt to get people to stop taking drugs. The aim, rather, is to provide addicts with enough opiate at nominal or no cost to allow him to maintain his customary habit. While drug addiction presents a real personal problem for the addict, it does not present a serious social problem in itself, and the problems created for society are the result of the high cost and attendant problems of maintaining a drug habit on illicit drugs. The vast majority of addicts maintain their habits on heroin, a totally illicit drug in the United States that is not even used in medical practice. Because it is available only through illicit channels, assurance of connections is one reason addicts get involved in deviant subcultures. As we have seen, the high cost of the drug implicates many addicts in income-producing crimes (Gould 1974). Stable employment at regular jobs for most addicts would not produce enough income to support their heroin habits. In addition to whatever strain the addiction itself puts on relationships with family and friends, the need to hustle to get the drug further jeopardizes normal relationships (family and friends are often the victims of the addict's thefts) and erodes the ability to hold down a steady job. Methadone maintenance programs promise to break the connection between addiction and these social problems: a legal opiate is supplied which is easily affordable or which can be dispensed free. Assured of a safe and steady supply at low cost, the addict is then able to hold a regular job, seek whatever other help he needs, restore social relationships, and in general become a contributing member of society. If the individual is thereby enabled to reduce or quit his habit, so much the better. But the goal would be accomplished if he simply maintained his habit indefinitely without creating problems for society.

Unfortunately, after a decade the methadone maintenance programs have not delivered on their promise. The first programs reported unqualified success, but subsequent re-evaluations of the early programs and evaluations of later programs show that such claims cannot be sustained. Many of the programs have not sufficiently controlled the supply and distribution

of the methadone to patients; consequently methadone has leaked considerably into the drug black market where it is now second only to heroin
in use. There is some evidence in some of the programs of reduced heroin
use, decrease in arrests, and self-reported criminal behavior. But the findings
are based on counting the behavior of only retained cases, and of course
illicit use of drugs and crime are prime reasons for people being dropped
from the programs. The programs have had mixed success in improving the
employment status of addicts.

The attrition (drop-out) rate is very high for all programs and it is the
older, longer-term addict who is most apt to stay in the program and benefit
from the assured maintenance of habit on methadone. The younger addict
still caught up in drug subculture is more apt to drop out, or if he stays in
the program he is more likely to continue use of heroin and to behave criminally. Much of the success of the programs is based precisely on the fact that
admittance is very selective: Only those with the best prognosis for stable
family life, employment, and conforming lifestyle are taken into the methadone programs. The less selective programs are less successful. Indeed, it
may be that "methadone is substantially a way station for the addict who is
maturing out of the heroin street scene [anyway]. . . . much of the improvement is a function of age" (Lukoff 1974:149). Much of the evidence that crime
has been reduced is suspect: The reduction appears to be primarily in arrest and incarcerations for drug law violation rather than in drug-related,
income-producing crimes. (For details and critical analyses see Epstein
1974; Lennard et al. 1972; Lukoff 1974; Gearing 1970; Glasscote et al. 1972.) In
short, it seems that maintenance assists addicts who are motivated to leave
the illicit drug world and try to live a straight life, but it is not the panacea
for the addiction problem as many of its supporters once believed.

Summary

Public policy on drugs in the United States has included both law enforcement and treatment approaches. The trend now is for decriminalization of
minor drug offenses such as possession of small amounts of marihuana. The
major treatment programs are institutional treatment (compulsory and civil
commitments), therapeutic communities, and methadone maintenance.
Neither strict law enforcement nor any of the treatment approaches has
provided a positive and demonstrably successful solution to drug problems.
Each, however, has been successful in achieving some of its aims with some
drug abusers.

Part Three   Drinking and Alcohol Behavior

133

10

Social and Physiological Aspects of Drinking Behavior

Social Norms and Effects of Alcohol

Drinking Norms in American Society: Definitions of Drinking and Deviant Drinking

Drugs have been used for a long time, but alcohol is the oldest and most universally available intoxicant known. If American society is in some ways a drug-saturated society, it is even more clearly an alcohol-oriented society. Alcoholic beverages are widely available, openly advertised and sold, regularly stocked in many homes, and used in a variety of social contexts. Moderate drinking for pleasure, recreation, and social purposes is an acceptable and integral part of American culture. The majority of the adult population (and in some areas the majority of the teenage population) use alcohol. However, considerable variation and ambiguity remain in the social definitions of drinking.

Total prohibition of alcoholic beverages prevailed as a public policy in the era of prohibition (1920–33) by virtue of the Eighteenth Amendment and the Volstead Act and state and local laws. The incorporation of the total abstinence norm into law was the result of the victory of "dry" organized pressure groups (for example, the Anti-Saloon League) against "wet" forces (Quinney 1970:90–92). Those supporting total abstinence norms have probably always been a minority in the United States, and they are now clearly without much political power (Plaut 1967:16). Nonetheless, strongly prohibitive norms hold sway in many communities and continue to influence the law and efforts to control drinking. Opposing the dry position is the view that drinking is not only permissible but serves positive social functions (Plaut 1967:8).

The range of moral evaluations placed on the drinking of alcoholic beverages is more complicated than the simple drink-abstain dichotomy. Although the wet-dry conflict has characterized much public debate and policy formation in this country, unqualified approval or disapproval of drinking is not typical. Rather, drinking is usually seen as conditionally or situationally right or wrong. The majority of people take the position that moderate drinking is permissible and even desirable, but that excessive drinking should be sanctioned negatively. The point at which drinking is considered to become excessive varies with the group and situation, however (Maddox and McCall 1964:58–76; Trice 1966:42–61). Thus there is an apparent lack of consensus on such basic issues as: Is drinking as such bad or dangerous? "Should it be postponed to later ages, or minimized, or eliminated? What constitutes acceptable or allowable drinking, and how can the other types of drinking be discouraged?" (Plaut 1967:10).

Despite the apparent ambiguity and disagreement in American drinking norms, one condition under which the use of alcohol is clearly disapproved is when it becomes abusive. Unlike drugs, for which any degree of nonmedical use is deviant, only extreme forms of drinking are deviant. To be deviant, drinking must be more than just habitual, for much socially acceptable drinking is regular and habitual. But there is substantial normative agreement that drinking which becomes "too much," "excessive," "heavy," "problem," or "alcoholic" should be considered deviant. Even those who see positive value in alcohol recognize that there are risks involved and disapprove when drinking becomes excessive, is combined with driving, or otherwise occasions injury or complications for the user or those around him. (For discussions of "acceptable" and "unacceptable" or "harmful" drinking see Plaut 1967:125–52; Akers [with King] 1967:57–66).

To some extent drinking by persons under a certain age is considered deviant. However, there is considerably less consensus on the deviance of underage drinking than there is on abusive drinking as deviant. There is disagreement about what age is considered old enough to drink (the common legal limitations are 21 and 18). Public opinion does not consistently abhor underage drinking, and the sanctions applied to it are much milder than those applied to drug use. In some groups children are routinely allowed wine and other beverages with meals, in religious ceremonies, and at other times in the home. Even in groups where this is not common practice, many adults do not strongly object to occasional underage drinking, although they may consider it premature. Nonetheless, the law does uniformly deny minors legitimate access to alcoholic beverages, most adults define unsupervised drinking by teenagers as undesirable, and most teenagers agree with them (Maddox and McCall 1964:73–75). Moreover, teenage drinking remains a perennial concern of adults and authorities, and public and semipublic programs of law enforcement and education to "do something" about the problem continue (Akers [with King] 1967:23–56).

Nature and Physiological Effects of Alcohol[1]

Alcohol and *alcoholic beverages* are generic terms which refer to the various forms commonly used in the United States. The major beverages are *wine*, made from fermentation of fruits and usually containing up to 14 percent ethyl alcohol, although wines can be "fortified" up to about 20 percent; *beer*, brewed from grains and hops and usually containing 3 to 6 percent alcohol; and *liquor*, whiskey, gin, vodka, and other distilled spirits usually containing 40 percent (80 proof) to 50 percent (100 proof) alcohol. The intoxicating effect is the result of the alcohol's *depressant* action on the brain and central nervous system, where it is carried by the blood.

Alcohol does not have to be digested; it can be absorbed directly from the intestines into the blood. Once absorbed, some is eliminated from the body in urine and breath, but most is used up, or oxidized, at a uniform rate. Food in the stomach, especially high-protein food, will slow passage to the intestine, but nothing like coffee, exercise, or deep breathing affects the rate of oxidation. Therefore, the only variables involved in the concentration of alcohol in the blood are how much absolute alcohol a person drinks in a given time period and his body size and weight. An average-size man can consume about three-fourths of an ounce of whiskey or a bottle of beer every hour without physiological effect. Drinking at this rate would result in an alcohol concentration of only .02 percent. The more the person drinks within a given time, the more noticeable and dramatic are the intoxicating effects. Supposedly the perceptual and coordinating functions of the upper brain are affected first. With a concentration of .10 percent (attained with about six drinks in a short period of time), the lower motor functions are dulled, resulting in slurred speech and blurred vision. A couple more drinks in the same time period makes it difficult for the person to walk straight. Enough drinks (about twenty ounces of whiskey in an hour) cause the loss-of-consciousness level of .40 percent to be reached. The effects are not accumulative, and when alcohol is gone from the body, the effects are gone.

Alcohol is an irritant to tissue lining in the mouth, throat, and stomach. Alcohol has no food value other than calories, and the neglect of nutritional foods which usually accompanies heavy drinking over a long period of time will produce malnutrition and ill health.

Drunken Behavior: Physiological and Social Factors

The behavior of a person who is drinking alcohol is only partly a function of direct physical effects. How one behaves depends also on how he has

---

[1] This section is based on Greenberg 1958 and Kendis 1967.

learned to behave while drinking in the setting and with whom he is drinking at the time. A person does not develop immunity, but an experienced drinker can learn to give the appearance of sobriety even when he has drunk enough to be definitely intoxicated. Thus variations in individual experience, group drinking customs, and the social setting combine with the physical effects to produce the observable behavior while drinking. The loss of coordination and motor control is largely determined by the physical assault of alcohol on the body, but the social learning factors become paramount in "drunken comportment"—the behavior of those who are "drunk" with alcohol before reaching the stage of impaired muscular coordination (MacAndrew and Edgerton 1969).

Does Alcohol Automatically Lower Inhibitions?

"No," say MacAndrew and Edgerton (1969). The conventional explanation for why people fight, commit sexual indiscretions, and do other things while drunk that they "wouldn't ordinarily do" is that the physiological impact of alcohol on the brain causes a person to lose his civilized control over his baser animal instincts. MacAndrew and Edgerton find no support for this argument. Rather, they find that the outcome of drunkenness may be no change, may be greater inhibition, or may be lowered inhibition, depending on what one learns to do under given circumstances. They state:

> In and of itself, the presence of alcohol in the body does not necessarily even conduce to disinhibition, much less inevitably produce such an effect. . . . We must conclude that drunken comportment is an essentially learned affair. . . .
> Over the course of socialization, people learn about drunkenness what their society "knows" about drunkenness; and, accepting and acting upon the understandings thus imparted to them, they become the living confirmation of their society's teachings (MacAndrew and Edgerton 1969:87–88).

Extent and Variations of Drinking Behavior

Extent of Drinking

Table 10–1 summarizes some findings from national, state, and community surveys of drinking behavior among adults that have been conducted over the past twenty years. The percentages of drinkers in the various samples shown in the table show fairly clearly that the majority, around two-thirds, of the adult population in the United States are not abstainers; an average of about 75 percent of the men and 60 percent of the women drink at least sometime. Although there is variability by year and sample, there are no consistent trends toward either increased or decreased drinking in the post–World War II period.[2] Relatively few in the population can be described as heavy drinkers (about 10 percent); fewer still (about 6 percent) are alcoholic drinkers; and less than 1 percent are addictive drinkers. Thus the modal pattern of drinking is nondeviant, light or moderate social drinking.[3] In the 1963 national survey 89 percent of those who drink at all do so lightly or moderately (Mulford 1964:642), and in the 1965 survey only 6 percent of the total sample and 9 percent of the drinkers were characterized as "heavy-escape" drinkers (Cahalan et al. 1967:8).

Although the deviant portion of all drinking is not great, the number of people who are problem or alcoholic drinkers is still impressive. If about 6 percent of the drinking population drink excessively enough to encounter the personal and social disruption of alcoholic drinking, there are about seven to nine million adult men and women who can be described as alcoholics (McCarthy 1964b; Straus 1966:267). The total number of alcoholics has increased, but the rate of deviant drinking seems to have stabilized over the past twenty-five years, and apparent increases in the total are due to increasing population and more effective reporting (Keller 1958:6).

These figures make it plain, however, that if sheer magnitude is any measure, alcoholism remains one of the most serious problems of deviance in American society. By contrast, the number of addicts is very small. But the rate of alcoholism tells only part of the story. The death toll on the highways attributable to drunken drivers is well known, and over half of all arrests in the United States are for public drunkenness and related offenses such as disorderly conduct.

---

[2]Mulford thought that his 1963 finding of 71 percent drinkers compared to the 65 percent figure obtained in the 1946 survey indicated an increase in the proportion of drinkers in the population (Mulford 1964:637). But the 1965 national survey found that 68 percent of the respondents drank at least sometime. The differences are probably due to sampling variability and measurement error rather than any real changes in the proportion of drinkers. Indeed, Mulford's two Iowa surveys conducted three years apart showed no change in the drinking portion of the population (Mulford and Miller 1963:51). Cahalan and his associates (1967) also believe that they detect a recent rise in the proportion of drinkers. They base this belief mainly on the Gallup poll results, which showed a steadily increasing percentage of drinkers from 55 percent in 1958 to 65 percent in 1966, an increase accounted for almost entirely by more women drinkers. However, the percentage of drinkers in the 1966 Gallup poll was two points less than in 1945. Also, there is almost as much difference between the Gallup poll and the Mulford study conducted about the same time as the eight-year difference in the polls themselves.

[3]But there has been a century-long trend toward a declining per capita consumption (McCarthy 1964b; Keller 1958).

Table 10–1
Percentages of drinkers and heavy drinkers from some surveys among adult populations, 1945–75

Location of sample	Year	Percent drinking			Percent heavy or problem drinking			Source
		Male	Female	Total	Male	Female	Total	
National	1945			67%				Gallup poll[a]
National	1946	75%	56%	65%	27%[b]	8%[b]		Riley and Marden 1959
Washington	1951	76	51	63	22[b]	9[b]		Maxwell 1952
National	1951			60				Gallup poll
Iowa	1958	68	50	59	14	4	9%	Mulford and Miller 1959
National	1958	67	45	55				Gallup poll
Iowa	1961	67	52	59				Mulford and Miller 1963
San Francisco	1962 –64	81	75	76	29[c]	13[c]	21[c]	Knupfer and Room 1964
							9[d]	Knupfer 1967
National	1963	79	63	71	13	3	8	Mulford 1964
National	1964	70	56	63				Gallup poll
National	1965	78	60	68	21	5	12	Cahalan et al. 1967
National	1966	70	61	65				Gallup poll
National	1967				15	4	9	Cahalan 1970
National (males 20–30)	1975	97			37[e]			O'Donnell et al. 1976
					8[f]			
					5[g]			

[a] All Gallup poll figures from Cahalan et al. 1967:30–31 and McCarthy 1964a.
[b] Listed as "regular," not heavy drinkers.
[c] Lifetime prevalence of frequent high intake.
[d] One or more problems related to current drinking.
[e] Lifetime frequent high intake.
[f] Been drunk for more than one day at a given time.
[g] Dependent on alcohol.

Social Correlates of Drinking Behavior

Age and sex.   As can be seen from table 10–1, drinking of any kind is disproportionately a male activity. More men than women drink in all age, religious, racial, social class, and ethnic categories and in all regions and communities. If they are not abstainers, women are more likely than men to be light drinkers. Even in the San Francisco study, which found the highest percentage of women drinking of any of the surveys, 63 percent of the women (compared to 43 percent of the men) were either abstainers or light drinkers (Knupfer and Room 1964:231; see also Mulford 1964:643; Cahalan et al. 1967:32). The difference between men and women is greatest in deviant drinking behavior. Table 10–1 shows that men are three to four times as likely to be heavy drinkers. Moreover, the ratio of alcoholic men to women is more than five to one (Keller 1958:6; Straus 1966:267). The percentage of drinkers is highest among both men and women in the young adult age groups. The

Gallup polls taken over the past twenty years have consistently found the highest proportion of drinkers in the twenty-one to twenty-nine age category and the lowest proportion among those over sixty years of age. The other drinking studies generally support these findings. The probability that a person will drink at all stays relatively high up to about age thirty-five to forty; after that the probability declines, with a precipitous drop among the elderly. The peak years for heavy and alcoholic drinking are middle to late forties, but there are relatively few heavy drinkers among persons sixty or older (Mulford and Miller 1959:717; Mulford 1964:640–41; Knupfer and Room 1964:228; Cahalan et al. 1967:34). Proportions of problem drinkers decline more sharply among women over fifty than among men of the same age (Cahalan 1970:41–45).

Region and residence.   All the national studies have found both drinking and the extent of heavy drinking to increase with the degree of urbanization and industrialization of the region and community. There is proportionately more drinking in urban and suburban areas than in small towns, and more in towns than in rural areas. In fact, the rate of drinking in the large cities is one and a half to two times that in farming areas. The urbanized regions of the Northeast and the Middle Atlantic states have the highest rates of drinking and heavy drinking, the South has the lowest rates, and the West and Midwest have intermediate rates (Mulford and Miller 1963; Mulford 1964:640–41; Cahalan et al. 1967:10).

Social class.   The proportion of men and women who drink at all, and to some extent the proportion of men who drink frequently, tends to be higher among middle-class and upper-class men than among those with low education, occupation, and income, but alcoholics or serious problem drinkers tend disproportionately to come from the lower socioeconomic strata (Mulford and Miller 1963:51; Knupfer and Room 1964:235–37; Knupfer 1967:982–83; Bailey et al. 1965:27; Lawrence and Maxwell 1962; Cahalan et al. 1967:9).

Race, ethnicity, and religion.   Although the proportion of drinkers is about the same for black and white populations (white females may be slightly more likely to drink than black females) (Cahalan et al. 1967:10), rates of excessive drinking and alcoholism are higher among blacks. The alcoholism rate for black males is from two to four times that for white males, and the female black rate is three to six times higher than the white female rate. This black-white differential in problem drinking remains even when age, socioeconomic status, and degree of urbanization of residence are controlled (Sterne 1967:71–72; Robins et al. 1968; Bailey et al. 1965).

Relatively high proportions of drinkers are found among members of the Jewish, Catholic, Lutheran, and Episcopalian religions. Relatively few fundamentalist Protestants, Baptists, Methodists, and Mormons drink. Of those who drink, Jews have low proportions of heavy and alcoholic drinkers; Catholics have high rates of alcoholism; and the probability is relatively high that once a Baptist or Mormon starts to drink he will become a problem drinker. The Irish in America have high rates of both drinking and alcoholism, as do the people in this country of Latin American origin. Italian-Americans drink frequently and heavily but apparently have little alcoholism (Cahalan et al. 1967:10–12, 62–80; Mulford and Miller 1963:51; Mulford 1964: 643–45, 640–41; Bailey et al. 1965:27; Knupfer 1967:982–83).

Table 10–2 summarizes some of the social correlates of adult drinking and heavy drinking. We turn now to the extent and variation in drinking by those in a particular age category—teenagers.

Table 10–2
Social correlates of drinking and heavy drinking [a]

Groups in the total population most likely to be drinkers	Groups among those who drink most likely to be heavy drinkers
1. Men and women 21–40	1. Men 40–49
2. Residents of Middle Atlantic, New England, East North Central, and Pacific regions	2. Residents of Middle Atlantic, New England, and Pacific regions
3. Residents of cities and suburbs	3. Residents of largest cities
4. Men and women of higher socio-economic status	4. Men and women of lower socio-economic status
5. White and black men, white women	5. Black men and women
6. Jews, Lutherans, Catholics	6. Catholics, Protestants of no established denomination
7. Italians, Irish	7. Irish, Latin Americans

[a] Adapted from Cahalan et al. 1967:12.

Teenage drinking.[4]   Table 10–3 makes it clear that much the same description that applies to adults also applies to adolescents. Although there is variation by time and place, all studies among teenage populations find at least a sizable minority (one in four at a minimum) and often a substantial majority (eight or nine out of ten in some surveys) have drunk some alcoholic beverage. However, the kind of exposure to alcohol experienced most often involves isolated (sometimes one time only) or infrequent use of low-content beverages, mostly beer. Approximately one-third to one-half of the high school boys and one-fourth of the girls drink to an extent that would be recognizable as a pattern of moderate drinking if done by an adult. Little

---

[4] This section summarizes findings from the studies cited in table 10–3. For a more detailed presentation of the extent and variation in teenage drinking see Akers (with King) 1967 and Akers 1968.

Table 10–3
Percentages of drinkers and heavy drinkers from some surveys among high school students, 1941–75

Location of sample	Year	Percent drinkers	Percent frequent-heavy drinkers	Source
Washington, D.C.	1941	25%	3%	McCarthy 1959
Washington, D.C.	1947	35		McCarthy 1959
National	1948	35		McCarthy 1959 (Purdue poll)
Utah	1952 ca.	31	2	Slater 1952
Nassau, N.Y.	1952 ca.	86		Chappel et al. 1953
Racine, Wis.	1955 ca.	64		Miller and Wahl 1956
Kansas	1956 ca.	50		Baur and McCluggage 1958
Wichita		56	9	
East Kansas		44	4	
Michigan	1956 ca.	92	6	Maddox and McCall 1964
National	1958	61	4	Maddox 1964 (Purdue poll)
Mississippi	1962	33		Windham et al. 1967
Tupelo		24	9	
Clarksdale		47	13	
Michigan	1963	61	4	Clay 1964b
New Hampshire	1964	71	8	MacKay and Clarke 1967
Boston	1965	82	2	Demone 1966
Utah	1967	45 (seniors)		Nelson 1968
National	1969	82 (male seniors)	6[a]	Johnston 1973
National	1974	63 (seventh-grade males)		National Clearinghouse 1974
		54 (seventh-grade females)		
		93 (male seniors)		
		84 (female seniors)		
National	1975	90 (seniors)	6[b]	Johnston 1975
		91 (male seniors)	8[b] (male seniors)	

[a] Use every day.
[b] Used twenty or more times in the past month.

of the drinking that teenagers do is high-frequency–high-quantity, and an average of only about 3 percent can be characterized as "problem" drinkers.

The social correlates of teenage drinking also parallel those of adult drinking. In every case boys are more likely to drink and to drink more frequently than girls. All the high school surveys have found that the proportion of drinkers increases from the early years (seventh and eighth grades) to later adolescence (eleventh and twelfth grades). By the time of high school graduation the percentage of adolescents who drink comes close to, and by the college years equals or exceeds, the percentage of adults who drink (Straus and Bacon 1953). As with adult populations, the probability of drinking and heavy drinking among teenagers is positively associated with the degree of urbanization and city size; the highest percentage of drinkers are found in the North and East and the lowest percentages are in the South; Catholic and Jewish adolescents are more likely to drink than their Protestant peers. Unlike adult populations, however, no consistent relationship of teenage drinking to social class and race has been found. Sometimes more adolescent drinkers are found in the higher social strata (Baur and McCluggage 1958); at other times disproportionate numbers of drinkers are found in lower classes (Maddox 1964). In some places both high-class and low-class youth are more likely to drink than the middle-class youth (Maddox and McCall 1964), and in other places variations in drinking by teenagers bears no relationship to their parent's occupation or education (Windham et al. 1967). There is some indication that black high school students are more apt to drink than white students, but as with social class the evidence on the relationship between drinking and race is mixed (Sterne 1967; Maddox and Berinski 1964; Globetti 1967; Windham et al. 1967).

Extent and Variations of Drinking Behavior: Summary

The majority of adults in the United States drink alcoholic beverages. The typical pattern is light or moderate drinking, but 6 to 10 percent are problem drinkers. More men than women are drinkers, and more men than women are alcoholic drinkers. For both men and women the probability that a person will drink is highest among young adult age groups. The peak years for alcoholism are the middle to late forties, and the elderly are likely to be neither drinkers nor alcoholics. The urbanized regions of the Northeast and Middle Atlantic states have the highest rates of both drinking and alcoholism. Drinking is more common among middle-class and upper-class persons, but alcoholic drinking is more common among lower-class persons. Catholics have high rates of drinking and alcoholism, whereas Jews have high rates of drinking and low rates of alcoholism. Depending on the location, from 30 to 50 percent of all teenagers have established a pattern of drinking that would be described as at least moderate drinking. The variations among teenagers in drinking resemble those among adults.

11

Learning to Drink

Just as we examined the whole process of drug use, our concern will be with the whole process of coming to try alcoholic beverages, using them regularly, and coming to drink excessively. The discussion will be in two parts. Initial, occasional, and habitual but still temperate drinking are not seen as problem drinking and are covered in this chapter on learning to drink. Alcoholism, or problem drinking, will be analyzed in the next chapter.

Social Reinforcement and Normative Definitions

As noted in the previous chapter, the normative definition of drinking does not parallel the drug situation. The general societal norm is antidrug, with minority, less powerful groups supporting drugs. In contrast, most phases of drinking behavior are not deviant (although normative ambivalence and conflict exist). Groups fostering strong antidrinking norms do not today command enough power to make total abstinence the prevailing morality or law. Only excessive, abusive, or alcoholic drinking is more or less universally condemned. The significance for a learning analysis of this difference between the cultural meaning of drugs and alcohol is the fact that there is no specifically deviant subcultural path along which the novice is introduced to alcohol analogous to the drug-oriented subcultures available as avenues to drugs. There are religious, ethnic, and other group differences, but all these are nondeviant variations. Underage drinking is at least mildly deviant (it is certainly illegal), and some have suggested that introduction to alcohol is part of participation in an antiadult adolescent subculture. But as we shall see, although the influence of adolescent peer groups is important in the beginning stages of drinking behavior, use or nonuse of alcohol in this context is still largely a conventional variation incidental to learning adult roles. For the majority of people in American society, sociable, moderate drinking is legally and socially acceptable adult behavior, and learning to use alcohol in this way is mainly a *conventional* part of socialization into adult role behavior.

Nonetheless, the same learning variables involved in hallucinogenic and nonaddictive drug use are involved in initial and habitual drinking. Specifically, before a person will use alcohol (1) it must be available, and (2) he must learn and apply either positive or neutralizing definitions to its use. He must further (3) have or acquire the ability to get the alcohol into his system for proper effect. Continuation after the initial experience depends on (4) the intrinsic or conditioned reinforcement of recognizable effects and/or (5) differential social rewards for drinking. The intensity and regularity of a person's drinking behavior will be determined by these variables, and the extent to which they are present depends on his exposure to drinking patterns and sanctions through his group associations.

Neither availability nor proper drinking technique is very problematic, as they are with drugs. Proper ingestion of alcohol requires no special learning; one need only know how to swallow liquids. By and large, alcoholic beverages are readily available through legitimate channels and require no special group associations. There are variations in the extent to which alcohol is available; for example, persons under legal drinking age and populations in dry areas have relatively less access. But even for them alcohol is still available through fairly easily learned techniques. At any rate, availability in the nonnormative sense of simply having physical access is less important in drinking than the way in which the drinking norms and customs of one's groups present it to him. Therefore, the following analysis concentrates on the group sources and types of definitions and reinforcement conducive to drinking behavior.

The research on drinking behavior shows that it is a social phenomenon in two related ways: (1) what one does with and thinks about alcohol is a function of his group membership and identification, and (2) almost all drinking takes place in social group settings which the drinker "believes make his drinking socially approved by the people who matter to him" (Cahalan et al. 1967:90).

The variations presented in the previous chapter testify to the socially patterned nature of drinking behavior. Within American society persons are subject to different group and cultural influences, depending on their location in the age, sex, stratification, religious, ethnic, and other systems. Both conforming and deviant use of alcohol are products of the general culture and the more immediate groups and social situations with which individuals are confronted. The cross-cultural and within-society differences in the rates of drinking and alcoholism reflect the varied traditions regarding the functions alcohol serves and the extent to which it is integrated into eating, ceremonial, and other social contexts (see Pittman 1967; Clinard 1968:424–44; Straus 1966:264–73; MacAndrew and Edgerton 1969). The more immediate groups within each of these cultural contexts provide learning environments in which the positive and negative social sanctions applied to behavior sustain or discourage drinking according to group norms.

Those who drink have been differentially associated with those who present them with definitions favorable toward drinking and with rewards conducive to drinking. Drinking is the expected behavior in many groups and situations, and as long as it stays within the acceptable limits of the group norms, it is accompanied by conviviality, acceptance, and other pleasant social sanctions and reactions. Although one may learn to drink in groups in which the reactions are uncertain, or neutral at best, as long as his behavior is not positively punished, starting to drink and proceeding to a regular pattern is based on positive social reinforcement. For some the initial response to alcohol is positive; even when their prior learning has been neutral, they like the taste and what they feel from drinking. But for many the initial reaction is dislike, or at least not noticeable enjoyment. If he does not initially like it, a person may acquire the enjoyment of the taste, smell, and effects of alcohol in the same way that the marihuana user learns to gain pleasure from use—through association with social rewards. Those who have been associated with groups in which drinking is not tolerated have a low probability of drinking.

But the behavioral and normative situation is more complicated than simply drinking or not drinking. A person not only learns to drink; he learns to make fairly fine distinctions among situations in which particular levels of drinking are or are not likely to be rewarded. His drinking becomes associated with a whole range of social and physical discriminative stimuli (in the form of situational norms and physical setting) which define what, where, how much, how frequently, and under what conditions certain kinds of drinking will be reinforced. He also learns how one is supposed to behave when intoxicated.

The most significant groups through which the general cultural, religious, and community orientations toward drinking have an impact on the individual are his primary groups—principally his family, peer, and friendship groups. In these groups a person is presented with social *sanctions* and a set of *definitions* favorable to or unfavorable to drinking, and through imitation and direct learning he acquires the appropriate behavior. The pattern of reinforcement, punishment, or tolerance (in the form of social sanctions) and the accompanying definitions discriminative for drinking (in the form of drinking norms) to which one is exposed in these groups can be classified into at least four types.

Types of Drinking Norms: Definitions Conducive to Drinking

(1) The pattern of norms and sanctions in which drinking behavior is prohibited can be characterized as *proscriptive* or abstinence. (2) *Prescriptive* normative patterns permit drinking, but at the same time provide definite

standards and limits on acceptable drinking. (3) *Ambivalent* learning environments present one with vague, incomplete definitions and sanctions which neither effectively prohibit nor adequately prescribe guidelines for proper drinking. (4) *Permissive* groups positively define and sanction drinking, including frequent and heavy drinking. The highest proportion of drinkers are found in prescriptive and permissive environments. However, in prescriptive groups, such as Jewish groups, controlled moderate drinking is differentially reinforced over intemperance (which is negatively sanctioned), and therefore those from such backgrounds have low rates of heavy drinking and alcoholism. Proscriptive groups, such as Mormons and fundamentalist Protestant groups, tend to have the lowest overall rates of drinking, but proportionately more of those who do drink become problem drinkers. This probably occurs because drinking of any kind leads to punishment, including group ostracism, which in turn leads to isolation from positive sanctions for abstinence and drifting toward groups which positively sanction heavy drinking or to groups in which drinking is relatively unregulated.[1]

The general American cultural orientation to drinking is best described as ambivalent. Those who have received their primary socialization in one type of normative setting become aware of and at one time or another may be exposed to different groups and definitions. Therefore, even among groups in which the prevailing norms are prohibitive, some still use alcohol, and in those groups in which some drinking is approved, there are still some who do not indulge. Nevertheless, one's drinking behavior is by and large congruent with the normative-sanctioning patterns of his primary groups.

The importance of definitions favorable to drinking is also supported by the findings on the extent to which persons' behavior is associated with their stated individual approval or disapproval of drinking. Those who abstain consistently define alcohol in negative terms—chiefly as morally or religiously wrong or as bad for one's health and happiness—disapprove of drinking in general, and see alcohol as harmful to society. Drinkers tend to report positive definitions of alcohol. They see it as promoting congenial social interaction, celebration, relaxation, and pleasure. More personal definitions of alcohol, such as "anxiety reduction," are less frequently reported; these reasons are associated with heavy drinking. At the same time, even those who approve of alcohol use are aware of counterdefinitions and recognize potential and actual negative aspects of drinking. However, these are seen chiefly as concomitant with excessive or uncontrolled drinking. Such negative definitions as applied to one's own behavior are neutralized by the acceptability and positive features of moderate drinking. "What alcohol as a narcotic was said to do *to* the individual and the groups to which he is

---

[1]The terminology used here is adapted from the studies of "norm qualities," mainly Larsen and Abu-Laban 1968, and secondarily from Pittman's (1967:5–13) discussion of "cultural positions" on drinking. The stated findings about rates of drinking and heavy drinking come from these sources and from Mizruchi and Perruci 1962 and Skolnick 1958.

associated was countered by what it was thought to do *for* the individual and his group associations" (Maddox 1958:6). Thus those who apply proscriptive or abstinent norms to drinking alcohol tend not to drink, and those who do drink tend to apply prescriptive or permissive norms, at least on a situational or conditional basis (see Cahalan et al. 1967:146–201; Riley et al. 1959; Maddox and McCall 1964:58–76).

Teenage Drinking

Although underage drinking is illegal, the preponderance of evidence from teenage drinking studies shows that for the most part it is behavior learned in conventional settings. Initial drinking behavior is conditioned most strongly by parental influence, and, as we have seen, drinking by teenagers conforms fairly closely to the adult patterns in the community, region, religion, and ethnic groups to which the teenagers belong. Peer group influence is also important for adolescent drinking practices, and the impact of other socializing agents seems to be less than that of family or peers.

It is generally recognized in the literature on drinking and adolescence that parents and peers exert the most salient influences on alcohol use, but there is some controversy over the roles played by them. Some argue that teenage drinking is "imitative" of adult patterns and place greater emphasis on the positive influence of parents and adults. Maddox and his associates have consistently supported the contention that drinking by teenagers is behavior learned principally from adult models and represents acceptance of, identification with, and anticipatory socialization into adult roles. Drawing from his own research in Michigan, national surveys, and studies in New York, Wisconsin, Kansas, and elsewhere, Maddox points to the findings which support this argument: the similarity in group variations in adult and teenage drinking; the high correlation between parental and offspring drinking habits; the increased probability of the adolescent drinking as he approaches adult age; the association of drinking with assumption of adult role responsibilities; the frequency with which first drinking experiences occur in the home with parental permission; and the frequency with which adolescents attribute drinking by teenagers to be attempts at acting "grown up."[2]

Maddox does not deny that much learning and drinking takes place in peer groups, but he maintains that peer groups do not participate in drinking as a form of rebellion or put irresistible pressure on the adolescent abstainer to begin drinking. Peer groups do provide the context in which drinking goes beyond what even prescriptive parents think acceptable for their sons and daughters. The pattern seems to be that many teenagers learn about alcohol as part of adult role-playing from observation of parents and other

---

[2]This approach is most fully developed in Maddox and McCall 1964 and in Maddox 1958. See also Maddox 1964; 1962.

adults, often drinking at home in the presence of and with the consent of parents. But they tend to describe their at-home use of alcohol as "tasting" or "sipping," whereas their use with peers is described as "drinking"—that is, consuming entire glasses or bottles of beer, wine, or whiskey. Boys tend to do more unsupervised peer-only drinking than girls, but for both, the

> peer groups only suggest that the teenager do prematurely what adults have already suggested that he may eventually do legitimately when he comes of age. . . . The basic model for his behavior comes from the adult world although part of his experimentation with drinking is done before audiences of his age peers as they move toward "coming of age" (Maddox 1958:8–9).

The imitation argument is countered by those who see adolescent drinking as *rebellion* against adult and parental authority or as the "expression of hostility toward the normative authority of the total society" (Alexander 1967:543; see also Globetti 1967:132). From this perspective, peers are the more important source of drinking influence, and adult models are important only in the negative sense of providing something against which to rebel.[3]

The differences in the two approaches may be due in part to differences in research settings. The research to which Maddox refers has been conducted among high school students in communities in which adults regularly drink and support essentially *prescriptive* drinking norms. In such an environment drinking serves to symbolize adult status, and it can be expected that most of whatever drinking there is by teenagers is conditioned primarily by the positive sanctions of and acceptability of drinking to adults. On the other hand, the research support for the "rebellion" explanation of underage use of alcohol comes almost exclusively from studies conducted in the *proscriptive* or abstinence cultural context of rural and/or southern communities (Alexander 1967; Globetti 1969; Globetti and Windham 1967; Sebald 1968:470–78). Because adults in such communities typically neither drink nor approve of alcohol use, it may be that for some youth drinking expresses or is part of a general alienation and rejection of conventional adult patterns.

Both the imitative behavior of adolescents in prescriptive drinking environments and the rebellious behavior of adolescents in proscriptive milieus are learned behavior. The main difference lies in the primary groups which provide the major source of reinforcement for and definitions favorable to drinking. In both cases, parents are carriers of and effective socializers into conventional normative standards. Where drinking is conventionally acceptable behavior for adults, a sizable portion of the teenage population will use alcohol; where abstinence is the conventionally expected behavior of adults, relatively few teenagers will drink. Moreover, insofar as there is a

---

[3]For an examination of this "imitation" versus "rebellion" argument as applied to both drinking and drug use by teenagers see Akers 1970.

teenage subculture in either situation, its norms and criteria for acceptance generally reflect those of the adult community (Windham et al. 1967).

Nonetheless, in both cases adolescents probably permit more drinking among themselves than adults would consider proper for teenagers. But in prescriptive communities drinking with peers is more in the nature of practice and training for the type of drinking considered appropriate by and for significant adults. Also, those with drinking parents are most likely to drink when they experience peer pressure to do so (Forslund and Gustafson 1970). Since the majority in the United States are raised in environments permitting alcohol use, this kind of socialization into conventional drinking patterns is typical. For most teenagers drinking is part of the general adolescent development and is related to other "transition-marking" behavior of moving into adult roles (Jessor and Jessor 1975). But among the minority who are raised in abstinence settings, the youth who drinks, if he is not rebelling against, certainly is not copying his parents. Because teenage drinking goes against the prevailing norms in such situations, it is more clearly deviant and may be rebellious by definition. The evidence is not certain that it results from some prior rejection of adult authority, however. At any rate, if teenagers in proscriptive environments drink at all, they must be relatively isolated from conventional adult influence and associated with groups— either adolescent peers or unconventional adults—that favor drinking.

The impact of family background continues through late adolescence and into adulthood; those who were abstainers in a proscriptive family context tend to remain abstinent, and persons from prescriptive drinking families continue to have a higher probability of drinking. However, drinking behavior comes more and more under the influence of peer associates. Drinking in college is sustained primarily by the influence of fellow students in friendship groups, on dates, at parties, and in fraternities and sororities. Adult drinking becomes very much a social activity with spouse, relatives, friends, and work and business associates (Straus and Bacon 1953; Haer 1955; Cahalan et al. 1967:90–94).

Summary

Learning to drink is a necessary step to learning to drink deviantly, and this chapter outlined the social learning process in teenage and adult drinking. The preponderance of drinking occurs in group settings, and drinking alcoholic beverages is socially and culturally patterned behavior which varies systematically by age, sex, race, religion, ethnicity, class, region, and community. These sociocultural influences on drinking or not drinking are transmitted to the individual first by the family and secondly by peer groups. In these and other primary groups a person learns definitions favorable to or unfavorable to drinking. The extent to which one continues to drink, once he starts, is a function of the social rewards attached to drinking and the reinforcing effects of the alcohol.

12

Alcoholism as Learned Behavior

Alcoholism is "repeated drinking of alcoholic beverages in excess of dietary and social uses . . . to an extent that interferes with the drinker's health or his social or economic functioning" (Keller 1958:2). Such terms as *alcoholism, problem drinking, excessive drinking,* and *alcoholic drinking*[1] will be used interchangeably.

Several physiological causes of alcoholism have been suggested: inherited tendencies, endocrine or metabolic abnormalities, chemical and nutritional deficiencies or imbalances, and alcohol allergy. Extensive knowledge of the physiology of alcohol in the body has not been of much help in tracing the etiology of alcoholism, and physiological explanations have not found empirical support (Greenberg 1958:30; Straus 1966:263). This conclusion is equally applicable to the research that has attempted to locate some personality pathology, characteristic, or type which makes a person prone or susceptible to alcoholism. No personality characteristics consistently differentiate alcoholics from other drinkers, and research has failed to find a distinctive or unique "alcoholic personality type" (Armstrong 1958; Symes 1957; Cahalan 1970:69–70).

A Social Learning Analysis of Alcoholism

Anomie, Stress, and Alcoholism

The sociological and anthropological literature almost universally assumes that heavy drinking is a response to stress, tension, and anxiety. Hence the relation of the sociocultural milieu to alcoholism is seen in the degree to which it exposes the population to stressful or anxiety-provoking situations. Although different terms are used, the various social character-

---

[1]See also conceptions of alcoholism and problem drinking in Jellinek 1960; Trice 1966; Straus 1966; Plaut 1967; and Cahalan 1970.

istics that set up stress-inducing situations conducive to alcoholism can be categorized under the concept of anomie or disorganization. To the degree that anomie prevails, the individual experiences "normlessness" and ambivalence about proper behavior, and this ambivalence supposedly produces anxiety.

Almost thirty years ago Bales (1949) suggested that high rates of alcoholism can be expected in sociocultural environments in which (1) social arrangements operate to produce problems of adjustment, such as anxiety, guilt, or sexual tensions; (2) the cultural traditions positively define drinking as a way of dealing with the tensions; and (3) there are few or no substitutes for alcohol with which to deal with the tensions. He pictured the traditional Irish society (and to some extent the Irish ethnic culture in this country), with its high rates of alcoholism, as providing all three of these conditions. Extreme problems were created for Irish men by the conflict and ambivalence resulting from the necessity of occupying a status of dependence on the father and delaying marriage well into adulthood. Drinking to deal with the tensions thereby created was culturally acceptable.

Others who have reviewed the considerable body of interethnic and cross-cultural studies have come to similar conclusions. Straus starts with the assumption that "alcoholism in its various forms is a manifestation of one or more of a number of underlying stress-producing conditions" (1966:262). From the observed cross-cultural and intrasocietal variations in levels of excessive drinking Ullman generalizes that in "integrated" cultures (where the drinking customs and sanctions are well established, are generally known and agreed upon, and are consistent with the rest of the culture) the alcoholism rate will be low. On the other hand, cultures with inconsistent and nonintegrated drinking patterns produce ambivalence and stress in individuals and are likely to experience high rates of alcoholism (Ullman 1958). Similarly, Snyder (1964) concludes that the more disorganized are the social conditions to which persons are exposed, the higher the probability of alcoholism is. To support this conclusion he cites, among other evidence, the low rates of alcoholism in societies with integrated kinship structures compared to the high rates in societies with more fragmented kin systems. Primitive societies disorganized by the impact of modern societies have more alcoholism problems than those which have remained more integrated. Snyder also explains the fact that the rate of alcoholism is slightly higher among Reform than it is among Orthodox Jews, because Reform Jews are more secularized, thus have less religious solidarity and cohesion.

The generalization linking alcoholism to conditions of anomie and the relative absence of alcoholism to sociocultural integration seems to fit most of the evidence, including much from recent studies on group and status variations in type of drinking (Madsen and Madsen 1969; Jessor 1968; Rushing 1969). It also fits fairly well the known variations in rates of alcoholism and heavy drinking. The ambiguous or inadequate normative guidelines which characterize groups with "ambivalent" drinking norms are most likely to produce problem drinkers.

On the other hand, the meanings of integration and anomie are not always clear in the literature and frequently are not measured. And exceptions to the generalization can be found (Lemert 1967). For some time the skid-row wino living in the disorganized, dilapidated section of the urban area has been viewed as a strong case for an anomie-disorganization explanation of alcoholism. However, new evidence raises serious questions about the extent to which the rate of alcoholism is in fact any higher on skid row than in other lower-class neighborhoods. Also, the skid-row drunk may not have had an especially unstable background, and he is often fairly well integrated into friendship, "bottle gangs," and other group situations. Thus anomie may not be an apt description for the condition of skid-row dwellers, or at best may be descriptive of the situation only for some alcoholics in skid-row areas (see Wallace 1968; Rooney 1961; Rubington 1968; Bahr 1969a, 1969b).

Negative Reinforcement of Alcoholism and Anomie

Assuming that anomie is one type of structural condition that may (but does not always) increase the probability of alcoholism, in what way can this be related to a learning process? If anomie produces anxiety, it may be related through the process indicated by the best-known learning theory of alcoholism, formulated some years ago by Conger (1956; 1958). Briefly his theory is that ambivalence produces anxiety; alcohol relieves anxiety; and this experience is rewarding and reinforces further drinking. Thus those who are anxious and who have access to alcohol will more often be rewarded in this way and become heavy drinkers. Although he recognizes that a person can become a "happy drunk," Conger's need-reduction theory is that alcoholism is behavior negatively reinforced by alcohol's reduction of anxiety or fear rather than behavior positively reinforced.[2]

Conger's theory is built on prior research with cats and his own research with rats, but he and others have applied the explanation to human consumption of alcohol (Kingham 1958; Clay 1964a; Cahalan et al. 1967). For humans, the theory holds that fear and anxiety created by social and personal conflict can be alleviated or escaped through drinking. Social interaction for many people involves a good deal of ambivalence; they are attracted to other

---

[2]Conger's theory seems to propose that alcohol can reduce both the *anxiety* created by conflict and ambivalence and the *fear* connected with any unpleasant situation. But from his own experiments Smart (1965) concludes that reinforcement comes from simply the alcohol-induced reduction of fear arising from exposure to any aversive stimulus, whether or not that situation also contains anxiety-producing conflict with positive stimuli.

people, but they fear rejection by them. Alcohol can be a social lubricant and can ease the interaction by reducing the anxiety in these situations. The experience of this relief reinforces further drinking, and the more a person drinks for the individual anxiety-relieving effect of alcohol rather than as an incidental accompaniment to sociability, the more likely he is to become a problem drinker. The evidence tends to support the contention that heavy drinkers drink more for personal effect, whereas moderate and occasional drinkers tend to drink more for the social rewards connected with drinking (Riley et al. 1959; Mulford and Miller 1960:493).

These personal effects are assumed to be fairly immediate, consistent, and frequent and should involve "more powerful operant conditioning than would be true of drinking for primarily social reasons."

> Since the "escape" drinker, by definition, is drinking primarily for the purpose of avoidance of personal anxiety or depression . . . it is inferred that the "escape" drinker ordinarily gets a greater immediate . . . reinforcing effect from drinking than does the nonescape drinker (Cahalan et al. 1967:214).

Some support for this hypothesis is found in the evidence that the great majority of nonescape drinkers fail to recall *any* effects, favorable or unfavorable, from drinking, whereas more escape drinkers recall definite personal effects from drinking. The more immediate effects, whether remembered later as good or bad, are more important for the heavy escape drinker than the nonescape social drinker (Cahalan et al. 1967:215–16). The rewarding effects of alcohol continue with increased drinking (supposedly even relieving the anxiety produced by concern over one's own drinking and the reproach of others) and are not offset by the negative sanctions of other people and additional problems connected with drinking bouts:

> Immediate reduction in anxiety . . . more than compensates for the punitive attitudes of a wife or boss the next morning and the physical punishment involved in a hangover (Conger 1956:303; see also Conger 1958:33).

Reduction of anxiety may not be the mechanism that reinforces heavy drinking, however. The procedure could be a straightforward process of negative reinforcement by escaping or avoiding unpleasant stimuli, whether or not drinking really relieves fear and anxiety. Research with human subjects is not available, but experiments with animals show that stable and frequent ingestion of large quantities of alcohol can be conditioned simply by letting the animals escape from a noxious stimulus only when they take a drink of alcohol (without regard to the reduction of "anxiety" in the animals).

It would seem then that alcoholism may be learned through *negative reinforcement*. That is, the individual avoids unpleasant situations or problems by or while drinking. The drinking may make the person less anxious or fearful or may simply be what he does when confronted with a problem. In either case, the fact that his drinking is connected with avoiding something aversive reinforces his drinking behavior.

> Each time he does this [reaches for the bottle] . . . the drinking response is reinforced and the tendency to repeat the act is strengthened. Eventually he may use alcohol to avoid every problem, large and small, and then he is a problem drinker or alcoholic (Kepner 1964:280).

To the extent that living under anomic conditions produces anxiety, adjustment problems, or is otherwise experienced as unpleasant, then, alcoholism may be related to anomie through negative reinforcement.

Group Reinforcement and Alcoholism

The negative reinforcement of drinking behavior may be combined with positive reinforcement of pleasurable effects and social rewards. If the taste of alcohol and its effects are not initially pleasurable, one may nevertheless learn to enjoy them. Eventually through both positive and negative reinforcement, drinking "like virtue, is its own reward" and is not likely to extinguish simply because no other rewards are contingent upon it (Kepner 1964:282).

However, there is some evidence that although the effects of alcohol may become positive reinforcers, other rewards continuing over a period of time may be enough themselves to produce excessive drinking. An illustration comes from research by Keehn (1969) in which he established and maintained strong drinking habits in rats by rewarding them with food for drinking high-content alcohol. The animals developed a preference for alcohol over a saccharin solution and reached the point of regularly ingesting intoxicating amounts of alcohol. When they were no longer positively reinforced for alcohol consumption their drinking fell back to low levels. Although in several cultural traditions drinking customarily accompanies eating, we cannot generalize from these animal experiments to conclude that human alcoholics are rewarded with food for heavy drinking. However, if the food reinforcers can be equated with other environmental conditions to which humans are exposed, it may be that "alcoholism in man is sometimes similarly maintained by reinforcement contingencies (inadvertently) set up by the community" (Keehn 1969:328).

One way in which the alcoholic's social environment can reinforce drinking is through the sympathetic actions and reactions of others, which reward the behavior and mitigate the consequences of drinking that would otherwise be punishing.

> Among these are the wife who regularly calls the boss to say her husband has a severe cold when he is suffering from a hangover; the spouse who buys liquor for her husband to help him "taper off"; the father who protects his son from the consequences of his drinking bouts by bailing him out of jail every week-end (Kepner 1964:285).

But this only begins to suggest the possibilities. Trice provides a thorough analysis of the way in which other people's reactions to a person's drinking can lead to alcoholism.

> More specifically, this social-psychological scheme for explaining alcoholism has the following parts: (1) personality features that set the stage, making one a candidate; (2) qualities of drinking-centered groups that uniquely attract and reward the use of alcohol for such persons, linking "readiness" with alcohol; (3) the uneven, but usually inevitable, shift from reward to rejection within drinking groups; and then (4) the seeking out of more tolerant drinking companions, providing continued support and protection for alcoholism to develop (1966:43).

"Drinking-centered groups" include tavern groups, formal and informal parties, neighbors, clubs, ceremonial and celebration gatherings, conventions, skid-row bottle gangs, and others. Several features of many drinking groups are attractive and rewarding for the drinker. They accept and legitimate the use of alcohol, permit congenial social interaction relatively free of competitive overtones, and provide the rewarding intimacy of "pseudo-primary" relationships. Some drinking groups hold that heavy consumption and the ability to drink more than others without appearing drunk are signs of virility, and they grant status to the one who can "drink like a man." At the same time the drinking groups are lenient with the heavy drinker and slow to apply negative sanctions to the person who drinks more than others in the group. Even persons who may become concerned about the developing alcoholic's drinking (wife, employer, friends, associates) fail to apply effective sanctions until it is too late, partly because the drinker does not fit the image of the skid-row derelict which they have learned is the "real" alcoholic. Thus the "negative sanctions that define and penalize undesirable drinking behavior are weak, irregular, and infrequent, contrasting clearly with the abundance of rewarding positive sanctions" (Trice 1966:53).

But at some point (varying from one group to another) a person's drinking begins to be seen as showing a lack of self-control, and sanctions short of rejection begin to give way to more severe reactions; eventually the person may be ostracized. He begins to seek out more congenial drinking groups which are tolerant of the level of drinking and kinds of behavior the previous group has come to consider excessive.

> Most come to reject a drinker as a future drinking companion due to certain kinds of drinking conduct: vulgarity, open aggression, sexual advances, excessive hilarity. At the same time the degree of acceptance before rejection varies widely between groups. Thus, if a developing alcoholic's drinking violates the norms of a rather conservative group, he can find emotional rewards by affiliating with more lenient sets of drinking companions. In the process his dependence on alcohol increases, but he is not confronted by realistic social controls with clear negative sanctions (Trice 1966:5).

This relocation may entail downward social mobility, but it need not; in fact, one may move to more permissive drinking situations without too much cost, simply by "making the rounds" of the taverns and bars. But as this shifting from group to group continues and the person's drinking becomes increasingly excessive, he becomes isolated from conventional social controls; to find ever more permissive groups he is propelled toward ever more deviant roles in groups clearly labeled deviant, such as skid-row drinking groups. The person becomes more excluded from avenues returning to sobriety.

We have seen the patterns of alcoholism. Now we will look at the social controls and treatment of alcoholism.

Control of Alcohol and Treatment of Alcoholism

Societal reaction to problems associated with drinking alcohol has revolved around basically two strategies: (1) control, regulation, and prevention in the general population, (2) control through the law and treatment programs directed toward specific deviant drinkers.

Control and Regulation in the General Population

Although the policy of total prohibition of alcohol was in effect only briefly (1919–33) in the United States, many local jurisdictions continue to control alcohol in this way. State and local regulation (but not criminalization) through control of alcohol sales and distribution is the typical pattern. All states and the federal government tax alcohol, primarily for revenue but also to regulate distribution and sales. All states (and many local jurisdictions) have a system of licensing the sale and consumption of alcohol on the premises of trade establishments. The licensing is used to control the character of the owners, managers, and patrons of the establishment. All states also have a minimum age for people to legally purchase alcohol.

There have also been alcohol education and alcoholism-prevention programs sponsored by the brewery and liquor industries and also by governments and school systems. Many of these programs are aimed at teenagers, attempting to convince them to wait until they are old enough to legally buy and consume alcohol. These have often concentrated on warnings of the negative consequences of illegal drinking (Akers [with King] 1967).

However, recently there have developed two different but overlapping approaches to the prevention of abusive drinking. Neither has yet been widely employed but each shows some promise. One emphasizes educating the public to use alcohol responsibly. This responsible use norm will not necessarily affect the overall level of consumption. But with consumption conforming to this norm, it would be more spread out among moderate and light drinkers and abusive drinking would decline. Even the manufacturers of liquor and beer are joining this campaign. They are taking out full-page ads in mass-circulation magazines and advising hosts not to encourage heavy drinking at their parties, teenagers to take it easy if they drink, and so on. The message is, "If you choose to drink, drink responsibly." The second approach emphasizes non-normative techniques of lowering overall consumption by (1) restricting availability through increasing the price of alcohol, (2) closing bars earlier, and (3) lowering the alcohol content of the beverages (see Whitehead 1975 for a review of both approaches).

Direct Control and Treatment of Problem Drinkers

Legal policy.   Legal policy traditionally has been directed toward controlling public drinking offenses, mainly through arrest and conviction of people drunk in public. This has become so common that until recently arrests for alcohol or alcohol-related offenses accounted for more than half of all criminal arrests. Thus, a considerable amount of police work (and hence public funds) has been devoted to dealing with problems having to do directly with alcohol (not to mention the role of alcohol in a whole range of other crimes, from check forgery to personal violence).

Arrests for driving while intoxicated (usually defined as at least .10 percent alcohol concentration in the blood) are directed toward curbing the high number of traffic accidents and fatalities attributed to drunk driving. It is popularly supported as a necessary police function that protects the public from drunk drivers. On the other hand, the other major police practice of arresting people for being drunk (or disorderly while drunk) in public is not popular with everyone; indeed it has come under intense criticism from many areas.

The typical pattern of arrests for public drunkenness is concentrated on the winos and bums of the skid-row areas of the city. These are a sort of floating population of arrestees who regularly are picked up by the police, held in the drunk tank, appear in court, receive a sentence of a month, serve it in the county jail or farm where they dry out, are released, go back to the streets, quickly get drunk again, and are re-arrested, to begin the cycle again. This "revolving door" of in and out of the courts and jails; punctuated with a round of the skid-row missions offering meals, ear-bending (sermons), and occasionally a place to sleep; is a way of life for most skid-row inhabitants. It is not uncommon for the "police case inebriate" to have been arrested over a hundred times in the same city, not to mention his arrest record elsewhere (Pittman and Gordon 1958; Bittner 1967; Wiseman 1970; Spradley 1970).

The police have encountered many of the same problems in controlling any "victimless" crimes, and the lower courts have become inundated with a seemingly endless parade of hopeless cases. The police have become increasingly annoyed at having to spend so much of their resources responding to behavior that is no real criminal threat to society and at most is just a public nuisance. Also, the system has been chastised as inhumane, unjust, and ineffective. In the past decade there has been a growing *diversion movement*—to get the chronic drunks entirely out of the criminal justice system by effectively diverting them from alcoholism. Some modification in that direction has taken place.

The diversion movement for controlling alcoholics.   In *Powell* v. *Texas* (1968) it was argued before the Supreme Court that the laws allowing for police arrest and conviction of people for public drunkenness are unconstitutional. The appellants argued that since the court had ruled earlier (*Robinson* v. *California,* 1962) that drug addiction is a disease or condition which cannot constitutionally be outlawed, the public drunk laws are unconstitutional since they, too, made a condition—alcoholism—illegal; therefore, to control the public nuisance of drunken comportment, the state would have to do it without the police-court system, that is, through a system of treatment and detoxification centers. The Court upheld Powell's conviction on drunkenness charges and ruled that the laws under which he was convicted were constitutional. The state laws make being drunk in public—not the alcoholism itself—illegal, although being drunk could have been a result of the alcoholism. The Court noted that there was no consensus on what constitutes the disease of alcoholism. Further, the Court found that at the time adequate treatment approaches or facilities did not exist, and involuntary diversion of the offender to a place where there is no treatment is the same as sending him to jail.

In spite of the decision in this case, the diversion movement accelerated after it. Many experts had not expected this reaction, although even before the case came to the Supreme Court local governments had met with some success in providing alternatives to jail. Some facilities were already in use and others were constructed. Also, the Court's reference in the decision to the need for real treatment facilities (and the objection mainly to the compulsory nature of commitments to them) and the dissenting opinion's emphasis on alcoholism as a treatable disease both provided impetus to get the chronic drunks out of jail and into treatment, even if on a more or less "voluntary" basis. Several states enacted statutes for police to take drunks to detoxification or treatment centers instead of jail, and allowing courts to give drunks the choice of undergoing treatment in lieu of sentence. Many communities set up new private and public programs to take care of cases referred from court or by the police. But to what are drunks diverted? Are the existing programs capable of stopping drunkenness at its source and thus alleviating the revolving-door process? Yes, there are programs, but they have not demonstrated unqualified success in treating alcoholics.

There are private and public programs that have existed for some time and some newer programs. (See Wiseman 1970 for a comprehensive study of the missions, treatment programs, and other "stations of the lost" through which skid-row drunks pass.) The best known is Alcoholics Anonymous (AA), a private organization of sober alcoholics helping others become sober. To AA, there is no such thing as an ex-alcoholic: Once an alcoholic, always an alcoholic. They urge alcoholics not to have even one drink because it will lead inevitably to another binge. The safest way to insure that one will not start uncontrolled drinking again is simply for him not to take another drink. However, research has not proven that this is necessarily true. In fact, many former alcoholics do successfully resume moderate drinking patterns (Hamburg 1975; see also *Newsweek,* June 21, 1976:58). AA's self-help approach has been successful with some middle-class and other problem drinkers who have family and financial resources (although the extent of this success is difficult to judge because records are not kept).

Private and public "hospitals" in which alcoholics can be placed also have existed in various localities for some time. These are state mental hospitals and psychiatric wards or sometimes special alcoholic wards of general hospitals. The publicly financed new detoxification and treatment centers are usually specifically connected to the court or jail and receive their treatment populations from these sources; the private ones take referrals both from official agencies and private sources. Some of these have been combined with existing skid-row institutions like the missions, usually without much success. There are residential halfway houses and nonresidential or drop-in centers. The therapy includes, singly and in combination: simple detoxification, traditional psychotherapy, individual and group counseling, and job counseling and retraining. Some have had success with particular problem drinkers, but for the type of chronic drunk who makes up the usual

police-case inebriate, the finding is usually one of ". . . overwhelming in-
effectiveness of efforts to intervene in the skid-row alcoholism problem"
(Fry and Miller 1975).

Alcoholism and Aversive Conditioning Therapy

We have examined the sources and kinds of conditioning that are involved in alcoholism. But whatever these are, it should be possible to treat
alcoholism by reversing the process. This is the assumption on which the
treatment of alcoholism by *aversion therapy* or *aversive conditioning* is based.
The basic idea is to create an association of the taste, smell, feel, or effects
of alcohol with aversive stimuli so that the person comes to experience punishing rather than rewarding effects of drinking.

This approach was first tried about forty years ago and was quite often
used in the 1940s. Its use declined, however, and was resumed systematically
again until the early 1960s (Franks 1963; Sanderson et al. 1963). In earlier
years the treatment relied on nausea-inducing (apomorphine or emetine)
or alcohol antagonistic (antabuse) drugs to cause the person to vomit when
he drank an alcoholic beverage. If this was repeated enough times, the alcohol itself would produce nausea, and the person could not stand to take a
drink. In more recent therapy, electric shock or in some cases a drug which
induces momentary paralysis and suffocation have been substituted for
the emetic drugs (Sanderson et al. 1963; Holzinger et al. 1967; Rachman and
Teasdale 1970:72–76). Aversion therapy has been used with some success
to train alcoholics either to abstain completely or to drink in moderation.
For those seeking abstention, electric shock is applied with each drinking
episode; the person seeking to become a moderate social drinker again receives no shock as long as he leisurely consumes a modest number of drinks
within a specified time period[3] (*Time*, March 15, 1971:54).

The results of these efforts have been mixed. Generally speaking, the
therapy has been more successful than no treatment or traditional psychiatric therapy. However, the rate of success varies considerably from one
group of treated subjects to another. Only in a few instances has the rate of
cure reached more than 50 percent (Chapman et al. 1969; Rachman and
Teasdale 1970:14–23; Bandura 1969:541). Part of this lack of success is due to
the way in which practitioners in this area have applied conditioning
therapy and carried out the evaluative research to determine how effective
their efforts were. After a review of eight studies in which electric shock was
used and ten studies in which drugs were used for aversive conditioning,
Chapman and his associates conclude that "most instances of behavior
therapy have carried over directly the precision of laboratory procedures to

---

[3]Sometimes the aversion treatment has been combined with *relaxation* and other behavior
modification techniques (Ashem and Donner 1968; Rachman and Teasdale 1969:97–105).

the clinic. The treatment of alcoholism is a notable exception. Gross errors are widespread in the literature" (1969:1).

But even when they are carefully conducted the aversion therapy sessions may simply cause the nausea or shock to become one more discriminative stimulus for the reinforcing effects of the alcohol.

> Drinking even though it is initially pleasurable and rewarding has many disagreeable punishing consequences built in, at least in our society. The alcoholic learns at a very early stage in his drinking career to associate both reward and punishment with drinking. Consequently, additional punishment for his drinking . . . can come to serve as a signal for renewed drinking. Evidently, punishment so employed will functionally operate as the secondary reinforcer, or as cue for reward, or as an arouser! (Blum and Blum 1967:105–6).

The subject's motivation to change and willingness to undergo the rigors of aversive conditioning and the number of "booster" sessions he undergoes are other variables in the success of aversive therapy, but they are not often taken into account in assessment of the treatment (Bandura 1969:542–44).

The mixed success of aversive conditioning therapy in treating alcoholism is probably also due to the fact that there is little systematic follow-up to deal with the variables, such as social influence, in alcohol behavior. Whatever aversive environmental features (anomie, anxiety-provoking conditions, problems, and so on) that have sustained the drinking in the past as negative reinforcement are not likely to disappear simply because someone has undergone contrived unpleasantness connected with alcohol. Positively reinforcing features (drinking groups, supportive wives, and friends) are also not likely to lose their potency because the person has undergone aversive therapy.

> Aversive counterconditioning alone has proved most successful with alcoholics who have developed their habituation by way of prolonged heavy social drinking, and who possess sufficient personal resources to derive adequate gratifications from sober behavior. . . . The major value of aversive procedures is that they provide a rapid means of achieving control over injurious behavior for a period during which alternative, and more rewarding, modes of behavior can be established (Bandura 1969:547, 554).

It is this differential reinforcement approach, rewarding sobriety while punishing alcoholic drinking, which seems to hold the most promise. In recent "broad spectrum" behavior modification programs, the emphasis has shifted from reliance on conditioning aversion to alcohol to promoting behavior that is incompatible with heavy drinking, and the success rate is considerably better than conventional treatment (Hamburg 1975). Such programs also probably work mainly with problem drinkers who have gotten into treatment on their own or through their places of employment (a growing number of businesses and industries are underwriting treatment of their employees with drinking problems rather than firing them). These drinkers have the motivation and have access to positive rewards for remaining sober. The outlook for the skid-row drunk remains bleak.

Summary

Alcoholic drinking may be reinforced through negative reinforcement by reducing anxiety and by becoming associated with the avoidance of stressful situations. Because it entails ambivalence, anomie may be one structural condition that fosters anxiety and hence promotes alcoholism. Alcoholism may also be positively reinforced. A series of drinking groups may, by first rewarding and then belatedly punishing the deviant drinker, progressively channel him into alcoholic behavior. Aversive conditioning therapy has been somewhat successful in the treatment of alcoholics but has not lived up to its potential.

Society has attempted to control alcohol through regulation and prevention programs in the general population and legal control and treatment of problem drinkers. An array of public and private treatment programs are available as alternatives to police and court control, but when treatment has been successful it has been primarily with problem drinkers with more stable family, occupational, and other social resources. The diversion movement for alternatives to the revolving door of the criminal justice system has resulted in getting some skid-row alcoholics into treatment, but successful treatment programs with this population have yet to be devised.

Part Four   Sexual Deviance

13

Sexual Norms and Society

Social Control of Sexual Behavior

Sex is both commonplace and exotic. It is basic biology common to all humans and to other animal species as well. Except that it is necessary only for the survival of the species and not also for the survival of the particular individual, it is on a par with breathing, eating, sleeping, and defecating as a common biological function. But the fact that sex is natural tells us little about actual customs and practices in society and what is natural or unnatural in what people think about and do with sex. The presumption in evolutionary theory is that the sex drive tends toward attachment to the opposite sex for the purpose of producing children. Nonetheless, there seems to be little biological imperative determining to what or whom people learn to respond sexually.

There is social regulation and control of sexual behavior in all societies. Everywhere, this control is linked to the structure of relationships and customs surrounding marriage and kinship. Marriage customs and family forms vary by time and place but one universal feature of sexual norms is the priority given to heterosexual behavior between adults within the marriage bonds. Thus intercourse between partners in a conventionally acceptable marriage-family system is always acceptable and nearly always the morally preferable ideal (Davis 1966:322–30). Nearly every other form of sexual behavior has at some time or place been tabooed. Some forms of sexual expression seem to be condemned universally, such as unbridled promiscuity and sexual violence against unwilling victims. However, the incest taboo, which is sometimes considered universal, has had historical exceptions (Bagley 1969; Fox 1962). Also, even such rare behavior as necrophilia (intercourse with a corpse) has not only been tolerated, but institutionalized, albeit in a highly ritualized way (Mantegazza 1935:60). Both the content and intensity of societal regulation of sexual behavior are subject to variation from one social and historical context to the next. While there are commonalities, social customs and regulations about the proper time, place, partner, manner, and occasion for sex show an amazing diversity across societies. Examples of cross-cultural differences abound (Ford and Beach 1951; Marshall and Suggs 1971; West 1967:17–32).

In traditional Irish society, sexual norms are highly restrictive and sex is saturated with religious injunctions. Although marriage is socially delayed into the mid-twenties for women and the mid-thirties for men, premarital sex is taboo and extramarital relationships are disapproved. Sex segregation permeates the community and sexual expressions of all kinds are repressed: Nudity is shameful and sinful, sex is seldom discussed (and never in public), and the *only* acceptable form of sexual behavior is genital-to-genital inter-course between husband and wife for purposes of procreation (Messenger 1971).

By contrast, in certain Polynesian societies sexual behavior is freely engaged in from an early age on and a dominant theme in the culture is achieving heterosexual satisfaction for both men and women. There is great interest in and activity based on genital matters and copulation. By accepted custom, the premarital period is a time of vigorous sexual activity. It is ex-pected that adolescent boys crawl to the huts of girls at night to engage in coitus. Sexual prowess is much admired in males: Unmarried females vie for lovers who can sustain long intercourse and many orgasms. There is com-petition among both boys and girls to be the first to have coitus with a visitor to the island. After marriage, interest in sexual gratification con-tinues and frequent marital copulation is the norm. Marital fidelity is ex-pected and negative sanctions are applied to publicly discovered adultery. Nonetheless, discreet adultery is tolerated and appears to be a regularity with both men and women (Marshall 1971).

Neither the traditional Irish nor the Polynesian societies tolerate homo-sexuality, but Davenport (1965) describes a society in the Southwest Pacific which does accept homosexual behavior. In this society, clear-cut distinc-tions are drawn between male and female mannerisms, behavior, and speech. Socialization is geared to sex-role training to achieve these distinc-tions in practice. There are strong sex taboos for men and women. During adolescence, sex segregation is strict: Young males reside in special men's houses. The norm for older persons is public separation. However, masturba-tion is openly encouraged and frequently practiced as an acceptable sexual outlet for young unmarried men. It is not as desirable but still tolerated in young women. Homosexual liaisons between women are disapproved, but they are normal and institutionalized between young men of the same age and between older unmarried men and seven- to eleven-year-old boys.

> At some time during his life, nearly every male engages in ex-tensive homosexual activities. Such experiences are readily and openly discussed for they are considered to be as normal as mas-turbation and marital intercourse. Homosexual activity usually be-gins with foreplay which consists of mutual or unilateral masturba-tion and ends with anal intercourse culminating in orgasm (Davenport 1965:199).

The homosexual relationships are seen as part of the normal male pattern of development and in no way contradictory to marriage, heterosexual relationships, and family responsibilities the males eventually assume.

To these examples could be added many other cross-cultural variations and the multiplicity of sexual norms that subgroups in society have developed. What is acceptable and common in one society may be abhorrent and rare in another. With sex, there is a wide range of other possibilities beyond those sanctioned by a given society. When we consider the myriad sources, objects, and techniques to which humans have become conditioned sexually, we recognize that neither the strength nor direction of the sexual response is directly determined by biological dictates. There would be no sex without the biological equipment, but what are sexually relevant events for the individual and the kind of sexual behavior he performs is learned from his socially patterned and idiosyncratic experiences.

Sexual Standards in American Society: A Sexual Revolution?

Aside from the variations across societies, is it possible to say what sexual norms prevail in American society? At one time, there was little doubt about the answer. The dominant morality was a *monolithic code* (Cuber and Harroff 1966:42) drawn primarily from a Judeo-Christian tradition which emphasized the sinfulness of *any* sexual activity prior to or outside of marriage. This code confined sex to reproductive functions and condemned all sex that is mainly for pleasure. In the monolithic code, sex itself is somewhat dirty and decent people do not discuss it openly. Certainly sexual matters are not to be portrayed or written and talked about explicitly. Married couples are supposed to engage only in normal (genital-to-genital) sex. Homosexuality, masturbation, sodomy, incest, and a host of other "perversions" are viewed as sins against nature — condemned by God and country alike.

Existing with this code is the so-called double standard. Patterned evasions from the code by men are tolerated and even expected, while women are expected to strictly adhere to the code. Thus, "sowing wild oats," using prostitutes, premarital adventures, and maintaining a mistress are all seen as necessary expressions of the more sexually vigorous nature of men. All heterosexual adventures of a man are tolerated, as long as he eventually settles down to married life and fulfills his obligations as husband and father. Women are to remain chaste until married, faithful to their husbands, and find the sex act an unpleasant duty to husband. Loose women are sinners who may be forgiven by God, but in the meantime are outcasts of decent society. This code was and to some extent still is enshrined in laws (now loosely enforced) which prohibit certain sex acts and promote censorship of erotic books, pictures, magazines, and movies.

Earlier in this century, writing on sexuality of all kinds, except for moral denunciations, was restricted. Even serious scholarly work tended to be filled with moralizing (Sagarin 1971). There was some erosion of this code following World War I, however, and freer expression of sexual matters was allowed. Then in 1948 the first of the famous Kinsey studies from the Institute for Sex Research at Indiana University, *Sexual Behavior in the Human Male* (Kinsey et al. 1948), was published.[1] The research itself encountered tremendous opposition from politicians, the medical profession, clergy, and others. There were attempts to stop the study, halt publication of the book, secure Kinsey's dismissal from the university, and dismantle the institute (Kinsey et al. 1948:11–12). The book openly discussed the full range of sexual behavior and documented that many men were engaging in acts in violation of the dominant sexual standards. It became a best seller and, along with the companion volume (*Sexual Behavior in the Human Female* 1953), became the standard reference on sexual behavior.

Some have argued that the success of the Kinsey volumes and their revelations on American sex habits produced a marked liberalization of attitudes toward sex (Sagarin 1969:82–83). Whatever the reasons, it is true that in the next two decades, the depiction and discussion of sex became a prime topic of public attention. The popular literature of the 1950s took on a more liberal tone regarding sexual subjects (Ellis 1961). Explicit sexual material became more and more part of the written word, and several men's magazines (the best known being *Playboy*) featuring frontal and provocative views of naked women were started. Even the more sedate news and general interest magazines began to print what formerly would have been considered dirty pictures. Following earlier Supreme Court decisions which held that nothing could be banned as pornographic unless it appealed primarily to prurient interest and was without redeeming social or literary value (Zagel 1973:399–407), the magazines became more explicit in the 1960s. Mass distributed movies came to include scenes once only seen in "stag" films. A whole range of deviant sexual themes, especially homosexual, received sympathetic and noncondemnatory treatment in the media. Sexual themes of various kinds came to occupy much of the movie and television fare.

In 1970 a national commission found that perusal of explicitly erotic materials was widespread (see page 178) and had no measurable negative effects on sexual behavior or on the development of criminal behavior. The Commission recommended that all laws prohibiting the distribution and voluntary use of erotica by adults be removed and replaced with simple regulation

---

[1]This cumbersome and expensive book with no pictures, no savory depictions of sex acts, no advice to the troubled, and laden with charts, graphs, and tables was bought by many and discussed by a great many more who never saw it. Controversy continued to surround the book even after it became a scientific and popular success. It was subjected to both deserved and undeserved criticism from public figures and from the scientific community as well. Even today after we are aware of the shortcomings of the Kinsey studies, the books remain basic sources of data on the incidence and frequency of conforming and deviant sexual behavior.

of the traffic. The X-rated and R-rated movies with close-up portrayals of homosexual, oral-genital, and other sexual scenes became big money makers (Commission on Obscenity and Pornography 1970). The pornography market boomed, slumped, and boomed again with increasingly deviant and violent content (*Time*, April 5, 1976:58–63). The men's magazines carried ever more revealing photographic layouts of women and men, and they were soon joined by pictures of nude males in women's magazines (Stephenson 1973).

> The major breakthrough came with full frontal male pictures followed shortly by . . . depictions of partial then full erections and simulated then actual penetration. Depiction of female pubic hair in *Playboy* represents one major breakthrough in the slick, mass circulated magazine; . . . *Playgirl*, the magazine for women, initiated in mid-1973 full frontal male centerfolds (Stephenson 1973:178).

Major Broadway theater productions featured live nudity and were quickly followed by live "nudie" shows of all descriptions, with simulated and actual intercourse, both heterosexual and homosexual. Nudity and overt sexual conduct were accepted at outdoor music festivals and other gatherings of young people (and there was, of course, the short-lived "streaking" fad). The media attention to every nuance of the youth counterculture meant that their freer sexual attitudes received widespread notice throughout society. The women's liberation movement openly espoused that equality for men and women meant free expression of sexuality by both genders; women were supposed to be as sexually alert and active and enjoy sex on its own as men were.

By the time of the early 1970s, then, it had become quite obvious that as far as public expression is concerned, the old monolithic code was no longer in force. The change had been going on for years but the 1960s witnessed a radical change in the sphere of public visibility of written, oral, and pictorial expressions of sex (Gagnon and Simon 1970:1). Does this mean that a "sexual revolution" has taken place in the lives of Americans? The evidence is that quantitative changes have taken place in sexual behavior and attitudes of society besides the change in the public media attention to sex. Whether or not one wants to call these changes evolutionary or revolutionary is a matter of word choice.

On the basis of the Kinsey research (Kinsey et al. 1948:384–447; 1953:298–302) and research from the 1920s to the mid-1960s, we can say that attitudes changed considerably over the decades toward more permissive standards but that actual sexual behavior of most people did not change much (Reiss 1967; 1970).

> Basic changes in the last forty or fifty years have more likely been in the areas of attitudes than in behavior. . . . The change in sexual revolution during the last century has not been a sexual revolution,

but rather, a gradual evolvement of a more equalitarian and more participant-run system, the basic parts of which were present a hundred years ago (Reiss 1967:175–76).

Previous research showed attitudes and behavior to be congruent, and it should not be surprising that behavioral changes followed the attitudinal changes. More recent research on both representative (Hunt 1974) and unrepresentative samples (Anthanasiou et al. 1970; Miller and Simon 1974) has, in fact, found that in some areas both attitudes and behavior have changed. There is now a more permissive orientation toward many forms of sex among large segments of the population, and higher proportions of both men and women are involved in premarital and extramarital sex. The change has been greater for women than men, and there has been a convergence in the male and female attitudes toward sex and in the incidences of premarital coitus. There is greater experimentation with sexual variation both within and outside of marriage. At the same time there has been no greater acceptance of violent sex, and there has been little behavioral change in some areas: Fetishism, group sex, homosexuality, and the more deviant forms of sexual behavior are still engaged in by very small proportions of the population. However, judging from the increased premarital and extramarital sexual activities among Americans that are following the ease of sexual standards about the activities, one would have to predict that if societal tolerance of many of these sexual acts continues to the point of acceptance, then it is likely that people will actually do them in the years to come.

Many segments of the society have not participated in the change. That at least public profession of the older code is still expected is testified to by the fact that as President, Richard Nixon flatly rejected the recommendations of the Commission advising liberalization of pornography statutes, and very few states have in fact changed their laws. Recent Supreme Court decisions (primarily *Miller* v. *California*, 1973) also have essentially reversed the liberal interpretations of pornography achieved by earlier Court decisions by allowing local communities to decide what is pornographic (Zagel 1973:399–407). Some local prosecutors are again vigorously cracking down on movies, magazine stands, and distributors of materials judged obscene by local standards. While a majority of the people now think it acceptable to have pornography available to adults (but not to minors), 80 percent of them would oppose it if it could be proven harmful, and 33 percent would still oppose it even if proven harmless. A majority believe that widespread availability of erotica leads to a breakdown in morality (Commission on Obscenity and Pornography 1970:190–91).

Nevertheless, the old code of strict intramarital sexual fidelity, premarital chastity, and the double standard no longer hold their old sway. There have been significant changes in behavior and attitudes. The moral preference is still for heterosexual relationships within marital bonds, ideally with romantic affection. But this does not mean that all possible deviations from this are disapproved, because other types of sexual involvement are no longer strictly forbidden. The norms of individual choice in our society tolerate individual preference for a wider range of sexual behavior. Thus a distinction needs to be made between the moral ideal that prescribes what people should strive for, and the tolerance limits that proscribe what people should not do and should be condemned for doing. The changes that have taken place in American sexual standards appear to be a broadening of the tolerance limits allowing for a variety of sexual relationships.

Sexual Deviance

If this conclusion is valid, then the total range of sexual behavior which can be considered deviant has been narrowed and the strong stigma attached to certain forms of sexual deviance has lessened. There are a number of signs that a behavior is socially defined as deviant: the existence of laws and use of criminal sanctions against it; public stigmatization and devaluation even when the behavior is not specifically illegal; when one performs the behavior he meets with gossip, ridicule, withdrawal of friendship, and the possibility of loss of job or status; the existence of publicly or privately supported organizations and professionals whose job it is to deter, change, or deal with those believed to have engaged in the behavior; expressed sentiments of disapproval in public even when many may not disapprove in private; and other verbal and behavioral indicators of prevailing community sentiment. By these standards such behavior as premarital and extramarital relationships, especially if they do not involve large numbers of partners, are not considered seriously deviant by most in our society and by formal structures of control.

By one or more of these signs the following kinds of sexual behavior tend to be defined as deviant in American society: (1) heterosexual deviations such as prostitution, incest, promiscuity, and group orgies, violent or forcible sexual attack like rape; (2) adult homosexual deviation by both males and females; (3) excessive autoeroticism and sexual fetishism; (4) fetishistic-like behavior such as transvestism (cross-sex dressing) and voyeurism (peeping Tomism); (5) publicly visible sexual indecencies and improprieties such as public nudity, exhibitionism, and sexual intimacy in public; (6) pedophilia (child molestation), whether homosexual or heterosexual, violent or nonviolent; and (7) a range of "perversions" such as bestiality (human-animal contact) and necrophilia and sado-masochism (from sadism, inflicting pain; and masochism, receiving pain for sexual gratification).

Of course, these are not equally deviant. The strength of disapproval and the severity of sanctions are not uniform across all types of sexual deviance. The strongest disapproval is of those acts which inflict pain or use force on an unwilling victim (for example, forcible rape). Even when no violence is involved, sexual activity with an innocent party (for example, most child molestation) is abhorred. Disapproval is likely to be relatively mild if the sexual activity involves willing and consenting partners, especially if both participants are mature or adult. Acts committed in public are more strongly disapproved than those out of public view. Indeed, behavior that is unacceptable in private becomes more offensive if done in public, and that which is perfectly acceptable behind closed doors becomes deviant when performed in public (the acceptance of simulated and real coitus on stage and in film notwithstanding). Thus, those harmless sexual acts engaged in by consenting adults in private, though viewed as distasteful, are most likely to be tolerated.

Incest, child molestation, exhibitionism, voyeurism, and highly aggressive sexual assault are examples of relatively low-frequency offenses, and they tend to be committed by individuals without group support. Male and female homosexuality and prostitution are major forms of what might be called *subcultural* sexual deviance. Homosexuality and prostitution may be engaged in by loners, but both are typically implicated in a recognizable and continuing social system which serves to recruit, teach, and provide support and opportunities for the deviant practice. References are made to other types of sexual behavior, but in the following chapters we concentrate on homosexuality and prostitution.[2]

Summary

Sexual behavior is controlled in every society but there are wide differences in the way this control is exercised. Sexual standards and behavior in American society have undergone noticeable (some would say revolutionary) change. Sex is more openly discussed now than in the past. The portrayal of sex in the mass media has become more explicit. People have a more tolerant attitude toward a wider variety of sexual acts, and there is greater involvement in sexual behavior such as premarital intercourse, which was once considered seriously deviant.

---

[2]See Gagnon and Simon 1967:9–11 for a classification of sexual deviance which "generates specific forms of social structure." For an illustration of a sexual deviance (voyeurism) which usually occurs as an individual practice but which can sometimes become part of a group activity, see Feigelman 1968.

14

Learning Sexual Behavior: An Overview

Conditioning in Sexual Behavior

The Kinsey researchers long ago recognized the conditioning of sexual deviance in what they called the "psychologic factors in sexual response" (Kinsey et al. 1953:643–89). They noted that the physiological ability to be sexually aroused and obtain orgasm is inborn, but

> apart from these few inherent capacities, most other aspects of human sexual behavior appear to be the product of learning and condition-ing. . . . In its early sexual experience with other individuals, the child begins to learn something of the rewards and penalties which may be attached to socio-sexual activities.
>
> Even some of the most extremely variant types of human sexual behavior may need no more explanation than is provided by our understanding of the processes of learning and conditioning. . . . Flagellation, masochism, transvestism, and the wide variety of fetishes appear to be products of conditioning (Kinsey et al. 1953: 644–46).

A variety of stimuli, such as sights, smells, sounds, tastes, types of food and drink, clothing, and physical settings, may become associated with sexual arousal. The Kinsey researchers found that American males seemed more readily conditioned to these associated stimuli than females. Specifi-cally mentioned stimuli include observing sexual intercourse and the oppo-site sex, portrayal of nudes, erotic art, pictures, shows, grafitti, and hearing and telling dirty jokes (Kinsey et al. 1953:649–81).

The recent national Commission on Obscenity and Pornography (1970) presents a more up-to-date description and analysis of the amount, variety, and effects of use of sexually associated visual and auditory stimuli in Ameri-can society. The research reported by the commission found that American men still use "pornography" more often than women. They also begin perusal of erotic materials earlier in life than do women. But the research failed to find significant differences between male and female in the sexual arousal to erotic stimuli; both men and women find "pornography" sexually arousing (Commission 1970:210). Indeed, it seems that the great majority of men and women in the United States have viewed and read pornographic materials and begin doing so before they are adults.

Americans' Experience with "Pornography":
Excerpt from the Commission's Report

Approximately 85% of adult men and 70% of adult women in the U.S. have been exposed at sometime during their lives to depictions of explicit sexual material in either visual or textual form. Most of this exposure has apparently been voluntary, and pictorial and textual depictions are seen about equally often. Recent experience with erotic material is not as extensive as total experience, e.g., only about 40% of adult males and 26% of adult females report having seen pictorial depictions of sexual intercourse during the past two years.

Experience with explicit sexual materials varies according to the content of depictions; depictions of nudity with sex organs exposed and of heterosexual intercourse are most common; depictions of homosexual activities and oral sex are less common; and depictions of sadomasochistic sexual activity are least common in Americans' experience.

Experience with explicit sexual materials also varies according to the characteristics of the potential viewer. Men are more likely to be exposed to erotic materials than are women. Younger adults are more likely to be exposed than are older adults. People with more education are more likely to have experience with erotic materials. . . .

Although most males in our society have been exposed to explicit sexual materials at some time in their lives, a smaller proportion has had relatively extensive experience with erotica. From one-fifth to one-quarter of the male population in the U.S. has somewhat regular experience with sexual materials as explicit as depictions of heterosexual intercourse. . . .

First experience with explicit sexual materials usually occurs in adolescence for Americans. . . . Roughly 80% of boys and 79% of girls have seen visual depictions or read textual descriptions of sexual intercourse by the time they reach age 18. . . . More than half of boys have had some exposure to explicit sexual materials by age 15. Exposure on the part of girls lags behind that of boys by a year or two. . . .

Recent research casts doubt on the common belief that women are vastly less aroused by erotic stimuli than are men. The supposed lack of female response may well be due to social and cultural inhibitions against reporting such arousal and to the fact that erotic material is generally oriented to a male audience. When viewing erotic stimuli, more women report the physiological sensations that are associated with sexual arousal than directly report being sexually aroused (Commission on Obscenity and Pornography 1970:23–28).

The Kinsey researchers emphasize classical, or respondent, conditioning, whereby any stimulus can be made to elicit the same sexual reflex action by pairing it over time with the stimulus originally eliciting the response. But their references to choice behavior and to social conditions indicate that they recognize that sexual behavior is also voluntary action. As with breathing and blinking the eyes, the sexual response is both a reflex, or *respondent*, and an *operant*, or voluntary, response. Tumescence is a reflex which can be conditioned to respond to a range of sexual *objects*; at the same time, the tumescence can be voluntarily controlled, and the various *methods* and behavior which bring about sexual arousal and orgasm are operants capable of reinforcement.

Therefore, both respondent and operant conditioning are involved. The process is the same for conforming and deviant sexual behavior. The sexual response can come to be elicited by a variety of stimuli. It can also be operantly conditioned so that a variety of activities are rewarded by achieving sexual pleasure and/or social sanctions while other sexual activities are punished or not rewarded. If the past and present rewards attached to an individual's particular sex act offset both the punishment attached to it and the rewards and punishment attached to alternative behavior, then that is the one he is most likely to perform when a proper opportunity arises. The most important of the discriminative stimuli are the learned definitions of the act as something that the individual should do or that it is all right to do.

Evidence of conditioning in sexual behavior is found not only in the Kinsey and other studies observing sexual arousal to deliberately erotic materials, but in other areas as well. Clinical studies of deconditioning treatment for sexual deviance indicate that sexual preferences can be learned and unlearned (see the discussion of treatment of sexual deviance in chapter 17). There is also some experimental evidence of conditioning individuals to become sexually stimulated by objects to which they were formerly sexually neutral (Rachman 1966). But the evidence from conditioning treatment and experiments does not demonstrate how the behavior is acquired in natural settings. The process whereby some people learn to behave in sexually deviant ways while living in the same society in which most people conform to sexual norms is the subject of the following section.

Learning Conforming and Deviant Sexual Behavior in Society

Left completely alone, only physiological limits and chance availability would determine who and what the sources, objects, and methods of sexual arousal and behavior would be. But of course in human society sexuality is never "left alone"; it is always surrounded by sociocultural restrictions. Social sanctions provide rewards and punishments in addition or opposition to the reinforcement for sexual behavior that comes from sensual pleasure. Sexual behavior is always implicated in a social normative context which defines certain parts of it as undesirable and directs it beyond the purely physiological level.

Only some of all possible sexual stimuli are socially valued. Social control and conventional sex training are meant to ensure that the objects to which people learn to respond sexually and the methods of sexual gratification they learn to prefer are within socially acceptable limits. The culture provides differential availability of sexual stimuli and thus affects the frequency and probability which certain actions have of being sexually reinforced. Social rewards are set up for reaction to acceptable sexual objects and employment of approved methods, and social punishments are set up for disapproved sexual behavior.

Thus, if the sexual behavior is legitimate and approved, three conditions exist: (1) It is more likely to be suggested verbally and through imitation as a way of gaining sexual pleasure, and the probability that it will be reinforced physically is increased; (2) the reinforcement of intrinsic physiological pleasure is intensified by the addition of social reinforcement, and/or (3) there is less chance that the positive reinforcement will be offset by adverse social reaction. Through sexual training then the individual learns to try only acceptable outlets. If he is deliberately or accidentally exposed to disapproved sexual activities, he may be so inhibited (he has learned to define the acts as sinful, evil, or revolting) that he derives no pleasure at all, even though he might if the actions were not so taboo. Or a person may find certain things physiologically pleasurable but find his enjoyment diminished by self-reproach or the apprehension of negative social sanctions. The pleasure gained from legitimate sex would then be so much greater than that gained from illicit sex that the acceptable form would be reinforced over the deviant form. This conditioning starts very early and continues throughout life, although after a while habit sets in, and the individual tends not to experiment and change.

Social Learning in Gender
Identification and Sex-Role Behavior

The most significant way in which society attempts to direct sexual behavior is in the part of the socialization process that involves sex-role behavior. Being masculine in American society includes being attracted and
attractive to women; it is an approved and expected component of the male
role. Likewise, the conventional expectation of those playing the female
role is that they will be sexually attuned to men. This strong cultural definition of the place of sexuality in the male and female roles leads to the popular
stereotype of the homosexual as somehow "feminine" and the lesbian as
"masculine," and it is also related to the special contempt for the homosexual
who completely reverses roles (Davis 1966:340). The cultural definition of
man and woman and the sex-role socialization society sets up to perpetuate
it are very important in understanding sexual behavior. Therefore, we turn
to an examination of how individuals come to think of themselves and to
behave as male or female.

Although each species uses a characteristic system of mutual male-female
signals in courtship and mating (Tinbergen 1965), whether animals develop
typical or "abnormal" patterns of sociosexual behavior depends on the conditions under which they are raised. The higher the animals are on the phylo-
genetic scale, the more determinative these conditions become. For instance,
Harlow (1965) and Harlow and Harlow (1962) found that compared to group-
reared and feral monkeys, isolated, laboratory-raised male rhesus monkeys
fail to develop social and sexual patterns considered normal for their species.
If the instinctual basis of sex-related patterns is questionable in infrahuman
animals, it is certain that sex-typed behavior is even less biologically determined in humans. In fact, male and female are only minimally biologically
defined categories in human society; the overwhelming part of their content
is based on culturally defined social roles.

There is some evidence of a "biological substrate" for behavioral difference between the sexes, but it is a secondary determinant. The impact of
culture on sex-role behavior

> does not necessarily disprove the presence of diffuse biological
> forces influencing gender behavior; it may be that the effects of rear-
> ing overwhelm and therefore hide the weaker biological qualities,
> rather than that the latter do not exist (Stoller 1968:13).

Thus biological limitations do exist, but whether the person acts and identifies himself as male or female is primarily determined by the sex role to
which he is socially assigned (initially by parents, later by others) and which
he learns to play. The high correlation between behavioral patterns and biological sex is based on the fact that others use physical signs (secondary

sex characteristics and external genital appearance) to define and react to a person as male or female.

The importance of socialization is shown dramatically in cases in which parents raise children in contradiction to their biological makeup either because they wanted a boy and had a girl (or vice versa) or because the child had a confused sexual biology. With a set of such cases Hampson plainly shows the primacy of the sex-role assignment in determining "psychosexual orientation," defined as "all those things a person says or does to disclose himself or herself as having the status of boy or girl, man or woman" (1965: 113). This includes, but is not limited to, erotic attraction to an appropriate partner. All the cases in Hampson's study were patients of an endocrine clinic who were all ambisexual—hermaphrodites or pseudohermaphrodites who possessed one or more sexual incongruities. Nearly all had achieved gender-role behavioral patterns congruent with the sex to which they had been assigned, whether or not that sex role was consistent with the person's secondary sex characteristics, external genital appearance, or internal sexual organs. Those who changed their sex identity during or after adolescence did so because they learned definitions different from their parents'.[1] Hampson concludes that there is no neurophysiologic evidence for a male-female brain center and that

> . . . an individual's gender role and orientation . . . does not have an innate, preformed instinctive basis as some theorists have maintained. Instead the evidence supports the view that psychologic sex is undifferentiated at birth—a sexual neutrality one might say—and that the individual becomes psychologically differentiated as masculine or feminine in the course of the many experiences of growing up (1965:119).

Even if the individual is not completely sexually neutral at birth, the evidence is clear that any inborn gender predisposition is highly modifiable and even reversible (Homberg and Lunde 1966:15–18; Sears 1965).

Mischel (1966) shows how this sex-typed behavior is learned. The sex differentiation starts very early in life. Parents and others very early distinguish between and react differently to boys and girls. Through observation and imitation the child begins to behave as a girl or as a boy, but only behavior considered appropriate in a given situation for the gender to which others believe he belongs has a high probability of being rewarded. Behavior considered inappropriate for his sex is likely to be punished. Through this process of differential reinforcement the individual's behavior is shaped in the direction of masculinity or femininity. The person learns the standards

---

[1]Stoller (1968:14–15) reports a rare case in which an individual who had been reared as female continued to identify as male through the years. Physiological examinations at puberty showed him to be biologically male, the sex he had wanted to be all along.

or norms applicable to his or her sex, the opposite sex, and both sexes, and which patterns of behavior are likely to be rewarded in which situations.

Initial socialization and later social controls are effective enough to guarantee that the vast majority of the population is heterosexual and attuned to normal sexual stimuli. Most of us have been effectively isolated from homosexual and other deviant opportunities. We have experienced rewards for conforming sexuality and have experienced or anticipated punishment for homosexual inclinations. However, sexual socialization may be conducted in such a way and certain institutions may be so arranged as to enhance rather than restrict the chances that some people will learn sexual deviance.

Sexual socialization.   The kind of sex training given to children may lead to sexual deviance in two ways: (1) the parents and others who socialize children into sex-role behavior may provide direct reinforcement (wittingly or unwittingly) for deviant sexual behavior, or (2) more commonly, they may conduct the heterosexual socialization in such a way that the individual is ill prepared for normal sexual behavior and is made a likely candidate for deviant alternatives.

The first way is illustrated by some of the more extreme cases reported in the literature. For instance, Bandura and Walters report a number of cases of sexual deviance which seem to be "the result of parental encouragement and reinforcement of inappropriate sexual behavior" (1963:154). There is the case of the mother who through affection and verbal approval for her little boy's dressing up in female clothing, make-up, and jewelry (including her own) trained him directly in transvestism. There is also

the case of a thirteen-year-old boy whose mother had actively fostered voyeuristic behavior toward herself by sleeping with the boy, by being physically and verbally seductive, and at the same time appearing in the nude before him. When the patient was six years of age, the mother had shown him her vagina a number of times at the boy's request, but had responded with disapproval when he suggested intercourse and from that time had discontinued her physically seductive behavior. The boy's strongly established voyeuristic habit had generalized to persons other than the mother. . . . Generalization of strongly reinforced homosexual responses was apparent in the case of a sixteen-year-old girl whose mother had throughout the girl's lifetime encouraged mutual stroking of the breasts and other erotic play.

[In another case of a seventeen-year-old boy] his mother took showers with her son, enjoyed exhibiting herself to him and in looking at his nude body, and described her anatomical attributes to him in great detail and commented on his, while at the same time demonstrating affection to him during these interactions (Bandura and Walters 1963:154–55).

These are extreme cases but they show how some individuals may learn sexual deviance directly from parents and others who ordinarily provide conventional sex training.

When parents and other adults who are supposed to provide conventional sex education actually foster deviant sexual behavior it is not usually in the direct way illustrated by the cases above, however. Rather, this production of deviant sexuality through normal socialization channels tends to occur when the sex training is not adequate for the individual to learn proper sexual behavior, and the way is thus opened to deviant sexual outlets. Sex-appropriate behavior then may be learned poorly or incompletely. A woman can learn to behave mostly feminine but also "like a man." A man can be a "sissy." Similarly, how a person is supposed to behave sexually and who or what are appropriate sexual objects can be inadequately reinforced. Thus the individual can come to act as the opposite sex does toward members of his own sex. Sex-role training may be effective in the nonerotic phases and at the same time be ineffective in the erotic aspects — for example, the lesbian can behave as a woman in all respects save her choice of partner. How well the individual conforms to the role expectations depends on how effective the sex-role training has been and the availability of alternative training. Generally, parents and other socializing agents in society are quite effective in teaching boys to become masculine in such respects as aggressiveness and girls to be feminine in mannerisms and dependency (Mischel 1966:72–80; Bandura and Walters 1963). But as Gagnon (1967) cogently argues, it is precisely the area of eroticism in which conventional sex-role learning is most ambiguous and ineffective. General moral standards are effectively transmitted, but children are not taught specific guidelines, information, or behavior. Thus in this area perhaps more than in any other the child and adolescent must learn on his own and through the shared ignorance of his peers.

The net effect of much sex education conducted by reluctant parents and others may be to conceal and cover more than is revealed. Strict moral training often does no more than convey the message that sex is "dirty." Because most parents have learned to associate sexual behavior with opposite-sex relations, their warnings, scolding, and discussions may have the effect only of inhibiting the person toward the opposite sex. An individual reared in this way may find that he can establish comfortable and rewarding relationships only with those of his same sex. Strong inhibition toward the opposite sex reduces the probability of satisfactory heterosexual relations, and attraction to the same sex opens the way for same-sex sexual relations.

Another way in which sex-role expectations and training may be conducive to homosexuality or other sexual deviance is that the strong emphasis on being sexually attractive to the opposite sex may backfire. Success with and attractiveness for the opposite sex is so important for acceptability in society that the stakes for successfully playing the game become too high for some people.

Sexual attractiveness becomes a valuable good not to be bargained away easily. To some persons, therefore, heterosexual attachments may seem almost unobtainable, or obtainable at too high a price; by contrast, uncomplicated homosexual relations may seem to them to provide an escape from such involvements (Davis 1966:343).

This is an especially relevant observation for male homosexuality. The male role is culturally defined as being sexually aggressive — young adult males especially are assumed to be in a continual state of tumescence, sexual readiness, and adventuresomeness. Females are taught to be more sexually constrained. The game of trying to find and seduce a female may be too troublesome compared to the easy availability of other men who, because of their training as males, are more likely to be sexually active.

Sex-segregated institutions. Other institutional arrangements in society tend to set up conditions increasing the probability of significant homosexual behavior. The sexes are partially or totally segregated throughout the life cycle, but often the period of greatest segregation occurs during the adolescent period following puberty — the time in which much sexual learning takes place. The homosexual behavior occurring under the condition of living in an all-male or all-female society in prisons and other correctional institutions for delinquents and criminals is only an extreme instance of what can be expected from sex segregation for a relatively long period of time (Giallombardo 1966; Ward and Kassebaum 1965). The one-sex boarding or public school arrangement, formerly the dominant and still a widespread educational situation in England, and the same-sex prep schools and colleges in this country are also cases of relatively extreme sex segregation which historically have produced considerable homosexual behavior. In some societies with strict sex segregation, homosexuality is so commonplace that it has become institutionalized, acceptable behavior (Davenport 1965). There is of course still much sex segregation in American society.

We unwittingly facilitate the formation of homosexual habits and attachments. Boys are encouraged to be with boys and girls with girls, in rooming and sleeping together in dormitories, prisons, youth hostelries, [toilets, camps, and so on]. This is intended to reduce heterosexual violations, but it causes the control of homosexual offenses to rest heavily on internalized norms (Davis 1966:343).

Even when adolescent experience in sex-segregated institutions is not the occasion for first involvement in homosexual behavior, the one-sex environment provides a major setting for "coming out" as a self-identified homosexual. In one study, 29 percent of the admitted homosexuals in the sample came out in the military (the biggest category with 19 percent), YMCA, boarding school, a mental institution, or prison (the smallest category with 1 percent), or some other one-sex setting (Dank 1971). **The one-sex characteristics and peculiar relationships toward the opposite sex found in some occupations such as strip-tease are also conducive to homosexuality (McCaghy and Skipper 1969).**

Other group contexts.   In voyeurism, fetishism, exhibitionism, rape, child molestation, and similar individualized deviance, the person's behavior is sustained primarily by self-reinforcement. He does not enjoy conventional sex or has not evolved satisfying social relationships with those from whom he could learn to enjoy it, and his reward comes from the sexual gratification from the deviant act itself and from masturbation while imagining himself committing the act. He finds justifications in the general culture and does not learn them from participation in a subculture. The rapist may claim that his female victim enticed him; the child molester may excuse his behavior by saying he was drunk (McCaghy 1968).

Premarital and extramarital heterosexual behavior are not disapproved of very much, and for most probably involve the same reinforcement and lack of neutralization involved in totally conforming sex. The partner(s) is from the same pool of eligibles as the person to whom one is married or will be married, and the liaisons often are gratifying affectional as well as sexual relationships. But that particular individual must redefine the behavior as justified and worth the risk if he feels he is doing something wrong or wants to conceal his relationships from others. Justifications for such behavior are abundant in the general culture, but learning them may involve association with approving and supportive others. For instance, premarital sexual activity is easily justified, given the lack of a marital partner and the general acceptance of successful heterosexual performance, but in addition:

> The courtship [peer] group has special characteristics which promote acceptance of premarital coitus, e.g. high exposure to temptation via privacy; dancing and drinking; youth culture approval of adventure and hedonism; . . . [P]remarital coitus results, in one sense, because it has subgroup support from the courtship group (Reiss 1970:83–84).

The one involved in extramarital relations may feel no guilt at all or justify his acts on a number of familiar grounds (for example, his spouse has affairs already, he was drunk, his wife doesn't understand him, etc.). Most extramarital sex entails no more than an individual finding for himself that such liaisons are more pleasurable than sexual relationships within his own marriage, and applying this definition to his actions. But something like wife-swapping evolves from a halting discussion to rationalization by man and wife to contact with others. This is often accomplished through organizational publications and learning an elaborate set of rationalizations for the behavior (makes life more interesting, strengthens their own marriage, etc.). For those who continue, both spouses find the swapping activity not only sexually rewarding but also exciting, entertaining, and approved by their new friends (Stephenson 1973).

Movement into other kinds of sexual deviance obviously means contact with those already participating in them. These people then provide social approval and subcultures with positive and justifying definitions. The most frequently studied of these are homosexual behavior and prostitution. These are considered in detail in the next two chapters.

Summary

The evidence supports the contention that sexual deviance is learned behavior, just as conforming sexual behavior is learned behavior—it is conditioned through experience with sexual stimuli and partners. Society's control mechanisms work to make most of us heterosexual and otherwise conforming to sexual norms, but inappropriate socialization and institutional structures work against this in some cases. The sexual response then may become conditioned to deviant stimuli, and deviant sexual behavior becomes differentially reinforced over conforming behavior.

15

Homosexual Behavior

Definitions and Misconceptions
of Homosexuality

Homosexuality Is Behavior,
Not a Condition

No one is a homosexual if by that is meant a kind of person who is qualitatively different from a heterosexual. *Heterosexual* and *homosexual* are distinguishable social roles, but people are not inherently one or the other; there is no "third sex" comprised of homosexuals.[1] As used here *homosexuality* and *heterosexuality* are only elliptical terms referring to social roles and behavior in which one's sexual partner is of the same sex or opposite sex.

Homosexual behavior is physical contact between members of the same sex which has direct sexual significance.[2] That is, it is activity which leads to or is meant to lead to sexual orgasm. It also includes the related behavior of sexual foreplay and afterplay, enticement, and seduction, such as kissing, petting, carressing, embracing, and fondling, as well as more forcible or violent acts. In short, homosexual behavior includes all those post-pubescent acts between members of the same sex to which we attach sexual significance when they occur between male and female.

A number of things which are sometimes thought of as homosexuality are specifically *excluded* from this definition: (1) same-sex friendship attachments, however strong or emotional; (2) the direct physical contact that occurs between members of the same gender without sexual connotations—

---

[1] Even male and female are not entirely qualitatively distinct in a biological sense. The only sense in which one may legitimately speak of a third sex is with respect to those whose gender is biologically ambiguous (Hampson 1965).

[2] For others who define homosexuality similarly see Kinsey et al. 1948:612–17; Davis 1966:336; Cappon 1965:1–8; Gebhard 1971:256. For the clearest conception of homosexuality as a social role see McIntosh 1968:182.

the patting, holding, and other contact between men in joking and athletic contexts and the embracing, hand holding, and kissing by which women sometimes show nonsexual affection for one another; (3) display of mannerisms and actions or physical appearances defined as characteristics of the opposite sex—femininity in men or masculinity in women—except when these occur in the course of homosexual courtship and dating (Schur 1965: 69); (4) the exploratory sex play of prepubertal children;[3] (5) covert or latent tendencies toward erotic attraction to persons of the same sex. All these may play a part in the etiology of homosexuality, but they are not themselves homosexual.

Within this conception it is possible to distinguish among degrees of activity, intensity of emotional attachment, or commitment to a homosexual way of life. It is also possible to distinguish among varieties of homosexual expressions, roles, and settings. Whatever the variety, the differences between heterosexuality and homosexuality are best seen as quantitative gradations on a continuum from a sex life devoted exclusively to opposite-sex partners at one extreme and entirely to same-sex partners at the other extreme, with many variations in between.

This is the basic idea behind the well-known Kinsey Scale, which marks off seven points on the continuum to denote rough categories of relative heterosexual–homosexual preferences (Kinsey et al. 1948:638).

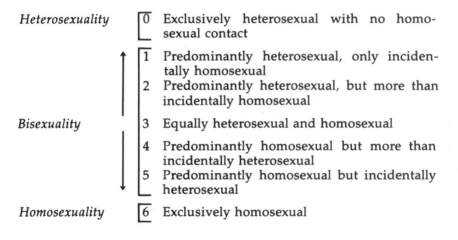

Heterosexuality	0	Exclusively heterosexual with no homosexual contact
	1	Predominantly heterosexual, only incidentally homosexual
	2	Predominantly heterosexual, but more than incidentally homosexual
Bisexuality	3	Equally heterosexual and homosexual
	4	Predominantly homosexual but more than incidentally heterosexual
	5	Predominantly homosexual but incidentally heterosexual
Homosexuality	6	Exclusively homosexual

This conception of homosexuality emphasizes that it is *behavior* which is to be explained, not some constitutional *condition* or pathology which underlies and is independent of behavior. Thus it is an essentially meaningless exercise to attempt to distinguish between the "true" homosexual and the

---

[3]This does not mean that prepubescent contact, heterosexual and homosexual, is always without sexual significance. We have known at least since Kinsey (1948:157–82; 1953:101–31) that even some infants can be sexually aroused and that a sizable minority of preadolescent children can be stimulated to orgasm. But regular sexual activity typically does not occur until puberty (Kinsey et al. 1948:219–20).

"pseudohomosexual," the person who is basically heterosexual but who happens for one reason or another to behave homosexually (McIntosh 1968: 182). A condition believed to be resident in some but not in others obviously cannot characterize those who are bisexual and cannot in any way explain degrees of heterosexuality and homosexuality.

Kinsey and his associates (1948:623; 1953:475) found that 37 percent of the white males and 13 percent of white females have at least one orgasm achieved homosexually somewhere between adolescence and age forty-five (rated between 1 and 6 on the Scale). Seventy-five percent of the men and ninety percent of the women in any given year will be exclusively heterosexual (rated 0 on the Scale). Ten percent of the men were rated more or less exclusively homosexual for a period of three or more years after age fifteen, but only four percent would rate 6 on the Scale throughout their active sexual life; two percent of the women would fall into this exclusively homosexual category. Kinsey's samples were selective and tended to overrepresent currently practicing homosexuals. His figures are strikingly similar to more recent and equally unrepresentative studies such as the survey taken among readers of *Psychology Today* magazine. In that research, 4 percent of the males and 1 percent of the females reported that all of their sexual outlet is and has been with same-sex partners; 37 percent of the men and 12 percent of the women reported at least one homosexual experience (Anthanasiou et al. 1970:50–51). Later studies of more representative samples of the general population, however, indicate that these figures are too high. In the only study of a representative sample of the national population reported so far, the proportion of females with any homosexual experiences was found to be about 13 percent, the figure Kinsey reported, but the proportion of men with at least one homosexual experience is 17 percent, not 37 percent as reported by Kinsey. Only 1, not 4, percent of the men are totally or mainly homosexual and .5 percent of the women, not 2 percent, are more or less exclusively homosexual (Hunt 1974:310–15).

Physiological and Psychiatric Explanations

Investigations designed to uncover congenital, neurological, biochemical, or chromosomal differences or abnormalities in homosexuality have failed. Studies have failed to reveal any consistent tendency for the twins of homosexuals also to be homosexual. Examinations of physical type, blood and urine samples, color blindness, taste threshold, and skin grafts have revealed no differences between the habitually homosexual person and the heterosexual person. Studies have found no connection between persons with deviant sexual physiognomy and homosexual desires or behavior. Persons with abnormal, ambiguous, or contradictory sexual makeup, internal sex structure, and secondary sex characteristics show no disproportionate tendency toward homosexuality. Attempts to detect some abnormality of the chromosomal structure in homosexuals have failed; homosexual males are just as likely as other men to have normal male patterns, and studies of men with an extra female chromatin have found them no more likely than others to be homosexual. No endocrinological differences between heterosexual and homosexual have been found; hormonal level and balance affect sex capacity but are unrelated to choice of sex partner (Cappon 1965:67–86; Kinsey et al. 1953:714–61; West 1967:44–48, 151–71; Hampson 1965; Schofield 1965:162–63).

There continue to be reports of research finding some chemical or other difference between exclusive homosexuals and heterosexuals. But because only subjects who have been exclusively homosexual for some time have been used in this research, the difference may be a result rather than a cause of homosexual behavior (*Newsweek*, April 26, 1971:54–55). Since sexual behavior has a physiological base and may be affected by physiological variations, it would seem reasonable to hypothesize that some of the variation would come out as behavior considered deviant by society. Possibly, some day a biochemical or other physiological factor will be found which differentiates the sexually conforming from the deviant. At this time, however, such a discovery has not been made.

Although psychoanalytic theorists are the first to point out the shortcomings of biological determinism, they still tend to hold that homosexuals as well as other sexual deviants suffer from some underlying pathological condition. Sexual deviance is viewed not just as behavior but as an expression of the person's whole psychosexual orientation or basic personality makeup. The behavior is not important, for it is merely a manifestation of an Oedipal or Electra complex, sexual immaturity, repressed guilt, fear of the opposite sex, narcissism, masochism, or one or more of a host of psychic disturbances and maladjustments. These are then traced back to some psychic trauma or to relationships with parents in early childhood. The judgment is that most, if not all, homosexuals are suffering from some form of neurotic disorder (see Cappon 1965; Oliver 1967; Caprio 1962). However, studies have produced contradictory and nonsupportive findings on such central contentions of the psychiatric explanation of sexual deviance as maladjustment, personality type, parental roles, and neuroses (West 1967:48–52, 172–215; Schofield 1965:122–28, 165–67; Schur 1965:73–74).

Comparisons of homosexual with general population samples have found no significant differences in self-acceptance, psychosomatic symptoms, or other psychological problems (Weinberg and Williams 1974:180, 202–3). The homosexual samples in these studies have come from the overt, committed segments of the homosexual community. They are not representative of all homosexuals and are more likely to include individuals who have adjusted well to their homosexuality. Other studies, however, have been unable to find a consistent homosexual psychological syndrome even when clinical and nonclinical populations of homosexuals are compared with matched control groups of heterosexuals (Riess et al. 1974). It may be that the average homosexual has greater emotional difficulty than the average heterosexual and that this preceded and caused his homosexual behavior; but at this time this has not been shown.

The "Latent Homosexual"?

Another common conceptual error is trying to define a category of "latent" homosexual—a practicing heterosexual who is "really" homosexual but who has yet to consummate a homosexual act. The notion *latent homosexual* may be true in the trite sense that everyone has the potential for sexual gratification by another of the same sex, just as everyone has the potential for heterosexuality. But the concept as used in the literature refers to latent inclinations, not potential. The latency does not necessarily refer to the tendency of someone to be consciously attracted to and erotically aroused by others of his sex without acting upon that attraction. Rather, it refers to the person who has unconscious homosexual desires of which even he is not aware.

This leads to a tricky diagnostic or research problem; if a person can be homosexual without behaving as one or can behave homosexually without being homosexual, how can it be determined that a case of homosexuality has been found? The error is compounded by using this unknown and unobservable condition of latency to explain other actions, such as other sexual deviance, attacking overt homosexuals, alcoholism, prostitution, and drug addiction (Oliver 1967:129–30; Caprio 1962:157–58; West 1967:216–18).

Learning Homosexual Behavior and Role

Our conception of homosexuality then is behavior which may become implicated in a social role, not a physiological or psychiatric condition. In the last chapter we presented some ways in which deviant sexual behavior can be learned directly from otherwise conventional adults, and we showed how deviant alternatives may be inadvertently fostered by ineffective socialization and sex segregation. We turn now to the social learning process involved in moving away from conforming sexual behavior toward a stable pattern of deviant sexuality within a subculture. Specifically, homosexuality can be seen to develop from occasional initial experiences to increased frequency of homosexual behavior to playing a full-fledged homosexual role in the homosexual subculture. Steele spells out the main features of this process:

> According to our theory the process of becoming a homosexual is based on a reinforcement pattern being established for a form of sexual response that is physiologically pleasurable. . . . As this pattern develops the person goes through several phases. . . . First

he is faced with the problem of rationalizing sexual behavior that he knows to be taboo in our society. Secondly, he begins to suspect that he may be different and he typically goes through a period of emotional conflict over this. Thirdly, he comes to the point where he realizes that he is homosexual and he must then attempt to adjust to this realization. The final phase for most homosexuals is exposure to the "gay" subculture and subsequent adjustment to their homosexuality (Steele 1967:9–10).[4]

Initial Homosexual Experiences

Homosexual behavior could result from exposure only to homosexual outlets, so that heterosexual behavior does not even have a chance for reinforcement, but this is not likely. The first homosexual experience may occur by chance; much preadolescent sex play is between boys or between girls, and the experience after puberty may take place in much the same unplanned way. On some occasions, although apparently not very often (Simon and Gagnon 1967a:255), the initial introduction to homosexuality is through "seduction" or tutelage by an older person, but typically it is with peers of about the same age. Many are made more receptive to deviant experiences by prior threatening experiences or learned inhibitions with regard to heterosexual relations, however.

Initial inhibitions toward homosexuality may be overcome by defining or redefining the behavior in ways that neutralize or play down its deviance. It may be rationalized as a "passing phase," "kid's stuff," not "really queer," or as otherwise unimportant to one's status as a heterosexual (Steele 1967). This neutralizing definition of homosexual behavior is facilitated for the male who voluntarily participates in homosexual contact as long as he is the "insertor" and not the "insertee" in homosexual action.[5] Such a definition may be maintained even beyond initial contacts. Illustrations of this kind of rationalization for the insertor role come from Reiss's (1964) study of lower-class teenage boys who make deliberate and self-conscious commercial contact with men whom they know are "queers"; Humphreys's (1970) study of "tearoom trade" — homosexual contacts in public men's restrooms — and Davis's (1970) study of homosexual rapes in a big city jail.

The peer subculture provides a rationale which permits the boys to remain integrated, straight members of the peer group even though as insertors they let homosexuals perform fellatio (genital-mouth contact) on them. The boy who acts as this sort of "trade" does not define himself and is not defined by his peers as homosexual as long as he does it for the money

---

[4] Steele's paper outlines somewhat different phases, but his emphasis is also on reinforcement and rationalizations.

[5] This terminology, *insertor–insertee*, is taken from Humphreys 1970, who refers to its use in earlier investigations.

alone, limits the contact to fellatio, and forms no emotional attachment to the queer (Reiss 1964).

The trades in the tearooms studied by Humphreys (1970) are also those who play the insertor part in the fellatio episode. Some of the trade are teenagers or young male "prostitutes" who demand payment from the insertee. But the typical trade is not an adolescent and does not expect payment. He is likely to be under 35, to come from a working-class background, and to be married and have children, and to maintain respectability in his community and neighborhood. His sexual relationships with his wife are minimally satisfactory and of relatively low frequency. He can continue to define himself as heterosexual and still occasionally stop off at the men's room in a nearby park on the way to or from work for a quick "blow job." But he does so only as the insertor.

> I find no indication that these men seek homosexual contact as such; rather they want a form of orgasm-producing action that is less lonely than masturbation and less involving than a love relationship. . . .
> . . . [He] may have learned this sexual game as a teen-age hustler, or else when serving in the army. . . . But to use one's own mouth as a substitute for the female organ, or even to express enjoyment of the action, is taboo in the trade code (Humphreys 1970: 115–16).

The man in the tearoom who plays the insertor role may or may not initiate the action, but he is not an "aggressor." The men who participate in forcible homosexual gang rapes in jails are clearly aggressors. The rapists in the jailhouse sexual assaults gang up and force their younger and weaker victims into sodomy (anal intercourse) with beatings and threats of violence. To the aggressors this kind of sexual behavior with another man does not constitute a homosexual slip from masculinity.[6] Indeed, in the one-sex society of jail it is one way of establishing dominance over others and asserting one's masculinity (Davis 1970).

> We were struck by the fact that the typical sexual aggressor does not consider himself to be a homosexual, or even to have engaged in homosexual acts. This seems to be based on his startlingly primitive view of sexual relationships, one that defines as male whichever partner is aggressive and as homosexual whichever partner is passive.

---

[6]The victim of homosexual rape is also likely to be straight and probably shares the insertor's definition of the insertee role as homosexual. But he is not faced with neutralizing this definition before engaging in such behavior; because he is forced into involuntary participation, neutralization is irrelevant.

It appears that need for sexual release is not the primary motive of a sexual aggressor. . . . A primary goal of the sexual aggressor, it is clear, is the conquest and degradation of his victim (Davis 1970: 122–23).

Subsequent Reinforcement and Rationalization of Homosexuality

If initial experiences, whether as insertor or insertee, are sexually rewarding, they are likely to be repeated. Homosexual behavior may also be reinforced through self-masturbation. Indeed, McGuire and his associates (1965) argue that the learning of deviant sexual behavior occurs "more commonly *after* the initial seduction or experience which plays its part only in supplying fantasy for later masturbation" (1965:195). Whatever materials, real or imagined, are used while masturbating will tend to become conditioned stimuli associated with and capable of arousing sexual pleasure. Subsequent masturbation increases the stimulus value of the homosexual sources, while arousal to conforming sources tends to disappear through lack of reinforcement.

Thus firsthand experience with deviant ways of gaining sexual pleasure offers vivid imagined stimuli for masturbatory purposes. What fantasy materials are used in conjunction with masturbation depend in part on the experiences one has had, and the masturbation in turn can reinforce inclination toward sexual arousal when the person is confronted with real situational stimuli similar to the imagined ones. The boy who has had a satisfying homosexual experience is more likely to think of other boys when masturbating, and if he does, masturbatory pleasure serves to condition him toward sexual excitation by other males. It therefore increases the probability that he will be sexually attracted to boys rather than girls.

These contentions are supported by a study of sexual offenders by Gebhard and associates (1965). Homosexuals, peepers, exhibitionists, transvestites, and fetishists all tended to intensify their sexual pleasure by masturbating while performing these deviant acts or while imagining themselves performing them. One sex act certainly reinforced by masturbation is masturbation itself. Although autoerotic and private, it is also socially acquired behavior. Self-discovery is not the only way one learns about masturbation; rather, observation of others, talking and reading, and being masturbated by someone else are all important sources of first learning of masturbation. A sex game of young adolescent boys is practicing masturbation in groups. For both nondeviants and sex offenders, fantasies while masturbating are akin to, but exaggerated beyond, actual experience. Significantly, the most important source of learning masturbation among homosexual offenders is being *masturbated by another male* (Gebhard et al. 1965:448–503).

Through both direct reinforcement and reinforcement through masturbatory imagery, then, the homosexual experience may be repeated. Each time that it results in positive outcomes, the probability of repeating it increases. Rewarded repetition and practice enhance the ability to attain pleasure from the homosexual acts of mutual masturbation, fellatio, and anal intercourse. Inhibitions toward homosexuality continue to decrease. Depending on how frequent and how pleasurable simultaneous heterosexual experiences are, each succeeding successful homosexual episode increases the probability of further homosexual involvement.

For many, initial and subsequent experiences involve both insertee (oral and anal) and insertor roles, and their further involvement in homosexual behavior will typically include the range of sexual acts. For the one whose initial contacts are only as "straight" trade—allowing another to fellate him but refusing to "go down" on someone else—continuation into homosexuality will often depend on his increasing willingness to play the insertee role. This change may occur at any time, but Humphreys found that when it occured among tearoom trade, it was apt to be due to the "aging crisis." The typical fellator in the tearoom is an older man, whereas the insertor tends to be younger and more physically attractive. As the participant in tearoom sex grows older he becomes less desirable as exclusively trade. If he continues such sexual encounters at all beyond his midthirties, then, he tends to play either the insertee or insertor, depending on the age and inclination of his partner (1970:108–11).

Along the way the individual learns new and more sophisticated definitions of his behavior, which help to further his homosexual development. The most common rationalization is some version of denial of responsibility: "I was born this way," "I can't help myself, this is just the way I am," "This is really me, why fight it?" He may come to see his behavior as not all that different from others or that "There is really nothing wrong with it, many others would do it if they had the chance." One notion of lesbians, for instance, is that most women secretly long for at least some homosexual experience, to have someone "do that little thing for them." These and other definitions may be part of a full-fledged homophile ideology. Parts of this ideology glorify homosexuality, defining it not as undesirable but unavoidable but rather as more noble and spiritual than the purely physical level at which heterosexuality is believed to operate. The emerging homosexual may pick up such definitions from scattered exposure to other homosexuals, but most likely he will acquire them through participation in the *homosexual subculture*.

Participation in the Homosexual Subculture[7]

There is a homosexual subcommunity in every sizable American city. Its characteristics vary somewhat from one city to the next, but its features

---

[7]This section on the homosexual community is based on Hooker 1967; 1956; Leznoff and Westley 1956; Simon and Gagnon 1967a; 1967b; see also Schur 1965:85–102; West 1967:107–14; Steele 1967; Helmer 1963; Dank 1971; Warren 1974; Weinberg and Williams 1974; 1975.

are uniform enough that it is possible to describe typical membership, location, structure, and operation. Many straight people have heard about, hold sterotypes of, and make jokes about the gay life. It is not surprising then that anyone who has had more than incidental homosexual experiences will sooner or later be confronted with the possibilities of participating in it. But he may not participate in it, or may participate either on the margin or at the core.

There are both lesbian and male homosexual societies. The male variety is the larger, more overt, and more active, but the two overlap somewhat, share a common deviant identity, and provide essentially the same functions for their members. But it is important to remember, as Simon and Gagnon point out, that there are differences in the lesbian and male homosexual subculture which reflect differences in conventional sex-role conditioning: the lesbian community is permeated with conventional femininity and the homosexual community is permeated with conventional masculinity. Other conventional differentiations and problems are also retained (Simon and Gagnon 1967a; 1967b).

The most visible and public locus of activity in the homosexual community is the gay bar. There are other meeting and rendezvous places such as beaches, parks, steam baths, certain streets or corners, theaters, gyms, and public toilets, but the drinking establishments are the hub of gay activities. Here friends are met, gossip is exchanged, invitations to parties are made, and the exercise of same-sex sociability generally takes place. Also, it is here that the most blatant and open displays of homosexual courtship and affection can be seen. Men are seen holding, embracing, and dancing with other men (and women with women). "Cruising" from bar to bar in search of "one-night stands" is probably the most common activity.

The gay bar is the likely place for the individual making his more or less public debut or "coming out," and for making the contacts and gaining the learning necessary for the homosexual way of life. Here he discovers

> large numbers of men who are physically attractive, personable, and "masculine" appearing so that his hesitancy in identifying himself as a homosexual is greatly reduced. . . . Once he has "come out," that is, identified himself as a homosexual to himself and to some others, the process of education proceeds with rapid pace. Eager and willing tutors—especially if he is young and attractive—teach him the special language, ways of recognizing vice-squad officers, varieties of sexual acts and social types. They also assist him in providing justifications for the homosexual way of life as legitimate and help to reduce his feeling of guilt by providing him with new norms of sexual behavior in which monogamous fidelity to the sexual partner is rare (Hooker 1967:179).

The gay bars are a common denominator and in some ways a defining feature of the gay world. But beyond this "overt" part of the subculture lies a less visible, or "secret," structure of private cliques of homosexual friends (Leznoff and Westley 1956). According to Hooker (1967), this is linked to the bar society by overlapping friendship networks and comprises three "layers" of organization. At the core are the close-knit groups of pairs, couples, and "marrieds." Then there are larger groups, some operating at the center but also at the periphery of the subculture, which are still relatively cohesive. Then there are still larger and looser networks of friends who meet only occasionally and who do not form cohesive groups. It is within these groups that more permanent relationships than those of the bar and street are sought and sometimes found. It is also within these groups that the "in" behavior of "camp" and "drag balls" (homosexual parties where men dress ostentatiously in female attire) take place.

In addition to these informally organized systems, there are formal homophile organizations, the first of which was formed right after World War II. The best known of the lesbian organizations is the Daughters of Bilitis, and the best-known male homophile organization is the Mattachine Society of New York (and One, Inc., formed as a result of a schism in Mattachine, devoted principally to publishing a magazine for homosexuals). There are now more than a thousand such organizations, but none is a national association. All together they can claim less than 1 percent of the homosexuals in America as members. These organizations have long been involved in political activity to promote legitimation of and reduce discrimination against homosexuals. The American civil rights movement has added emphasis to the relatively long-standing idea that homosexuals are an oppressed minority, discriminated against for something over which they have no more control than over skin color. This has become part of the homophile ideology supported by the organized groups. While many are content to be service organizations facilitating social and sexual contact among homosexuals, others are more militant and promote a "gay liberation" front (Sagarin 1969:79–110; Weinberg and Williams 1974; Humphreys 1972).

A sizable portion (but not all) of those who progress beyond the occasional and incidental stage of homosexual involvement will gain first-hand exposure to this subculture. The person who does become incorporated into it displays his homosexual behavior more visibly and runs a greater risk of job loss, alienation from friends and families, and police arrest. But substantial rewards offset these problems. In addition to a better organized set of justifications for his homosexuality, the homosexual community provides him with a ready sexual marketplace, social reinforcement, and group support for a deviant sexual activity. The gay world provides him with a supportive refuge in the realization that he is not alone. He can find a congenial atmosphere of acceptance where he can relax his "straight" front and become part of a network of friends with similar inclinations. As some say, "The only time I don't feel queer is when I am with other gay people." He learns patterns of interaction, the gay style, manners, and jargon which enable him to recognize other homosexuals and make rewarding social and sexual contacts with little risk of being repulsed or exposed.

Summary

Social and physiological reinforcement and rationalizing definitions are involved at each stage of development from initial homosexual contacts to participating in the homosexual subculture. The homosexual subculture offers strong social support and a homophile ideology for a stable homosexual role.

16

Prostitution

The oldest cliché in the world is none the more accurate for being old. Prostitution is not the oldest profession in the world — the priesthood is. It is true, of course, that some form of exchange of sexual favors for other rewards is a very old practice, and some form of the social status of prostitute has been known in nearly every society. The practice of "prostituting" oneself specifically for money has been around for a long time, but the more or less specialized and stigmatized role of earning a living from this is a relatively new development.

Activities of several different types have been called prostitution, and no special plea is made for restricting its use to one type. But the following seem acceptable definitions:

> [A] prostitute is an individual who will engage in sexual activity with strangers or other persons with whom the individual has no affectional relationship in exchange for money or other valuable materials that are given at or near the time of the act (Gebhard 1971:258).
>
> [Prostitution] can generally be defined as the granting of nonmarital sexual access, established by mutual agreement of the woman, her client, and/or employer, for remuneration which provides part or all of her livelihood (Winick and Kinsie 1971:13).

That is, as used here, *prostitution* refers to a specific type of economic transaction — not to the exchange of sexual intercourse for social rewards, affection, or popularity or to the several historical varieties of concubinage, sacred prostitution, and the like (Henriques 1963). Prostitution in contemporary American society is not a profession in a meaningful sense; rather, it is a low-level, semiskilled (but relatively high-paying) occupation in which one more or less regularly sells or is hired to provide a sexual service for monetary return (Bryan 1965:296; Winick and Kinsie 1971:29). In this chapter prostitution refers to female prostitutes; although there are also male prostitutes, we will not consider them in our discussion.

At the time of the 1948 Kinsey research, 69 percent of white males had had at least some experience with prostitutes sometime between the beginning of adolescence and old age, and about 15 to 20 percent visited prostitutes during any given year. About 20 percent reported frequent sexual relations with prostitutes and such relations accounted for some 40 percent of the total sexual outlet for men. Since the Kinsey studies, there has been a drop in the proportion of men whose first coital experience is with a prostitute and a reduction in the number of visits to prostitutes per man. In spite of the prostitute's oft-repeated claim that she services mainly married, middle-aged men and hence salvages bad marriages, younger single men are the most likely to visit prostitutes. However, the recent data show that even in this category, the percentages having intercourse with prostitutes have decreased; only about 25 percent of the men under thirty-five have ever had coitus with a prostitute, and only 3 percent of those under twenty-five have been with a prostitute in the past year. The highest proportion of males who have intercourse with prostitutes is found in the least educated population; those with college educations (both at the time of the Kinsey studies and now) are least likely to be prostitutes' customers (Kinsey 1948:351, 595–609; Winick and Kinsie 1971:165; Geis 1972:186; Hunt 1974: 144–45).

There are about 1,000,000 prostitutes in the United States; about half of these are more or less full-time and half are part-time. Together they entertain an average of about 300,000 clients each night (Winick and Kinsie 1971:14). Prostitutes tend less to work in brothels now (which reached their peak in the 1930s) and are more likely to be call girls or streetwalkers. Official and unofficial data indicate a decline in the average age of prostitutes, and there is evidence of a considerable amount of teenage prostitution ("baby pros"), some by girls as young as thirteen years old. Nonetheless, about 33 percent of the prostitutes are over the age of thirty and 5 percent of the active prostitutes are over fifty. Even though they have been glamorized in autobiographies and in magazines, prostitutes have been and remain mainly unattractive, overweight, and in poor health. They are recruited disproportionately from the poorly educated, lower-class, and minority groups (Winick and Kinsie 1971:29–92, 142–43; Gray 1973; Davis 1971).

Learning Prostitution

A number of questions could be raised about prostitution, including why prostitution exists at all (Davis 1966:355). However, our attention here focuses on the process of becoming a prostitute. Specifically, we examine the relevant sources and kinds of justifying definitions and reinforcement in the process of entering and practicing prostitution.

No one seems to have seriously advanced the idea that there is some biological cause that explains why some women become prostitutes, although Freudian and other psychiatric explanations of prostitution are as pervasive as those for homosexuality. Frigidity, Oedipal fixation, maternal rejection, latent homosexuality, dependent personality, and other psychiatric problems have all been offered as the underlying cause of prostitution (Jackman et al. 1963:151; Winick and Kinsie 1971: 81–85).

Economic and Social Reward

However, entry into and maintaining a prostitution career are not accounted for by explanations of "emotional problems." Rather they are better explained by the relative rewards of prostitution. It is not simply a matter of money because other social rewards may also influence the decision to go into prostitution.

> It was the attractiveness of certain things about prostitution that led the young girl into exploring possible entry into the life. . . . initial attraction for the girls in this study was social as well as material. Reasons such as being drawn to the "fast life," liking her pimp, seeing a "way to be somebody important" or becoming someone "to be admired" were as likely to be mentioned as the money or clothes. . . . Social rewards are recognized as readily as material rewards by the girls even prior to their entry into prostitution (Gray 1973:411).

Hence, sometimes very complex interpersonal relationships reinforce, both positively and negatively, a woman's entry into prostitution. The economic incentive in prostitution should not be discounted, however. Some form of economic reward is always involved; money is not the only positive reinforcer, but it is a necessary one. This may sound trite or overly simplistic, but the nature of the monetary incentive in prostitution is often misunderstood. The women need not be in dire or desperate economic straits; escape from poverty is only one way (and probably a relatively infrequent way) in which prostitution is economically inspired. Because the choice is not usually "prostitute or starve," some see the prostitutes' talk of money as rationalization simply as a cover for the emotional problems which are the "real" motivation. The choice is most often between a low-paying, "respectable" job and the relatively high economic rewards of prostituting.

> The work done by the woman before she became a prostitute tends to be fairly unskilled—domestic service, waitress, and so forth. The sectors of the entertainment industry which produce some prostitutes involve little status. Inadequate income is common in the immediate previous work background of prostitutes (Winick and Kinsie 1971:40).

The amount of money earned by prostitutes is easily and too often exaggerated, and the income of the typical prostitute is not really very high judged by conventional standards. Winick and Kinsie (1971:14) estimate the average annual income from prostitution in 1970 to be about $6,000 net. Nevertheless, some prostitutes have very high incomes and many keep seeking the fantastic fees they think some receive. The nearly complete loss of respectability that goes along with being a prostitute is, of course, punishing enough to deter most women from taking up prostitution. But for many, their social status is already low, and the loss of status is more than offset by the rewards of prostitution compared to other available economic opportunities (Davis 1966:361–62).

What the prostitute does with the money after earning it is another matter. The money will be used in exchange for other reinforcers — expensive clothes, paying for a drug habit, supporting a pimp, maintaining an apartment, and other things of value to her. Seldom is anything saved. The reinforcement comes from the lucrative payoff which allows her to buy these things, not from possible economic security. Saving enough to buy a legitimate business or to set herself or her man up in a respectable profession or to otherwise "get out of the game" is often thought and talked about, but its accomplishment remains the exception rather than the rule (Hirschi 1962).

To say that prostitution is economically rewarding is not to say that it is entered into in an economically rational way. Some prostitutes may one day have surveyed their economic situation and prospects, rationally calculated the probable gains from prostitution as compared to other reasonable opportunities, and finding the balance in favor of the former, set up shop in an apartment or started walking the streets. But even legitimate occupational choices are seldom made in this way. The starting points and the backgrounds of prostitutes are as diverse as the atrocity tales that each can tell (Hirschi 1962).

For some girls who become prostitutes at a young age there is not much of a time lag between their very first sexual experiences and their first acts of prostitution. Often there are practicing prostitutes in the family — sister, aunt, cousin, or sometimes even mother — who serve as models for the girls to imitate. They may have been incarcerated for a time in a delinquency institution and learn from other girls who had already done some prostituting (Hilton 1971). For others there may be a longer period of preliminary promiscuity during which prostitutionlike behavior is learned. The reinforcement for continuing this behavior becomes increasingly pecuniary, and the woman begins practicing prostitution regularly. Thus a girl stops sleeping around for dinner and consideration and starts doing it for money; the drug addict drifts toward it as one of the few ways she can consistently get enough money to support her habit; the habitually unfaithful wife may take it up after losing her husband and family. The middle-class housewife who does it part-time to supplement the family budget is probably mythical.

(For the variety of concrete ways in which the process is acted out see the biographies in Murtagh and Harris 1957; Young 1967; Adler 1953; anonymous 1960.)

Initial Contacts and Level of Entry

Although most women learn that men are willing to pay in one fashion or another for sexual relations, the specific prospect of becoming a prostitute for the gains to be had is usually not the solitary decision of the individual. She may make some preliminary forays and attempted solicitations, but entrance into prostitution on a regular basis nearly always involves someone else from whom the novice learns and who has a hand in persuading, suggesting, or (seemingly rarely) forcing the move. This may be an older sister, a friend, or a boyfriend, but the real helping hand into prostitution is someone already in it: the main contacts are practicing *prostitutes* and *pimps* (Bryan 1965:289–90; Young 1967:114–15).

The relationship between the pimp and his prostitute (or more usually his "stable" of prostitutes) at both the initial and later stages of prostitution is a complex one which will not be described in detail here. The pimp is not just a procuror, as popularly believed, although he may sometimes take part in securing customers. Rather, his relationship to the prostitute is a combination of leech, friend, lover, protector, teacher, business manager, boss, exploiter, and abuser. (For the best description see Murtagh and Harris 1957:105–68.) Madams figured prominently in earlier times, but with the decline of brothels (except in such places as Nevada) their role has diminished.

The world the prostitute enters is stratified: at the top (in terms of income and affluency of clientele) are the call girls who operate in their own apartments or in hotels, at the bottom are the streetwalkers, and in between are the remaining house girls and the bar girls. Within each of these types there is further stratification. There is some movement among these levels, mainly downward with advancing age, but the tendency is to practice at the level at which the prostitute first enters.

> The novice's [call girl] initial contact is someone at the level at which she will eventually enter the occupation; not a streetwalker but a call girl; not a pimp who manages girls out of a house of prostitution, but a pimp who manages call girls (Bryan 1965:289).

Apprenticeship

After entry there is a period, usually short, during which the prostitute becomes further socialized into the life of prostitution. This is often done under the explicit tutelage of the prostitute or pimp who was the initial contact. During this period the prostitute learns (1) the techniques of prostitution and (2) the positive definitions glorifying and the neutralizing definitions justifying her deviance.

Techniques.   The techniques needed to practice prostitution are not very complex. Beyond some instruction in simulation of enjoyment or how properly to "grunt and groan" (Young 1967:109) and how to perform fellatio, there is little in the way of learning specialized sexual techniques (Bryan 1965:293). The prostitute usually has learned the prerequisite sexual behavior before entering the occupation. Also, there seems to be only a limited and nonspecialized language to be learned (Maurer 1939). The techniques learned depend partly on the level at which the person enters prostitution. For instance, how to make optimal use of the telephone is vital for call girls (Bryan 1965:293) but is not a problem for streetwalkers and bar girls.

There is also a set of techniques for dealing with the others who, along with the prostitute, play the roles in the social organization of prostitution. She must learn how to relate to other prostitutes and to pimps, how to approach and solicit customers and how to satisfy them effectively, how to deal with "kinkies" or "freaks," how to recognize a detective from the vice squad, how to deal with cab drivers, bell hops, and other connections. These interpersonal techniques are important because on-the-job relationships provide the social reinforcement for continuing in prostitution.

Definitions and occupational ideology in prostitution.   The definitions available in the occupational culture and used by prostitutes are summarized by Hirschi (1962) into two main categories: the functions prostitution is believed to serve for society; and attacking the integrity, honesty, and goodness of the "squares" in society. These two categories correspond to (1) those definitions that place the deviance in a *positive* light and (2) those which *neutralize* the acknowledged social stigma attached to the behavior and which justify it.

Positive definitions of prostitution.   The positive verbalizations about prostitution attempt to identify it with conventional values. This is done in two ways. First, the financial success of prostitutes, the ability to buy expensive and fashionable clothes, and the wherewithal to engage in leisure activities are emphasized (Jackman et al. 1963:154–55). Second, prostitution is said to support the marriage and family institution and to provide an important social "safety valve" function for men who are inadequate in normal sexual relationships and for assorted sexual "nuts." It is believed to add to the stability of marriages by offering the variety a man cannot find with his wife, temporary "understanding" of the man in a troubled marriage, and help in achieving a better adjustment with his wife.

I could say that a prostitute has held more marriages together as a part of their profession than any divorce counselor (Bryan 1966:443). (See also Young 1967:131–32.)

The therapeutic values which prostitution is believed to provide for the lonely, the deformed, and others are illustrated by these quotes:

> If I have a hunchbacked client, I always keep my eyes on his face. . . . I can't look at his hump and I can't look away from him; he'd notice it at once and feel it (Young 1967:130).
> We girls see, like I guess you call them perverts of some sort, you know, little freaky people and if they didn't have girls to come to like us that are able to handle them and make it a nice thing there would be so many rapes. . . .
> I believe that there should be more prostitution . . . and then we wouldn't have so many of these perverted idiots, sex maniacs, all sorts of weird people running around (Bryan 1966:443).

This "it keeps the nuts away from our daughters" argument in favor of prostitution is also given by those who support legalization of prostitution and by citizens supporting prostitution in communities where prostitution is not only tolerated but forms an integral and important part of the local economy.

Neutralizing definitions of prostitution. Societal reproach may be neutralized by maintaining that prostitutes are just like other working women — they must support children, elderly parents, and others dependent on them in the only way they know how (Jackman et al. 1963:157–58). Most often neutralizing definitions take the form of "condemning the condemnors." The "upper world" is itself immoral and is not justified in derogating prostitutes. Prostitutes are really no worse than anyone else, for everyone has a "hustle" and is dishonest in some way. The difference is that the squares are hypocritical about it; at least prostitutes are honest about what they are doing. Sexual relations are seen as nearly always a form of prostitution: wives, girlfriends, and other women really practice prostitution, they just do not call it that.

> Little chippies in bars give it away for a couple of beers (Jackman et al. 1963:153).
> Ask me, the only difference between me and some of these wives is that they don't keep the bargain and I do (Young 1967:132).
> Actually all women are whores in my opinion whether they get married for it or whatever it is. There are just different ways of being a whore (Bryan 1966:444).

It's a good deal for the guy and it's a good deal for me. People lie to each other and use each other all over the country, everyday. At least what I do is honest and it doesn't harm anyone (Winick and Kinsie 1971:50).

Men, particularly the "johns," or customers, are defined as exploiting, deceitful, and out to get what they can. The subterfuge used by the prostitute to get what she can out of the man is therefore justified (Bryan 1965:291).

Men are . . . shrimps. Show me the man that's worth killing and I'll do the job (Jackman et al. 1963:153).

Although it is fairly clear that an occupational ideology something like that just described exists, is learned by, and can be verbalized readily by prostitutes, it is not clear how it plays a role in the process of becoming and remaining a prostitute. It is part of the prostitute subculture, but there is considerable variation in the extent to which prostitutes are exposed to it, and it appears that after a while most do not subscribe to it privately (Bryan 1966). It is probably the case that the ideology helps to overcome societal reproach and individual misgivings of prostitution in the beginning, when the woman first enters and is learning prostitution. After she gets into it, the economic rewards, the lessened alternatives, fear of her pimp, and the network of interpersonal relationships are more than enough to sustain her behavior, even after she no longer believes the ideology.

While the professional ideology is learned and perhaps serves a function during this apprenticeship period, it is doubtful that it remains of equal importance throughout the call girl's career. . . . Once entrance into prostitution has been accomplished, there are many reasons to reject such beliefs (Bryan 1966:448).

Summary

A major source of reinforcement for prostitution is economic reward. But the network of relationships the prostitute builds up with other prostitutes, pimps, and others offers additional social reinforcement and provides tutelage in the techniques and definitions favorable to participation in prostitution.

17
Control and Treatment
of Sexual Deviance

The Law and Sexual Deviance

The laws regulating sexual behavior, with the exception of those prohibiting sexual violence and sexual relations between adult and child, serve primarily symbolic rather than instrumental functions. That is, strict enforcement of them to curb behavior is secondary to their importance as a symbolic statement of a public moral stance against that behavior (Gusfield 1967). Legal prohibitions against homosexuality and prostitution in particular tend to be largely symbolic. The language of the laws is filled with nonspecific references to unnatural fornication, cohabitation, sodomy, crimes against nature, and so on. Penalties for homosexuality are relatively severe and penalties for prostitution relatively light. But except for periodic cleanups, the laws are not stringently enforced. Indeed, sex laws in general are among the least enforced of all statutes. There is probably a good deal of public tolerance of prostitution and homosexuality, but lack of enforcement results from other factors as well. Sexual behavior, both deviant and conforming, is mainly performed in private, and is unreported and undetectable. Sometimes, as with rape victims, the victims are reluctant to press charges because there is often as much stigma attached to the victim as to the perpetrator. Finally, many of the sex offenses are crimes without victims. These simply do not involve innocent and injured victims who are willing to press for justice. Therefore, enforcement depends largely on police surveillance and practices that border on entrapment. They turn out not to be very effective.

In addition to legal sanctions, sexual deviants also face the possibility of informal punitive reaction. The convicted rapist, especially one who has inflicted severe injury on his victim, is scorned by those who know of his offense. The person convicted of child molestation, incest, or another offense with a child victim meets with contempt of his neighbors and family and, if imprisoned, is also subjected to cruelty by his fellow prisoners. The homosexual may be dishonorably discharged from the military, victimized through blackmail, beatings, robbery, may lose his job, and is the subject of ridicule and jokes (Geis 1972:29–34; Williams and Weinberg 1970). But for many sexual deviants, these negative sanctions remain more threat than actual experience. In one study of homosexuals, 75 percent of them had never been arrested, 83 percent had not lost any job and most had not encountered any major problems in informal social interaction due to their sexual preferences (Weinberg and Williams 1974:140).

When the law forbids acts against identifiable victims as in sexual violence, there is little disagreement that the law is performing its proper function. However, there is a continuing controversy over whether consensual unions in private by adults are any business of the law (Geis 1972). Many who personally disapprove of such behavior still feel that it is a matter of personal choice and should not be governed by public morality: The law should not force one conception of morality over another. It is clear that laws which create sexual crimes without victims (Schur 1965) incorporate the more conservative standards of sexual morality and that repeal or liberalization of these laws is seen as a weak stand on public morality and is tantamount to approving of the behavior itself. When a group attempts to change the law, a number of interests surface and affect the outcome. An illustration of the diversity of political interests that vie with each other at various stages in the formulation and execution of sex laws comes from Roby's (1969) case study of the revisions and enforcement of the New York state law on prostitution.

After four years of study a Code Commission, specially appointed to study and recommend changes in the New York penal code on prostitution, proposed a revision which, among other things, reduced the maximum sentence for prostitution from three years to fifteen days. Later, in response to some individuals and a representative of an organized group who came forward at a public hearing, the bill was changed to include "patronizing a prostitute" as a violation and was passed into law. After passage of the law the police in New York City began making fewer arrests of prostitutes and stopped having policemen prosecute prostitutes in court. This was followed by a supposed "invasion" of prostitutes into New York. A number of groups — politicians, City Hall, downtown businessmen, and the Hotel Association — began to complain about prostitutes in Times Square and pressured the police to clean up the area. When the police did this, by arresting alleged prostitutes by hundreds on charges of loitering and disorderly conduct, the Civil Liberties Union, Legal Aid Society, and some judges publicly opposed the round-up as consisting of unconstitutional arrests. When the district attorney refused to prosecute most of those arrested, the police began pressuring his office to prosecute. Although the district attorney's office responded with taking more cases to court, the judge dismissed them as illegal arrests. A few were taken in, but patrons of prostitutes were largely ignored. Both the police and a special mayor's committee filed legislative amendments

to reclassify prostitution back to higher maximum penalties, but the bill died
in committee.

Thus in addition to the Code Commission itself, the groups which
became involved at one point or another included a "social health" association, a hotel association, city politicians, the police department, judges, the
Civil Liberties Union, the Legal Aid Society, the district attorney's office,
and a mayor's committee. Roby concludes:

> Throughout the development of the New York State Penal Law,
> Section 230, numerous interest groups and individuals worked dili-
> gently in an effort to have the law written or enforced in the manner
> they desired. . . .
> . . . During the five stages in the formulation and enforcement
> of the Penal Law concerning prostitution, power shifted from first
> one interested group to another (1969:103, 108).

This is a case where in spite of the recognition of the widespread violation and nonenforcement of the laws, any attempt to revise them has usually
met with resistance. This resistance has usually been successful: Organized
proposals for revising the criminal codes on sexual behavior have existed
for at least twenty years, and as yet there has been little liberalization in the
statutes (although there has been liberalization in police and court action).
Only three states have legalized homosexual behavior between consenting
adults in private and only in Nevada (and then only by specific local ordi-
nances meeting certain specifications) may houses of prostitution legally
operate. A 1971 poll in California found more support than opposition to a
proposal to legalize prostitution and there are liberal model penal codes on
homosexual behavior and prostitution being considered in several states.
Therefore, some changes may be forthcoming (Geis 1972:45–46; Winick and
Kinsie 1971:187–214). There are organized pressure groups, organizations
of deviants, civil liberties groups, feminist groups, and others. They have
increasing political power and are active in promoting liberalization of the
laws on prostitution, homosexuality, and pornography. The existence and
activity of these groups, too, indicate some change in the law is coming. But
as yet, they have not very often been able to prevail over the conservative
pressure groups that want the laws to stay the same or become still more
strict (Quinney 1970:89–90; Zurcher et al. 1971).

Is the Sexual Deviant Sick?

A key part of the controversy over legal changes has to do with decrimi-
nalizing private, consensual adult sexual behavior. Much of the argument has
revolved around whether sexual deviants are evil, depraved people who
threaten public morality or simply misguided, sick people who deserve

help, not condemnation, by the law. As we have seen in the previous chapter, traditional psychiatric theory holds that sexual deviants are people who are in some degree sick or mentally ill; usually neurotic rather than psychotic, but ill nonetheless.

> It is generally agreed that most sexual deviates present psychological or psychiatric problems of one type or another. . . . [S]exual deviation represents a symptom rather than a cause of underlying emotional difficulties and usually represents an outlet or relief from tensions (Oliver 1967:46–47).

This theory has been applied to rapists, child molesters, prostitutes, exhibitionists, and other sexual deviants, but especially homosexuals. This theory is based mainly on the cases of sexual deviants who are already seeing psychiatrists. There is little valid evidence supporting it.

In recent years the view of the deviant as sick has come under increasing attack. Homosexuals, particularly those who are leaders or members of homophile organizations, have voiced the strongest opposition to the idea that they are sick. Some social scientists and even some psychiatrists have come to reject the sick concept of homosexuality. Indeed in late 1973 the trustees of the American Psychiatric Association voted to change the classification of homosexuality in the standard diagnostic manual from a "mental disorder" to merely a "sexual orientation disturbance." The rejection of the illness concept in homosexuality has come about primarily on ideological grounds, however, not on scientific grounds that the theory is simply wrong.

It is understandable that objections to the sickness label are often not scientifically based. After all, it is stigmatizing to homosexuals to be called sick in this sense. While they might prefer being considered sick to being considered evil, some feel that the sickness label means society wants to have an excuse to attempt to *force* homosexuals to change. Recall from chapter 15 that part of the homophile ideology is that homosexuals simply *are:* They cannot change themselves or be changed by others. They argue that they should be viewed as exactly the same as racial minorities: If discrimination against racial minorities is wrong then discrimination against homosexuals is wrong. If homosexuals were to admit that they are sick, then, by implication they can be cured or changed—this is the very concept they deny. To support their campaign for acceptability, they must persuade others that their sexual orientation should be seen as simply an alternative lifestyle to heterosexuality. Their view is that if they do have any problem at all, it is because they are the objects of harassment of a hostile society; whatever psychological problems they have will disappear as soon as there is greater acceptance by society. Therefore, homosexuality is neither a cause nor an effect of emotional difficulties (Sagarin 1969:98–108).

Thus, it seems that the sickness concept is rejected because denying that homosexuals are sick is a liberal or radical position to take. Indeed, much of the recent literature on homosexuality adds little to the scientific question of whether or not the psychiatric theory is valid. Rather it tends to consist of denunciation of the psychiatric theorists—the "bad guys"—by the "good guys" (liberals and radicals), who hold that homosexuals differ from other people only in that they pursue a persecuted lifestyle. (See Sagarin 1973 for a review of several books which illustrate the "good guy" vs. "bad guy" nonscientific controversy quite clearly.) Some are so anxious to show that they are liberal in this regard that they sometimes take extreme positions or ignore their own evidence. For instance, an extreme position is taken by one psychiatrist who disagrees with many of his colleagues. He not only argues that *all* homosexuals are well adjusted and normal but that anybody who believes otherwise is himself sick, suffering from the invented disease of "homophobia" (Weinberg 1972). One study on the "sociology of homosexual liberation" is primarily a song in praise of homophile organizations and an almost total acceptance of their viewpoint (Humphreys 1972). The authors of another study show that homosexuals in more tolerant European countries have as much trouble from psychological problems as do homosexuals in American society, which is supposedly repressive of homosexuals. And even though the psychological problems thus cannot be attributed to a rejecting society, the authors ignore their own data and conclude that homosexuals should receive "positive support" and acceptance by society and that will alleviate the psychological problems they have from rejection. The authors say that we should accept the homophile organizations' contention that homosexuals are the same as other minority groups—that this is the first step in the right direction (Weinberg and Williams 1974).

This position taken by the homophile organizations and some social scientists contains some internal inconsistencies and leaves them in an untenable position. The basis for the position, as we have discussed, is that homosexuality is an inherent condition in some individuals. Therefore, it is as useless to try to change homosexuality as it would be to try to change skin color. To be in this category, the homosexual condition would have to be inborn and result from genes as specific and identifiable as those for skin and hair color. As noted earlier, there is no evidence of genetically determined homosexuality. But, if it is found that the condition is physiologically inherited or is a biochemical or neurological abnormality not found in "normal" people, then it is by definition a sickness—a physical sickness. Physical sickness of course can be treated and there is often a possibility of cure. Further, if homosexuality is a condition over which there is no control, how can it be a freely chosen alternative lifestyle at the same time?

One may reject the sickness concept without holding that it is the result of an unchangeable condition and becoming entangled in these inconsistencies. The more tenable conception is that there is:

> no such thing as a homosexual. . . . What exists are people with erotic desires for their own sex, or who engage in sexual activities with same-sex others, or both. The desires constitute feeling, the acts constitute doing, but neither is being. Emotions and actions are fluid and dynamic, learnable and unlearnable . . . [They] are constantly in a state of change, flux, development, and becoming. . . . (Sagarin 1973:10).

Research on bisexuality indicates that individuals are, in fact, capable of moving back and forth among homosexual, heterosexual, and bisexual behavior and identities in a manner that argues against the immutability of sexual orientations (Blumstein and Schwartz 1976a; 1976b).

Conceiving of homosexuality as simply *behavior* also opens the door directly to the issue of decriminalization of consensual sexual acts. In this light, it can stand on its own merits rather than on whether or not homosexuals are a minority oppressed for a condition they cannot change or whether or not they are sick. For purposes of the law, it really matters little if the homosexual is sick and curable or if he is not. The question is, *does the state have the right to intervene coercively through the criminal law in support of one side or the other on a moral issue such as sexual preference when the behavior in question does no demonstrable harm to others?* In this sense, then, the question of the psychological adjustment or maladjustment of the homosexual is:

> . . . itself out-of-order . . . ill or otherwise . . . homosexuals are making an adaptation of choice. Society may choose to persuade the homosexual to change. . . . [T]he homosexual [may] elect to accept the invitation. . . . But it seems clear that if the homosexual decides not to change his orientation it cannot be insisted, by the use of forceful coercion, that it is to his own best interest to do so. For one thing, such a viewpoint is not necessarily . . . true; for another, it is unjust (Geis 1972:28–29).

Treatment of Sexual Deviance

It is clear that attaching criminal sanctions to homosexual behavior or other sexual deviance has little ability to make the person stop his actions. Whatever the therapy, there is little prospect for change after forced treatment (Freund 1960). But what if the homosexual or other sexual deviant accepts the invitation to change? Are there successful treatment strategies for him? The answer is a qualified yes. If the person is highly motivated to change, has not persisted in his deviant sexual pattern for many years, has conforming alternatives available to him, and can be insulated for a time from the circumstances which produced his deviancy in the first place, then the chances are good that he can change his behavior.

One usual treatment for the sexual deviant is some form or another of traditional psychotherapy: Over several months or years, the person talks to a psychiatrist, who can then interpret the deeper meaning of the deviant's problem. Confronted with the real unconscious motivation for his deviancy, the patient ideally can then deal with it rationally, resolve his difficulties, and stop the behavior (Oliver 1967:223–24). Some have argued that this procedure is the best treatment for homosexuality and claim high cure rates (Cappon 1965:250–65), but the evidence generally does not support traditional talk therapies as being successful in treating sexual deviance (West 1967:230–46; Schofield 1965:166–68; Freund 1960:312–15).

Some form or another of behavior modification in deconditioning sexual deviance seems to offer better success. One common technique is *aversive conditioning* (Rachman and Teasdale 1970).

One of the first cases of successful application of aversion therapy to homosexuality typifies this approach (James 1964). A homosexual male rated 6 on the Kinsey Scale came for treatment and was placed in a dark room and given apomorphine and brandy to produce nausea. When the sickness set in, a light illuminated pictures of nude men, and the man was told to imagine and relive his homosexual experiences. A tape recording every two hours during the nausea period explained his homosexuality and traced its development and its adverse effect on his life. The tape ended with such words as "sickening," "horrible," and "stupid" and finally with the sound of someone vomiting. This therapy was continued for thirty hours, followed by a day's rest, and then another thirty-two-hour session. The idea, of course, was to make the homosexual stimuli and thoughts become associated with the sick, unpleasant feeling produced by the emetic drugs. The man was encouraged to seek heterosexual relations. A follow-up nine months later found that he had not returned to homosexual relations but had been dating women, successfully achieving heterosexual intercourse, and generally improving his social relationships (James and Early 1963).

This therapy has been used a number of times with some, but far short of perfect, success. It is a strenuous and taxing treatment that can, in fact, be dangerous. There is at least one case of a homosexual who died of a heart attack while undergoing such treatment (West 1967:258). Because of the physical strain involved in the use of nauseating chemicals, subsequent therapies have begun to rely more on mild electric shock as the punishing stimulus. But although this variation has had more success than has chemical aversion, serious ethical problems remain with this style of treatment (Rachman and Teasdale 1970:24–28, 153–63; Bandura 1969:551–52).

The success of such treatment also depends on the person's motivation to change, the availability of heterosexual alternatives, how long and to what degree he has been homosexual, and other variables outside the treatment setting. In an English study of twenty homosexuals who were made by enforcement authorities to undergo such aversive conditioning, only three showed any change from homosexuality afterwards, and those three did so for only a short time. But of the group of thirty-one male homosexuals in the same study who volunteered for treatment, only twelve showed no improvement and eleven achieved long-lasting (more than three years) aversion to homosexuality (Freund 1960).

Merely increasing a person's aversion to homosexuality does not necessarily mean that he will turn to heterosexual outlets. Not only is the homosexual attracted to same-sex partners, he is also *not* attracted to opposite-sex partners; indeed, he may have a distaste for heterosexuality. Reducing his homosexual attractions while leaving his heterosexual inhibitions might only result in making him completely sexually inhibited. Thus, after reducing his homosexual inclinations it may be necessary to overcome the negative reactions he has been conditioned to make to the opposite sex (Gold and Neufeld 1965; Stevenson and Wolpe 1960). The most effective way of changing behavior from homosexual to heterosexual patterns has been to combine aversive conditioning with positive reinforcement for heterosexual behavior (Ramsay and Van Velzen 1968; Thorpe et al. 1964; Herman et al. 1974).

Another approach to therapy which holds some promise for particular kinds of sexual deviance is that used in the treatment of homosexual pedophiliacs at the Atascadero Hospital in California. Rather than attempt to modify behavior toward heterosexual partners, the aim is to redirect the homosexual preference away from children and toward other adult homosexuals. This pilot behavior modification project, which as yet has no follow-up evaluation, utilizes both modeling and direct reinforcement but not aversive conditioning. Volunteers from the local gay community participate as role models, role-playing homosexual interaction in a simulated gay bar setting. The patients and the staff observed these simulations and identified specific target behavior needed to relate socially to adult homosexuals. Videotapes allow the patients to see themselves in that setting and to model the behavior of the volunteers more accurately. They are then directly rewarded with praise and privileges for practicing the appropriate behavior (Serber and Keith 1974).

Whatever the particular behavior modification technique, humans, unlike animals, can recognize the difference between the unnatural conditions in the treatment environment and what happens to them in real life. Whatever changes are produced by the therapy may not last outside of that setting and the "patients would revert to homosexuality without the concomitant [therapy-induced] shock" (Sagarin 1973:6). Success in the treatment setting will produce lasting results only if conditions after treatment sustain them. The treatment may be to no avail if the person has no available conventional heterosexual alternatives. Also, what happens in the relatively artificial therapeutic setting may not be strong enough to overcome years of reinforcement for homosexuality or lasting enough to withstand the sexual enticement and social reinforcement of homosexual friends if they are rejoined. For these reasons all the studies have found the best prospects for therapy are relatively young bisexual persons or young homosexuals who are married to women — those who have not established strong ties in the homosexual community.[1]

Behavior modification techniques have also been used successfully with exhibitionism, sexual impotence, transvestism, fetishism, and child molestation.[2] Not all of those treated have been volunteers — some have been incarcerated offenders. The ethical problems encountered here are more severe than in the free community. The ethical problems can be resolved if behavior modification treatment is used only with patients who freely and voluntarily elect to undergo it, with full knowledge of the nature of what they are undertaking. But within the confines of a coercive environment, the degree of voluntariness is open to serious question. Therefore, even though behavior modification can be successful with even repeat offenders, particularly when combined with procedures like group therapy, the ethical problems demand that such intervention in a closed institution be minimal and done on as voluntary a basis as possible — for example, not tying release to participation in the treatment program (Wolfe and Marino 1975). Besides the ethical issue, in order to be successful, conducting treatment among inmates incarcerated for sex offenses has to surmount important obstacles: If the treatment environment itself causes problems, it does not improve when embedded in a highly restrictive and unusual environment like prison.

> Expecting a man with sexual problems to benefit from an environment deprived of any but abnormal sexual stimulation is logically absurd. In this setting his only practical and regular sexual outlet is masturbation which, paired with aberrant fantasies, are what we theorize led to the behavior in the first place (Wolfe and Marino 1975:83).

Prostitution is viewed typically as a law enforcement problem and there has been very little done in the way of offering treatment for prostitutes who want to change. The usual traditional psychotherapy has been used, but is not applicable for most prostitutes. Rehabilitative programs offered by social agencies and private groups have included halfway houses, group sessions, and vocational counseling, but these have been sporadic and not very carefully done. Also, sound judgment of their success is not really possible because of the lack of data on outcome of the programs (Winick and Kinsie 1971:75–85). It seems that behavior modification techniques have not been used with prostitutes.

---

[1] For other illustrations of behavior modification with homosexuals see Feldman and Mac-Culloch 1964;1965; Solyom and Miller 1965; McConaghy 1971; West 1967:256–60; Rachman and Teasdale 1970:39–71; Bandura 1969:335–38; Barlow and Agras 1973.

[2] See Blakemore 1964; Blakemore et al. 1963; Bond and Hutchinson 1964; Glynn and Harper 1964; Kushner 1965; Lazarus 1965; Raymond 1960; Wolfe and Marino 1975.

Achievement of change in sexual behavior ultimately depends upon the willingness of the one who is troubled by his own sexual tendencies to seek out help and to establish relationships which will sustain him in integrating into his daily life the conforming sexual activities with which he is comfortable. The various behavior modification techniques have been more effective than the talk therapy of psychoanalytic practice. They will become even more successful when they recognize the impact of the conditioning variables operating in the person's larger social environment.

Summary

Laws regarding sexual behavior, except violent sex or sexual advances toward innocent partners, serve mainly symbolic functions. They are unenforced or underenforced. Changes in them are slow and have met with pressure-group resistance. The extent to which the law should try to regulate sexual behavior has been confused by the debate over whether or not sexual deviants are sick and whether or not they should be viewed in the same light as racial minorities. From a behavioral perspective, the sexual deviant is not sick, but if he wants, his behavior may be changed by appropriate treatment techniques.

Part Five

Some Types of Criminal Behavior

18

White-Collar Crime: Crime in Business, Occupations, and Professions

In this chapter we examine one type of crime, white-collar crime; professional crime, organized crime, and violent and "compulsive" crimes are examined in the next three chapters. These do not represent the entire range that would be included in a comprehensive typology of crime, but they do represent different enough types so that showing how social learning theory applies to them should lend support to the contention that the theory is applicable to all types of crime. Also, other topics usually a part of general discussion of crime are not broached here.[1]

As with the previous discussions, the emphasis in this and the following chapters on crime is on describing and explaining the behavior. But one illustration of how power and group conflict contribute to the legal definitions themselves is given. (See pages 235–36.)

Definition, Types, and Extent of White-Collar Crime

The term *white-collar crime* is usually associated with Edwin H. Sutherland, who was the first to use the term and to study the type of crime systematically. He began formulating ideas about and doing research on white-collar crime more than forty years ago, about fifteen years before his first publication on the subject (Cohen et al. 1956:44; Sutherland 1973). Indeed, references to the type of behavior now usually included under the name *white-collar crime* can be found in the last century and the very early part of this century (Hartung 1953:31–36; Bloch and Geis 1962:381–82; Morris 1968; Ross 1968).

The concept of white-collar crime has been called too vague. It has been

---

[1] For convincing reasons for the need to develop typologies of crime which include the full range of types see Clinard and Quinney 1967; Gibbons 1965; Gibbons 1968. For further reading on crime in general the reader is referred to the leading texts in criminology, for example, Sutherland and Cressey 1974; Reckless 1967; Bloch and Geis 1970.

charged with referring not to "real" crime but merely to behavior in violation of some government regulation or simply to some sharp business or unethical practice to which a particular investigator happens to object (Tappan 1960:7–10; 1947a; 1947b; Caldwell 1958). Other objections have been raised because the offenders are not "really" criminals; neither they nor society define them as such (Burgess 1950). Furthermore, it has been noted that it is incongruous to call respected business and community leaders criminals (Vold 1958:253).

Much of this controversy is extraneous to the central purpose of white-collar crime research, which is to extend criminological research and theory (Cressey 1961:vii). Far from attempting to identify persons, research has focused on the criminal behavior, not on the criminals (Newman 1958:747). White-collar offenses have been shown to be "real" crime; they are acts which are defined as socially injurious and for which punishment is provided. They differ from the other crimes chiefly in the way many of them are handled — that is, by enforcement boards, commissions, departments, or other government agencies rather than by regular criminal courts (Sutherland 1949:29–56; Clinard 1952:226–58). Little controversy remains today; white-collar crime is now generally recognized as an important problem of deviance (President's Commission 1967; Bloch and Geis 1970; Geis 1968).

White-Collar Crime as Occupational Crime

Sutherland's first (1939) definition of white-collar crime simply referred to "crime in the upper or white-collar class, composed of respectable or at least respected business and professional men" (Sutherland 1956:46). But it was clear that he intended ordinary crimes committed by these upper-status persons to be excluded; only offenses committed as part of the job were to be included:

> White-collar crime may be defined approximately as a crime committed by a person of respectability and high social status in the course of his occupation. Consequently, it excludes many crimes of the upper class, such as most of their cases of murder, adultery, and intoxication, since these are not customarily a part of their occupational procedures (Sutherland 1949:9).

Contending that most white-collar crime involves "violation of delegated or implied trust" in one form or another, Sutherland includes a range of law violations by those in business, politics, the professions, and other occupations (Sutherland 1956:49). However, his chief research on white-collar crime concentrated on the crimes committed by business corporations, including violations in restraint of trade, infringement and manipulation of patents, trademarks, and copyrights, rebates, advertising misrepresentations, unfair labor practices, black marketeering, pure food and drug violations, and others. In addition, he analyzed the fraud perpetrated on consumers and investors by utility holding companies (Sutherland 1949).

After Sutherland, a number of others investigated and offered conceptions of white-collar crime which have modified its meaning, both adding to and subtracting from the list of offenses (Clinard 1952:viii, 16–27; Hartung 1953; Aubert 1952:266; Cressey 1953:20; Newman 1958; Geis 1962; Quinney 1963). These modifications have not consistently adhered to the criterion of high social status of the offender, but two essential defining characteristics have been retained: (1) White-collar crimes are law violations, not breaches of contract, torts, or unethical behavior which may be immoral but not illegal; (2) white-collar crime is that which occurs during occupational activities (Newman 1958:737). Recognizing that the violation occurs as part of or as a deviation from the violator's occupational role—whether it is blue-collar or white-collar, lower-class or upper-class—Quinney suggests that the more general term *occupational crime* be used (Quinney 1964:210; Clinard and Quinney 1967:131).

With this in mind, occupational crime (white-collar crime) is defined here as *violation of legal norms governing lawful occupational endeavors* during the course of practicing the occupation. The reference to norms governing the occupation is meant to exclude violations of the usual criminal law, such as arson, murder, and assault, while on the job, unless the law applied to the occupational behavior—for example, theft or embezzlement of funds. The reference to lawful occupations is meant to exclude the activities of those whose entire job is illegal, such as prostitutes, con men, professional forgers, thieves, and organized criminals. The term *white-collar crime* will be retained here as a synonym for *occupational crime*, since most of the specific research and discussion relates to white-collar occupations. But obviously the definition includes the whole gamut of legitimate occupations—blue- and white-collar employees, business owners, executives, and professionals. Thus we are referring here to *crime in business, occupations, and professions.*[2]

The legal definitions which distinguish some occupational behavior as criminal are contained partly in the common law and in regular criminal statutes, but more often they are contained in federal and state statutes regulating food, drugs, goods, and services; in federal laws regulating monopolies, securities, and interstate commerce; and in state public health and licensure and practice laws regulating occupations. These statutes usually provide a different system of adjudication, so that most white-collar crimes (other than embezzlement and employee theft) are not handled by the regular criminal courts (although they may wind up there); rather, the enforcement of the law is mainly in the hands of civil courts and government agencies.

---

[2]Organized crime is *business in crime;* career and professional crime are *occupations* and *professions in crime.*

Types of Occupational Crime

The varieties of occupational or white-collar crime can be placed in two major categories: *crimes against the public* and *intraorganizational crimes*.

Crimes against the public.   These are offenses committed by managers, executives, or agents of legitimate corporations in their own and the firm's behalf or by the individual businessman or professional practitioner for himself and his practice or business. The "public" against whom the offenses are perpetrated includes clients, patients, customers, other businesses, the government, the public in general, or whomever is the immediate or ultimate consumer of goods or services. Two subtypes are included as crimes against the public:

Corporate and Business Crime

Monopolistic restraint of trade (conspiracy)

Manipulation of stocks and securities

Commercial and political bribery and rebates

Patent and trademark infringements and manipulations

Misrepresentation and false advertising

Fraudulent grading, packaging, and labeling

Short weights and measures

Tax frauds

Black marketeering

Adulteration of food and drugs

Fraudulent sale of unsafe and injurious products

Illegal pollution of environment

Crimes by Individual and Professional Practitioners[3]

Obtaining fees, payments, or charges through fraud or deception

Deceiving or defrauding patients, clients, customers

---

[3] Except for the first two, the offenses in the list pertain only to licensed professionals.

Fraud, forgery, deception in securing licenses

Immoral practices in relations with clients

"Unprofessional" conduct and malpractice

Fee splitting

Advertising violations, misleading advertisement, misuse of titles, and so on

Criminal operations, abortions, ghost surgery, and so on

Falsification of statements on vital documents

Intraorganizational crimes.   These are crimes against employers or management by employees, or conversely, by employers or management against employees. In general they are violations of financial trust by employees or employers within the organization for their own gain against the organization or other members of the organization. Two subtypes are discernible:

*Employee and Management
Theft — Embezzlement*

Employee theft of funds

Inventory theft by employees

Misapplication of funds in receiverships, fraudulent bleeding of company funds, and so forth by managers and their agents against investors and stockholders

*Employer and Management
Offenses against Employees*

Violation of labor practice laws

Unfair, fraudulent, or discriminatory employment practices

It should be noted again that in addition to their illegality and occupational character, all these white-collar offenses are characterized by deception, fraud, or violation of explicit or implied trust.

Extent and Costs of Occupational Crime

Statistics on white-collar crimes are not collected and reported on a regular basis as are statistics on other crimes. For this reason we do not know exactly how much occupational crime exists and how much loss society suffers from it. But Sutherland pointed out long ago that white-collar offenses are pervasive in American society and in the end are much more harmful than the usual "major index" crimes reported in crime statistics (Sutherland 1949:10–13). Certainly health hazards, personal injury, and even loss of life result, and it is difficult to measure these losses. But the cost to society from occupational crime just in dollars is enormous, far outrunning the losses due to "traditional" crimes. For instance, the President's Commission on Law Enforcement and the Administration of Justice estimates losses to the public through tax fraud at $25 to $40 billion annually; securities fraud, $500 million to $1 billion; fraudulent and misrepresented drugs and medical devices, $500 million; fraud in home repair and improvement, $500 million to $1 billion; fraud in auto repair, $100 million. As unreliable as these estimates are, they clearly dwarf the less than $1 billion annual loss to all robberies, burglaries, auto thefts, larceny, and forgeries combined. A single large-scale corporate crime can cost the public vastly more than the take of thousands of armed robbers and auto thieves (President's Commission 1967:102–3).

The classic and still the most comprehensive study of corporate crimes is the one by Sutherland, which covered many years up to 1948. By carefully scrutinizing a number of official and unofficial reports and newspapers, he was able to secure a fairly good statistical compilation of recorded violations by seventy of the country's largest manufacturing, mining, and mercantile corporations. All but two of the companies were charged with more than one count of law violation, and most had violated the law repeatedly. The average number of times the corporations were cited for violations by an official agency or court was fourteen. There were 307 cases of restraint of trade, 97 of false advertising, 222 of patent infringement, 158 of unfair labor practices, 66 of illegal rebates, and 130 cases of other offenses (including wartime black market crimes) (Sutherland 1949:17–28). An examination of the records also revealed 38 instances of defrauding consumers or investors among fifteen utilities companies up to about 1940 (Sutherland 1949:185–213).

Because of the difficulties involved in scouring the many sources, no one has completed a recent survey as complete as Sutherland's to bring the record up to date. But enough instances of crimes by corporations come to light to remind us that this type of activity continues on the scale documented by Sutherland.

It should also be remembered that the statistics above represent only a part of occupational crimes. To these must be added the intraorganizational crimes. No one has yet done an exhaustive study of the frequency and take of embezzlement, "inventory shrinkage" due to employee theft, and other intraorganizational crimes. But in a book written about fifteen years ago (Jaspan 1960) the head of a management consultant firm reported that his company's experience in advising airlines, manufacturers, hotels, banking firms, and government agencies revealed time and again huge profit drains from employee theft.

In a more recent study of employee theft in department stores Robin (1969) found that of the nearly $400,000 loss of cash and merchandise, executives and white-collar clerks stole the largest average amount (Robin 1969:26–27). The typical employee thief had been employed only a short time by the store, was discovered or reported by a fellow employee or an "integrity" shopper (hired by private detective firm), stole relatively little at a time (average of less than $41) but more than an average shoplifted item (about $7), and had stolen from his employer previously (Robin 1969:20–26).

Occupational Crime as Learned Behavior

Few would quarrel with the contention that occupational behavior in general is normally learned behavior which is sustained through social and economic reinforcement. In fact, business and occupational behavior is seen as archtypically rational, economic behavior. We intend to show that the criminal aspects of occupational behavior can be understood in the same way. *Occupational encumbents*, those new to occupational crime, learn criminal behavior and definitions from others in similar positions. In addition to whatever social support they get from these others, the major source of reinforcement for their criminal behavior is economic. Whatever the exact figures turn out to be, it is clear that there is strong economic reward involved in crimes among businesses, occupations, and professions. This will be illustrated by examples from embezzlement and crimes of corporations.

Corporate Crime

Recently, the American public has become increasingly aware of crimes by large American and multinational corporations. For years, several large grain export companies have made illegal profits by artificially inflating the price of grain sold to foreign customers (by short-weighting wheat and mixing poor quality with the good quality grain). Packing companies bribed Army meat inspectors to give a higher grade rating to the low-grade meats they sell to the military, so the packing companies could then charge premium prices. The inspectors pocketed the bribes, the meat packers received the illegal profits, the military personnel ate the inferior meat, and the taxpayers footed the bill. Several corporations, most notably ITT, as well as Gulf Oil, Phillips Petroleum, Ashland, and other oil companies, admitted making illegal contributions to candidates during the 1972 presidential campaign. Lockheed and other multinational corporations bribed businessmen and government officials in several foreign countries to secure contracts and sales. These bribes were covered by tax deductions as business expenses and inflated prices. These few examples only hint at all of the high-level corruption in business, the magnitude of which dwarfs anything that previously had been uncovered in corporate crime. And more can be expected in the future.

As the succession of payoffs, under-the-table deals, and law violations hit the headlines and executives testify before Congressional committees, they provide further evidence for Sutherland's analysis of some thirty years ago. Corporate crimes are organized and may become part of the deliberate policy of the company (Sutherland 1949:217–33). These systematic violations of the law are not controlled or are controlled sporadically and belatedly by a diffuse, unorganized public response. Therefore, corporate crimes exist in the first place due to this "differential social organization" of procriminal and anticriminal forces in society (Sutherland 1949:255–56).

Because his study was mainly a compilation of the collective acts of corporations, Sutherland did not have data suitable to testing the differential association part of his theory. The most recent disclosures of corporate crime do not contain the kind of information needed to test a social learning explanation of the behavior of the individuals who executed the crimes. How do the executives learn the techniques and definitions conducive to their committing illegal acts on behalf of their companies? Sutherland contends that they were relatively isolated from definitions against their crimes on the job, and that they learned from others in the business who transmitted to them the techniques and rationalizations for violating the law. In support of this, however, he offers only biographies and autobiographies of minor executives and employees (Sutherland 1949:235–40). In some cases of corporate crime, more is known about the criminal behavior of top executives over a period of years and these show that:

> many of Sutherland's ideas concerning the behavior of corporate offenders also receive substantiation. His stress on learning and associational patterns as important elements in the genesis of the violations receives strong support (Geis 1967:149–50).

Geis refers to the antitrust violations twenty-nine leading electrical companies had been committing for many years but which were not discovered and acted against until 1960–61. The companies involved included big companies such as General Electric, Westinghouse, and Allis-Chalmers as well as some less well known ones. They fixed prices, rigged government bids, and entered into a "conspiracy" in restraint of trade and suppression of competition in the multi-billion-dollar heavy electrical equipment market.

The facts emerging from this case support the contention that social learning accounted for the process of promoting and sustaining the law-violating behavior.[4]

It is clear from the accounts of the case that the violations in the electrical conspiracy had been repeated time and again over more than thirty years and that the price-fixing agreements with competitors were consistently rewarded with high profits for the companies. When profits were not maximized for a given company through participation in the antitrust conspiracy, that company withdrew from its illegal agreement. When competition proved more profitable than price agreements and fixed bids, open and legal competition flourished. When the market slumped and prices dropped cutthroat competition was restrained, and the conspiracy was formed again to keep prices and profits high. Within the same company, such as General Electric, only some divisions (mainly the heavy transformer and circuit breaker division) stood to gain by illegal activities, and only those divisions engaged in the illegal agreements with competitors. Divisions in which the payoff was greater through legitimate business practices did not conspire with their competitors. Of course the actual and potential profits from the illegal activities would have been jeopardized and further costs would have been incurred if the conspiracy was discovered and acted upon by enforcement officials. There was not much risk of this until 1959 and 1960, but at certain times previously it appeared that company legal officers or government investigators might uncover the conspirators' activities. At these times meetings were curtailed and the agreements were terminated or restricted. When the heat was off the pricing agreements commenced again in full force. The ups and downs of the conspiracy over the years provide a clear-cut example of differential reinforcement: when legal behavior brought greater rewards it was maintained; when the illegal behavior paid off better and the probability of adverse consequences was low the illegal activities were maintained.[5]

The same pattern of reward for illegality is seen in the stories of the individual executives involved. Price fixing was established practice in the company when they came on the scene. They were specifically introduced to the idea and given training in the techniques and rationalizations of the practice by their directors, immediate superiors, and coworkers. They simply learned to meet with competitors as a part of learning the job. They soon learned, if they did not know it before taking the job, that the way to promotion, increased salary, and approval of peers and superiors was to violate the

---

[4]Perhaps the best account of the case is that written at the time (1961) by Richard Smith for *Fortune* magazine and reprinted in Wolfgang et al. 1962:357–72. For the most sophisticated sociological analysis see Geis 1967. For the account with the most detail about the investigation leading up to disclosure of the case and the mechanisms used in price fixing and bid rigging see Fuller 1962. See also Bloch and Geis 1970:309–12.

[5]For similar arguments see Lane 1953 and Dershowitz 1968.

antitrust laws. If the person was not "broad-minded" enough to go along with the practice he was shunted out of his position. For instance, one man was dismissed because he did not go along with the violations (although this was not the official reason for his demotion), and another was promoted to his high-level job because, as he said, "They knew I was adept at this sort of thing. I was glad to get the promotion. I had no objections" (Smith 1962:361).

The executives learned that one way to meet the pressure for increased profits and net return on sales was to agree with competitors on how to slice up the market so that all could raise prices and still keep their company's usual share of the market.

> We did feel that this was the only way to reach part of our goals as managers. . . . We couldn't accomplish a greater percent of net profit to sales without getting together with competitors. Part of the pressure was the will to get ahead and the desire to have the good will of the man above you. He had only to get the approval of the man above *him* to replace you, and if you wouldn't cooperate he could find lots of faults to use to get you out (Smith 1962:363).

The difference between what the equipment would sell for under normal conditions of competition and the inflated fixed price represents the loss to customers (many of whom were cities and municipalities), the government, and the public.

These executives were otherwise law-abiding men who had been brought up in environments which led them to define the law as something to be obeyed, not broken. Many were pillars of their respective communities, leaders in their churches, members of school boards, and respected participants in citizens' affairs. They would not dream of engaging in strong-arm robbery, burglary, or other usual forms of theft or violence, yet they knowingly broke the law. They learned complex and intricate skills to do so successfully and went to elaborate effort (faked expense accounts, use of public phones, secret meetings, coded messages, plain paper, and so on) to conceal their actions and prevent detection. "I didn't expect to get caught and I went to great trouble to conceal my activities so that I wouldn't get caught." When they first started, some individuals were not sure or believed that they were not really breaking the law. At some point, however, all knew full well they were breaking the law.

Those who could not redefine what they were doing as all right discontinued their participation in the conspiracy. But those who continued to break the law did not define themselves or what they were doing as criminal. The rationales involved defining their behavior as illegal but *not really criminal,* as only *technically wrong,* as *necessary* to curb cutthroat competition and to stabilize prices, as *not really injurious to the public;* or they defined the laws themselves as *bad laws*.[6] The individual manager did not need to invent these rationalizations any more than he needed to invent the techniques of carrying out the antitrust actions; he found them already available and supported by others in the company.

How Do Executives Justify Corporation Crimes?

Getting together with competitors was looked on as a way of life, a convention. . . . It was considered easier to negotiate market percentages than fight for one's share, less wearing to take turns on rigged bids than play the rugged individualist. Besides the rationale went, they were all "gentlemen" and no more inclined to gouge the consumer than to crowd a competitor. Admittedly, all of them knew they were breaking the law. . . . Their justification was on other grounds. "Sure, collusion was illegal," explained an old GE hand, "but, it wasn't *unethical*. It wasn't any more unethical than if the companies had a summit conference the way Russia and the West meet. Those competitor meetings were just attended by a group of distressed individuals who wanted to know where they were going" (Smith 1962:359; italics in original).

"Illegal? Yes, but not *criminal*. I didn't find that out until I read the indictment. . . . I assumed that criminal action meant damaging someone, and we did not do that. . . . I thought that we were more or less working on a survival basis in order to try to make enough to keep our plant and our employees"(Geis 1967:144, italics added).

In summary, it can be seen that the illegal behavior of the electrical company executives was differentially rewarded, and they learned the requisite techniques and definitions from associations with other antitrust violators.

They had to perceive that there would be gains accruing from their behavior. Such gains might be personal and professional, in terms of corporate advancement toward prestige and power, and they might be vocational, in terms of a more expedient and secure method of carrying out assigned tasks. The offenders also apparently had to be able to neutralize or rationalize their behavior in a manner in keeping with their image of themselves as law-abiding, decent, respectable persons (Geis 1967:150).

---

[6] In his study of lower-level white-collar offenders Spencer (1968) found the most common rationalization used by the offender was that he was merely doing what everyone else did.

The influence of the nature of the market and occupational context on white-collar crime shown in the case of these corporate executives is also apparent in other cases. Quinney (1963) shows how the pharmacist's location within his occupational group (that is, oriented toward business or professional aspects) is the best predictor of prescription violations. Leonard and Weber (1970) explain the frauds perpetrated by franchised auto dealers in servicing automobiles to be a reflection of market forces. The "racket" in auto repair is the way in which auto dealers attempt to maintain profit and reduce losses, given the extreme emphasis on sales which goes along with their franchise from the automobile manufacturers.

> The dealer and his sales people may receive bonuses for superior sales performance, but there are no financial rewards for good service. . . . The direction in which the incentives operate is clear: enhance sales and downgrade service. . . .
>
>   In many industries and trades, criminal behavior in an occupation is conditioned by the concentrated market power of producers capable of establishing terms of employment and rewards for the occupation (Leonard and Weber 1970:412).

Other illegal activities in the car sales industry such as kickbacks to used car wholesalers also appear to result from the pressures on the car dealer created by company policy of high volume and low per-unit profit (Farberman 1975).

Embezzlement

Shortly after Sutherland completed his study of corporation crime, Cressey completed the classic and nearly definitive study of the process by which persons in positions of financial trust violate that trust (1953). Cressey defined the phenomenon he wanted to explain as "violation of a position of financial trust" which had been taken originally in good faith.

    The processual theory Cressey evolved through his analysis of this type of criminal behavior is succinctly stated:

> Trusted persons become trust violators when they conceive of themselves as having a financial problem which is nonsharable, are aware that this problem can be secretly resolved by violation of the position of financial trust, and are able to apply to conduct in that situation verbalizations which enable them to adjust their conceptions of themselves as user of the entrusted funds or property (1953:30).

"The entire process must be present." The nonsharable problem is not enough, for many with such problems do not violate trusted positions. The knowledge that embezzlement would resolve the problem and the ability to act on that knowledge still is not sufficient. Before he will then go on to violate financial trust the person "must first apply to the situation a verbalization which enables him to violate the trust and, at the same time, to look upon himself as a non-violator" (Cressey 1953:31–32). The theory then is that the embezzler passes through three steps in the process of coming to steal from his employer. There must be (1) a nonsharable problem or problems, (2) opportunity for trust violation, (3) a set of rationalizations which define the behavior as appropriate in a given situation.

The nonsharable problem. One main type of nonsharable problem the trust violators in Cressey's study had prior to their offense is "violation of ascribed obligations." Certain kinds of behavior are considered improper for one in a position of financial trust, such as frivolous activities, maintaining a mistress, and heavy gambling. If one in such a position incurs debts through these actions which he is unable to meet, the financial crisis that is created is difficult for him to share with his wife, boss, or friends. He does not want to admit to them that he has not lived up to obligations of personal propriety which are ascribed to his position.

Another type of problem is the building up of insurmountable debts in "status-gaining" behavior—attempting to present a front of affluency and status that one's real income will not permit. Thus the man in a trusted but moderately paid position who maintains membership in expensive clubs, frequents prestige restaurants, contributes lavishly to charities, dresses his wife well, and buys an expensive house is living well beyond his means. He cannot present his problem to those who might be able to help solve it without disclosing the false front of affluence he has been upholding. Other problems are personal failure, business reverses, and employer-employee relations. Any of these may present the individual with a financial problem which he dares not share with others to seek a solution (Cressey 1953:33–76).

Opportunity for trust violation. The notion of opportunity here includes being in a position and having the requisite skills to perform an embezzlement. The skill needed to embezzle is already possessed by the trusted person. It is the same skill, applied to a different end, that is needed to hold the job in the first place. Likewise, the person's position of trust in handling goods or money places him strategically for converting them to his own use without discovery, at least temporarily. The key element then is the recognition that this skill and opportunity to violate the financial trust can be utilized to solve or alleviate his problems. The possibility of embezzlement as a solution to a financial problem is widely known, of course, and it can be learned by those not in, as well as by those in, a trusted position. But more specifically, the individual may have observed the dishonest behavior of his associates on the job; he may have learned of someone in the office or in the same job who has been embezzling, or he may have engaged in "technical violations" as part of his job. Knowledge gained in this fashion then can be applied in his specific situation (Cressey 1953:77–92).

The violator's "Vocabulary of Adjustment."[7]   Whether or not the person will act upon this knowledge by embezzling depends on whether he defines or redefines the situation so that he sees his trust violation as essentially noncriminal, as justified, or as not really his responsibility. This function is served by "vocabularies" which rationalize, such as: "I am just *borrowing* the money, I will pay it back soon," "The money is *really mine*," "It is only *fair* that I get something more, I'm certainly not getting paid what I'm worth" (Cressey 1953:93–138).

> Each trusted person does not invent a new rationalization for his violation of trust, but instead he applies to his own situation a verbalization which has been made available to him by virtue of his having come into contact with a culture in which such verbalizations are present (Cressey 1953:137).

Cressey's empirical support for this theory rests on depth interviews with convicted trust violators. Thus there is no evidence from cases of embezzlement which were not discovered or information from cases (if there are any) in which the three steps were present but embezzlement did not occur. However, all of the cases of known trust violation in Cressey's study conformed to the process—there were no contradictory cases. Cressey also examined the cases reported in the literature in sufficient detail to test the theory and found no negative cases. Also, he was unable to find a negative case among the more than two hundred embezzlement cases in a file collected over a period of years by Sutherland. All the cases in Jaspan's files also conformed to Cressey's processual theory (Jaspan 1960). The theory has been known and widely cited for years, and to date no negative cases have been reported in the literature. Thus it appears that trust violation does not occur in the absence of the three steps spelled out in Cressey's theory (although it may be that trust violation does not always occur in the presence of the three steps).

Later research found that rationalization is also involved in theft by blue-collar employees. While plant workers see taking personal property from a co-worker and stealing what is clearly defined as company property as wrong, pilfering things of "uncertain" ownership from the plant is rationalized as not really being theft. A number of other neutralizing definitions are also applied to pilfering by the workers: The company is big and

---

[7]For an analysis of white-collar crime which draws heavily from Cressey and emphasizes vocabularies of motives see Hartung 1965:125–36.

won't miss the stolen items; stealing from a person is wrong, stealing from a company isn't; the company expects stealing and doesn't mind; and so on (Horning 1970).

Although he had reservations about the extent to which an "excess" of definitions favorable to trust violation exist, Cressey did conclude that his theory was in general consistent with differential association (Cressey 1953: 147–51). It should also be clear that Cressey's careful analysis of this type of white-collar crime is consistent with the differential association–reinforcement explanation of deviant behavior. A full-scale analysis of trust violation in terms of learning principles would build on Cressey's formulation but go beyond it to say more about the monetary and social reinforcers, the specific sources from which the individual learns the techniques and verbalizations of trust violation, and the contingencies which lead one person to define his problems as nonsharable and another to define them as sharable. Such a full analysis will not be attempted, but the following remarks about the nonsharable problems illustrate the tack the analysis would take.

Obviously the nature of the problem does not wholly determine whether or not it will be shared. The same problems which the violators in Cressey's study did not share have plagued many others who worked them out by means other than trust violation. The individual will avoid sharing his problems to the extent that this type of behavior has been differentially reinforced in the past. The person who in the past has sought and received help from others (friends, relatives, and employers) in solving his difficulties is likely to continue to do so. On the other hand, the person may have previously attempted to solicit the aid of others and found that (1) he received no help, (2) he was castigated for not being able to handle his own problems, or (3) he received some help but it was given grudgingly, and the amount of negative sanctions which accompanied the help more than offset whatever positive reinforcement for sharing problems may have come from the aid. Someone with this kind of history who finds himself in a difficult situation is likely to attempt his own solution. His previous problems need not have been precisely the same as his current ones, but he will have learned that he can successfully share some types of problems and other problems he cannot. If the problem precipitating his embezzlement falls into this category, he will keep it secret and will become vulnerable to trust violation as a solution.

Embezzlement Was Not Always a Crime: The Impact of Social Change on the Law

Even some legal norms which today are deeply embedded in folkways were originally established as the outcome of power shifts in society. In his classic study, *Theft Law and Society*, Jerome Hall shows how the concept of embezzlement evolved as one powerful segment of English society gave way to another. When the large landholding baronial or nobility class was most powerful in England, there was no such thing as the crime of embezzlement. Theft was legislated and interpreted by the courts to mean only trespassing on and carrying away another's property—literally taking possessions from someone else's property. The large landholders were concerned only with stationary property and the possessions located there. What money they had was handled by themselves or by trusted servants. They had no employees as such, only bonded servants and serfs tied to the land on which they worked. The nobility was the most powerful segment of English society—indeed, the King could hardly keep them in check. The law and the courts generally reflected the interests of and were subservient to the militant power of the nobility.

But with the increased importance of mercantilism, commercial exchange, and manufacturing this situation began to change. During the fifteenth century a rising middle class of merchants began gaining power through their control of expanding trade and industry. The King himself became a merchant involved in international trade, and he and Parliament became increasingly indebted to and sympathetic toward mercantile interests. The most important legislation and court decisions of the day came to reflect commercial interests, particularly those of the wool trade. The increase in commerce meant a greater reliance by the merchants on strangers, agents, and employees rather than trusted servants. The merchants stood to lose if these agents converted the money or goods entrusted to them to their own use. At this time then, first in court decisions and later in legislation, violating financial trust by embezzlement came to be defined as a criminal offense. It was no longer necessary actually to go onto another's property to be guilty of theft; converting funds entrusted to one also became and remains theft (Hall 1952).

Watergate: White-Collar and Political Crime

The American public is now very familiar with the series of crimes committed by people in the highest levels of the federal government during the Nixon administration. These have come to be known as the Watergate crimes.[8]

---

[8]The name comes from the Watergate apartment-office-shopping complex in Washington, D.C. where the national offices of the Democratic party were located. These offices were burglarized by men on the payroll of the Republican Committee to Re-Elect the President (CREEP), a committee which was set up by and directed from the White House. The burglars were caught

While some similar crimes were probably committed in previous presidential administrations, the Nixon group reached new heights of offenses against the American people and their political institutions and traditions. The offenses began in the first Nixon term, continued through the election year of 1972, and went on throughout the following cover-up right up to Nixon's very last days in office. The story is a complex one and has been well told; we will undoubtedly hear more about it, as it is a major set of events in American history. But this is not the place to recount it or the more recently revealed criminal abuse by the CIA, FBI, and other intelligence agencies. Rather the task here will be: (1) to conceptualize Watergate-type crimes as political crimes similar to but somewhat distinct from the other white-collar crimes discussed in this chapter, and (2) to offer a social learning explanation of the criminal behavior of the offenders in the Watergate crimes.

The evidence in the presidential tape transcripts and in congressional testimony shows that the crimes were part of an organized conspiracy directed from the White House. The crimes included burglary and break-in, illegal wiretaps, payoffs, obstruction of justice, domestic spying and invasion of privacy, abuse of power, failure to uphold the constitutional requirements of office, illegal use of governmental agencies to disrupt groups and harass American citizens who opposed the Nixon administration, and other offenses. The intelligence community kept secret files on U.S. citizens and engaged in domestic and foreign covert operations. The people involved were not just low-level people who were essentially hired hands, but also middle-level and higher-level officials. Some were elected and appointed governmental officials, and some were nongovernmental personnel employed by CREEP (Committee to Re-Elect the President). Some of the offenses are ordinary crimes and some, such as political bribery, have long been considered as subclasses of white-collar crime. But the Watergate offenses are of such moment and magnitude that it seems they have outgrown the general classification of white-collar crime. They may be better conceptualized as political crimes.

---

and their trial first revealed connections with the White House. This led then to discovery of a conspiracy to cover up these connections, obstruct justice, and the other crimes.

The revelations started in 1972 with reporting by Carl Bernstein and Bob Woodward of the *Washington Post* and reporters from other newspapers. The Senate (the Ervin Committee) began investigating in 1973. A special prosecutor's office was created for investigation and prosecution of the conspiracy. The special Watergate Grand Jury, working with the prosecutor, named Richard Nixon as an unindicted co-conspirator. Nixon attempted to withhold the evidence that consisted of taped conversations he had secretly recorded in the White House, and the House of Representatives voted three major articles of impeachment against President Nixon in 1974. The publicly disclosed information from witnesses combined with Nixon's own words on tape made it very clear that he would be impeached for "high crimes and misdemeanors" as provided by the Constitution. He resigned in August 1974 before he could be impeached and was almost immediately pardoned by President Ford. The interested reader is referred to the news coverage of these events, particularly the *Time* and *Newsweek* stories. Of the many books which have now appeared, see especially Bernstein and Woodward 1974; White 1975; Presidential Transcripts 1974; and the *New York Times* 1974. The descriptions in this section are based primarily on these sources.

The Watergate crimes are white-collar crimes in the sense that they were carried out in the course of otherwise legal occupations. But when these occupations are political or governmental occupations, the occupational crimes become political crimes. Just as the distinction between white-collar crime and organized crime can blur at some points, the distinction between white-collar and political crime blurs at other points. There are no political crimes in the United States in the same sense that there are strictly political crimes in other countries, in particular, communist and totalitarian nations. That is, it is not a crime here, as it is elsewhere, to belong to an outlawed political party or association, to dissent from governmental policy, to express antigovernment sentiment, and so on. Also, although some have suggested that we call everyone from minority or disadvantaged groups who is convicted of any crime a political criminal, it makes little sense to do so. There are offense patterns, however, to which the label *political* can be legitimately applied.

Political crime is best defined by Minor (1975): It is a law violation motivated by the desire to influence existing public policy or power relations. This includes the common crimes of burglary, property damage and theft, murder, etc., committed with this in mind; and crimes such as treason or violent overthrow of the government, committed only to change the existing system. *Political crime* may be committed by those who oppose the existing system and want to do away with it or change it. *It may also be committed by people in governmental or other official positions in the attempt to defend the status quo or to change the system toward the direction they want.* The Watergate and related crimes are plainly political crimes of this latter type. To some extent they are also *politicized justice* in that these crimes used law enforcement agencies unfairly against groups and individuals that were perceived as threats to the authority and power of the established regime (Minor 1975:393). It is this political motivation that permeated the entire range of Watergate offenses and similar conspiracies and makes them political crimes. Crimes by public officials for personal gain would ordinarily be counted as occupational crime, and part of the motivation for some offenders was personal, monetary, or career advancement. Personal gain was a major objective for only some of the lower-level participants.

The evidence also reveals that the combination of political and other payoffs for the crimes and the rationalization used for them more than offset the perceived risks. For the lower-level offenders — the burglars, bag job men, field operatives, etc. — the rewards were monetary, personal, and political. The Watergate burglars were well paid and got paid even more for keeping quiet. CREEP and the White House staff controlled enormous amounts of money, and monetary incentives were certainly not confined to the lowest level. There was also a certain amount of "command influence," in which offenses were committed and then covered up to please and gain the favorable opinion of one's superiors. At the lowest levels this sometimes involved simply doing what one was ordered to do. At the middle levels it involved a calculated "getting along by going along" to advance one's own career in the political hierarchy and move closer to the center of power. The payoff for those at the top was gaining and retaining power. The crimes started in the latter part of the first Nixon administration. Their purpose was to prevent the political damage from the protest over Vietnam and civil rights from affecting Nixon's renomination. The Watergate break-in was part of a general campaign of illegal and dirty tricks to disorganize the Democratic opposition campaigns and insure Nixon's re-election.

The potential and actual rewards were not countered by actual or perceived negative consequences. Everyone was aware that there would be some negative consequences if the actions became widely known. But apparently no one believed that these were likely or would be very severe. From beginning to end, all the conspirators believed that the risks were minimal. They believed that even if they were caught, the consequences could be avoided: Criminal charges against them could be fixed with executive clemency and pardons. Sentences, if served, would be short, and the individuals would be well taken care of. Any embarrassing information could be concealed. A cover-up could be effectively carried out, because the law enforcement agencies were under presidential control. Congressional inquiries could be stymied by exercise of executive privilege. The secret tapes would never come to light and could be used selectively to counter charges. Attacks on the press would neutralize press reporting. "Stonewalling" and perjury would keep evidence from the courts and the Congress.

Of course, for a long time the consequences were *not* grave; the cover-up worked and penalties were contained. Eventually, many lost their status, positions, and incomes. The ultimate loss, of course, was power and esteem. But only one or two received severe sentences. Most did not suffer long-term punishment or financial loss. Nixon escaped impeachment conviction and received a pardon before any criminal charges could be brought against him. The important point, however, is that at the time none of these adverse consequences were anticipated—no one imagined the conspiracy would come to national attention. But the same rewards sought by these men are sought and accomplished by others by legal means. Why did they resort to crime? Apparently, none defined the actions as legal. They were aware of the improper or criminal nature of what they were doing and tried to cover it up. But they defined the situation as warranting effective means—criminal means, if necessary—to achieve the ends. These definitions favorable to criminal behavior are in the same class as the neutralizing and positive definitions used by other deviants for their behavior.

The rightness of the cause and the value of team loyalty spread from the highest to the lowest levels. The violators often appealed to the necessity of protecting national security and the office of the presidency. Some of the lower-level operatives felt they were defending democracy against Castro. The neutralizing definitions included the one common to many forms of deviance—"everybody else is doing it." The strong belief, buttressed by

FBI evidence, was that this was common practice in previous administrations. Protest groups, Vietnam dissenters, and civil rights activists were breaking the law all the time in the name of a higher cause; this justifies doing the same to promote the Nixon presidency. In testimony submitted in a civil case related to the telephone taps by the Nixon administration, the ex-President maintained that the sovereign can do certain acts as he believes necessary which would be criminal if committed by an ordinary citizen. This resurrected version of the divine right of kings suggests an interesting new rationalization for crime which, obviously, not many deviants can use. The conspirators saw themselves in a war of "us" against "them." Opponents and dissenters were not just legitimate opposition but were the enemy — to be defeated by any means necessary.

Finally, one definition conducive to these crimes has little to do with neutralizing moral apprehension; rather it represents the absence of moral reservations. Probably one of the most common conceptions they had, especially among the top leaders, was not that it was moral or immoral, only that it was necessary or not necessary. The evidence revealed that hardly anyone ever stopped to ask "Is it wrong?" or to say "It may work, but it isn't right." The whole affair was permeated with a certain pragmatic amoral conception of the presidency and power. It emphasized what would work, not what was right.

Summary

The two major categories of occupational crime are (1) crimes against the public, including corporate crime and crimes by individual or professional practitioners, and (2) intraorganizational crimes, including embezzlement and employee theft and crimes by employers against employees. Corporate executives, individual practitioners, employees, and others who are implicated in these two types of crimes learn to violate the law as they learn and carry out their normal occupational behavior. There is strong economic reward involved in both types of occupational crime. In addition, occupational encumbents who violate the law have received social support and learn definitions justifying their criminal behavior from others in similar positions or even in the same organization.

The Watergate crimes are a type of white-collar crime because they are crimes against the public by individuals who carry out otherwise legal occupations, but they are actually political crimes of which the aim is to support the group in power. Whereas in corporate crimes maximization of profit is the aim, only some of the Watergate criminals sought monetary gain. For the others the primary aim was the maximization of political power by keeping the Nixon administration in control of the government.

White-collar offenses bring crime into otherwise legitimate occupational endeavors. In this sense they can be described as crimes in business, occupations, and professions. In the next chapter we discuss crime pursued as a living and a way of life somewhat on the traditional model of a profession — the profession of crime. Next we discuss crime on a more or less business basis. This "organized" crime can be described as business in crime.

19

Professional Crime

Types of Professional Crime

Professional crimes are characteristically property, not personal-violence, offenses. There are those who kill for hire and who are sometimes called "professional killers"; however, they are more clearly part of organized criminal syndicates rather than separate professional operators. Violent thieves, such as armed robbers, sometimes achieve an occupational identity and organization, but they still do not qualify as professional thieves (Einstadter 1969; Roebuck and Cadwallader 1961; Conklin 1972:59–68). Rather, the crimes typically committed by professionals are *nonviolent theft.* Certain kinds of professional crime, such as the big con, would not even be attempted by amateurs, but many of the same offenses practiced by professionals are also committed by nonprofessional thieves — for example, there are systematic professional check forgers and there are also "naive" check forgers (Lemert 1958; 1953); just as there are professional shoplifters ("boosters"), there are also amateur "snitches" who regularly shoplift (Cameron 1964). On rare occasions, a self-taught amateur may even successfully make it as a pickpocket ("gun") (Maurer 1964:165–68). Thus the professional and the nonprofessional may commit the same offenses and may even use much the same modus operandi, but the following constitute the major types of professional theft (Maurer 1962; 1964; Sutherland 1937:43–81; Bloch and Geis 1970:173–85; Inciardi 1975:12–30):

Confidence games[1]
  Big con — wire, rag, payoff, Spanish prisoner swindle, and so on

---

[1] The *big con* and *short con* categories are taken from Maurer 1962. The basic distinction between the two is that in a big con game the "mark" is put "on the send" to draw out his savings, cash his bonds, sell his property, or otherwise secure all the money he can. The short con beats the mark for what he has on him. See Maurer 1962 for further explanation and detailed descriptions of how these crimes are carried out.

Short con—smack, tat, huge duke, tip, pigeon drop, high dice, and so on

Theft involving mainly manual or mechanical skills and with little contact with victim—safecrackers (boxmen), counterfeiters, jewelry thieves (penny weighters), and so on

Pickpockets (whiz mob, guns, cannons)

Shoplifters (boosters, heels)

Forgers

Small-time grifters of all sorts—circus grifters, railroad grifters, exclusively short con men [2]

Characteristics of Professional Crime

Professional crime emerged out of the changes from feudal to modern economic systems and urbanization. It can be traced specifically to the Elizabethan era of English history and has persisted in the United States in forms that can be clearly identified in the earlier historical periods (Inciardi 1975:5–11, 75–82). Systematic social scientific analysis of professional crime dates from the publication in 1937 of Edwin H. Sutherland's *The Professional Thief*, based on the life of one thief. David W. Maurer's studies of criminal jargon and organization published in 1940 and 1964, based on interviews with con men and pickpockets, are other sources of information. Sutherland and Maurer distinguished professional theft from other crime by definite social and technical characteristics.

The regular commission of crimes to make a living and as a more or less full-time occupation is obviously necessary for a profession of crime. But to designate any criminal pattern which meets this criterion as *professional* crime means that any habitual or career criminal, however petty or amateur, would be called a professional. This conception confuses *full-time* with *professional* and would include such a variety of offenders that there is nothing to distinguish professional crime from other types. For example, in 1966 the President's Commission studied a sample of thieves in prison with three or more convictions: Although these convicts had attempted to make a living from crime working at it on a more or less full-time basis, they were petty, unsuccessful criminals. Thus, we learn something from this study about ordinary habitual offenders. We learn nothing about professional thieves. The use of such an ill-conceived category accounts for the

---

[2] I exclude "hustling" of either the poolroom variety (Polsky 1967) or of the street variety (Williamson 1965), although the first is included by Clinard and Quinney (1967:468–79), and Bloch and Geis (1970:185–86) include the latter, presumably because both involve "conning" to some extent.

fact that the President's Commission survey failed to add more up-to-date and systematic data on the understanding of professional crime (President's Commission 1967:96–101).

More recent studies have followed the Sutherland and Maurer model more closely. They rely on socio-historical data (Inciardi 1975), case studies of individual thieves (King 1972), or interviews with a limited number of thieves currently or recently in prison (Shover 1973; Letkemann 1973). Therefore, we are still largely dependent on biographies, autobiographies, and other case-study accounts and interview data for the delineation of professional attributes in crime. The following outline of those attributes is based primarily on the Sutherland (1937) and Maurer (1962; 1964) studies; later studies essentially confirm them. (In addition to these, see the literature reviews in Clinard and Quinney 1967:428–37; Bloch and Geis 1970:167–73; Quinney 1970:270–73.) This outline, then, is a description of a style of crime which may be dying out and about which much of our knowledge is not recent. (Inciardi [1975:76] argues that it has been declining since the 1940s, but Chambliss [King 1972:168] argues that it is as viable today as ever.)

As we have seen, neither the kind of crime nor the engaging in it on a full-time basis completely distinguishes professional from other crime. Rather, the distinctive features of professional crime are the characteristics of the perpetrators, their social organization, and the degree of skill in criminal occupations they possess. The usual analogy is that this type of crime compares to other crime as conventional professions compare to other legitimate occupations. But perhaps the more accurate analogy is to the skilled craft trades or semiprofessional occupations rather than to full-fledged professions. Nonetheless, in delineating the following characteristics the term *professional* will continue to be used.

1. Relatively *complex and highly developed skills* and techniques enable thieves to perpetrate crime with a certain finesse, or "class," and above all *success*. These techniques are never "heavy" or strong-arm. They involve theft through nonviolent means; they never cause physical harm to individuals and only occasionally cause property damage. Rip and tear methods are viewed by professionals as evidence of amateurism and lack of class. Professional skills are of two basic types. For many crimes, especially the confidence games, *interpersonal* and *role-playing* skills are used to swindle, manipulate, and outwit the victim, or "mark." For other crimes, such as those committed by "boxmen" (safecrackers) and "whiz mobs" (pickpockets), *manual* or *mechanical* dexterity is needed. In either case, skilled planning and execution are necessary. There is a selective pattern of recruitment and a period of training to acquire these skills.

2. The professional criminal enjoys high *prestige* compared to the low-skilled burglar, the amateur shoplifter, the mugger, the purse snatcher, the jackroller who preys on drunks, and the street hustler. There are also status distinctions among the various forms of professional crime. For instance, higher prestige is accorded the con men and boxmen than the shoplifters

and forgers. The high status of professional thieves is recognized not only by those in the underworld but also, to some extent, by the police, the press, and the public.

3. Theft is pursued as a *way of life*. Not only is crime committed on a regular basis as a means of livelihood, but the thief's life and identity are organized around these occupational pursuits. The thief's *friendships* and *associations* are primarily with other thieves. He shares with them a mutual identification, a certain esprit de corps, and an overall *ideology* or set of sentiments and attitudes toward crime, society, and victims.

4. This way of life is sustained through a network of communication and interpersonal relations among professional criminals, the hallmark of which is a specialized jargon or *argot*. This network allows the thief to know who is who, at least by reputation. Consequently he is able to locate other thieves a short time after arriving in a new city.

5. The practice of crime as a way of life could not exist without the active cooperation of certain persons in the conventional society. This means that an important part of the professional thief's occupation is the purchase of job security insurance through proper connections and the *fix*. This is an important, even vital, aspect of professional crime. Becoming a professional thief does not only mean learning the technical training, learning the professional ideology, and becoming incorporated into the system of theft. It also means learning how to put in the fix with law enforcement authorities, chiefs of police, detectives, prosecuting attorneys, judges, juries, sheriffs, witnesses, or even the mark himself (Maurer 1962:179). Usually the fix is put in at the lower levels of the law enforcement system, partly because the higher one has to go in the system the more difficult and expensive it is to fit the "tin mitten" (the hand of the corrupt official).

The fix by a professional is most apt to be on a job-by-job basis and is accomplished most often through a fixer (criminal lawyer perhaps) in the locality. Sometimes he will even "work on the sneak" without a fix. Professional thieves have neither the organizational permanence nor the wealth to put in a more lasting fix by the long-term corruption of key people in a city or state in the manner used by organized crime.

6. Professional theft is committed within the framework of a definite *social organization* or structure. This organization is not as elaborate as that of organized crime; rather, it is the organization of the small working group. The professional thief seldom works alone, and within the professional mob there is a division of labor. There are traditional roles within each theft specialty. For instance, the boxman (safecracker) will attempt a score alone only in unusual circumstances; usually he works with at least two other persons. The boxman's role is to plan the crime and to actually open the safe. He will nearly always have a "point man" working with him who is stationed in a strategic location to signal a warning if the police or someone else shows up. He will also have a helper with him at the safe. The "whiz mob," or pickpocket gang, will include the "tool" or "wire," the person (man or woman) who actually takes the money from the mark's pocket, one or

more "stalls," the ones who bump up against and maneuver the victim into position, and a "dukeman," someone to whom the money is passed. Some tools become especially adept at "left front breech" pockets or the "pit," the inside coat pocket, although they do not confine themselves to these pockets. Some "gun molls," female pickpockets, become expert stalls, and others become regular tools. Con games are played with at least one accomplice, and some of the big con games can involve as many as twenty people, including inside men, outside men, steerers or ropers, and shills.

Learning Process in Professional Crime

Few would disagree that the process motivating and sustaining professional crime is similar to that which keeps anyone working at an occupation or profession. The necessary skill, ideologies, and connections are learned in association with practicing professional criminals. It should also be clear from the foregoing that not only is professional theft sustained by the positive reinforcement of monetary return but also the social reinforcement of recognition, prestige, and identity with other thieves as well as the respect of the police and others. It is true for many kinds of criminals, but especially true of professional thieves (and organized criminals), that partly because of the cooperation of law enforcement, the positive consequences of their criminal behavior far outweigh the negative consequences. Professional criminals are sometimes caught and punished, but the frequency, probability, and amount of reinforcement for continuation in crime are far greater than this sporadic, uncertain punishment.

Learning professional theft, whether it is confidence games, picking pockets, or opening safes, typically requires a period, sometimes a rather long period, of socialization and training—*tutelage and apprenticeship*—under an accomplished thief (Maurer 1964:153–72; 1940:142–75). The training model is that of the master-apprentice common to skill crafts and to the professions at an earlier period of history.

> Professional thieves have no policy of recruiting for the profession. . . . On the other hand, a person can become a professional thief only if he is trained by those who already are professionals. . . . He knows nothing of the racket, its technique, or operations, and he can't learn these things out of books. . . . He is first filled in for a day's work on a particular job of no great danger and calling for no particular ability. . . . If he does this unimportant part well, he may be called on later for more important parts, and gradually acquire the expert skill of the professional (Sutherland 1937:21–23).

We have seen that during this period of apprenticeship the prospective professional learns a number of things—skills, the fix, the argot. Of most interest is the belief system of professional theft, which contains definitions conducive to lawbreaking. Part of the belief system has to do with codes relative to acceptable behavior of a professional—for example, "Don't grift on the way out," "Always put aside the fall dough," "Don't burn or double cross a partner or member of the mob," "Help another professional in distress." A significant portion of the belief system of professional theft comprises definitions justifying crime. The con man maintains earnestly that "You can't cheat an honest man" and "Every mark has larceny in his heart." The notion that "Everybody has his own racket" or "Everybody is a crook, but at least we thieves are honest about it" is a central part of this rationalization system,

> which is made up of verbal justifications for a way of life which he is aware elicits disapproval from a large segment of the society. . . . In particular, the professional criminal is likely to re-define his own behavior as being equivalent to behavior by a majority of persons in the society. . . . Professional criminals often catalogue at length the wayward behavior of some politicians and the exploitative techniques employed by many businessmen, and they are acutely aware of deviations from ethical conduct by the group with which they have their most emotional contact—the law enforcement officers (Bloch and Geis 1962:192–93).

Summary

Professional crime is characterized by the pursuit of theft for a livelihood and as a way of life, relatively complex skills, high prestige, a specialized argot, and a criminal ideology. Varieties of professional crime include confidence games, safecracking, pocket picking, shoplifting, and forgery. Professional crime involves a high probability of economic reward, a low probability of legal punishment, and the social reinforcement of others in a criminal subculture. Learning often includes a period of apprenticeship or direct tutelage in which the novice learns the skills and ideology to become a professional.

20

Organized Crime: Business in Crime

The Criminal Activity of Organized Crime

The following descriptions make clear that organized crime is a continuing multi-billion-dollar enterprise that is perhaps the most costly crime. White-collar crime is certainly costly in dollars, but the systematic theft, fraud, extortion, and murder committed by organized criminals are certainly the most treacherous in American society.

> In many ways organized crime is the most sinister kind of crime in America. The men who control it have become rich and powerful by encouraging the needy to gamble, by luring the troubled to destroy themselves, . . . by maiming or murdering those who oppose them, by bribing those who are sworn to destroy them. Organized crime is not merely a few preying upon a few. In a very real sense it is dedicated to subverting not only American institutions, but the very decency and integrity that are the most cherished attributes of a free society (The President's Commission 1968:485–486).

Supplying Illicit Market Demands

The central activity of organized crime is the essentially monopolistic supply of the market demand for illicit goods and services (Vold 1958:226; Reckless 1967:320–23; Cressey 1969a:72–108; The President's Commission 1968:440–42). Whenever the law prohibits the legal production, distribution, or sale of some commodity or service for which there remains a more or less inelastic public demand, the conditions are set for organized crime to move in and supply that demand at a tremendous profit. Other market conditions and the nature of the product are also involved in the extent to which an illegal business can be organized on a large black-market scale (Schelling 1967). But the erection of legal prohibitions means that only those who are organized and willing to operate illegally and who have the wherewithal to corrupt enforcement officials will enter the field and succeed. This basic ingredient has been the backbone of organized criminal behavior at least since Prohibition, when organized crime as we know it today began by monopolizing the production, distribution, and wholesale of bootleg alcohol. When alcohol was legalized and bootleg profits declined, organized crime moved into gambling (Bloch and Geis 1970:198–205; Reckless 1967:322; Sellin 1967; Bloch 1967; Cressey 1969a:74–76). *Gambling* remains the single most important source of revenue for organized crime; it provides the wealth needed to underwrite ventures in other areas. The two most profitable types of gambling controlled by organized crime are *off-track betting* on horse races and the operation of *illegal lotteries*—"policy" and "numbers" (Sellin 1967). But illegal gambling of any kind—unlawful casinos, gambling establishments, or betting on sports events—is likely to be controlled by criminal syndicates. It has been estimated that as much as $50 billion is bet annually in all forms of gambling and that organized crime realizes a profit of about $7 billion a year from it. (The President's Commission 1968:441).

Organized criminal syndicates have moved more into "loan sharking"— loaning money for usurious rates (usually 20 percent per week!) and ensuring repayment through force and intimidation (as Cressey says, the loan applicant puts up his body as collateral) (Cressey 1969a:77–91; Bloch and Geis 1970:208). Although loan sharking is not of recent vintage, it has only recently become enormously rewarding—a multi-billion-dollar racket which ranks second only to gambling as a source of income for organized crime.

Smuggling and wholesaling illegal *drugs*, principally heroin, is the third major black market enterprise of organized crime (Cressey 1969a:91–95). Although trafficking in drugs returns the biggest percentage of markup per sale, there are not enough addicts in the country to make the total income from it comparable to that from gambling or loan sharking. Nonetheless, the drug traffic does return an annual profit to organized criminals of more than $20 million (The President's Commission 1968:441).

Due to a combination of factors, including decreased patronage and the diminishing role of houses, control of *prostitution* is not as important to organized crime as it once was.

Racketeering

The basic principle of racketeering is to extort a levy or tribute from an unwilling victim through intimidation, duress, and physical force (Vold 1958:228; Reckless 1967:323–26; Cressey 1969a:95–99). Its simplest form is the *protection racket*, whereby an owner or manager of a business is "sold" insurance against property and personal damage in his business. The "protection" sold is against the harm the racketeer will certainly commit unless he is paid the tribute. Another form is *business and labor racketeering*, in which the racketeers gain control through force of the leadership positions of a union and extort all or a large portion of the union "dues" from the membership, without in any way providing the usual union functions such as wage bargaining with employers. Indeed, the racketeer may combine the labor racket with extortion of the employer; providing labor docility and guarantee against strikes in return for a levy in the form of payments to "labor relations consultants." No one is able to estimate the extent or amount of financial return from racketeering, but it certainly ranks close to black market activities and probably close to a related type of organized criminal operation—infiltration of legitimate business.

Fencing and Organized Theft

Fencing of stolen goods has long been an activity of organized crime, and it is now conducted on an international scale. The syndicate buys stolen goods and money from other thieves and then markets them through various outlets including otherwise legitimate business fronts. Recent activities of this type include fencing of merchandise stolen from large airports and of securities from Wall Street brokerage offices; indeed, it appears from reports in the popular media that the syndicates may now be organizing the actual theft as well as arranging for the selling.

Incursion into Legitimate Business Enterprises

Although organized criminals do sometimes get into legitimate business and operate legally, they also gain control of and run legal businesses illegally (Bloch and Geis 1970:205–8; Reckless 1967:326–29; Cressey 1969a: 99–107; The President's Commission 1968:443–45). Certain kinds of businesses have long been heavily influenced or controlled by members of crime syndicates—cigarette vending machines, juke boxes, pinball machines, the garment industry, linen supplies and cleaning, construction, and bakeries. More recently encroachments have been made into large manufacturing, commercial, and banking concerns. Sometimes the entry into lawful businesses is accomplished simply through racketeering—extorting part or whole ownership. Sometimes a businessman is cut off from further legitimate sources of loans, borrows from a loan shark and is unable to repay the loan, and then finds that the debt is foreclosed through the acquisition of an unwanted partner—the loan shark. Organized criminals also enter legal businesses by investing the gains from their criminal enterprises. By whatever method they get in, they use their control of the business in various illegal ways: forcing businesses who are customers to buy their product; using the business as a front for tax evasion; operating bankruptcy frauds, and so on (Bloch and Geis 1970:209; Cressey 1969a:105–6).

When organized crime operates a legal business illegally its activities shade into a form of white-collar crime. But there are crucial differences between the white-collar and the organized criminal: The white-collar offender commits crimes as a part of his business, but the organized offender operates the business as a part of his crimes.

> Some of the laws against white-collar business practices are not meant to be enforced, and they are violated frequently. But if this is corruption at all, it is very different from the corruption induced by Cosa Nostra bribes. White-collar criminals are not organized for corruption, . . . and even when they are organized for crime, they do not kill witnesses or potential witnesses against them (Cressey 1969a:312).

All the illegal activities of organized crime are interrelated, and the continuation of all depends on the fix and corruption of enforcement and political officials. As noted earlier, the fix put in by organized crime is a more permanent and elaborate procedure than that employed by professional criminals. It is so pervasive and thorough that organized crime may corrupt key personnel at all levels of the government—not just the beat policeman but also the police chief and the prosecutor; not just the court clerk but the judge; not just members of the city council but members of state and federal legislatures; not just the mayor but also the higher administrators of state and federal government (Cressey 1969a:248–89).

The Structure of Organized Crime

Much nonprofessional crime occurs within a more or less organized group setting; for example, white-collar crime is often part of an organized and systematic conspiracy, and much other crime is organized in the sense of being socially structured group behavior. But to include all of this crime in the concept of *organized crime* is misleading (Sellin 1967:406). Rather, the label *organized crime* refers to a particular kind of "organization for profit and power" (Vold 1958:220–42).

> The criminal syndicate is a relatively stable type of business organization. Its business is to integrate and co-ordinate existing crime opportunities, practices, and personnel into a smoothly functioning large-scale enterprise devoted to the assurance of a high level of profits for the organization (Vold 1958:226–27).

Although every social scientist interested in the problem knows that such a criminal apparatus exists, there is little agreement on the proper descriptive label. In some respects it is analogous to corporate or semicorporate business structure, but it has also been likened to a syndicate, feudal organization, a patriarchal kinship system, a confederation, a military organization, a government system, and a cartel (Vold 1958:224; Reckless 1967: 329; Cressey 1969a:16–24 and elsewhere; Clinard and Quinney 1967:383). Perhaps the most accurate description is that of an authoritarian, nepotistic business organization.

Cressey offers the best definition of organized crime. It includes everything that organized crime is generally conceded to be and yet is precise enough to allow distinction between organized crime as such and other types of criminal organizations.

> An organized crime is any crime committed by a person occupying, in an established division of labor, a position designed for the commission of crime, providing that such division of labor also includes [but is certainly not limited to] at least one position for a *corrupter*, one position for a *corruptee*, and one position for an *enforcer* (Cressey 1969a:319, original all italics).

The division of labor in organized crime can become fairly intricate, but Cressey allows for this in his definition. Furthermore, he specifies the three organizational positions without which organized crime could not exist. The corrupter puts in the fix with officials to ensure immunity for members of the organization against enforcement action; the corruptee is the official so corrupted; the enforcer is the illegal equivalent of policeman–executioner. These positions, especially that of the enforcer, presuppose a division of labor which is somewhat hierarchically arranged. The corrupter is simply a subordinate in a system of command, and the corruptee, while he stands to some extent outside the direct chain of command, is still under its control. The enforcer carries out the "judicial" decisions made by those at the top against lower-level violators of the unwritten code, the organizational rules, against competitors (Cressey 1969a:127–40; on the nature of the code see pp. 162–85). Thus Cressey's definition would more accurately reflect what he intends to include if he were to make explicit the hierarchical division of labor.

This conception fits all of organized crime and successfully distinguishes it from other divisions of labor in crime. Professional crime is organized and is tied into a system which includes corrupter and corruptee, but these positions lie outside the professional criminal group. Moreover, the organization of professional crime does not include a systematic role of enforcer, and it is relatively flat or horizontal. The characteristic professional crime organization is the small working group. The "leader" of a whiz mob or safecracking crew is a more informal position and carries none of the command privileges of the "boss" position in organized crime.

Cosa Nostra:
The Structural Core of Organized Crime

Sociologists have long been skeptical, and justifiably so, of the existence of a nationwide organization that autocratically controls all crime. They have been particularly wary of the cultural myth that this system is the more or less directly transplanted Sicilian *mafia* (Bell 1962; Bloch and Geis 1962; Albini 1971; Morris and Hawkins 1970; Tyler 1962:323–36; Smith 1976). It is true that much of the reference to the *Black Hand*, the *Mafia, Unione Siciliane*, and other terms has carried a good deal of fanciful journalistic freight. There has not been and there is not now one single, tightly knit organization which monopolizes all organized crime in the United States. It is also true that there has never been a monopoly in organized crime by any ethnic or nationality group (Gardiner 1970; Homer 1974); the racial and ethnic composition of organized criminal groups continues to undergo change (Ianni 1975). However, there is some evidence of a nationwide network of inter-related organizations which, in some sections of the country, virtually monopolize the kinds of crime we are discussing. Spotty, unconfirmed evidence for a nationwide criminal organization goes back some time, but not until Cressey's reports for the President's Commission did the nature of this organization become clearer. Cressey's data and conclusions continued to be disputed but his analysis is still most thorough, careful, and convincing (Cressey 1969a; 1972).[1]

Just as there is some uncertainty about what to label organized crime in general, there is also disagreement about what to call it (Reckless 1967:332–33; Bloch and Geis 1970:210; Cressey 1969a:16–24). Even its members refer to it by different names in different parts of the country. It has historical ties, through immigration, with the Sicilian and Italian Mafia, and its core members are still exclusively of Italian descent. But it is not simply the old-world Mafia transplanted; rather, it is a new-world phenomenon. It has thrived and evolved in America and has become increasingly bureaucratized, reflecting general social changes (Anderson 1967; Cressey 1969a:8–28). *Cosa Nostra* ("our thing," "our affair"), the term Cressey prefers, is as good as any name to use, despite the misdirected indignation of some Italian-Americans over names which connect Italians with organized crime.

Cosa Nostra does not equal all organized crime; much crime is organized outside the boundaries of Cosa Nostra and contains members of non-Italian descent. The President's Commission survey revealed that organized crime of some type exists in 80 percent of American cities with more than one million population, in 20 percent of cities with populations between 250,000 and one million, and in more than half the cities with populations of 100,000 to 250,000. Many of these organizations, particularly in the smaller cities, are not Cosa Nostra organizations, but Cosa Nostra forms the core of

---

[1]This section is based almost entirely on Cressey 1969a:109–40. See also Anderson 1967.

organized crime in the United States. No other criminal organization or complex of criminal organizations even begins to rival Cosa Nostra on a large scale. The localities organized by non–Cosa Nostra syndicates seldom exceed the boundaries of one city. In contrast, Cosa Nostra controls criminal activity in entire states and regions of the country. Indeed, Cosa Nostra directly or indirectly controls nearly all interstate illegal gambling and the illegal importation and wholesale distribution of drugs. No other criminal combine has the power and wealth to corrupt officials at all levels of government — federal, state, and local. Any criminal system which fits our definition of organized crime is organized, whatever its scale of operations, but the definition fits Cosa Nostra best. The structure of organized crime then is best exemplified by the structure of Cosa Nostra.

The basic organizational unit of the Cosa Nostra style of organized crime is the *family*, a designation which is a carry-over from earlier days when real family ties were combined with organizational ties. Today real kinship is likely to be combined with fictive kinship. The authoritarian head of the family is the *boss*, and at least in the bigger families, there are one or more *underbosses*. The next level of authority and command is the *caporegime* or *lieutenant* or *head* (other terms are also used). Each caporegime has a *section chief*, or deputy lieutenant, and under each will be a number of *soldiers* or *button men*, who occupy the lowest recognized position in the family. (This "lowest" position is likely to be occupied by a millionaire!) Working with or for the button men are the street-level workers — bookies, numbers runners, dealers, and so on — who may feel that they are part of the syndicate, but they are just as likely to be non-Italian and they are not "in the book" as "members" of the family.

The Cosa Nostra family is located and operates in a fairly restricted geographical area, usually within a city (New York has five families). There is no single nationwide family, but the activities of the families are interrelated and to a large degree answerable to and controlled by higher levels of organization. The next step above the family is the *council*, composed of the bosses from several families in a given region or area (councils exist only in some parts of the country). The highest level of organization and the one which gives the Cosa Nostra its national coordination is the *commission*, which comprises the bosses from the most powerful and wealthy families. (Usually there are eight to twelve members on the commission; the current commission includes three from New York families and one each from Newark, Buffalo, Philadelphia, Detroit, and Chicago.)

Other key roles are recognized, but they are more informal and in some ways are not directly in the "line" positions and hierarchy of control. One of these is the *consigliere*, or advisor to the boss, who occupies a rank equivalent to underboss. The *buffer*, who is an intermediary between the boss and other top-echelon people and the lower-level participants in the organization, is another underboss-level position. The *corrupter* may be anyone from an underboss to a soldier, but one who operates as corrupter for an entire family is likely to have fairly high rank. The *corruptee* is really an integral part of the organization, but he is not likely to be thought of as such be-cause he is outside of the family. The *enforcer* is another informal role which may be played by anyone but is most often filled by a person of lieutenant rank or below.

At least twenty-four established families in the United States effec-tively organize the following regions: New York and the surrounding states down through Pennsylvania and west as far as Ohio and Michigan; Illinois and some adjoining states; Florida; the Southwest; southern California, Nevada, and Colorado. In some crimes, such as gambling, their reach is in effect national. The membership in a given family (from boss down through soldiers but not counting corruptees, street-level workers, and others) ranges from about 20 to about 700; the twenty-four families have an esti-mated 5,000 Cosa Nostra members.

The present structure is a direct outgrowth of the system that was de-vised in 1931–32 as a compromise and a policy of "peaceful coexistence" after a series of battles over territory. Somewhat by historical accident, the largest, most powerful criminal syndicates by the time of Prohibition were Mafia-style Italian groups. They first succeeded in conquering through "war" and assassination nearly all of the non-Mafia groups, and then they began fighting one another. The killing that took place under the old guard, the "mustachios" or "mustache Petes," was diminished by the newer breed, who wanted to do things the American way—namely, by reaching rational agreements over territory and profits and by curtailing cutthroat competition. The leaders who took over as the new guard more than forty years ago are aging but are still in control, although many changes have taken place since (Cressey 1969a:8–9, 29–53, 141–61; Anderson 1967:424–25).

Recruitment and Training in Organized Crime

Organized crime as an economic enterprise in American society is main-tained because the continuing demand for certain illegal goods and services ensures great financial rewards and the corruption of officials which this wealth makes possible minimizes the risk of punishment. This pattern of differential economic reinforcement as the basis for individual entry into organized crime is similar not only to other criminal behavior but also to conventional occupational and business behavior. To it is added, again, as with other behavior, the social reinforcement of group ties. Through differential association one is exposed to, becomes eligible and acceptable for, and favorably defines securing these rewards through criminal rather than conventional pursuits. As differential opportunity theory reminds us, illegal and legal opportunities are not equally distributed in society, and a person's social location strongly influences which are available to him. For the person who enters it, organized crime represents the most effective way of achieving financial and social rewards.

The social situation most conducive to entering organized crime has been a lower-class area where successful and admired criminal models abound and where one may receive initial training and orientation by participating in criminally oriented delinquent gangs (Cloward and Ohlin 1960; Spergel 1964; Geis 1966:89–93; Cressey 1969a:236–38; Clinard and Quinney 1967:384–85; Quinney 1970:268). Organized criminals traditionally have recruited from among these young lower-class, principally white, males in the urban slums.

> The most successful recruitment processes are those which do not appear to be recruiting techniques at all. These are the processes by which membership becomes highly desirable because of the *rewards and benefits* the prospective members believe it confers on them. Some boys grow up knowing that it is a "good thing" to belong to a certain club. . . . Other boys grow up knowing that is a *"good thing" to become a member of* a criminal "family" (Cressey 1969a:237, italics added).

But only a few boys in this situation will aspire to organized or other criminal careers. For most, even those who may sometimes get involved in delinquent gangs, conventional socialization is strong enough that a criminal career is not acceptable. Others simply do not acquire the attributes which make them acceptable to the members of organized crime. The informal selection policy of organized crime places an initial premium on the ability and willingness to use violence.

> In the lower-class gang, the future organized criminal learns the utility of violence and is recruited into groups which train him in other social and personal attributes of importance to a career in organized crime. These traits later assume a certain priority over direct physical coercion for successful work in organized crime, necessitating a balancing of adroitness and violence by the leadership (Geis 1966:86).

After acceptance into the organized criminal circle, the individual who continues to evince a particular aptitude for using "muscle" may become specialized as a killer or enforcer. For others, continued success means learning other organizational skills. To the more or less "achievement" criteria by which persons are recruited into organized crime in general, Costa Nostra adds additional "ascriptive" criteria—Italian ancestry and real or fictive kinship. But the "books have been closed" for some years on Cosa Nostra family membership. The increased bureaucratization of organized crime has brought an increased emphasis on and reward for business and organizational competence. Indeed, organized criminals increasingly recruit not only from slum gangs but also from among college graduates, or they underwrite college educations for existing members. Whatever the source of entry and whatever the skill involved, the behavior of members is controlled through financial reward and loyalty to the "code" and the organization on the one hand and the certain severe punishment for deviation which an authoritarian group can mete out on the other hand (Cressey 1969a:221–47).

Summary

Organized crime is characterized by a more formal structure and a more definite leadership hierarchy than other criminal groups. Organized crime is involved in gambling, loan sharking, the drug traffic, and racketeering and is moving increasingly into formerly legitimate businesses. Organized crime continues because supplying the demand for illegal goods and services guarantees financial rewards, and the risk of legal punishment is reduced by corrupting law enforcement officials. The pattern of differential economic and social reinforcement for individual recruitment into organized crime is similar to that for other criminal behavior, such as professional crime, and also to that for entry into conventional occupations and business.

21

Violent and "Compulsive" Crimes

The types of criminal behavior discussed thus far are apparently committed for reasons we can easily understand. It is not difficult to demonstrate, then, that white-collar, organized, and professional crimes are normal, learned behavior committed by emotionally stable and psychologically "normal" individuals. In this section we analyze a category of criminal behavior which theorists suggest does not have these characteristics. This category is usually labeled *compulsive crime*. We attempt to show that even this type of deviance can be understood as learned behavior.

Compulsive crime is a vague, ill-defined category of offenses characterized not by similarity of overt behavior but rather by the assumed irrationality of the offenders who commit the acts. As Cressey (1954) noted, *compulsive crime* is a "wastebasket" label that is applied when the motivation of the offender is not quite understandable to others.[1] The concepts of compulsive irrationality are

> no less "wastebasket categories" than is the "psychopathic personality" concept. Casual observation indicates, at least, that the application of the "compulsive crime" label often accompanies the inability of either the subject or the examiner to account for the behavior in question *in terms of motives which are current, popular, and sanctioned in a particular culture or among the members of a particular group within a culture* (Cressey 1969b:1112).

Because the person is believed to have committed the act for no recognizable or "valid" reason, it is assumed that he was impelled to do so by some inner force he was unable to resist.

> Such acts are considered as irrational because they are thought to be prompted by a subjective morbid impulsion which the per-

---

[1]Cressey more than anyone else has offered a sound sociological analysis of "compulsive" crimes, showing them *not* to be exceptions to differential association. His central ideas were first presented in Cressey 1954; a revised version appeared in Cressey 1962 and later in Cressey 1969b.

son's "will" or "judgment" or "ego" cannot control. . . . Thus, the overt act is considered as prompted entirely "from within" and present contact with values concerning morality, decency, or correctness of the overt behavior in no way affects the actor, in the last analysis, either in deterring him from acting or in encouraging him to act (Cressey 1969b:1115).

Some kinds of extreme or bizarre sexual deviations, suicide, shoplifting (kleptomania), and arson (pyromania) are often included under compulsive crimes. But acts of savage personal aggression such as crimes of passion and senseless killings are nearly always included, and we emphasize these "compulsive" violent offenses.

Hartung recounts the case of a young man who after an altercation with his girlfriend's mother turned on her, strangled her, and stabbed her with a pair of scissors. He later told the police, "I just blew my top" (Hartung 1965:137–39). The compulsion explanation would agree with the man and say that his behavior was a senseless, uncontrollable act with no precedent in his background. But it could be argued that this explanation is no explanation at all, but simply a case of labeling a behavioral occurrence that is not understood and thinking that it has thereby been explained. It appears "senseless," and the tendency then is to write off the event by saying that the man "doesn't know what he is doing" or "must be crazy." When we learn that a man has entered the apartment of eight young women, stabbed and cut them to death in a methodical, brutal manner, the first reaction is likely to be, "He must be nuts." We know he is crazy and compulsive because he did a crazy and compulsive thing.

This answer is understandable as a first reaction, but it is not an adequate answer to why he did it. It cannot be accepted as a scientific explanation because no evidence is adduced to support the contention other than the very behavior the explanation is meant to explain. This circular logic is characteristic of the compulsion explanation of behavior (Cressey 1954; Hartung 1965:193–97).

But rather than just dismissing the compulsive theory of violent behavior, we offer an alternative theory—a social learning explanation. Our theory is not precisely worked out, and it admittedly leaves unanswered questions, mainly because the empirical evidence in this area is still insufficient to provide a base for a closely reasoned argument or a base from which to test the theory. However, the learning hypothesis fits into a general theory of behavior which has been empirically supported and which can be tested.

Learning "Compulsive" Violence

Of course no one has produced homicide, either "senseless" or otherwise, in a controlled situation in order to study the variables leading to its occurrence. But experimental research has shown that very aggressive behavior which on the surface could be described as equally impulsive and uncontrolled, although not as destructive, is acquired and extinguished through the social reinforcement contingencies surrounding it. Both physical and verbal aggression have been conditioned, inhibited, and reproduced by manipulating reinforcement and punishment. It has been found that violent and aggressive people have had such behavior reinforced in the past or have imitated it after observing that it was rewarded when practiced by others. Studies have discovered that aggressive adolescents have parents who actively encouraged and rewarded their children's violence. Nonaggressive people have not been exposed to violent models and had parents who responded with approval to nonviolent acts. Both the intensity of violence and the situation in which it is likely to occur may be manipulated through social reward (Bandura 1973).

Violence to the point of brutality and homicide is not simply the result of parental socialization, although it is fairly clear that the kind of socialization received is relevant to the commission of outwardly violent acts (Gold 1958). Rather, the person who commits violent acts has come into contact with other persons and social situations which differentially reinforce such action. Through participation and imitation in certain social and cultural contexts he learns that violence is defined as "all right," and if it is not rewarded, at least it is not punished in some situations. When he is confronted with similar situations he is likely to respond violently. Thus, when a person reacts with seemingly senseless violence to something or someone, on examination we may find that the same behavior, or something similar to it, is an already established part of his behavioral repertoire. The seemingly irrational homicide

> will likely be found to have learned and practiced his violence more or less frequently before committing his present criminal homicide (Hartung 1965:151).

The person who "blows his top" and assaults or kills another person will be found on close scrutiny

> . . . to have engaged previously in physical violence in interpersonal relations. . . . Negatively speaking, such a person is not controlled in his behavior by the moral injunctions against the use of violence in interpersonal relations. Positively speaking, he has learned violent patterns of thought and action (Hartung 1965:140).

Learning to be violent does not mean that the homicide or other violent act was premeditated in the sense of careful advance planning. Indeed, research has shown that assault, homicide, and other violence often is not carefully planned and occurs in the course of an argument. But the same research shows clearly that the offense is not completely unplanned and that the offender (and often the victim too) has a long history of interpersonal violence (Wolfgang 1957; Pittman and Handy 1964; Voss and Hepburn 1968). Moreover, it is found that the seemingly "'insane murderer' does *not* execute his crime *with a more conspicuous lack of planning, motivation, or rationale* than the murderer whose mental faculties are not in question" (Curvant and Waldrop 1967:163; italics added).

Learned Definitions Conducive to Violence

The definition of what are "usual" motives for committing homicide varies from one culture to another (Bohannan 1960; Wolfgang and Ferracuti 1967:273–84). Within the same society some situations are defined as calling for aggression, whereas others are defined as inappropriate for it. In our society fiercely aggressive performance is encouraged and rewarded in the boxing ring, on the football field, or in combat, but it is likely to be disapproved otherwise. Knocking a man senseless through savage repeated beating which results in death in the boxing ring differs from the same act in the street chiefly in the setting and the way it is defined. We tend to accept as reasonable the boxer's rationalization that he was just defending his title. But just as the behavior of the boxer has been both positively and negatively reinforced under the discriminative stimuli of the "fair fight" in the ring, the actions of the street assailant may have been reinforced in past situations similar to the one in which he attacked his victim.

This tendency to respond violently under given conditions is not randomly distributed in society. Rather, it is subject to socially patterned variations by race, nationality, class, sex, age, social status, relationship between victim and offender, time of year, week, or day, and place (Wolfgang 1957; 1958; 1961; Pittman and Handy 1964; Amir 1967a; 1967b; Clinard and Quinney 1967:20–31; Voss and Hepburn 1968; Wolfgang and Ferracuti 1967:258–66). This social regularity in aggression has led some theorists to posit the existence of a *subculture of violence* in which violence is rewarded and one learns definitions conducive to violent behavior (Wolfgang and Ferracuti 1967; Hartung 1965:144–46; Amir 1967a:69–73; Gastil 1971). Wolfgang and Ferracuti have most systematically espoused the subculture of violence formulation:[2]

---

[2]See their fullest statement in Wolfgang and Ferracuti 1967. Portions of this book and the original (1962) statement of the theory have been reprinted. See Wolfgang 1967; Wolfgang et al. 1970; Arnold 1970.

> Our hypothesis is that this overt (and often illicit) expression of violence (of which homicide is only the most extreme) is part of a subculture normative system, and that this system is reflected in the psychological traits of the subculture participants (1967:158).

The mechanism by which the violence in this subculture is transmitted is identified by Wolfgang and Ferracuti as differential association:

> The development of favorable attitudes toward, and the use of violence in a subculture usually involves learned behavior and a process of differential learning, association, or identification (1967: 160).

The subculture of violence is carried mainly by lower-class (and disproportionately nonwhite) males in their teens and young adulthood. It is characterized by values which condone physical aggression. From childhood one learns to approach other people and life's problems with the alternative of physical violence always present. A high percentage of participants in the subculture own weapons, and the use of aggression, with or without weapons, is the expected, approved, and rewarded response in a wide variety of situations. The participants learn rationalizations which not only define violence as all right but place positive valuation on it as a sign of masculinity, upholding honor, personal autonomy, and toughness. Even occurrences which seem trivial to a person outside the subculture may be interpreted as threats to these values and the occasion for violence. An argument, an unpaid debt of a very small amount, a slight insult, dispute over the ownership of a bottle of beer, or any number of other confrontations can lead to a "senseless" beating. The subculture of violence may also exist mainly in a region where rates of homicide and other violent crimes are especially high, such as the South. However, recent research casts doubt on the validity of the subculture of violence thesis of both the regional (Doerner 1975) and class type (Ball-Rokeach 1973; Erlanger 1974).

But one does not have to learn the behavior and rationalization in a subculture of violence. The *general culture* provides ample training and justifications for aggression. Indeed, the justifications found in the subculture bear striking resemblance to some of the "norms of evasion" for the moral injunctions against violence found in the general culture. That is, there is a generalized norm against physical attack, maiming, or killing others, but at the same time there are familiar excuses for doing just that. Thus violence is justified if it is "unavoidable," "in time of war against the enemy," or "in self-defense," or if "legitimate channels are closed off," "that is the only way to get things done," "the other person deserves it," "you are forced into it." Generally held values (at least by American men) justify violence under a number of different circumstances. Many see violent behavior as unnecessary most of the time, but justify violence by authorities to maintain social control. A minority of people define violence as necessary to promote fast social change (Blumenthal et al. 1972).

These categories of acceptable exceptions to the general antiviolence norm may be learned and applied by individuals as techniques of neutralization justifying violent behavior. But they may apply the definitions to situations where others do not agree that the aggression is justified. In these cases the person is apt to be described as engaging in "senseless" violence. The killer of the enemy during wartime is a hero because in that situation, the consensus is that the action is justifiable. Everyone knows that the dangerous enemy deserves to be killed. But if the soldier comes home, climbs a tower in Texas, shoots the same number of people, and defines what he has done as killing the "enemy," we are likely to disagree and suspect that he is nuts. However, his definition of the act as excusable does not differ from the war hero who defines his killings as excusable. In both cases definitions discriminative for behavior have been learned and serve to increase the probability that the individual will commit the act. The difference is that we agree with the war hero's application of the definition; we do not agree with the other person's application, and thus he is "crazy."

> If they accept his rationalization they will define his behavior as "understandable," even if they disapprove of or condemn it, and even if they may think him "stupid," or "not very smart." If others reject the criminal violator's rationalization, they will define his behavior as "unintelligible," or "senseless," or "impulsive," or "unmotivated" (Hartung 1965:132).

That he may at the time or later define his own actions as crazy, beyond his control, the spontaneous outburst of "losing his mind," or as otherwise not quite understandable to himself does not necessarily argue against this approach. First, the person may indeed not know or understand why he has committed such acts; his behavior may truly be as "senseless" to him as to others. It should not be surprising that a person may not be able to explain his behavior even to himself, that he will sometimes develop responses to certain stimuli based on prior reinforcement without knowing or understanding the stimulus-response relationship. Second, he may define his actions as beyond his control because he has learned the belief that certain acts result from uncontrollable outrage or compulsion—a belief which itself has become an acceptable excuse for such behavior. From a number of sources, including the mass media, control and treatment agents, and other people in the general population who have come to believe the "pop" psychology of the impulsive act, persons learn that their actions may be acceptably excused as the result of irresistible psychic forces.

Chapter Twenty-one: Violent and "Compulsive" Crimes   265

Research will reveal that in the past decade in the United States the statement, "I was drunk," has been superceded by "I just blew my top," "Something snapped in my head," "I broke down," "I blew up," and similar ungrammatical and misleading physical metaphors that are taken literally (Hartung 1965:159).

This plea of nonresponsibility and irrational motivation has become an increasingly respectable excuse not only for "motiveless" violence but also for shoplifting, setting fires, and other acts when they are not obviously economically inspired (Cressey 1954).

Summary

The label *compulsive crimes* is ordinarily placed on violent and other acts which seem to be without rational or understandable motivation. We apply it to the behavior of persons in certain situations in which there is no immediately apparent rational reason for their actions. But the implication that they therefore were impelled to such actions by some irrational and uncontrollable internal compulsion is not warranted. The analysis here suggests that when an individual responds in a seemingly senseless violent way to a situation, knowledge of his life history would reveal that he has learned definitions conducive to and has been reinforced for such behavior under similar situations in the past.

Part Six   Suicide

Chapter Twenty-four

22

Suicidal Behavior: Definition, Variations, and Prevention

Suicidal Behavior

Definition of Suicide

In his classic sociological study of suicide in 1897, Durkheim discussed various nuances in the meaning of the word *suicide*, the difficulty of determining suicidal intent, and the problem of distinguishing suicide from similar behavior. He then offered this formal definition of suicide:

> death resulting directly or indirectly from a positive or negative act of the victim himself, which he knows will produce this result (Durkheim 1951:44).

His discussion has a modern tone, for nearly all subsequent attempts to define suicide have confronted the same ambiguities that Durkheim faced, and some modern writers conclude that Durkheim's definition is still correct (Gibbs 1968:12). Most of the others, although they do not take over Durkheim's definition wholecloth, arrive at something very similar to it. The general conception of suicide today is still that it is self-inflicted death knowingly and willfully precipitated by the person; the person more or less deliberately kills himself or places himself in a sure-death situation (Douglas 1967:350–83; Farber 1968:4; Stengel 1964:12). However, ambiguous motivations, feigned suicides, unsuccessful attempted suicides, accidental self-inflicted deaths, and other events confound attempts to define suicide.

The difficulties revolve around ambiguities in the usual definition, in which suicidal *intent* is coupled with suicidal consequences or *acts*.[1] Self-

---

[1] The emphasis on intent as the symbolic connection between one's action and its outcome has raised the intriguing philosophical question (Durkheim and others dwell on it at length) of whether animals can have self-destructive intent and thereby commit suicide. No one has yet answered the question adequately. However, an interesting approach to it has been offered by

caused fatalities include the person who quickly ends his life with a lethal weapon, the person who slowly kills himself by overindulgence in tobacco, alcohol, drugs, or hard work, and the one who quickly, but accidently, dies by his own hand. However, both the overindulgence and the accident are instances in which the overt act of self-inflicted death is not often seen as suicide by either common-sense or scholarly definitions, because they are not based on suicidal intent. The suicide by deliberately driving an automobile over a cliff is "caused" by the conscious actions designed to end in death (however fuzzy the thinking which led to the cliff drive); the automobile accident over a cliff is not caused, it just happens. The behavior is the same in the two events, but the intent is different. The death of the person who without wanting to die knowingly pursues an occupation or activity that carries a high risk of fatality is seen as different from the death of a person who does the same thing hoping to die. Again, the end is the same, but the intent is different. Also, a death by the hand of another is observably different from death by one's own hand, but the intent to die may be the same—for example, martyrdom. The person may vacillate between a firm resolve to kill himself and the sincere desire to live, or he may hold both intentions simultaneously. Deliberate suicide shades imperceptibly into unintended or accidental death; one may feign suicide and accidently succeed. Probably only a minority of suicides are firmly resolved to die right up to the very last. The typical suicide places himself in a situation of greater or lesser risk, rather than of certainty, of death (Wilkins 1967:287); the actual outcome then may depend upon factors other than the suicide's intention.

The variations in intent and likelihood of death combine to produce the central problem in defining suicide—what to do about *behavior that is suicidelike* (either suicidal in intent or in action) but does not fit the description of full intent successfully carried out in the act of suicide. Specifically, what is to be done with suicidal attempts, threatened suicide, self-injurious but nonfatal acts, and similar behavior? Are all to be categorized together as essentially the same behavior? Can they be arrayed along a continuum of increasingly serious intention and destructiveness? Or are they to be clearly separated from completed suicide and their relationship left an open empirical question? A number of different solutions to this problem have been offered.[2] There is no one best answer, but the following discussion provides one way of including the range of suicidal behavior while allowing meaningful distinctions to be maintained.

Schaefer (1967), who asks, "Can a Mouse Commit Suicide?" He attempted to train rats first to discriminate between lethal and nonlethal environments and then to choose the lethal environment. He achieved the first step, discrimination training, but was not able to train the rats to choose death over life.

[2] See, for instance, Douglas 1967:350–83; Durkheim 1951:42–45; Gibbs 1968:10–13; Farber 1968:4–10; Schneidman 1967:510–39.

Self-Injurious Behavior, Suicidal Behavior, and Suicide

The most inclusive class of suicide-relevant behavior might be labeled *self-injurious*. The term *self-injurious behavior* would include any and all cases in which a person's own actions present threatened or real destructiveness to himself (without reference to intent, degree of injury, or lapse of time). Subsumed within this general category are two subclasses of suicidal behavior, both of which are characterized by self-caused death as the apparent, threatened, or real outcome within a relatively short time after the omission or commission of some act. One subclass is *suicide* proper, defined as the completed act of intended, self-precipitated fatal injury. Although the awareness of risk of fatal outcome and the seriousness with which death is sought vary, suicide has at least some element of these in proximate relationship to actual death. The second subclass is *nonfatal suicidal behavior*. This would include suicide *attempts*, defined as any overt self-injurious act with a relatively high risk of death coupled with a relatively serious intention to take one's own life. But it would also include *suicidal gestures* — attempts to make others believe that one will take his own life, although he has a low level of suicide intent and engages in low-risk acts. Finally, suicidal behavior includes suicidal *communications* and warnings — verbal threats that one plans to take his life but without overt acts, regardless of the degree of real suicide intent.

Traditionally sociological research and theory have concentrated on group rates of completed suicide. The usual interest is to account for variations in these rates, measured by official suicide statistics, by reference to variations in social structure. Sociologists have been much less concerned with the suicidal process (Douglas 1967:3–163). It is very difficult to reconstruct the motivational process leading to suicide on the basis of completed cases alone, because the victim is not available for interviewing, and competent observation of a case over time up to the point of suicide is not possible. Therefore we rely on self-observations, suicide notes, and other forms of evidence left behind by the suicide, and on information supplied by those who know something about the background, events, and conditions surrounding the person prior to the act.

But these after-the-fact reconstructions may not be sufficient to provide the knowledge needed to understand the entire suicidal process. Rather, the cross-sectional and retrospective study of suicide may serve only to explain how given group conditions promote or prevent suicide among certain persons (Wilkins 1967). We need to combine this kind of knowledge with the study of suicide attempts and other suicidal behavior if we are to understand the motivations to suicide. The extent to which this is possible depends on the correlation between suicide and nonfatal suicidal behavior, to which we now give consideration.

Empirical Relationship of
Suicide to Other Suicidal Behavior

There are no regularly compiled statistics on attempts and other non-fatal suicidal behavior. Official suicide statistics, based on coroners' reports, deal only with completed suicides. The police receive some reports on attempted suicide (Schmid and Van Arsdol 1955), but only a small portion of attempts come to the attention of the police. Schneidman and Farberow (1961) surveyed physicians and hospitals on the assumption that most of the serious attempts, at least, would be reported for medical aid. They were able to locate a great many such cases in Los Angeles, to make estimates of the total number of attempts, and to make comparisons of attempters' social characteristics with those of suicides. They estimate that there are about eight attempted suicides for each completed suicide, a ratio that agrees with other studies of attempted suicide, which have found the ratio to range between four to one and nine to one, depending on how completely the investigator was able to locate attempt cases (Wilkins 1967: 289–90; Stengel 1964:75).

However, none of these studies used representative samples from the general population to locate cases of attempted suicide without depending on reports of enforcement and medical personnel. For this reason they do not provide a sufficient basis for determining how many in the community as a whole have attempted suicide. The only research to use random samples from the general population to ascertain the prevalence of persons who have attempted suicide is that reported by Mintz (1970). He reports that 3.9 percent of those in his random sample of adults over fourteen in Los Angeles had made one or more suicide attempts in their lifetime. Mintz does not report the number of attempts for a given time period, say for a given year, and therefore it is difficult to compare this rate of attempts with the rate of suicide, which is calculated per year.[3] That he found nearly four people out of a hundred who at some time had attempted to take their own lives indicates more clearly than any other data that suicidal behavior is about as common as other deviant behavior that is generally considered a major problem, such as drug addiction and alcoholism.

Schneidman and Farberow found that although 70 percent of the completed suicides were male, this sex ratio was almost exactly reversed among

---

[3]The estimates which can be calculated from this percentage of attempts in the adult population over a lifetime come surprisingly close to the eight-to-one ratio of attempts to suicide estimated by Schneidman and Farberow. For instance, 3.9 percent is the equivalent of 3,900 suicide attempts per 100,000 population. This is of course an accumulated prevalance covering an unknown number of years. However, if we assume that the years reported on covered an average of thirty years (the median age in Mintz's sample was thirty-seven), there was an estimated average of 130 attempts per 100,000 per year in Los Angeles. If we multiply the official rate of approximately 17 suicides per 100,000 per year that occur in Los Angeles by 8 (from the eight-to-one ratio of attempts to suicide) we arrive at a figure of 136 (see Akers 1971).

attempters. The suicide rate is highest among older age groups, but suicide attempts are most apt to be made by younger men and women (modal age of thirty-two for men and twenty-seven for females). Married persons are underrepresented in both types of suicidal behavior, but single people are more likely to attempt than to complete suicides, and the formerly married are more likely to complete suicide than they are to attempt it. Blacks are underrepresented in both completed and attempted suicides. Men employ more lethal methods than women in suicidal behavior, and certain methods, such as gunshot, hanging, and jumping, preferred by men in suicide are seldom used in attempting suicide. Less fatal techniques such as cutting the wrists and taking drugs are most likely to be used in attempted suicide (Schneidman and Farberow 1961:28–32). Essentially the same differences between completed and attempted suicide have been found in other studies (Stengel 1964:76–78; Schmid and Van Arsdol 1955; Pokorny 1968; Kalish 1968). The typical attempter is a white female in her twenties, single or currently married, not employed outside the home, who attributes her suicidal actions to marital difficulties and attempts to take her life with barbiturates. The usual suicide, on the other hand, is a white, forty-year-old, unskilled or semiskilled male who takes his life by hanging, carbon monoxide, or gunshot and who either in a note or prior to his death indicates marital problems or ill health (Schneidman and Farberow 1961:45).

The differences in the social patterning, methods used, and setting between suicide and attempted suicide lead some to assert that the two should not be considered as in the same class of behavior. The argument is that attempters form a group different from completed suicides. Suicides are not just a subgroup of attempters who happen to have been successful; the process and intent of attempting are different from those in completing suicide (Gibbs 1968:12; Stengel 1964:67–71).

Others contend that all forms of suicidal behavior are relevant to the study of suicide (Farber 1968:8). In the most thorough and systematic appraisal of the relationship between suicide and nonfatal suicidal behavior, Wilkins dismisses the notion that suicides and attempts differ in intent. In neither is the intent clearly focused on death — in both cases one places himself under the risk, not the certainty of death (1967:287–88). His review of the major studies reveals that among completed suicides who had been patients in mental hospitals at one time, between 30 percent and 77 percent had known prior histories of attempts. Studies of suicides among nonhospitalized population have found smaller proportions of suicide cases with known histories of attempts — from a low of 7 percent to a high of 33 percent.

The figures from general population samples probably represent only cases for which it could definitely be established that attempts had been made. The actual percentages are bound to be higher, for they would include attempts which did not come to anyone's attention. The higher percentage of suicides with known-attempt histories among former mental patients is probably because they had been under closer observation over a period of time, and hence their attempts were more likely to be discovered. But even if the real percentage of suicides with prior attempts is higher, it still remains that a sizable portion of people who commit suicide did not make any attempts before the fatal one. They succeeded the first time they tried (Wilkins 1967:288–89).

Another way to measure the relationship between completed and attempted suicide is to determine the proportion of people who attempt suicide and who go on to complete it later. Depending on how much time has elapsed between a known suicide attempt and the effort to locate the case for follow-up, up to 12 percent of nonhospitalized attempters subsequently commit suicide. Thus the attempter is not very likely to become a suicide; if he engages in any further suicidal behavior, it is much more likely to be further attempts. Two out of every five attempters had made at least one prior attempt and substantial numbers had made more than two prior attempts. Between 50 percent and 80 percent of completed suicides and more than half the attempters give some warning (Wilkins 1967:290–94).

The following outline summarizes the empirical relationship between completed suicide and other suicidal behavior.[4]

A. For every 100 who commit suicide, about 800 will attempt it.
B. Of 100 completed suicides
   1. At a minimum, from 7 to 33 had attempted suicide previously (a majority would have such a history if they were former mental patients).
   2. At a minimum, from 50 to 80 gave warning that they were contemplating suicide before committing it.
C. Of 100 attempted suicides
   1. At least 30 had attempted suicide previously.
   2. More than 50 gave some forewarning.
   3. From 5 to 12 (or from 22 to 69 if they are former mental patients) will complete suicide later.

It appears then that the most common suicidal behavior is gesturing, warning, and attempting. Completed suicide is a relatively rare event; only a small portion of those who attempt to take their own lives succeed. But because the number of attempters is so much greater than the number of suicides, this small percentage of people with prior attempts could contribute considerably to the total number of suicides (Wilkins 1967:294).

Keep in mind, however, that with the exception of certain special populations like former mental patients, a *minority* of successful suicides are drawn from the population of *known* attempters. Even if we admit that the percentage of suicides with actual attempt histories is greater than the percentage with known histories, it is still debatable whether more people

---

[4]Based on data from a number of studies reported in Wilkins 1967.

commit suicide only after attempting it than commit suicide on the first try. This may mean that there are at least two different paths to suicide. One path is followed by those who practice attempts before going on to complete suicide. The other path to suicide is without attempts, and the study of as yet unsuccessful suicide attempters may not tell us very much about those who follow this course. Both patterns are discussed again in chapter 24.

Variations in Suicide Rates

Statistical data on officially known completed suicides have been regularly compiled and reported for more than a century. But nearly every investigator of suicidal phenomena recognizes the pitfalls in using these official statistics. The researcher must depend on the definition used by coroners and others who decide that a death is the result of suicide and not some other cause. Insofar as both the investigator's and the coroners' definitions derive from the common-sense concept of suicide, this does not present a serious problem. However, the specific bases for deciding whether death is suicidal, accidental, homicidal, or natural may vary from one reporting district to another. Moreover, some forms of suicide, such as drowning, are especially difficult to distinguish from accidents. There are also problems of underreporting and overreporting cases. This does not mean that official data are completely unusable, as Douglas (1967:163–231) argues. Officially compiled information is the best available in the absence of other sources of data for many forms of deviant behavior, and it is the best available for studying variations in suicide rates.

Cross-Cultural Differences

Statements about suicide in nonliterate societies usually cannot go beyond noting that suicide is "common" or "rare," describing the presence of suicidal practices, or noting the instances where suicide is the custom, such as following dishonor, disgrace, or the death of a husband (Cavan 1928:56–76; Dublin 1963:83–92). But with few exceptions (Bohannan 1960) ethnographies do not include enough information to make confident statements about the actual frequency of suicide (Gibbs 1966; Labovitz 1968). It does appear that at least some nonliterate societies have suicide rates equal to those of literate and industrialized societies. There are cultural differences in methods and acceptable motives, but the range of differences is not great (Dublin 1963:76; Palmer 1968; Bohannan 1960; La Fontaine 1960; Fallers and Fallers 1960).

Much better data are available for modern nation-states. These show that while rates are not entirely constant and changes have taken place for some

countries, differences in relative frequencies of suicide around the world
have been fairly stable in the twentieth century. (These are summarized in
table 22–1.) Generally, highest rates of suicide are found in Northern and
Western European countries. North America experiences moderate rates, and
low rates prevail in Central and South America. Suicide rates by nation are
directly correlated with the degree of urbanization and industrialization
(Quinney 1965).

Table 22–1
Levels of suicide rates in selected groups of countries

Level of suicide rates	Countries
High rates (about 20 per 100,000 or more)	Austria, Denmark, Finland, Hungary, Japan, Sweden, Switzerland
Moderate rates (about 10 per 100,000)	United States, England and Wales, Uruguay, Ceylon, New Zealand
Low rates (about 5 per 100,000)	Colombia, Chile, Italy, Netherlands, Norway
Very low rates (less than 2 per 100,000)	Taiwan, Ireland, Mexico, Peru

Source: Gibbs 1966:296–97; Labovitz 1968:60–61; Cavan 1928:46).

Age, Sex, and Marital Status

In the United States, as in all the world, two generalizations about
suicide rates have held true since they were first systematically recorded:
(1) the great majority of suicides are committed by men, and (2) children
(under fifteen) commit virtually no suicides. The ratio of male to female
suicides varies considerably throughout the world, and the female rate in
some high-suicide countries is actually higher than the male rate in some
low-suicide countries. But within a given country the male rate is always
higher than the female rate, and in the United States completed suicide is
overwhelmingly a male phenomenon. About 70 percent of all suicides in
this country are male (although, as we have seen, this male-female ratio is
reversed for attempted suicide). After childhood, for both sexes, the rate at
which persons take their own lives increases with each succeeding age
group, at least until the sixth decade of life. The rate for men continues to
climb throughout, so that the oldest men are also the most suicidal. But the
female rate does not increase after about age fifty-five; at that age it stabilizes
and actually decreases somewhat among very old women. Except for those
who are married and young, marriage (especially if it results in children)

protects against suicide. For both sexes and at all age levels, the divorced and widowed have the highest suicide rates, and with the exception of the under-twenty-five group, suicide is more prevalent among the single than among the married (Dublin 1963:22–29; Labovitz 1968:63–66; Maris 1969a: 91–98, 107–8; Gibbs 1966:298–300, 304–5; Cavan 1928:306–19; Schmid and Van Arsdol 1955; Pokorny 1968).

Race and Religion

The rate of suicide among the white population of the United States is about twice that among the black population. (The white rate is not higher and in some instances is lower than other ethnic groups, such as Orientals.) This disproportionate representation of whites among suicides remains even when other variables such as age, sex, region, and marital status are controlled. But cross-classifying some of these variables produces interesting variations. For instance, the rate among all males is high enough to offset the racial difference, so that black males commit proportionately more suicides than do white females. On the other hand, the regional differences are great enough to make the suicide rate for white females in the West higher than it is for black males in the South, and the black rate in some Western cities is higher than the white rate in some Southern localities. Protestants tend to be more prone to suicide than either Catholics or Jews, but again there is variation from one country to another, from one region to another, and from one time to another (Maris 1969a:101–2; Labovitz 1968: 64–67; Dublin 1963:30–35, 74–79; Gibbs 1966:300–304; Kalish 1968; Breed 1970).

Occupational Status, Mobility, and Economic Conditions

The data on occupational status (and related indexes of socioeconomic status) and economic factors in suicide in the United States are not as readily available and do not show as consistent patterns as the data on other variables. Some investigators report higher rates for lower-status positions (Maris 1969a:122–23; Breed 1963:202); other investigators report higher rates at both the upper and lower ends of the occupational hierarchy and lower rates in the middle-level categories (Gibbs 1966:303; Labovitz 1968:68–69; Powell 1958); and others report both patterns (Dublin 1963:61–66). No one has found the highest rates to occur in the middle occupational levels.

It appears that at least for white males the highest rates of suicide are among the unemployed and the downwardly mobile (Breed 1963; 1967; Labovitz 1968:69; Powell 1958; Maris 1969a:127). Rates tend to rise during times of economic depression and to decline in periods of war and relative prosperity (Henry and Short 1954:25–44; Dublin 1963:65–66; La Fontaine 1960:119; Gibbs 1966:308).

Place of Residence

Until the early part of the twentieth century in the United States urban suicide rates were much higher than rural rates, but the urban rates declined until the difference became quite small. Rural and urban rates have been about the same (in some places the rural rate is higher; in others the urban is higher) since around 1960 (Dublin 1963:49–55; Gibbs 1966:301–2; Labovitz 1968:66). The highest suicide rate is in the West, the South and Midwest have intermediate rates, and the lowest rates occur in the Northern states (Labovitz 1968:62). The proportionately larger number of suicides in the West is affected by the especially high rates in the large coastal cities— Los Angeles, San Francisco, Portland, and Seattle (Dublin 1963:52, 223–25). Some locations within the city traditionally have high rates. Suicide occurs most frequently in the skid row and "disorganized" areas of the city in and near the central district. Relatively few suicides occur in the black community, in residential areas in the outer parts of the city, and in suburban areas (Cavan 1928:77–105; Schmid and Van Arsdol 1955:276; Maris 1969a:136,

Table 22–2
Social status, economic conditions, and residence correlated with suicide in the United States

Status	Status with relatively high rate of suicide	Status with relatively low rate of suicide
Sex	Male	Female
Age	Old	Young
Race	White	Black
Marital	Divorced	Married
	Widowed	
Religion	Protestant	Catholic
		Jew
Occupation	Low-level	Middle-level
	High-level	Employed
	Unemployed	

Economic conditions	Condition with relatively high rate of suicide	Condition with relatively low rate of suicide
State of the economy	Depression	Prosperity

Area of residence	Area with relatively higher rate of suicide	Area with relatively lower rate of suicide
Region	West	North
City area	Central	Suburbs
	and	
	adjacent	

Source: Adapted from discussion and sources cited in text.

156; Dublin 1963:54; Seiden 1967). (This discussion of suicide rates by status, economic conditions, and place of residence is summarized in table 22–2.)

Temporal and Seasonal Variations

The suicide rate in the United States (approximately 11 per 100,000) is about the same as it was in 1900. The rate per 100,000 increased to over 16 by World War I, declined, and then increased again, reaching a peak of over 17 in the depths of the depression. It dropped in the late 1930s and continued to fall through World War II. Since then it has remained between 10 and 11 (Dublin 1963:18–19). There is some indication that suicides are most frequent in the spring and in the first or middle of the week, but there is little consistent relationship between suicide and temperature, season, or month of the year (Dublin 1963:56–60; Schneidman and Farberow 1961:33–36; Pokorny 1968:235; Maris 1969a:76–90; Schmid and Van Arsdol 1955:280).

Suicide and Homicide

The nature of the relationship between suicide and homicide has been the subject of empirical and theoretical debate for more than a century (see Durkheim 1951:338–52). Are groups that have high rates of suicide the same as or different from those that have high rates of homicide? Both are obviously violent acts, but are they linked in some way? Henry and Short (1954) found that in the years when suicide rates were high in the United States, homicide rates were low. Homicide correlated positively with the business cycle, whereas suicide correlated negatively with the business cycle. Suicide was concentrated in high-status categories and homicide in low-status categories. These findings led them to view suicide and homicide—both aggressive acts flowing from frustration—as opposing phenomena negating each other.

Studies and theories of the general homicide-suicide relationship have continued, and some attention has been given to the special situation in which persons follow up their commission of homicide by committing suicide (Gold 1969; Teele 1965; Wood 1961; West 1966; Cavan 1928:254–62). It is still not clear, however, that there is a consistent empirical relationship between homicide and suicide. At one time statistics showed an inverse correlation, and much effort was expended to explain this. However, in the twentieth century this clear negative relationship has tended to disappear in many parts of the world (Bohannan 1960:17–18). Both rates have been moderate and stable in the United States for some years now; both rates are low in some societies and in some social categories (for example, among women) and high in other societies and groups (for example, among men).

Although both may be related (either in the same or opposite direction) to some third variable, it appears that no necessary or causal connection exists between suicide and homicide (Quinney 1965).

Issues in the Prevention of Suicide

Recently a movement has emerged which pictures suicide as an act of cool deliberation, that people should have the right to commit suicide without interference from the state. This "death by choice" (Maguire 1975) is part of the "death with dignity" movement. Basically the argument is that death by individual choice is more dignified and humane than life as a human vegetable or under unbearable circumstances.

It is obviously in the interest of the society as a whole to protect life and to prevent self-destruction. And, although one who takes his own life may adversely affect the lives of others, the only direct victim of successful suicide is the suicide himself. It is in the same category of "crimes without victims" as drug use, homosexuality, prostitution, and so on. Therefore, the question is whether or not the state should legally or coercively prevent people from taking their own lives. At one time the answer seemed clear: Only God and the state have the right to take life and it was a sin and a crime to attempt or complete suicide. Suicide attempters could be prosecuted for a misdemeanor, and the state could confiscate the property of one who committed suicide and deny his heirs their inheritance.

Suicide is still widely viewed as an irrational act of desperation by a person with a sick mind and is considered by many to be the ultimate sin. But the state no longer treats suicide as a problem of criminal law. If the state does intervene, it is through the lunacy hearing boards which commit individuals to institutions for mental incompetency; danger to oneself is one major criterion for determining involuntary incarceration in a mental hospital. The state is also apt to support private efforts to dissuade or help attempters and prevent potential suicides. In addition to the traditional medical-psychiatric treatment for those who have attempted suicide, *suicide prevention centers* or crisis clinics have been established within the past decade.

The first suicide prevention clinics were opened in Seattle and Los Angeles in the 1960s. Other cities followed them in quick order. Many of these have expanded into or merged with more general purpose "crisis" or "hotline" centers to react to other crises as well as suicide. Now these exist in most major cities and in many smaller ones. They began mainly as private institutions (often funded through the local United Way), but often now combine private support with public funding. They are staffed by a few professionals and mostly volunteers, who might have been given some elementary training in dealing with suicidal behavior. Their principal service is what may best be described as "telephone talk therapy." The idea is that people who are contemplating suicide will "cry for help"; they desperately need someone who will answer that cry because suicide results when no one responds. Therefore, simply dialing the phone to get help should prevent suicide. The volunteer tries to convince the caller to come to grips with his problem, that there is hope, and that constructive action can be taken. If the caller has already committed some life-threatening act, such as taking an overdose of barbiturates, then the volunteer tries to locate him and to send medical help. Some centers have counseling staff and will sometimes urge the caller to come to the center for face-to-face counseling. But the main technique is simply to converse on the telephone. If this is done properly, the potential suicide can be talked out of taking his own life.

The actual operation of the centers is confronted with a number of problems which frustrate their aim of suicide prevention. One common problem is that a great many of the calls have nothing to do with suicide or any other imminent crisis. The caller hangs up when the telephone is answered, there are obscene phone calls, and some callers make sick jokes. There are some chronic callers who call several times every day, just wanting to talk to someone. Some centers get as many as 100 of these kinds of calls a day.

The call from someone who is really on the verge of suicide is actually not very common. Indeed the typical serious call is from someone who is at best a moderate risk of suicide. The great majority of calls are from people who are not serious about suicide; they seem to be suicide attempters and communicators who, as we have seen, are not necessarily those who are most likely to commit actual suicide.

Therefore, because centers are not reaching the people they were meant to reach, they have not had much impact on the suicide rates. Their ideology is that all the effort is worthwhile if just one person is reached and saved. The effectiveness of the suicide centers is very rarely studied, but what evidence there is suggests that they have not successfully curtailed suicides even among the people that they do reach. The idea seems sound but before the centers can be expected to accumulate much of a record of success in diverting people from actual suicide, they must deal with more serious suicide victims than they now do (Maris 1969b; Lester and Lester 1971; Jacobs 1971).

Summary

The most general category of behavior relevant to suicidal phenomena is self-injurious behavior. Suicide proper is defined as the completed act of intended, self-precipitated fatal injury. Nonfatal suicidal behavior includes suicide attempts, gestures, and communications. Nonfatal suicide attempts are about eight times more frequent than completed suicide, and up to one-third of those who commit suicide have attempted it at least once before.

The highest rates of suicide are found in countries in western and northern Europe. Men are much more likely to commit suicide than women, but women are more likely than men to attempt suicide. Unmarried men and women tend to take their own lives more than married persons. The suicide rate among whites is double that among blacks. Protestants are more prone to suicide than either Catholics or Jews. Suicide rates are low in times of economic prosperity and high during depressions. Suicide is unrelated to temperature, season, or month of the year. At one time suicide rates tended to rise as homicide rates fell (and vice versa), but this is no longer true.

The suicide prevention clinic is a new way in which society is attempting to control suicide. The suicide center has professional and volunteer staff on hand to answer calls from those contemplating suicide, although thus far the suicide prevention centers appear to have had little effect on the suicide rate.

23

Theories of Suicide

Sociological Theories

Durkheim: Classic Statement
of the Sociological Perspective

The classic sociological study of suicide is that of Emile Durkheim, in *Le Suicide*, first published in French in 1897. It set the tone, the issues, and, to some extent, the methodology, and it became the standard reference for all subsequent sociological interest in suicide, although it was not translated into English until 1951 (Durkheim 1951). Durkheim's chief concern was to use the study of suicide to illustrate that sociology is and ought to be an independent and positivistic science separate from psychology and biology. If suicide, an obviously unusual and individual act, could be shown to be fundamentally caused by social factors rather than by biology, climate, heredity, or psychopathic states, other less "individualized" behavior should be even more dependent on "social facts." To Durkheim this was possible because he conceived of the *rate of suicide* in a social group or category as a fact above and independent of the individual motives leading a given person within that group to take his own life. Moreover, so capricious and complex were the individual circumstances and motives leading to suicide, only a general theory of suicide rates was possible. This general theory would refer directly to "the states of the various social environments . . . in terms of which the variations of suicide occur" (Durkheim 1951:151).

In concrete terms these social environments are the family, religion, the state, the occupation, and the economy. Durkheim studied the way in which the suicide rate differed among these social environments. The general theory was then arrived at by positing collective properties of the groups to account for their higher or lower suicide rates. The collective properties were identified by Durkheim as of three basic types—*egoistic, altruistic,* and *anomic*. The extent to which a group was egoistic, altruistic, or anomic was seen as the social cause of its suicide rate, and because he argued for a theory of suicide based on what causes it, Durkheim applied these same labels to denote three basic types of suicide (1951:145–51).[1]

Egoistic suicide was caused by a lack of social *integration* of the group. For instance, Durkheim explained the higher suicide rate among Protestants (as compared to Catholics) by reference to the lesser degree of integration or solidarity among Protestants (Durkheim 1951:152–70). His explanation of differences in suicide rates between married and single persons (controlling for age), between families with children and those without, and between one political entity and another followed the same line of reasoning (Durkheim 1951:171–216). His overall explanation of egoistic suicide then was that

> suicide varies inversely with the degree of integration of religious society, . . . of domestic society, . . . of political society. . . . The cause can only be found in a single quality possessed by all these social groups, though perhaps to varying degrees. The only quality satisfying this condition is that they are all strongly integrated social groups. So we reach the general conclusion: *suicide varies inversely with degree of integration of the social groups of which the individual forms a part* (Durkheim 1951:208–9, italics added).

Durkheim placed *altruistic* suicide at the opposite pole from egoistic suicide. Persons committed suicide not because they were insufficiently integrated into a society but because they were too well integrated; they obediently followed the "social requirement" (obligatory or optional) of taking or sacrificing their own lives under certain circumstances (Durkheim 1951:217–40). Durkheim gave several illustrations of historical and contemporary customs of altruistic suicide for "social ends," but he had statistics only on the military, which he saw as a "special environment where altruistic suicide is chronic" (Durkheim 1951:228–40).

Anomic suicide was for Durkheim the consequence of a lack of social *regulation* of "desires." The variations which he felt were indications of anomic suicide were those which occurred with changes in the economy, among occupations, and with war. But he also posited that the high rate of suicide among the divorced was a result of the anomic situation of being severed from the social control of marriage and a family (Durkheim 1951: 241–76).

Durkheim did not propose a theory of suicide and then set out to test it. Rather he constructed a *post hoc* explanation through a study of the suicide rates. Although he carefully defined suicide, Durkheim did not clearly define or measure either degree of integration or regulation. He was therefore left with no operational way, apart from the rate itself, to determine if a group

---

[1]A fourth type of suicide, "fatalistic," was recognized in a footnote but was discussed nowhere else by Durkheim (1951:276). See Breed (1970) for a recent discussion of fatalistic suicide. Breed maintains that black suicide in the United States is fatalistic suicide.

whose high suicide rate he said was caused by egoism was in fact not well integrated. He could not measure the extent to which a group was so well integrated that it could impose altruistic suicide on its members or had become so deregulated that it presented a social environment for anomic suicide. His method was simply to argue on an essentially common-sense basis that Catholics were more integrated than Protestants, that suicides in the army were of an altruistic nature, that married persons were more socially integrated than single or divorced persons, and so on. Thus, although Durkheim is still recognized as a pioneer in sociology, his study of suicide has been criticized for a number of theoretical and methodological shortcomings (Douglas 1967; Johnson 1965; Martin 1968; Maris 1969a).

Post-Durkheim Sociological Theories of Suicide Rates

Cavan: Disorganization and suicide.   Although American sociologists do not often explicitly recognize its Durkheimian basis, their *disorganization* is essentially the same thing referred to by Durkheim's *anomie* (lack of regulation) and *egoism* (lack of integration). Cavan's study (1928) of variations in suicide around the world, in the United States, and in Chicago, along with such pioneering studies as that of Schmid (1928), can be taken as classic statements of the disorganization theory of suicide.

Cavan distinguished between "institutionalized" suicide (altruistic?), which she believed was the characteristic mode of suicide in primitive and some contemporary Eastern societies, and "individualized" (egoistic? anomic?) suicide, which she believed was the typical form of suicide found in Europe and the United States (Cavan 1928:12–105). Individualized suicide is explained by disorganization in the community or in the life of the individual. The basic argument is that suicide rates will be high in communities, groups, and social categories where disorganization prevails, because social control is insufficient to check deviant impulses.

> Whenever community organization breaks down there is an especially good opportunity for personal disorganization to occur. Vagrant and normally inhibited impulses are permitted free reign in a way not possible in a well-integrated community. . . . [C]onduct typical of the highly suicidal areas . . . are symptoms of a general condition of personal and social disorganization which in the end may lead to suicide. There is in these areas a concentration of unsatisfied and disorganized persons, and therefore the probability of more suicide than in communities well organized as to community life and the characters of individuals.
>
> [In disorganized groups] which have conflicts in social codes and confusion of customs . . . the individual stands out as a separate entity, driven by unregulated impulses and wishes and often unable to find satisfaction for them. . . . In times of social disorganiza-

tion the difficulty is increased and many people who travel happily along under normal conditions find themselves unable to adjust to confused and conflicting standards. It is these people . . . who contribute to the increased suicide rates in communities where social disorganization prevails (Cavan 1928:103–8).

Henry and Short: Restraint and suicide.   The theory of Henry and Short (1954) is a sociopsychological theory of homicide and suicide as forms of aggression. They accept the hypothesis that aggression is the inevitable result of frustration and postulate that both homicide and suicide are aggressive products of frustration. This frustration is created by the relative loss of status from the ups and downs of the economy (Henry and Short 1954:54–65). Thus suicide and homicide are opposite directions in which aggression can flow, and they are linked by the common cause of frustration. The direction of the aggression—suicide or homicide—depends on the presence or absence of sociological and psychological *restraints.*

When psychological restraint is present in the form of a strong superego or "internalization of harsh parental demands and discipline," outward aggression is not legitimized, and the probability of suicide is increased. When sociological restraint is present in the form of external social control, just the opposite is true: the probability of suicide is decreased. The highest rate of suicide is predicted for those who operate under weak external restraint and strong internal restraint; the highest rate of homicide is predicted for those with weak internal but strong external restraint (Henry and Short 1954:69–121).

Although Henry and Short include both internal and sociological variables in their theory, they are rightly regarded as following in the Durkheimian tradition. They quote Durkheim in hypothesizing that persons of higher status have higher suicide rates because they are under less external regulation than lower-status persons. Therefore, men with higher status than women have higher suicide rates, whites with higher status than blacks have higher suicide rates, and so on. To explain other high rates in which status positions seem irrelevant (for example, high rates among the unmarried), Henry and Short use the concept of "degree of involvement in relationships with other persons," or "strength of the relational system," as the equivalent of Durkheim's notion of social integration. Those, like the unmarried, who are not involved in a strong system of interpersonal relationships such as the family are more apt to commit suicide. In both cases— lower status and strong relationship system—individuals are externally restrained and are less likely to commit suicide.

The external restraint theory has also been subject to criticism (Douglas 1967; Gibbs 1966; Martin 1968). The theory has not really been tested, because neither Henry and Short nor anybody else has devised good measures of internal and external restraint related to suicide. Henry and Short assumed their presence or absence. Also, the theory has been questioned on the grounds that it does not explain many variations (for example, among nations) and that it assumes that higher-status people are not restrained.

Maris: External constraint and suicide.   Although he is critical of Durkheim on some points, Maris's approach is self-consciously Durkheimian. The "modest systematic theory" he proposes is also presented as directly derived from Durkheim's theory of social integration and suicide (Maris 1969a: 177–89). The theory as stated, however, is more in the nature of Durkheim by way of Henry and Short, for it is almost the same as the "external restraint" part of their theory.[2]

> Our crucial postulate or general proposition is that the external constraint in a group (or of an individual) varies inversely with its suicide rate (his suicide potential) (Maris 1969a:185).[3]

To Maris, *constraint* is by definition the equivalent of Durkheim's integration-regulation. Thus *lack of constraint* by definition means anomie and egoism. The less the constraint, the higher the probability of suicide is. Maris assumes that greater constraint is present when there is a greater "number of interpersonal dependency relationships" and the "more subordinate one is" ("the less power he has") (Maris 1969a:180).[4] However, as was true of Durkheim and of Henry and Short, Maris has no direct measures of his independent variable—constraint. He too assumes greater or lesser constraint from such variables as marital status, age, sex, and race. For example, the low suicide rate of married people with children is explained by the constraint based on the greater number of interpersonal relationships implied in that status.

Maris does introduce a new element into the theory—namely, the notion of the "suicidal career" (Maris 1969a:12). This idea helps to explain instances of suicide which occur under apparent conditions of strong external constraint, such as fatalistic suicide. For example, in a suicidal career the person could start out under conditions of excessive regulation (too much constraint), become alienated as a result, begin to lessen ties with others,

---

[2] Maris seems not to recognize the great similarity between his and the Henry-Short theory. He cites Henry and Short only when he discusses the problem of "internal restraint" as a possible individual variable which must be taken into account in predicting suicide from lack of external constraint (Maris 1969a:183).

[3] Actually this statement implies that external constraint is caused by high suicide rates. It should read, "Suicide varies inversely with external constraint."

[4] Again these two notions of interpersonal relationships and subordinate status very closely echo Henry and Short's ideas about the "strength of the relational system" and "status position."

and enter a stage of anomie and diminished constraint. Therefore, at the point of committing suicide the person is under weak constraint, even though the objective facts about his social characteristics (such as being young or black) would classify him in a high-constraint group.

Gibbs and Martin: Status integration and suicide.   In the most significant modern theory of suicide rates, Gibbs and Martin offer "status integration" as an empirically measurable form of social integration (Gibbs and Martin 1958; 1964; Martin 1968; Gibbs 1969). They interpret Durkheim to mean that suicide varies inversely with the "strength of individuals' ties to society" or the "stability and durability of social relationships." But they contend that these are unmeasurable and then move through a series of assumptions and postulates to something which is measurable.

Basically their argument is: (a) durability and stability of relationships depend on how well persons are able to conform to normative expectations; (b) conformity is inversely related to degree of role conflict; (c) if a greater number of people occupy compatible statuses they experience less role conflict; (d) if a population is made up of individuals who occupy various compatible statuses within "status configurations," the degree of status integration in that population will be greater. Finally, the testable hypothesis is: "The suicide rate of a population varies inversely with the degree of status integration in that population" (Gibbs and Martin 1958:143).

They reason that persons will avoid configurations with conflicting statuses and will gravitate to those which are internally harmonious. Therefore, if a particular status configuration is not very often occupied, it must be because it is not "integrated"—that is, it contains statuses which are incompatible. People who find themselves in these situations are more prone to suicide, supposedly because people who experience role conflict commit suicide more often than those who do not. For instance, if 70 percent of Protestant, white men aged twenty-five–thirty-five and working at white-collar jobs are married, then the most integrated marital status which one who fits this religion–race–age–occupation description could have is "married." If 20 percent of the men in this status configuration are single, and the remaining 10 percent are divorced or widowed, then being single is less integrated, and being formerly married is the marital position least integrated with the other statuses. Therefore, the prediction would be that among people fitting this particular age, sex, occupational, religious, and racial combination, the highest rate of suicide would be found among the formerly married, the next highest among the single, and the lowest rate among the currently married.

The status integration theory is the most formalized theory of rates, and both the earlier data (Gibbs and Martin 1964) and more recent data

(Gibbs 1969) analyzed by Gibbs and Martin tend to support the basic proposition that more integrated statuses have lower rates of suicide. However, the theory has been criticized for not recognizing that some status configurations may be infrequently occupied simply because they are undesirable or have low prestige, rather than because they are not integrated. Also, critics argue that the research testing the theory does not properly measure status integration (Douglas 1967:84–91; Chambliss and Steele 1966; Gibbs and Martin 1966; Hagedorn and Labovitz 1966; Gibbs and Martin 1968; Gibbs 1969).

Summary of Sociological Theory

Johnson (1965) shows that the two variables of regulation and integration which Durkheim saw as independent social causes of suicide turn out to be just two labels for the same thing. A well-integrated group is also well regulated, and even using Durkheim's own concepts, anomie and egoism cannot be clearly distinguished (Johnson 1965:882–84). Therefore, according to Johnson, Durkheim is left with only "one cause" of suicide: lack of social integration. The sociological theories reviewed here seem to recognize this and do not maintain Durkheim's distinctions. To all intents and purposes the collective variables by which sociological theories explain suicide rates (solidarity, integration, restraint, and so on) all refer to social integration (combining Durkheim's integration and regulation).

Anomie or disorganization characterizes groups with high rates of suicide, and strong social integration characterizes those with little suicide. At least for societies and groups with norms against suicide, when strong ties hold people to a common bond and when individuals are involved in integrative social relationships, there is less likelihood of suicide. When this integration is lacking or when it is disrupted or lessened by crises and problems, the likelihood of suicide increases. This theme runs through all the post-Durkheim sociological theories and overrides their differences.[5]

This Durkheimian emphasis has meant that sociological theories have been devoted mainly to accounting for variations in rates of completed suicide and have been tested mainly with statistical analysis of suicide rates. Because they have been addressed to the structural question, these theories only indirectly attempt to explain why some individuals take their own lives. The theories do sometimes contain notions about individual acts of suicide, but these are not formal components of the theories. Individual motivation to suicide has been the focus of other theories, and we now discuss some of them.

---

[5] For a review of pre- and post-Durkheim sociological theories see Douglas 1967:3–163. For a review of latter day sociological theory see Gibbs 1966; Martin 1968; Bohannan 1960; Beall 1968.

Psychological and Social
Psychological Theories of Suicidal Behavior

A Note on Psychiatric Theories of Suicide

The psychoanalytic approach contains a variety of perspectives, but the basic psychoanalytic explanation of suicidal behavior is that it is the outcome of some form of mental disorder, psychopathology, or personality disturbance. Most psychoanalytic theorists do not accept the common-sense idea that a person "must be crazy to commit suicide." Nevertheless, a person who commits or attempts suicide is likely to be diagnosed as suffering from some type of neurosis, extreme depression, unconsious wishes to kill or to gain revenge, repressed guilt, or other intrapsychic disturbance, and to have his psychic difficulties traced to some childhood experience.[6]

The presumption among some writers is that the way to answer the questions of both group rates and individual motivation is to devise some combination of sociological and psychoanalytic perspectives. For instance, in his introduction to the English translation of Durkheim, Simpson says:

> It is the basic hypothesis here that interrelating psychoanalytic discoveries on the motives for suicide with the social conditions under which suicide occurs offers the most fruitful method of advancing our knowledge of the phenomenon (1951:22–23).

Likewise, noting the century-old split between the "psychiatric thesis" and "sociological thesis," Martin aptly sums up the distinctive features of each:

> Anomie, social isolation, the strength of external restraint over behavior, lack of status integration, secularization, and social disorganization in the sociological literature are matched by morbid anxiety, pathological depression, hopelessness, alienation, and guilt as central notions in psychology and psychiatry. The sociological terminology focuses on "weak" social relations, while the notion of personality traits is the other common denominator (1968:94).

---

[6] For the person who wishes to read more about this approach, which is admittedly slighted here, the following sources should be helpful. The entire second part of Schneidman and Farberow 1957 is entitled "Clinical Considerations" and contains exclusively psychoanalytic analyses. The same is true of the entire part two of Farberow and Schneidman 1961, which presents different psychoanalytic interpretations of the same case. The bibliography on pp. 325–88 of Farberow and Schneidman should also be consulted. In addition see Menninger 1938; Kilpatrick 1968; Stengel 1964:97–116; Dublin 1963:153–76; Beall 1968.

Although he is not entirely optimistic about the prospects, Martin suggests that social structural determinants be combined with psychoanalytic conceptions of personality determinants. Beall (1968) also notes that sociologists continue to emphasize social structure without taking into account the "basic internal struggle" which suicides undergo and that social psychological theories should combine the two. Finally, Hendin (1964) believes that psychoanalytic insights into motivation must be fused with knowledge of sociocultural forces for an adequate understanding of suicide, and he makes one of the few serious attempts to do so.

However, there is no reason why the process whereby an individual comes to the point of taking or attempting to take his own life must necessarily involve intrapsychic pathologies as traditionally conceived in psychoanalytic theory. Moreover, there have been some notable attempts to devise a social psychology of suicide which focuses on the impact of interpersonal relationships rather than on the mental health of the individual. Some of these will be discussed here as a prelude to the presentation of a social learning analysis of suicide and suicidal behavior.

Cavan: Disruption of life organization.   Just as she anticipated many later sociologists in studying suicide rates, Cavan anticipated by many years most of the themes that figure prominently in social psychological theories of suicide — life crisis, hopelessness, disrupted life organization, despair, socialization of aggression, and the interplay of these with the reactions of others to the suicide's behavior. Cavan's idea was that the varying rates of suicide reflected the extent to which categories of persons were (1) faced with life crises and loss of hope, and (2) exposed to attitudes favorable to suicide. In essence, she thought that the suicide process was one of personal disorganization growing out of (a) a major disturbance in adjustment of the person's environment, (b) thwarted wish or ambition, (c) disconcordant life interests, or (d) some break in a previously satisfactory life organization. When these disorganizing experiences are met by someone who has developed (learned?) a "favorable attitude to death, and particularly to suicide, as a commendable means of ending crises," suicide is apt to result (Cavan 1928:320–27).

Douglas: Social meanings and suicide.   Douglas (1967) attempts to direct the study of suicide to the concrete situations and meanings involved in the suicide process. To do this he proposes to construct a theory of "suicidal actions as socially meaningful actions." The three prime subjects to which he directs his attention are *general dimensions* of meaning, *common patterns* of constructed meanings, and the *suicide process*. The general dimensions of suicidal meaning are that: (1) suicidal actions are meaningful, (2) suicidal actions mean that something is fundamentally wrong with the situation of the actor, and (3) something is fundamentally wrong with the actor (1967: 271–83).

The common patterns of meanings in suicidal actions are: (1) suicide is a way of transforming oneself to another world—for example, religious suicide; (2) suicide is a way of transforming the "substantial self," to show how sincere or committed one is about something—for example, atonement suicides; (3) suicide is a means of achieving "fellow-feeling," to get pity or some other response from others—for example, suicidal actions as an appeal for help; (4) suicidal actions are a way of seeking revenge on someone (1967:284–319).

Douglas's attention to the suicide process is not directed toward spelling out the steps or stages leading up to suicide; rather, it is directed to the interactions and communication which lead to constructing specific meanings of suicide by individuals. He does not show how these communications lead to meanings, but he notes that because suicidal thoughts and statements are very common, most people do not impute real suicidal intent to others unless the others have a suicidal history or have previously communicated serious suicidal intent. However, there are "typical suicidal situations" in which suicidal intent is likely to be imputed before the person himself has given any signals of intent. The only one Douglas mentions is the situation of sudden, great personal loss. Also, "specialists' communications" include the mental illness context, in which patients are likely to be suspected of suicide intentions even without suicidal acts or communications.

Breed: Symbolic interaction and loss.   Warren Breed (1963; 1967) stresses that some form of "loss" is the crisis which precedes suicide. His primary emphasis has been on loss of status through downward occupational mobility (1963), but he also recognizes loss of important and satisfactory social relationships (either through the loss of another person or through the inability to maintain relationships) (1967). Somehow this loss represents a failure to live up to role expectations (for example, the expectation of males that they will be employed and will fulfill an occupational role), and the reactions of others to this failure make it difficult for a person to maintain a favorable self-image. The destruction of the favorable self-concept leads to the destruction of life.

Farber and Kobler and Stotland: The end of hope.   Farber (1968), like Breed, posits loss of competence in interpersonal relationships and role performance as an element in suicidal potential. But for Farber this is related to suicide through its impact on hope. Hope is a function of (a) a sense of competence and (b) threat in life conditions. When competence is low and threat is great, hopelessness sets in, and "it is when the life outlook is of despairing hopelessness that suicide occurs" (1968:12).

Kobler and Stotland (1964) recognize that external circumstances can push people to loss of hope, but they are less concerned with original causes of hopelessness and more with how others react to the individuals' communication of that despair. To Kobler and Stotland, suicide results less from a crisis or loss of hope as such than from an inadequate response of others to the person's pleas for help, indicated by suicide threats, warnings, or attempts. If the response communicates to the suicidal person that there is hope and that suicide is not expected of him, suicide usually will not occur.

> Our conception views suicidal attempts and verbal or other communications of suicidal intent as efforts, however misdirected, to solve problems of living, as frantic pleas for help and hope from other people; help in solving the problems, and hope that they can be solved. Whether the individual then actually commits suicide— and this is our central concern—seems to depend in large part on the nature of the response by other people to his plea. If the response to the plea is hopeless and helpless, suicide is more likely to occur. It is our conviction that an implicit or explicit fear or expectation of suicide is most often communicated by a hopeless, helpless response, and that this communication is important in facilitating suicide (Kobler and Stotland 1964:1).

Jacobs: Suicide as trust violation—unsolvable problems and verbalizations. Jacobs (1967) has devised a theory which comes closer than any other to spelling out a step-by-step process by which individuals come to the point of attempting or completing suicide. He combines the elements of despair, crisis, loss, hopelessness, and relationships with others with a differential association concept of coming to acquire rationalizing definitions favorable to suicide. Indeed, his theory is a direct application of Cressey's theory of trust violation to the "conscious deliberations" that take place before the individual is able to consider and execute the act of suicide. Just as persons turn to financial trust violation to solve a nonsharable problem, suicides turn to self-destruction as a resolution of nonsharable, insolvable life problems. But in a society which condemns suicide, one's life is seen as a sacred trust, and as with violations of financial trust, the person contemplating suicide must "reconcile the image of himself as a trusted person with his act of trust violation—suicide" (1967:64).

As Jacobs sees the full process, the individual must:

1. be faced with an unexpected, intolerable, and insolvable problem;

2. view this as not an isolated unpleasant incident but within the context of a long biography of such troubled situations, and expect future ones;

3. believe that death is the only absolute answer to this apparent absolute dilemma of life;

4. come to this point of view (a) by way of an increasing social isolalation whereby he is unable to share his problem with the person or persons who must share it if it is to be resolved, or (b) by being isolated from the cure of some incurable illness which in turn isolates him from health and the community, thereby doubly ensuring the insolubility of the problem;

5. overcome the social constraints — that is, the social norms he had internalized whereby he views suicide as irrational and/or immoral;

6. succeed in this because he feels himself less an integral part of the society than the others and therefore is held less firmly by its bonds;

7. succeed in accomplishing step 6 by applying to his intended suicide a verbalization which enables him to adjust his conception of himself as a trusted person with his conception of himself as a trust violator;

8. succeed in doing this by defining the situation so that the problem is (a) not of his own making (b) unresolved, but not from any lack of personal effort, and (c) not given any resolution known to him except death . . . ;

9. in short, define death as necessary by the above process and in so doing remove all choice and with it sin and immorality;

10. make some provision for ensuring against the recurrence of these problems in the afterlife (1967:67).

This process was reconstructed by Jacobs through an examination of suicide notes. He recognizes several "forms" used to recount the suicide's

---

Suicide Notes

It is hard to say why you don't want to live. I have only one reason. The three people I have in the world which I love don't want me. . . . I love you all dearly and am sorry this is the way I have to say goodbye. Please forgive me and be happy.

Your wife and your daughter

Dear Dear Jane: You are ruining your health and your life just for me, and I cannot let you do it. The pains in my face seem worse every day and there is a limit to what a man can take. I love you dear.

Bill

You Bob and Jane caused this — this all.
Mary, I hope you're satisfied.

Bill

I have gone down to the ocean. Pick out the cheapest coffin Jones Bros. has. I don't remember the cost. I'll put my purse in the trunk of the car.
Please do not disturb. Someone sleeping.

(From Jacobs 1967)

---

reasons and rationalizations for taking his life. Of these, "firstform" notes contain all or nearly all the steps of the full process and invariably ask forgiveness for the deed. In other forms some elements may be missing. For instance, when an incurable illness is the insolvable problem, pleas for forgiveness are apt to be missing because the illness itself is seen as sufficient and acceptable justification for suicide. "Direct accusation" notes place the blame for the suicide squarely on someone else's shoulders, and therefore no responsibility and need to ask forgiveness is felt. Other notes concentrate on the last step — precaution against meeting the same problems in the afterlife by asking God's forgiveness, requesting prayer, repudiating the concept of afterlife, and so on. However, of all the notes studied, only a very small proportion (such as those that simply left instructions or last wills) did not contain the essential elements of the process (Jacobs 1967:68–72).

As long as there is some possibility of resolving the problems, suicide will not be contemplated and attempted seriously. When a person's life is defined as offering no possibility of resolving the difficulty — through repeated experience with failure to resolve difficulties and the lack of others' help — it becomes a serious consideration. But before the consideration is carried further and acted upon, the individual must rationalize suicide as a justifiable act, something a trusted person would do and for which he could be absolved. It should be noted that Jacob's theory of suicide as trust violation does not have to contend with verbalizations as after-the-fact rationalizations. The rationalizations had to be offered before the suicide (in the note) because the person cannot justify his suicide afterward.

Summary

All the sociological theories of suicide rates are derived from Durkheim. Variations and refinements of Durkheim's explanation of suicide rates as reflection of social integration and regulation can be found in modern theories of disorganization, restraint, constraint, and status integration. Sociological theories maintain that suicide rates will be low in groups and societies which are highly integrated and will be high in those which are loosely integrated.

No such common thread runs through social psychological theories of the process by which an individual comes to take his own life. One or more of these theories include an emphasis on: personal disorganization; exposure to attitudes favorable to suicide; the meaning of suicide as atonement, revenge, or an appeal for help; personal tragedy or loss; hopelessness; failure to live up to role expectations and to maintain a favorable self-image; the responses of other people to suicidal attempts; suicide as an effort to resolve nonsharable, insolvable problems; rationalizations of suicide.

24

A Social Learning Analysis of the Suicidal Process

Suicide presents an intriguing challenge to a learning theory of deviance which relies upon reinforcement as the major element of motivation. Completed suicide by its very nature is not a repeatable or recurrent behavior. Therefore, *the act of taking one's own life, as such, cannot have been reinforced in the past.* In this sense one cannot learn to kill himself or develop a habit of killing himself. Although all the evidence and all the theories presented in chapter 23 argue convincingly that suicide is a profoundly social act based on and precipitated by events the person has experienced in his past and which confront him in the present, these events cannot have included the environmental consequences of the completed act of suicide.

Suicidal behavior is based on social learning, however. There are at least two learning paths to suicide: (1) learning to behave suicidally, but not fatally, and ultimately reaching the point of suicide, and (2) learning about and developing a readiness to suicide and completing it without prior practice in specifically suicidal behavior. If an explicit recognition of the reinforcing and nonreinforcing actions and reactions of others were added to it, the ten-step process posited by Jacobs (see pp. 293–94) would probably apply to both avenues to suicide. The essential features of the suicide process, with or without overt attempts before suicide, then would be: (a) learning and applying cultural definitions of suicide, (b) the real or perceived existence of chronic or acute problems of loss and life crises, (c) the loss of hope for their solution, (d) reinforcing or punishing reactions of others to the person's suicidal behavior and attempts to communicate that he wants help for his problems.

The roads to suicide are discussed below. The discussion of suicide after previously learned nonfatal suicidal responses emphasizes the social reaction to such behavior; the discussion of the other way to suicide emphasizes the learning of cultural definitions conducive to suicide. These two do not exhaust the ways in which people come to the point of committing suicide. There are cases of suicide in which there has been neither prior practice of suicidelike behavior nor any particular learning of suicide-prone definitions. These cases must be taken as exceptions to the social learning analysis which follows. However, the analysis does provide a way of incorporating the basic items in the theoretical and empirical knowledge of the suicide process (reviewed in chapter 23) and articulating it with that of suicide rates.

Suicide Resulting from Previously Learned Nonfatal Suicidal Behavior

This route to suicide is most clearly based on prior instrumental learning: successive approximations to suicide are made by repeating rewarded nonfatal suicidal acts. The individual's conditioning history produces a class of nonfatal responses similar to the final act of suicide—indeed, different from it often only through happenstance. But whereas other behavior once shaped is capable of subsequent direct reinforcements, suicide is self-terminating.

The clearest evidence for the control of self-destructive behavior by its reinforcement in a social environment comes from work with autistic and retarded children (Tate and Baroff 1966; Lovaas et al. 1968; Lovaas and Simmons 1969; Bijou 1965). These children have developed extremely self-injurious behavior patterns—banging their heads against walls and other solid surfaces and objects; gouging their eyes with fingers or objects; self-beating; biting their fingers, arms, legs, toes; severe pinching of flesh; and other forms of self-mutilation committed both sporadically and chronically. The severity of the behavior should not be underestimated because children are doing it. The self-inflicted harm can be quite serious—blindness and other eye injuries can result; chunks of flesh have been bitten or torn out; limbs and fingers are mutilated; bones and noses are broken; and brain concussions are caused. In fact, in some cases it is plain that the child would *eventually kill himself* unless physically restrained by a vigilant parent or other adult.

Because we are uncertain whether the child knows or intends his behavior to be fatal, it could be argued that even if death were to result from such behavior it should not be considered suicide. None can deny, however, that even if it is short of suicide, this self-inflicted injury is in the category of behavior which could lead to suicide. This kind of

> self-destructive behavior showed a great deal of lawfulness which could be accounted for by considering the self-destructive behavior as learned social behavior (Lovaas and Simmons 1969:144).

The learning takes place in a context in which *social attention* typically follows and reinforces the self-mutilating behavior. The attention initially may come from a parent who comes to comfort any injury, however mild and from whatever source, suffered by the child. If this continues, the child learns that he will be immediately attended to in a warm and affectionate way by parents and other well-meaning adults if he appears to be hurting himself. He may begin to concentrate on self-inflicted harm to gain attention, to the exclusion of other behavior. More severe self-injury brings more attention, which serves to reinforce further self-injury. After a while, apparently a fairly short while, the child develops a self-sustaining repertoire of ever more destructive self-directed aggression that cannot be ignored. For this reason, those who have attempted therapy with these children find that initial treatment cannot simply be nonattention; rather, electric shock is given each time the child engages in self-destructive acts. This tends to decrease and then stop the behavior, but ceasing the shock and reinstating the social attention increases the behavior again; only after the behavior is extinguished and then ignored will the child stop mutilating himself (Lovaas et al. 1968; Lovaas and Simmons 1969). Recently, conditioning techniques have been used to control self-destructive behavior in severely retarded adults, using both aversive control of self-mutilation and positive reinforcement for alternative noninjurious behavior (Tanner and Zeiler 1975; Azrin et al. 1975).

If this kind of self-mutilating behavior can be controlled by social reinforcement, it is understandable that wrist-slashing, drug overdosing, shooting, hanging, and other suicidal behavior can be learned and sustained through the same kind of social reward. Indeed, both common-sense and scholarly conceptions recognize that the desired consequence of much nonfatal suicidal behavior (communications, feigned suicide, and attempted suicide) is social attention. The attention-gaining purpose of much of this behavior has been called the *appeal function* of suicidal action. Both nonfatal and fatal suicidal behavior may include this appeal function (Stengel 1967).

> Most people who attempt, and many who commit suicide, remain within the social field, i.e. near others. . . . Regular and predictable consequences of a voluntary act such as attempted suicide are apt to play a part in its motivations. It often leads to a belated upsurge of affection, in short many of the things happen which some of the people contemplating suicide envisage in their phantasies, and sometimes ask for in their suicide notes. . . . [T]*here is nothing like a suicidal attempt to call forth helpful reactions* from the environment (Stengel 1967:37, italics added).

There is a great deal of truth to the well-worn story of the individual who dramatically announces to others who are very much in a position to rescue him that he intends to do away with himself, then exits to the bathroom to cut his wrists, to the kitchen to stick his head in the gas oven, or teeters on the bridge's edge and thereby succeeds in gaining concern and attention. Suicide threats have produced all sorts of desired changes—marriages have been kept intact; marriages have been prevented; military service has been escaped; others have been made to comply with one person's wishes; individuals have gained favored treatment over others; others have even fussed enough to call in doctors and arrange expensive hospitalization (Wilkins 1967:294; Stengel 1964:89–96; Kobler and Stotland 1964:7). One sure-fire way to gain notice, at least temporarily, is to threaten or to attempt suicide, especially if you can make the attempt seem real.

This is not to imply that all attempts are pseudosuicidal—a game played simply to gain attention. The attempted suicide can be a very serious cry for help. Even a person who has a low intention of killing himself knows that at least the appearance of some crisis is needed for his attempt to be credible enough for others to react in the desired way. This reaction may not only positively reinforce suicidal behavior through social attention, as we have seen; it may also ease the crises and problems of the attempters.

Suicidal gestures, threats, and attempts are reinforced through the attention and other active responses which their enactment brings from other people. In this way, people learn behavior that carries real suicide potential and which in many cases does result in suicide. The individual has built up a repertoire of previously nonfatal behavior which for some reason in the fatal instance is not met by the attentive, protective, and rescuing responses it received in the past, and death results. This is most likely to happen to individuals with maximal intent who use very lethal methods, but even those with minimal intent may die.

Suicide without a History of Nonfatal Suicidal Behavior

If all or most suicides had histories of overt attempts, accounting for the suicidal process would be essentially as just outlined. But all cases of completed suicide are not the result of engaging in behavior which in the past has had some other outcome, but which this time ends in death. Learning to engage in self-injurious but nonfatal behavior most often leads only to continuation of the same behavior, not to death. Moreover, many who attempt suicide receive the proper response from others so that they discontinue suicidal actions and develop other ways of maintaining social attention. Nearly all completed suicides do give prior warning by communicating suicidal intent; but less than half actually attempt suicide before the fatal effort. The cases in which there have been no prior attempt are obviously not based on direct reinforcement of the particular behavior which produced death. However, learning is still involved.

In some instances of suicide without prior attempts suicidal acts may be imitated by persons who have observed others "solving" problems or at least avoiding them by committing suicide. This is essentially the explanation used by Blachly et al. (1968) to account for suicides among physicians, especially the high rate of suicide among psychiatrists. They note that the psychiatrist, "being in frequent, intense emotional relationships with suicidal patients, learns better than most that suicide is a way of solving problems" (1968:9).

> Thousands of times the doctor will learn that death solves problems; that it is pain and illness that causes them. He will rarely have stayed with families after death to learn of the problems that death causes, particularly if it is premature, particularly when self-inflicted. As his enemy—the concept of death—grows older, he may reconsider its significance, particularly when he is apt to be losing his children, his energy . . . (Blachly et al. 1968:16).

The learning explanation of suicide is applicable not only to suicide by physicians.

> To view suicide as a learned way of solving problems . . . helps explain . . . (1) Epidemics and contagiousness of suicide; (2) those persons who have the greatest experience with suicide and violence have the highest rate; and (3) why suicide is chosen as a problem-solving maneuver rather than some other action (Blachly et al. 1968:14).

Direct contact with suicide is not necessary for imitation processes to operate. Indirect suggestion of suicide can be gained from a number of sources including the mass media. It has long been observed that the publicity given to suicide cases, especially of famous or well-known people, is often followed by a "wave" of suicide. (For this reason, many newspapers now relegate suicide stories to the back pages or do not carry them at all.) And although Durkheim remained unpersuaded that imitation is a factor in suicide, and the data have been somewhat inconclusive, the only study to utilize national data demonstrates convincingly that publicizing suicide in the media inspires other people to commit suicide (Phillips 1974).

This study examined suicides by following front page coverage in the national news. Of thirty-three front page stories studied, twenty-six were followed by an increase in suicides over the average (the average of suicides in the same month the year before and the year after the one-month studies). The upsurge in suicide always occurred after not before the suicide story, it began in the month of the story, started declining one month after, and returned to normal levels two months after the story. The longer the story runs, the greater the increase in suicide. American suicides increase more than British suicides after stories publicized in the United States but not Great Britain (in the two cases when the same stories were also printed in Britain, British suicides also went up). The relationship cannot be explained by the "bereavement effect" in which the suicides are a result of the grief produced by the publicized deaths. Also, prior conditions cannot account for both the front page stories and the suicides following them because the stories are not published in the middle of a suicide wave, but before the wave. Also, there is no evidence that the publicity simply influenced coroners to classify doubtful cases as suicide more readily; the alternative categories of death by accident and homicide do not decrease during the suicide wave. Finally, the stories simply do not inspire a wave of suicides at an earlier date among those who would have taken their own lives anyway, because there is no noticeable decline in suicides in later months. But because of the many other sources of inspiration for suicide, the imitation effect increases the overall rate in the United States by less than 3 percent. But for some stories the increase (such as the one following Marilyn Monroe's death) can be as much as 12 percent (Phillips 1974).

Few people have directly observed suicidal acts, yet most of us have learned that there may be social utility to suicidal behavior; that people take their lives by hanging, shooting, jumping off bridges, and drug overdoses; and that chronic or terminal ill health, loss of a loved one, financial ruin, and other crises, as well as "selfless" sacrifice for a cause or to save others are "good and sufficient" reasons for suicide. These "social meanings" of suicide (Douglas 1967) may be fairly standardized "folk explanations" or "culturally defined motives" which help make sense of suicide, and they vary somewhat between cultures (Bohannan 1960:26–27).

Thus, simply through the media and socialization into the general culture one learns approximately the lethality and appropriateness of various techniques (for example, shooting is an effective and "manly" way to take one's life) and the various definitions favorable to suicide. At least one "neutralizing" and two "positive" sets of definitions are acceptable motives for suicide. The two types of positive definitions of suicide relate to situations in which it is the honorable and acceptable (if somewhat sad) thing to do. The first is *obligatory suicide* (altruistic in the Durkheimian sense), which is the expected, institutionalized response to certain situations—the widow in historic India who burned herself on her dead husband's funeral pyre; the Japanese who because he brought disgrace on himself or his family commits a ritualistic suicide by sword; the Prussian officer who, having failed, shoots himself in the head. Obligatory suicide may be considered unfortunate, but the suicide is not morally condemned; rather, he is thought well of because he has done the "right thing." *Sacrificial suicide* (altruistic in the sense of serving others) is the second type which is likely to be defined positively. The soldier who knowingly gives his life to save his buddies, the father who sacrifices his life to rescue his child from the path of a speeding car, and the student who starves himself to protest a war or to call attention to some other cause are all instances of sacrificial suicide. This type of suicide is seen as more optional, but it probably carries equal or greater heroic approbation than obligatory suicide. The individual may commit either obligatory or sacrificial suicide without suffering personal loss and without contemplating suicide.

Both these types of positive definitions of suicide are part of American culture, but they are rare. For the most part, our society condemns suicide, and therefore the definitions conducive to suicide are usually neutralizing ones which rationalize it as justifiable, excusable, or forgivable. Most people gain knowledge of these definitions, but they do not use it. The knowledge is offset by counterdefinitions which place suicide in a wholly unfavorable light, and other, more effective and less harrowing ways of gaining desirable social responses and solving problems are learned. The person who attempts or commits suicide, on the other hand, finds himself in a situation to which he can apply a definition justifying it. Ill health, tragic loss, or unrelieved problems may justify suicide, other people may be blamed for it, or the person may believe he is not responsible for it (Jacobs 1967). Other people provide no hope or convincing counterdefinitions to the individual. If the individual attempts without completing suicide, others' reactions may reinforce further attempts and ultimately death. Or a person may learn and apply a definition justifying suicide to his situation and may attempt and complete suicide the first time, without the possibility of others affecting his behavior.

Possible Relationship between Suicide Rates and the Suicidal Process

Self-injurious behavior may be operantly conditioned so that a person develops a pattern of self-destructiveness. Building on this basic proposition, the social learning analysis of the suicidal process may be recapitulated as follows: (1) The person must have knowledge of suicidal techniques, and which are appropriate to be used — for example, what is right for men, for women; what is generally available, and so on. (2) General cultural definitions of suicide are available, some of which define suicide under certain conditions as honorable and some of which define suicide as understandable or justified under certain conditions. Many individuals learn these definitions but are not likely to apply them to their own situations unless (3) they have experienced acute or chronic loss or crises and can find no hope for any other solution. (4) If the crisis is such that the culture defines it as an "obligatory" suicide situation or such that giving one's life is the only way to save others, the positive definitions are applied. (5) The justifying definitions are likely to be applied to the crisis or loss in which the person can "find no other way." All such persons will communicate their intention of applying a suicidal definition — that is, "Suicide is justified in my case since there is no other hope." (6) Whether or not a person will continue and actually attempt to complete suicide depends on the reactions of others. If the response of others is such that the definition is not counteracted and no hope for solution is communicated back to the person, he will attempt suicide. (a) He may complete it the first time, or (b) if he does not, whether he tries again also depends on the reaction of other people. They may increase their attention to him without necessarily solving the crises and thus reinforce further attempts, or they may reinforce his belief that there is no hope. In either case he is likely to attempt again, and one of these attempts may be fatal.

If this formulation is reasonably accurate, the suicidal process may be articulated with group rates in at least three ways. (1) The differences in rates of suicide may reflect the differences in the extent to which individuals who are members of a given group or social category are apt to be faced with crises, loss, and hopeless situations. (2) A person's group membership or social location may determine how seriously he is exposed to or isolated from definitions favorable to suicide as a problem-solving technique. It is not clear that the groups with the highest rates are the most crisis-ridden, and it is difficult to determine what constitutes a hopeless loss or crisis, for hopelessness and crises are relative. The assumption in the social learning explanation of suicide is that techniques and definitions are generally available, but exposure to definitions favorable to suicide may be unevenly distributed in the same way that suicide rates are. (3) However, our hypothesis is that the crucial link between process and rate is a third possibility — that *the extent to which the reaction of others is likely to reinforce suicidal behavior is positively related in obligatory and sacrificial suicides and negatively related in other suicides to the degree of social integration.* If the suicide rates do reflect social integration (regulation, constraint, restraint, and so on) as sociological theory would have it, greater integration of the group or status configuration may prevent nonobligatory and nonsacrificial suicidal behavior. An individual who is integrated into a network of social relationships is more likely to receive helpful solutions and hope and less likely to have to resort to suicide as either an attention-getting or a problem-solving maneuver.

Summary

The social learning explanation presented in this chapter incorporates the disparate elements in social-psychological theories and offers a way of relating the suicidal process to suicide rates. The essential features in the suicidal process are: learning and applying definitions of suicide, chronic or acute problems of loss and life crisis, the loss of hope for solving them, and the reactions of others to the person's suicidal behavior and attempts to communicate a desire for help with the problems.

The analysis sketched the interplay of these features by portraying two ways in which the person who comes to commit suicide may proceed: (1) by developing a pattern of suicide attempts, one of which is fatal; (2) by learning about suicide, developing a readiness to attempt it, and completing it on the first attempt.

Part Seven | Mental Illness

25

Conceptions of Mental Illness:
The Medical and Behavioral Models

What Is Mental Illness?

Some people have always behaved in ways that are bizarre, highly unusual, seemingly out of touch with reality as others perceive it, and generally disturbing to themselves and others. Throughout history societies have labeled such people "possessed by demons," "witches," "insane," "crazy," and a host of other pejorative names. But beginning in the nineteenth century and continuing until today, such behavior has come to be defined as a medical problem — that is, as an illness which should be handled by physicians applying physical and psychological medical science. In this century the mental hygiene movement has tried to convince people that insanity is not deviant at all, that it is "just like any other illness" and should be treated as such. This message has been widely accepted in Western societies, but the public still holds a stereotype of the mentally ill as insane and dangerous. To be "mentally ill" (whatever else it may be) is to be deviant and stigmatized (Nunnally 1967; Scheff 1966). The existence of public and private organizations (some of which are indistinguishable from prisons) for the voluntary and involuntary incarceration and "treatment" of mental patients demonstrates that mental illness is a form of deviant behavior about which great concern remains and about which it is believed "something should be done."

But it is a peculiar form of deviance. For at least a century and a half, the medical-psychiatric (and for the last seventy years, largely Freudian) view of the deviance as "mental illness" has prevailed among the professional workers and agents of society in the field (and to a large extent among the public). Yet as an increasing number of critics of this view have pointed out, this behavior may be *neither mental nor illness*. At least, it is not more "mental" than any other deviant behavior and is "illness" only in a metaphorical sense.

Moreover, as we see when we discuss the medical model, the label *mental illness* (mental instability, disorder, disease, or defect) is not just a way to refer to a cluster of similar behavior; rather, the illness analogy is taken literally. Calling someone mentally ill carries with it an assumption about the cause of his behavior—namely, that his actions are the symptoms of an underlying sickness. But if the illness analogy is not to be taken seriously, what assumption-free descriptive term can we use for the troublesome behavior and problems which are themselves real enough? Also, what alternative explanatory scheme do we use once we have defined and described the behavior in which we are interested?

After a discussion of the medical model of mental illness, an attempt is made to answer the first question. Then after a presentation of the variations in rates of mental illness in chapter 26, an answer to the second question is proposed in chapter 27.

The Medical Model[1]

Although differences between insanity and other forms of deviance have long been socially recognized and given different names, not until the latter part of the eighteenth century were the insane treated differently from the criminal. They were incarcerated together with law violators, held equally responsible for their behavior, and punished in much the same way. Insofar as they were reacted to differently, they were likely to be persecuted as witches, heretics, or as servants of the devil. But in the eighteenth century people began to recognize that insanity (and childhood) excused criminal responsibility, and a movement which has been called "moral treatment" for the insane began. Moral treatment involved removing the insane from prisons and dungeons and placing them in a "re-education and moral training" social milieu in special institutions. Moral treatment did not define the persons as ill or as patients. Rather, they were defined simply as people who had lost their rationality through insufficient moral training or subjection to severe stress. Hence they were subjected to different and more uplifting influences, given job skills, and given sympathetic, friendly counsel. All available evidence shows moral treatment to have been remarkably effective.

By the middle of the nineteenth century the medical profession had made tremendous gains in the treatment of physical illness and was moving toward a scientific basis for practice. At this time the insane came to be defined as ill and hence amenable to treatment by physicians. The analogy from physical illness to behavioral problems was given its major impetus

---

[1]This section on the medical model is based on a number of sources which are admittedly critical. The presentation is a fair one, however, which accurately depicts this model of mental illness, subject only to distortions arising from the need to simplify somewhat to conform to space limitations. The student is referred to the original sources cited in the following references. The clearest and most concise portrayal of the medical model is in Ullmann and Krasner 1965:2–15, but see also Ullmann and Krasner 1969:121–70; Bandura 1969:2–69; Milton and Wahler 1969:3–16; Ullmann 1967:19–39; Szasz 1961:21–113; Wolpe 1964:5–10; Scheff 1966:7–31; Eysenck 1960:4–22; Rotter 1954:66–73.

by the theories of Freud in the late nineteenth and early twentieth centuries. Later psychoanalytic theorists and practitioners embellished and elaborated on the Freudian conceptions, but the major part of the current medical model of mental illness is essentially a psychoanalytic model based on Freud (Adams 1969:46–48; Ullmann and Krasner 1969:121–41; Ullmann 1967: 19–39).

There are two aspects of the model: The first relates to "organic disorders" and is nonpsychoanalytic, and the second relates to "functional disorders," which are defined entirely in psychodynamic terms. There is little disagreement about the first aspect, but the second one refers to all but a tiny portion of the "mental disorders" and it is characteristic of the medical analogy.

Although some researchers continue to search for a physiological basis for all forms of mental illness, at least at this time firm evidence for neurological lesions exists only for general paresis (slight paralysis caused by syphilitic infection) and organic brain damage or defects. These are rare occurrences (particularly since the advent of penicillin treatment of syphilis) and compose only a very small number of cases labeled mental illness (Ullmann and Krasner 1969:130–39). The search for genetic, anatomical, and chemical causes of more common categories such as schizophrenia continues. Thus far research has failed to find any consistently significant physiological factors in all mental illness (Mosher et al. 1970; Wyatt et al. 1971). Moreover, as Szasz notes, the "organic disorders" are not defined by applying a physical illness analogy to mental phenomena—they *are* physical illness in which specific brain or tissue pathology can be found (Szasz 1961:15–16; Szasz 1967:243–44). To the extent that research has established a genetically transmitted anomaly or chemical imbalance in schizophrenic or manic-depressive behavior as some claim (Gove 1975b:49–50), then these disorders are not mental illnesses. They are physical illnesses in the same sense as other organic disturbances. If the term *mental illness* were confined to a meaning synonymous with organic disease, there would be little disagreement about the term and the theory behind it. But this is not done. Rather, the same term *mental illness* is also applied to the whole range of "functional disorders."

The central feature of this model is that the bizarre, unusual, and inappropriate behaviors are merely *symptoms of an underlying psychic disease, pathology, or illness* within the individual, primarily in his unconscious. Just as physical pain, high blood pressure and fever are signs of the body's attempt to control infection or physical ailment, certain behavior (including even some physical ailments) is believed to be a sign of some disturbance in the proper functioning of the psyche. Also, in physical illness the sickness may be due to contact with illness-causing agents in the environment, but once contracted, the symptoms are due to the sickness, not to the environmental factors. Likewise, in mental illness the features of the environment are secondary. Experiences in infancy and childhood, especially as these relate to the unconscious sexual attraction and jealousy toward parents and to toilet training, are seen as the most important molders of psychic materials. But after that the social context becomes relatively unimportant except as it contains stress factors precipitating psychotic or neurotic episodes.

> Thus, the psychoanalytic model of neurosis is basically a system of behavior that is contained within the individual. The external situation in which the individual is involved is seen only as an almost limitless source of triggers for a fully developed neurotic conflict within the individual. Psychoanalytic theory, like most contemporary theories of mental illness, whether they are psychological or organic, locates the neurotic system within the individual (Scheff 1966:11).

The form this psychic illness takes is believed to vary considerably, but the basic problems involve conflict between and among intrapsychic forces which produce anxiety, guilt, and other problems with which the person must deal, consciously or unconsciously. If one adheres closely to a Freudian approach he is likely to say that these conflicts are caused by the repression of instinctual or sexual forces (id, libido) or the "unnatural" unfolding of life stages. All behavior is an outgrowth of coping with the psychic problems, but there are healthy ways and unhealthy ways of resolving these internal conflicts. "Abnormal" behavior, including criminal and delinquent behavior, sexual deviations, alcoholism, and all the symptoms of mental illness, are manifestations of unhealthy resolutions. They are functional (that is, they allow the individual to compromise with the guilt or conflict with the least psychic cost) but nonetheless "sick" resolutions.

The connection between the underlying difficulty and the symptomatic manifestation of the individual's unconscious attempt to handle it is nebulous. Almost any psychic pathology can produce almost any symptom, for the symptoms are "symbolic" of or "substitutes" for the "real" motives, which are driven from the consciousness because they are too painful for the ego to bear. The real, repressed guilt or anxiety is converted to and relieved by more acceptable and less painful manifestations.

Nonetheless, the way the individual overcomes the sickness is to bring the "real" reasons for his behavior to conscious awareness so that he may deal rationally rather than irrationally with his problems. This process is called *gaining insight,* and the patient is helped to do this ideally through *interview therapy* (Bandura 1969:52–53). By talking with the therapist over a long period of time the patient can vent his pent-up emotions and reveal the hidden motives to the therapist, who can interpret the meaning of the patient's behavior—that is, of what it is expressive or symbolic. This interpretation gives the patient the needed insight; he can bring the problem out of his unconscious into the light of conscious day, examine it, deal with it rationally, and rid himself of it. Once this is done he is cured of his sickness and his symptoms will disappear.

Gaining insight, then, is the key to treating the sickness. Indeed, because treating the symptoms leaves the underlying illness untouched, it is foolhardy and dangerous merely to treat the symptoms; new symptoms will develop to substitute for the repressed symptoms, and the person remains sick. The behavior itself is unimportant; symptoms are relevant only to the extent to which they can be grouped into syndromes which allow diagnosis of the basic mental pathology.

Although no case will evince all the symptoms in a syndrome and widely different forms of behavior are judged to be part of the same syndrome, a fairly standardized nomenclature for diagnostic categories of syndromes has evolved within the medical model. (For summary discussions of these categories see Clausen 1966; Ullmann and Krasner 1969.) There are a number of categories of "functional disorders." The prime syndromes, *psychoses*, *neuroses*, and *psychosomatic* ailments ("psychophysiological autonomic and visceral disorders"), are summarized by Clausen:

> the psychoses, which entail a gross derangement of mental processes and inability to evaluate external reality correctly; the neuroses, which entail impairment of functioning often of a segment of behavior, but no sharp break with reality; and the psychosomatic disorders, which entail very real organic symptoms and malfunctions caused at least in part by psychological processes (1966:32).

Psychotics probably conform closest to popular notions of people who are nuts or crazy. The most frequently diagnosed psychotic disorder is schizophrenia, which is characterized by intellectual and emotional disassociation and inappropriateness. Schizophrenia is further subdivided into simple, undifferentiated, paranoid (delusions of persecution and grandeur), catatonic (extremely withdrawn or mute or the opposite), and hebephrenic (silliness) types. If a person of middle age shows psychotic problems he is apt to be typed as an involutional psychotic (if older, probably senile). The manic-depressive psychotic syndrome is characterized by extreme shifts from deep moods of depression to heights of hyperactivity and maniacal craziness.

Neuroses are defined primarily in terms of specific or free-floating anxiety and fear. The most frequently diagnosed (and the best known to the public) are phobias—"unrealistic" fear or avoidance of something—and hysteria—"conversion reaction," in which the person acts as if he is paralyzed, blind, deaf, and so on without specific organic damage.

In addition to psychoses, neuroses, and psychosomatic diagnoses there are personality disorders ("pathological trends in personality structure"), including pattern disturbances, trait disturbances, and psychopathic or sociopathic personalities. (Sexual deviation and drug or alcohol addiction are defined as sociopathic personality disturbances.)

It is important to remember that these diagnostic categories are not viewed as simply syndromes or symptoms: they are believed to be *disease entities.* The psychodynamic conception of the nature of these disease entities as causes of the symptoms is built into the nomenclature. This set of terms is nearly always referred to in discussions of mental illness. According to this scheme the label of mental illness is not a metaphor; the set of phenomena to which it refers *is* illness — an indwelling sickness with all the characteristics of physical sickness except that it is psychogenic.

Critiques of the Medical Model

The medical model is still the predominant view of mental illness in American society, but it has come under increased criticism in recent years. The critical response to the medical model has come from two major sources — certain sociologists and behavioral psychologists. Both have found the medical model unsatisfactory for much the same reasons and have offered similar alternatives. It is not surprising, therefore, that the ideas of behavioral psychologists are discussed approvingly by sociologists (Scheff 1966:19–23; Taber et al. 1969) or that sociological conceptions are accepted by psychologists (Ullmann and Krasner 1969; Milton and Wahler 1969; Bandura 1969; Szasz 1961; Ullmann 1967). The views converge on the idea that the kinds of behavior called mental illness are simply learned adaptations to the social and physical environment; they are products of a social and behavioral process which can be understood better without reference to disease processes.

The critiques of the medical model from these two sources revolve around two major interrelated axes: (1) The critics have evaluated the theoretical and empirical adequacy of the medical model as a theory and its practical effectiveness as a therapy and have found it to be *scientifically inadequate* and *therapeutically ineffective.* (2) The critics have judged the impact of the medical-psychiatric approach on individuals and society and have concluded that adherence to the medical model as the major orientation has had *undesirable social consequences.*

Scientific and therapeutic inadequacies.   One frequently noted shortcoming of the medical-psychiatric approach as an explanation of deviant behavior is that it ignores important variables in the social milieu (Milton and Wahler 1969:6–7; Scheff 1966:174–75). Even sociologists who basically accept the assumptions of the medical model are dissatisfied with its lack of attention to sociocultural factors in the behavior labeled mental disease and to its inadequate conception of the relationship between the individual and society (Clausen 1966; Weinberg 1967b:4; Dunham 1965:26–27). But the illness concept not only neglects social variables in the causation of deviant behavior; it also contributes to a failure to understand that the diagnosis, categorization, and labeling of mental illness are themselves profoundly social acts and that other social factors besides the behavior itself affect the informal and formal process whereby persons are judged to have a mental pathology (Ullmann and Krasner 1969:2–23; Mechanic 1967; Scheff 1967:5–6).

This tendency to regard "mental illness" as an internal, autonomous entity with determinate power over behavior illustrates the logical error of *reification* — making concrete or treating as real an abstract or a hypothetical construct. Rather than serving only as a convenient label for observed regularities, *mental illness* has been made an actual disease. Szasz (1967; 1961) perhaps more strongly than others underscores the extent to which this reification has taken place by calling mental illness a *myth*. He and others argue that while the interpersonal problems are real enough, no such thing as mental illness, as currently conceived, actually exists (Adams 1969; Zinberg 1970). Thus the beliefs about mental illness and its cure function in much the same way as religious or magical beliefs (Scheff 1967:13–14; Silverstein 1968:2). Bandura illustrates the ease with which any mythical entity can be substituted for mental illness without changing a thing:

> Let us designate behaviors in which persons violate social and legal codes of behavior and frequently engage in assaultive activities as the external expressions of an inferred *zoognick*. Based on prevailing clinical practices, the zoognick would come to represent an intrapsychially functioning agent. An honorific causative power would be conferred upon this hypothetical zoognick whereas the observed behavior from which its existence is inferred would be depreciated as superficial behavioral manifestations (1969:72).

Using the mythical illness (or zoognick or sicoglop or whatever) as an explanation of behavior creates the problem of circular reasoning. An unobservable agent, mental illness, is inferred from certain deviant acts and then is used to explain these acts. Because the connection between the alleged illness and its symptoms remains nebulous, psychiatric diagnosis and prognosis are highly unreliable. And it is difficult to refute directly assertions about the illness.

However, there are some indirect ways of judging the validity of the medical model. One of these is to assess the *effectiveness* of *treatment* by the interview therapies which are predicated upon the medical model. Judged by this criterion, traditional psychotherapy has proven to be ineffective. Some research indicates that persons released from mental institutions against psychiatric judgment do as well as those who are released because psychiatrists have judged them cured (Steadman 1972). There is little evidence that cure, improvement, or change by treatment is any greater than that achieved by no treatment. Moreover, the evidence is fairly clear that this treatment method is much less effective than learning-based behavioral modification procedures (Bandura 1969:52–61; Eysenck 1960:4–22; 1964:1–20; Wolpe et al. 1964; Ullmann and Krasner 1965:1–39). Another way of evaluating the medical model is to examine the evidence on the *symptom substitution* hypothesis. The evidence is negative. When symptoms are treated and behavior changed without regard to the assumed underlying illness, there is no evidence that other symptoms develop to take their place as expressions of the same illness (Eysenck 1960:10–13; Ullmann and Krasner 1969:157–60; Bandura 1969;48–52).

Another way of judging the medical model is to see to what extent *social and behavioral* variables play a role in psychiatric decisions. If mental illnesses are scientifically diagnosed and treated disease entities, then the degree and progress of illness should be the only or major variables in admission to and length of treatment. There is no research directly measuring (aside from imputations of illness by mental health professionals) the existence and degree of mental illness. But some research shows that decisions to admit and release (at least for predominantly voluntary patient populations) are related to staff judgments of psychiatric impairment (Gove and Fain 1975; Gove and Howell 1974). However, the preponderance of evidence is that other variables also play important roles. Evaluations of mental impairment seem to have less to do with staff decisions to release patients or to keep them hospitalized than the wishes of the patients' families (Greenly 1972a; 1972b). Further, social class, marital status, and legal status (voluntary or involuntary) are predictive of both admission decisions and length of hospitalization, even controlling for psychiatric judgment of mental illness (Hardt and Feinhandler 1959; Rushing 1971; Rushing and Esco 1975).

This logical and empirical inadequacy of the disease model means that there are *no objective criteria of illness*. To diagnose someone as mentally ill is not to apply scientific measurement against objective standards of health, but to make a *social, legal, or moral judgment of undesirability*. The label *sick* simply replaces other labels such as *bad* or *crazy* and is no more or no less scientific (Szasz 1961:17–20; Goffman 1961:323–86).

One study (Rosenhan 1973) illustrates dramatically the lack of objective criteria for distinguishing between mental health and illness. In this study, eight people who were in every sense sane and "normal people" presented themselves to several different hospitals for diagnosis and possible admission for psychiatric treatment. They initially faked symptoms of hearing voices, but in no other way acted or said things out of the ordinary. They gave false names, vocations, and employment, but everything else they said was true. Their feelings, background, family relationships, interaction with others and so on were described as they actually were. In each case the person was admitted to the hospital as sick and in need of psychiatric treatment. All except one were diagnosed as schizophrenic (a severe psychotic diagnosis). After admission, each pseudopatient stopped faking any symptoms and behaved as normally as could be expected under the circumstances of living in a psychiatric ward. The schizophrenic diagnosis colored the nurses' and psychiatrists' interaction (which was impersonal and brief) with them. The staff reports interpreted the pseudopatients' otherwise unexceptional personal histories as being filled with pathology. They interpreted the behavior on the ward as due to the presumed illness. Although they were kept hospitalized for up to two-and-one-half months, the hospital staff never believed that they were perfectly normal (but many of the real patients detected their subterfuge). They were released and diagnosed as having "schizophrenia in remission." At one hospital, the staff was told that during the next three months one or more pseudopatients would seek admission and was asked to rate all incoming patients for that time as real or fake patients. No actual pseudopatient came, but of the nearly 200 real patients during that period, 41 were judged by the staff to be pseudopatients. This study does not, of course, prove that psychiatric professionals can never distinguish between the "sane" and "insane" or that they apply the mental illness label in a totally arbitrary or random way. It does demonstrate how slippery psychiatric diagnostic categories can be. The line between mental health and illness must be thin, indeed, if even very mild, faked symptoms can be interpreted as evidence of the need for hospitalization.

Because the concept is fuzzy and value-laden the medical approach to mental illness is less a scientific body of theory and research and more an *ideology* or belief system and a *social movement* for the promotion of a particular set of values and beliefs—namely, conformity, problem solving, thrift and hard work, control of emotions, striving and planning ahead, and community participation (Davis 1938; Gursslin et al. 1964).

Undesirable social consequences. The preoccupation of psychiatrists and other helping professionals with diagnosing people who come to them as mentally ill has meant that many people who want and could accept help with their problems do not receive it. Many with treatable behavioral difficulties are reluctant to undergo the stigmatized labeling process which is so often the prerequisite for help. They must accept being defined as "ill" and being treated as sick or be thought "resistive" and uncurable. Seeking professional help often means social rejection (Phillips 1963). Understandably, then, many people prefer not to seek help, and the problems they have and are causing others are not alleviated (Bandura 1969:17).

But the social harm that results from deterring voluntary requests for help is minor compared to the damage to those who are involuntarily hospitalized or treated. In these cases psychiatrists function not as agents of the person but as agents of others and the state; the police power of the state backs up the psychiatrists' decision that a person is mentally "incompetent" and should be incarcerated. Identification and incarceration of those who are allegedly mentally ill does not differ significantly from social control of crimes (Silverstein 1968:4). There is evidence that many individuals are involuntarily confined as "criminally insane" even when they present no more danger to themselves or the community than those who are released by the psychiatric staff (Steadman 1972). But even when there is no question of criminal behavior, the belief that the involuntary commitment to a mental institution is a medical procedure which is for the "good" of the person (not punishment for wrongdoing) and faith in the psychiatrist have led to incarceration and denial of freedom with minimal and perfunctorily applied safeguards for civil rights during commitment procedures and hospitalization. Legal ideology says that it is better to make a mistake by releasing a guilty person than to make a mistake by convicting the innocent. The medical ideology, on the other hand, fosters the idea that it is better to hospitalize someone who is not "really sick" than to fail to treat one who is sick. The legal model presumes innocence; the medical model presumes illness. This presumption leads to a very high probability that one will be judged mentally incompetent by the psychiatric hearing board in the civil commitment process and to a conservative bias in release decisions, tending to keep people in longer (Szasz 1961:19; Scheff 1966:105–68; Mechanic 1967; Miller and Schwartz 1966; Fein and Miller 1972).

**   *Pervasiveness and defense of the medical model.*   The foregoing outline of critiques of the medical model should not be interpreted to mean that the medical model is discredited; indeed, the opposite is true. The medical-psychiatric conception continues to dominate the entire field and to be accepted more or less uncritically by social scientists (see, for instance, Gove 1970; 1975b). This acceptance continues despite the fact that the critiques have not been satisfactorily answered. (There have been attempts to respond to the critiques but they have not been convincing [Ausubel 1961].)**

Mental Illness as Behavior Disorders and Residual Deviance

The behavior to which mental illness refers is of interest to the sociologist because it is a socially defined category of deviant behavior. But how can we define it in such a way that the same sort of behavior is included without implying that it is illness (and encountering the difficulties just reviewed)? Maybe *troublesome behavior* is good enough, but much that is troublesome is not defined as deviant, would not be called mental illness, or could be easily placed in another category of deviant behavior. The central objective feature of mental illness is that it is *deviant behavior socially defined as unacceptable and undesirable* (Taber et al. 1969; Silverstein 1968:5). Scheff (1966:31–54) proposes that mental illness be defined as *residual deviance*.

> The culture of the group provides a vocabulary of terms for categorizing many norm violations: crime, perversion, drunkenness, and bad manners are familiar examples. . . . After exhausting these categories of behavior, however, there is always a residue of the most diverse kinds of violations, for which the culture provides no explicit label. For example, . . . the typical norm governing decency or reality . . . literally "goes without saying" and its violation is unthinkable for most. . . . These violations may be lumped together into a residual category: witchcraft, spirit possession, or, in our own society, mental illness. In this discussion, the diverse kinds of rule-breaking

for which our society provides no explicit label, and which, there-fore, sometimes lead to the labeling of the violater as mentally ill, will be considered to be technically, *residual rule-breaking*. (1966:33–34, italics in original).

In some ways this definition is misleading, for it is a bit contradictory. If society provides a label of *mental illness*, then it thereby provides one that is every bit as explicit as the labels of crime, perversion, drunkenness, and bad manners. The norms in question are more than just decency and reality, and their violation is not "unthinkable." There is the cultural expectation that people will relate to the environment in a way that is culturally defined as rational, competent, and understandable. When they do not the label *mental illness* is apt to be used to describe them. Such behavior is not so much unthinkable as it is considered irrational. Mental illness is not a residual category in the sense that names can be applied to other deviance but that this brand is unnameable.

But there is no doubt that the mental illness label is often a *leftover, waste-basket category* to be used when more clearly delineated terms are not appro-priate. In this sense it is residual deviance. An observer can examine this residual category to determine *what kinds of behavior* under what circum-stances typically are viewed as mental illness and the nature of the *social reaction* which distinguishes this class from other classes of deviance.

The Behavior

The kind of behavior to which the term *mental illness* is typically applied is what Szasz calls "problems in living" and "*communications* expressing unacceptable ideas" (1967:249–50) and what Lemert calls a "disorder in communication between the individual and society" (1967:197). These con-ceptions of mental illness as deviations from situational and communicative appropriateness were anticipated by several years by Faris and Dunham (1939:155–58).

Problems in living, inappropriate communications, maladaptive be-havior, and others may all be subsumed under the rubric *behavior disorders*, which is free of the illness assumptions (Milton and Wahler 1969; Rachman and Teasdale 1970). The behavior included under this rubric which is likely to be labeled symptomatic of mental illness is apt to be characterized by one or more of the following: situational inappropriateness, behavioral deficit, presumed irrational motivation, inappropriateness to one's age, sex, and other attributes, and self-defined as based on emotional disturbance (Bandura 1969:3–9). A similar listing includes: not attending to correct stimuli, inaccurate labeling of the situation, lack of behavioral and role skills, inadequately reinforced behavior (Ullmann and Krasner 1969:92–105).

The Social Reaction

The kind of social reaction involved in the behavioral disorders called mental illness is concisely captured by Ullmann and Krasner:

> There is an area of behavior, however, where formal rules may not be broken but where unexpected behavior is seriously upsetting to other people, such as friends, parents, spouses, neighbors, teachers, and policemen. [This type of] abnormality is the sort of deviance that calls for and sanctions the professional attention of psychiatrists, clinical psychologists, and other "mental health" professionals (Ullmann and Krasner 1969:1).

This definition does not sufficiently differentiate mental illness from other forms of deviant behavior such as delinquency, crime, drug use, and so on, which also may be defined as calling for psychiatric treatment. But it does describe what most people have in mind when they talk about the mentally ill. And we in fact are interested in much the same behavioral phenomena as that which is believed to need the attention of psychiatrists and for which legal-medical procedures have been provided by society. This does not mean that we must accept at face value that the mentally ill are "those who are confined in mental hospitals or who consult psychiatrists in their private offices" (Szasz 1961:ix). Rather, we approach the study of mental illness, as Scheff (1967:9) does, in the anthropological sense of studying "folk medicine." We are interested in the behavior defined by society as mental illness and labeled as such by psychiatrists and other socially sanctioned agents of control, but without accepting either's assumption about disease and causation.

The term *mental illness* will continue to be used here because it is so established in everyday and professional language that it would be difficult to discuss the problem without it. But its use implies no more; it is used simply as a *label for behavior.* To underscore this, other terms, such as *residual deviance, behavioral problems, behavioral disorders, insanity,* and so on, will also be used. In each case the reference is to the residual category of deviance of personally or interpersonally troublesome behavior. This behavior is characterized by irrational inappropriateness which typically is believed to warrant the attention of "mental health" professionals.

Summary

The medical model views the kind of deviant behavior discussed in this chapter as disease or illness; the behavior is seen as the symptom of an underlying sickness. Although it is still the prevailing approach to "mental illness," the medical model has been subjected to extensive criticism as being scientifically and therapeutically inadequate and as having undesirable social consequences.

As an alternative to the medical model, a behavioral model consistent with the social learning approach is proposed. What is called mental illness may be defined as residual deviant behavior; it is a wastebasket category for labeling deviance that may be used whenever more clearly defined categories are inappropriate. The behavior which usually receives this label includes communication of unacceptable ideas, maladaptive behavior, behavioral deficits, and other actions which are troublesome to the person or others. In the behavioral model mental illness is simply those behavioral disorders which are socially defined as requiring the attention of "mental health" professionals in addition to or instead of other social control agencies. There is no assumption that the behavior in question is literally illness.

26

Variations in Rates of Mental Illness

Incidence and Prevalence:
Methods of Case Finding

Whereas the studies of other types of deviance only occasionally acknowledge the difference between "incidence" and "prevalence," studies of mental illness have consistently maintained the distinction. *Incidence* refers to the number of new cases found or arising within a given time period; *prevalence* refers to the total number existing and new cases within a time period.

Two methods are used to find and count cases. First, the number of *in-treatment* persons—those who are in state, federal, other public, and private hospitals and asylums; those who are clients of outpatient clinics; and those who are under the care of a private physician or psychiatrist—is counted. This method results in the number of persons being treated or at least known by the agencies in a given locality, city, or state. The other method is to survey samples of the general population and to determine how many are "psychiatrically impaired" without regard to their known treatment status. This results in a count of largely *untreated* cases, although the survey might turn up people who are past or present clinic outpatients or patients of a private psychiatrist and people who are ex-patients of an in-residence institution.[1] Counting all the cases who are either treated or untreated results in a closer approximation to the *true* prevalence and incidence in an area.

Whether the findings are based on in-treatment or untreated populations, the definition of mental illness used is that which would be called mental impairment by a psychiatrist. Indeed, the researcher who makes the decision about the mental health of untreated cases surveyed in the community is almost certain to be a psychiatrist. The dependence on mental hospitals, clinics, and other psychiatric caseloads for data on the distribution of

---

[1] Indeed, reported past hospitalization or agency contact for mental disorder is likely to be taken as evidence of current mental illness (Langner and Michael 1963:55).

mental illness in the social structure is similar to the dependence on official agencies as sources of information and study populations on drugs, crime, and suicide.

But there are differences. One is that police and coroners can record cases of crime and suicide regardless of their theory about the causes of crime and suicide. In the case of mental illness behavior is not recorded; rather, a presumed illness is recorded, the definition and existence of which are at least partly determined by adherence to a particular theory of causation. This in itself would not cause great difficulty if the clarity and precision of definition and theory matched that of regular medical diagnosis. But the evidence shows that psychiatric case finding and definition are highly unreliable (Ullmann and Krasner 1969:219–26). Nonetheless, all the studies rely on the deviation from clinical norms as determined by a psychiatrist and share the major handicap of using a fuzzy, ill-defined dependent variable (Manis 1968; Clausen 1966:59–60; Scheff 1966:176).

Incidence and Prevalence of Mental Illness in Various Locales

Dunham (1965) reports on the prevalence and incidence rates found in various studies in North America, Europe, and Asia. The studies show *prevalence* rates ranging up to 9,000 per 100,000 population in Europe, 920 in Asia, and 650 in North America. The rates for schizophrenia (the most frequently diagnosed disorder) are from 190 to 960 in Europe, from 210 to 380 in Asia, and from 100 to 230 in North America. The *incidence* rates of treated cases found in studies in the United States range from 35 to 175 for all categories of psychoses and from 10 to 47 for schizophrenia. In his own study of Detroit he found new cases of schizophrenia to range from 20 to 163 among various subcommunities (Dunham 1965:15–23; 76–79).

As these figures and the ones presented in table 26–1 indicate, there is considerable variation in the prevalence and incidence rates of diagnosed mental illness. Variations in the actual amount of residual deviance account for only some of the differences found; much variation is due to the general confusion about what mental illness is and to methodological differences from one study to another. Therefore, the figures on the new cases and total cases need to be viewed with a great deal of skepticism. It is especially difficult to compare incidence and prevalence cross-culturally, for it goes without saying that "insanity" is relative to the culture. Even when commonalities in cultural meaning of mental illness can be found, there is cultural variation in what categories account for most of the total and in the symptomology within the same categories (Murphy et al. 1968).

Even within the same country or even the same city, how many cases are found depends on how narrow or wide is the definition of what constitutes a case. For instance, in the Manhattan study the figure based on the

Table 26–1
Prevalence and incidence of mental illness in selected studies

Authors	Date Published	Location	Case Finding Method	Prevalence (Per 100,000)	Incidence (Per 100,000)
Faris and Dunham	1939	Chicago	First admissions to public and private hospitals		From 48 to 499
Hollingshead and Redlich	1958	New Haven	Cases under treatment in public and private hospitals and clinics and private psychiatric care	798	104
Jaco	1960	Texas	First admissions to private, teaching, public, VA, and state hospitals and to private care		73
Dunham	1965	North America	Summary of several studies of treated cases of psychoses	From 130 to 650	From 35 to 175
Srole et al.	1968	Manhattan	One-day census of public and private hospitals and clinics and office therapists; sample of general population, those judged "impaired" by symptoms checklist	From 1,060 to 1,703 23,000	
Pasamanick et al.	1959	Baltimore	Sample of general population, clinical evaluation of subsample	9,300	
Levy and Rowitz	1973	Chicago	First admissions to public and private clinics and hospitals		300

Sources: Faris and Dunham 1939:23–37; Hollingshead and Redlich 1958:210–13; Jaco 1960:32; Dunham 1965:15–23; Srole et al. 1968:108–9. Pasamanick et al. 1964:43; Levy and Rowitz 1973.

total number under treatment is high enough. But 23 percent of those in the sample survey of the same study were judged sufficiently impaired that they should be under treatment. This would mean that the true prevalence rate in Manhattan is close to 23,000 per 100,000 which is close to unbelievable. But the Manhattan researchers went even one step further and judged that more than 80 percent of the sample were suffering some degree of impaired mental health. If this expanded notion were taken seriously, prevalence rate would be 80,000 (Srole et al. 1967:34). Obviously these figures on the amount of mental illness in society border on the nonsensical. Indeed, even a finding in the Baltimore research that 10 percent of the population at any given time is mentally ill (5 percent severely ill) need not be taken seriously.

Social Class and Community Ecology

By far the most frequently studied correlate of behavioral disorders is social class, measured either by socioeconomic status (education, occupation, income) or by area of residence in the city (central area, middle-class area, suburbs, and so on). In the community studies area of residence is studied not only as an indicator of class but also of community organization or disorganization. Lower-class areas are invariably described as disorganized, and middle-class or upper-class areas are described as organized communities.

The classic sociological study of the distribution of diagnosed mental disorders in the city is that by Faris and Dunham (1939). The methods and findings of this study have formed the model for all subsequent studies of urban residence and insanity. Faris and Dunham found (in the late 1920s and early 1930s) that admissions from Chicago to public mental institutions came disproportionately from the central, lower-class districts of the city, and admissions to the private asylums were concentrated in the higher-class districts. When the public and private cases were combined for overall incidence rates, the rates were highest in the central district and they became progressively lower toward the outlying areas of the city. This pattern was duplicated for rates of admission on a diagnosis of schizophrenia. But unlike the overall rates and the schizophrenia rates, admissions diagnosed as manic-depressive showed no patterned distribution (Faris and Dunham 1939: 23–81). Although only admissions to a state hospital were used, essentially the same pattern was found in Providence, Rhode Island (Faris and Dunham 1939:143–50).

A negative relationship between social class and mental illness was also found in a now famous study in New Haven by Hollingshead and Redlich (1958) and their associates. In the New Haven study socioeconomic status was related to psychiatric diagnosis, referral patterns, type of treatment, incidence, and prevalence of mental illness. Patients from the upper classes were most likely to be in private asylums, diagnosed as neurotic, and to be referred for treatment by private physicians, family, and friends, whereas lower-class patients were likely to be in state hospitals (often involuntarily), diagnosed as psychotic, and to be referred from social agencies and clinics (Hollingshead and Redlich 1958:186, 220–302). There were disproportionately high numbers of new and existing psychiatric patients in the lowest class, disproportionately low numbers in the highest class, and proportionate numbers in the middle classes. This relationship remains even when age, sex, race, marital status, and religion are controlled (Hollingshead and Redlich 1958:199–213). Some have been critical of the New Haven research and findings on social class (Srole et al. 1968:110–14; Miller and Mishler 1964), but other research confirms the findings on the relationship between class and psychiatric treatment, even in circumstances in which the cost of treatment is not a factor (Brill and Storrow 1964).

The more recent study in midtown Manhattan found the same *inverse* relationship between social class and the prevalence of *"impaired" mental health* as measured by a symptom checklist. One's class of origin (parental socioeconomic status) and even more, his present social class standing, were related to the likelihood that he would be mentally impaired (Srole and Langner 1967:34–39). However, the probability of being a *psychiatric patient* was found to be *positively* associated with social class; the higher one's class, the more likely he is to be a mental patient. Two facts account for this: there is an abundance of office therapists and attendant private facilities in Manhattan, and upper-status people are more apt to seek psychiatric care and to advise friends and family to seek care, and if they become patients, they are more likely to be under private office or hospital care or outpatients. Lower-status persons tend not to seek help for themselves or to advocate psychiatric help for others; if they do become patients, they are much more likely than upper-status persons to be involuntary patients of a public hospital or outpatients of a public clinic (Srole et al. 1968:108–20).

Jaco (1960) also found that lower-status persons are overrepresented in the public hospitals in Texas, but when patients in private care and hospitals are added there is not a straight negative relationship between socioeconomic characteristics and the number of mental patients. He found the highest combined incidence rate among the unemployed. Among the employed, the highest rate was found in the higher-status occupations (professional and semiprofessional); the next highest patient rates were found in low-status occupations (agriculture, service, and manual); and the lowest rates were found in intermediate occupations (clerical, sales, managerial). Jaco also found that the highest rates are at both ends of the educational continuum (highest among those with little or no education and next highest among the college educated) and the lowest rates are among those with intermediate levels of education (1960:125–73).

The Baltimore study located a greater prevalence of psychoses among lower-income groups and a lesser prevalence among upper-income groups, but this inverse relationship with class was not found with neuroses. Rather, a U-shaped pattern prevailed: those judged neurotic were most apt to be in the lowest or highest income levels and the least likely to be in the middle-income strata (Pasamanick et al. 1964).

A lower-class area of Boston had a higher rate of hospitalized but a lower rate of nonhospitalized patients than another area or an upper-class Boston suburb. When hospitalized and nonhospitalized cases were combined the lower-class community still had a higher proportion of psychiatric patients (Kaplan et al. 1968).

Dunham found that the subcommunities of Detroit with high rates of psychoses and schizophrenia are located in the areas adjacent to the down-town, central district, and the subcommunities with low rates are in the out-lying and suburban areas. But he found no relationship between social class and schizophrenia (as diagnosed by a psychiatrist who collaborated in the study) within each of two communities (one a central-district, high-rate subcommunity and the other an outlying, low-rate subcommunity) selected for more intensive study. Moreover, when length of residence in each sub-community is controlled, the impact of living in an organized or disorgan-ized community is not significant (Dunham 1965:86–198). However, these findings must be largely discounted because they are based on a total of only 63 cases of schizophrenia (39 in the "high"-rate neighborhood and 24 in the "low"-rate neighborhood).

After reviewing studies in such disparate communities as Chicago, Providence, St. Louis, Cleveland, Omaha, Kansas City, Milwaukee, and Peoria, Weinberg concludes that the findings fairly consistently show that (1) the overall rates of psychoses and of schizophrenia are highest near the central areas of the city and decline as one moves outward toward the suburbs; (2) rates of schizophrenia are highest in the low-income and dis-organized areas; (3) the differences in rates are not explained by the per-centage of foreign-born persons, male-female ratios, and other variables; (4) there are no consistent patterns for manic-depressive and some other diag-nostic categories (Weinberg 1967a:22–25). "Despite variations in the types of subjects studied and the methods used, one persistent finding has been the existence of an inverse relationship between socioeconomic status and rates of schizophrenia" (Weinberg 1967a:20).

Social Class Mobility, Aspiration Discrepancy, and Stress

The preponderance of mental patients in the lower class could be due to their downward mobility, or "drift," to a lower status because they are un-able to maintain their status in an achievement society. But neither Faris and Dunham (1939) nor Hollingshead and Redlich (1958) found much support for this drift hypothesis. The neurotic and schizophrenic patients in the New

Haven study were more mobile than nonpatients in the general population, but they were as likely to be upwardly as downwardly mobile (Hollingshead et al. 1967). Downward mobility was found to be related to overall "impairment" in Manhattan (Srole and Langner 1967:40–41), but some symptom classifications (such as obsessive-compulsive and schizoid) included relatively greater numbers of those who had moved up in social status (Langner and Michael 1963:425–30). Langner and Michael include mobility and a number of other childhood and adult experiences as "life stresses." They and others (see Clausen 1966:65–66) hypothesize that mental illness symptoms are formed as defenses against social stress.

Failure to achieve mobility aspirations is also related to mental illness. The greater the discrepancy that exists between what one hopes to achieve and what he can realistically expect to achieve occupationally and educationally, the greater the probability that he will be a mental patient (Hollingshead et al. 1967; Rinehart 1968; Kleiner and Parker 1967). This aspiration-achievement discrepancy, which is a form of anomie, could be a stress factor resulting in mental breakdown. But Rinehart (1968) offers the reasonable alternative hypothesis that a person seeks out the mental illness role as an excuse for his failure to realize his aspirations.

Age and Sex

There is some indication that males are more likely to be mental patients than females (Faris and Dunham 1939:38–81; Kaplan et al. 1968). However, the incidence rate was higher for females in Texas, and there were no differences in prevalence of mental disturbance by sex in the Manhattan study (Jaco 1960:32; Langner and Michael 1963:77). Overall rates of mental disorders tend to increase with age, but functional psychoses level off in middle age and decline thereafter; schizophrenia and the neurotic diagnoses reach a peak sooner (Clausen 1966:33–34; Jaco 1960:32–39; Langner and Michael 1963:77; Pasamanick et al. 1964).

Other Social Characteristics

Catholics and Protestants tend to be somewhat overrepresented and Jews somewhat underrepresented in psychotic cases, but Jews seem to have higher rates of neuroses. The rate of mental illness is higher among whites than it is among blacks and other minority groups. Whites living in areas where blacks are in the majority are more likely than those living in all-white or predominantly white areas to become schizophrenic patients. And although earlier studies also found that schizophrenia is more prevalent among blacks in all-black areas than it is among blacks living in racially integrated areas, a later study found that admissions of blacks to psychiatric facilities are greater in areas with smaller percentages of black residents; admissions were fewer in more segregated areas (Levy and Rowitz 1973). Rates of mental illness are highest among the divorced and maritally separated and are lowest among the married (Langner and Michael 1963:77–79; Jaco 1960:40–59, 109–24; Wanklin et al. 1968; Roberts and Myers 1968).

Conclusion: Mental Illness
Rates and Individual Behavior

The connection between the variations in rates and the processes of becoming a mental patient is fairly clear—psychiatric diagnoses and treatment are affected by the social characteristics of the persons being considered for the patient role. For instance, those in the upper and middle classes tend to be diagnosed as neurotic and tend to seek and be given private office or hospital care. The lower classes tend to be judged psychotic and to be given public clinic or hospital care. Because the judges are psychiatrists and related professionals, the behavior of lower-class persons is more apt to seem different, strange, and "sick" to them. The connection between the rate patterns and the actual deviant behavior is not so clear, and in fact there may be no connection. Even in the community surveys the diagnostic predilections of the psychiatrist intervene between the social variables and the reported behavior, so that the behavior itself only incidentally is included as a variable. Therefore, all that the studies may tell us is that the behavior of certain persons, whatever it is, is more likely than that of other persons to be called symptomatic of illness by the psychiatrist, who bases his judgment on his training and social values.

But insofar as certain kinds of behavior (that is, disruptive, inconvenient, or troublesome to others or to self) influence the diagnosis, then there should also be a relationship between the behavior and the social characteristics. The medical model would lead one to believe that the relationship is simply one in which the rates reflect the probability of being sick. An alternative is to view the connection between group rates and the "symptoms" of individuals as a behavioral relationship. One's social environment differentially shapes and maintains his behavior which leads others to define him as mentally ill. This social learning explanation is the topic of the next chapter.

27

Mental Illness as Learned Behavior

In the behavioral model the "symptcms" are taken as the problem to be explained, not some presumed underlying illness. When the symptoms are removed, the psychoses or neuroses by definition are removed. Although there are variations in emphasis and interpretation among learning-based theories and the behavior modification therapies of mental illness, all view and treat the symptoms as conditioned responses to the environment. They may be behavioral deficits or deficiencies or annoying and unnecessary behavior surpluses; they may be disturbing, disruptive, and unpleasant; but they result from the same cognitive and behavioral processes as normal, "healthy" behavior.

> Briefly, the behaviorist regards neurotic behavior as learned behavior: conditioned emotional, verbal, and motor responses have resulted from a history of aversive events and are maintained by immediate reinforcement of behaviors that are instrumental in preventing extinction of conditioned emotional responses. . . . In describing the behavior called neurotic as learned, the emphasis is on indicating that this behavior is initially the result of various external operations such as reinforcement, generalization, and continuity rather than on postulated unobservable inner forces (Reyna 1964: 171).
>
> From a social-learning perspective, behaviors that may be detrimental to the individual or that depart widely from accepted social and ethical norms are considered not as manifestations of an underlying pathology, but as ways, which the persons have learned, of coping with environmental and self-imposed demands (Bandura 1969:62).

Mental illness involves one or more of the following behavior patterns: (1) autonomic, visceral, and emotional responses which have been conditioned to respond to stimuli which ordinarily do not elicit them; (2) inappropriate or unusual actions which have been learned through (a) imitation and modeling, (b) direct social attention and socialization, (c) avoiding aversive situations; (3) behavioral deficits (failures to develop adequate repertoires of social skills); (4) "delusional," symbolically constructed definitions of the situation which are directly reinforced (either positively or negatively reinforced by providing excuses for not performing roles and so on), or which are discriminative for other behavior.

The process may start and end simply as behavioral idiosyncrasies either not very distinguishable from other individual differences or not sufficiently different to be defined as serious deviance. But some individuals tend to move toward and take on (and move out of) a stabilized deviant role. Whether a person does or not is determined by the nature of his interpersonal relationships, not the unfolding of the imperatives of a dynamic illness. The development, maintenance, and extinction of the residual deviance reflects the functional relationship with the person's environment.

A number of things may shape the behavior progressively toward more prominent actions which are disturbing to the person himself or to others. Psychosomatic complaints may be very effective in bringing attention and sympathy that is otherwise lacking or as excuses for avoiding unpleasant jobs. Other people may in fact behave conspiratorially or otherwise validate and further reinforce a person's initial paranoid hypotheses about them. Becoming more and more withdrawn and mute may be an efficient way of avoiding and closing out an unrewarding world; playing the schizophrenic role may serve well to handle contradictory parental expectations (Lu 1967).

The usual reaction to this behavior, even by those who are knowingly or inadvertently reinforcing it, is to deny that it is unusual, abnormal, or seriously deviant (Scheff 1966:80–84; Gove 1970:877). But at some point either the person himself or others close to him become upset (or the accommodations to the behavior are disrupted) enough so that they entertain the idea that illness is involved and that the deviant person needs the attention of mental health professionals (Yarrow et al. 1968; Sampson et al. 1968). When this idea is formally validated by psychiatric diagnosis, treatment, or hospitalization, the person becomes more firmly *labeled* mentally ill. This means that he is assigned, and may seek and accept, the *social role of the mentally ill.* This adds another dimension to his social interaction, and others come even more to reinforce behavior believed appropriate and to punish behavior believed inappropriate to that role. Among the people who reinforce the deviant role are the physicians, psychiatrists, nurses, aides, ward attendants, and other patients, who constitute the major social actors in the world of the formally labeled mentally ill. Behavior interpreted as sick may develop as the patient's adaptation to the strange world of the mental hospital and to help him attain the limited rewards mediated by the staff. Thus "treatment," especially hospitalization, may perpetuate the behavior it was meant to extinguish. Return to conventional roles may prove difficult after the label has been assigned (Scheff 1966:85–93).

It is not clear, however, to what extent assignment to the stigmatized role and hospitalization simply stabilize and prolong the individual's career in the mental illness role. The labeling theory of mental illness maintains that it is a frequent if not the most common outcome of being formally labeled mentally ill (Scheff 1966; 1974). This contention (along with the one that nonpsychiatric variables influence the application of the label) has been a major source of controversy between supporters of the labeling theory and supporters of psychiatric theory. (See the exchange in Gove 1970; Scheff 1974; Gove 1975a; 1975b; Scheff 1975.) There is not much research on this issue, but an objective reading of the literature leads to the conclusion that the labeling hypothesis is not supported. Discontinuation of the mental illness role is more frequent following hospitalization or treatment than the labeling theory hypothesizes. However, this does not mean that therefore the medical model view is correct—that people hospitalized even against their wishes are in fact mentally ill and are cured by hospitalization. Rather the data can be readily interpreted in terms of social learning without assumptions of psychiatric impairment.

The illness definition often allows the individual's family to come to terms with his behavior and to change it. People are reluctant to apply a stigmatizing label to those close to them, especially when it means involuntary incarceration, and they therefore use that label (and seek to have it legitimatized through psychiatric diagnosis) only after the behavior has become troublesome enough to warrant action. After the one defined as ill undergoes the "cure" and is released from treatment, the person may be defined as no longer ill, and family relationship may change so that he is no longer rewarded for behaving that way and is supported in his attempts to resume his conventional duties. The nature of the social environment confronting the patient and the extent to which he is able to forge independent roles after his release are more important in keeping him out of the hospital than the diagnostic label or supposed seriousness of his illness before and at the time of treatment (Maisel 1967; Freeman and Simmons 1959; Dinitz et al. 1961; Davis et al. 1957).

The evidence supportive of this learning explanation of mental illness comes from (1) case studies and experiments in behavior modification, (2) sociological observations in the community, (3) sociological studies of mental hospitals, (4) specifically designed and experimentally evaluated social organizations utilizing learning principles—"token economies."

Behavior Modification

Learning-based behavior modification therapies have been used to change "sick" behavior and induce "healthy" behavior quite successfully. An examination of the reports on these treatment procedures (an abundance of which has now accumulated) shows that nearly the entire range of "symptoms" from the mildest, least disturbing psychosomatic and neurotic reactions to the severest, most impairing behavior has been responsive to the manipulation of eliciting stimuli and reinforcers and punishers. The behavior affected has been verbal, visceral, motor, imaginal, symbolic, and simple and complex. Excessive and surplus behavior such as obsessive-compulsive actions (for example, constant washing of one's hands) has been eliminated or reduced. Extreme "anxiety" behavior such as fear and avoidance reactions (phobias) to cats, snakes, rats, rabbits, and other animals and objects has been allayed. Chronic stuttering, facial tics, hysterical blindness (and other conversion phenomena), asthma, amnesia, sleepwalking, enuresis, and anorexia (refusal to eat) have been effectively counteracted. Persons experiencing depression, delusions, withdrawal, muteness, and apathy have responded to behavior modification. The behavioral therapies have used both operant and respondent conditioning. Several have been carefully conducted therapeutic experiments, but many of the reports are simply case studies (experiments producing previously nonexistent psychotic and neurotic behavior are understandably absent). Taken together they represent an accumulation of demonstrated successes in a short time that cannot be matched by the long history of traditional psychotherapy.[1]

Thus the evidence is accumulating that not just the side effects—mildly disturbing concomitants of illness—but the *central defining symptoms* of all the major psychiatric categories of mental illness are conditioned behavior patterns which can be increased, decreased, and produced again (Ullmann and Krasner 1969:377–413). This is as true of schizophrenia as it is of any other diagnostic category, and schizophrenia is the most frequently assigned diagnosis; it is considered the "sickest," the most chronic and deep-seated form of mental illness, with the most pessimistic, hopeless prognosis. Yet when "organized" responses by persons diagnosed as schizophrenic are systematically rewarded through social attention and verbal response, they significantly increase (as compared with control and nonreinforced groups) and approach normal patterns. Similarly, both verbal and motor apathy (bland, limited, or no responsiveness to the environment) of schizophrenic patients are readily modified and replaced with interested and interesting behavior through differential reinforcement. Social withdrawal, even in its extreme, mute form, can be changed through behavior therapy in the direction of normal social behavior, talking, and attentiveness to the social milieu. Finally, patients can be made to verbalize in ways usually taken as signs of schizophrenia when they are reinforced for "sick" talk (bizarre, unrealistic, nonlogical, discontented, and so on) or aversive talk (grouching, griping, and so forth). They come to respond normally when reinforced for "healthy talk" (Ullmann and Krasner 1969:398–408).

All the therapies and experiments have been performed with patients in a hospital or some other treatment setting. Experimental data are lacking on the production and extinction of mental illness in social situations outside

---

[1] See the collection of cases and reports in Eysenck 1960; 1964; Wolpe et al. 1964; Ullmann and Krasner 1965; and Krasner and Ullmann 1965. See also the summary discussions in Bandura 1969:217–554; and Ullmann and Krasner 1969:273–572.

the treatment milieu. However, if the "symptoms" of mental patients can be modified by deliberate changes in learning conditions, there is reason to believe that the same sort of environmental influence is operative before arriving at the point of treatment. Indeed, the therapies have relied heavily on essentially the same variables probably operative in the natural environment.

> Many of the experiments . . . made use of verbal conditioning, a procedure in which a relatively trivial reinforcing stimulus (usually a smile, a nod of the head, and/or an "Mmh–hmm") is emitted contingent upon the subject's behavior. The very fact that such a small environmental change is effective seems inconsistent with a picture of the schizophrenic as withdrawn and socially unresponsive. . . . In verbal conditioning experiments more than in most situations, the experimenter is the instrument, the source of reinforcing stimuli. . . . If what has been done with a smile, a head nod, and a grunt is fact, what can be done with stronger and more continuing reinforcing stimuli? (Ullmann and Krasner 1969:408)?

Observations in the Community

The evidence from observations in natural settings supports the importance of the quality of the individual's interaction with others in the etiology of his problems. He develops residual deviance through the reinforcement of some acts and the nonreinforcement of other acts and thoughts by those in the primary and secondary groups with which he is differentially associated. A good illustration comes from Lemert's (1967) observations based on interviews with several individuals diagnosed as paranoic (none of which, however, involved reports of hallucinations or intellectual impairment). Lemert disagrees with Cameron (1943) that the paranoid person builds a completely imaginary pseudocommunity of hostile actors. He found that paranoic behavior was the outgrowth of an interactional process in which the person was gradually excluded from normal communication with the other group members. The actions and reactions of the others in fact involved *real* covertly organized, hostile, suspicious, and conspiratorial behavior toward the person before, during, and after he engaged in "paranoid reactions." Paranoia is generated and maintained in a process of exclusion which denies the person the proper informal feedback on the consequences of his behavior, which is confusing and disorienting.

> The general idea that the paranoid person symbolically fabricates the conspiracy against him is in our estimation incorrect or incomplete. Nor can we agree that he lacks insight, as is so often claimed. To the contrary many paranoid persons properly realize that they are

being isolated and excluded by concerted interaction, or that they are being manipulated. However, they are at a loss to estimate accurately or realistically the dimensions and form of the coalition arrayed against them (Lemert 1967:207).

In an effort to get a more accurate estimate and to clear up the confusion the person may be led to direct accusation and confrontation. This only leads to his further exclusion, to being defined as insulting, difficult, and strange, and to receiving even more evasive and ambiguous communications. Thus as the individual constructs a conspiratorial definition of the situation to explain the exclusion he is experiencing and starts behaving toward others accordingly, they engage in a process of communicative exclusion and ambiguous action which only serves to confirm his suspicions. His paranoid reactions are reinforced, and he becomes more set in the role of the mistrusted and mistrusting.

This formulation is in substantial agreement with that by Laing and Esterson in their detailed study of cases based on many interviews with mental patients and their families. In one of these cases the behavior of a woman diagnosed as paranoid schizophrenia (for which she had at the time been incarcerated for ten years) was found to be quite understandable reactions to the actions of her parents prior to hospitalization (Laing and Esterson 1967). For example, the woman was thought to have "delusions" that her parents were trying surreptitiously to "influence" her. Laing and Esterson found that in fact the parents did believe she could read their thoughts, did try to influence her with "experiments," and yet denied that they were doing so when she confronted them. (This took place when she was a teenager, prior to her hospitalization at age eighteen, and continued in the interview situations repeated in the following quote.)

> When they were all interviewed together, her mother and father kept exchanging with each other a constant series of nods, winks, gestures, knowing smiles, so obvious to the observer, that he commented on them after twenty minutes of the first such interview. *They continued, however, unabated and denied.*
>
> These open yet unavowed non-verbal exchanges between father and mother were in fact quite public and perfectly obvious. Much of what could be taken to be paranoid about Maya arose because she mistrusted her own mistrust. She could not really believe that what she thought she saw going on was going on (Laing and Esterson 1967:138–39, italics in original).

We recognize the behavior of the parents as a direct analogue to the behavior of the experimenter in operant conditioning experiments in which the symptoms (especially verbal) of hospitalized schizophrenics can be readily changed with smiles, nods, and words. It is easy to see from this quote how the behavior of the parents—their open collusive behavior coupled with denial that they were behaving out of the ordinary—was confusing to the woman and reinforced her "paranoid delusions." That the woman and not the parents was hospitalized and defined as sick reflects mainly their greater social power and the fact that committing officials sided with their definition of the situation rather than with the woman's.

This may be an unusual case, but the power of interactional influence on behavioral "symptoms" which it illustrates is not unusual and is probably operative, in more or less subtle ways, in most cases. In addition to the strictly behavioral aspects, the reactions of others shape the person's conception of what is happening to him. The paranoid's constructed meaning of the situation is simply one which is not shared by those in a position to label him paranoid. The diagnosis of paranoia, then, is based on the fact that the one diagnosing does not agree that the person's fears and suspicious definitions have any basis in fact; he believes them to be unreal, delusional, and so on. The same person with the same behavior, thoughts, and story will be diagnosed sane if he is believed, insane if he is not believed. Therefore, there is no difference in the behavior or thoughts themselves; the difference is only in the extent to which they jibe with others' beliefs.

Of course, an individual's notions about what was or is happening to him can be tested against data, and their objective truth or falsity can be ascertained. Some will be false, others will be true, and still others will remain unresolved. It may be independently determined that the individual's story is false or a lie, but as the scientist who holds a false hypothesis about the subject he is investigating is no different from the one who holds the correct hypothesis, *a false belief is no more pathological than a true belief. It is only not true.* The mental and behavioral processes involved in a "paranoid" belief differ from a "nonparanoid" belief only in that they are not taken as plausible by others and that the one holding them is defined as disruptive.

Studies of Mental Hospitals

Studies of institutions for the incarceration of mental patients also show how symptoms are shaped by social consequences. The office therapist can and does (usually inadvertently) reinforce "sick" verbalizations. But the control by the institutional staff over patients in a mental hospital is much more complete and hence more dramatic in its impact. The situation is somewhat different for those in private asylums and for voluntary patients, but for those involuntarily incarcerated in one of the large state-run institutions, the stay may be the most deviance-producing experience he ever had.

Whatever his condition is at the time of admission, it is clear that his behavior afterward is based much more on an adaptation to the hospital environment than it is on previous experiences or on some presumed psychiatric disturbance. The "total institution," to use Goffman's (1961) term, begins almost immediately to strip the patient of his identity, individuality, and control of his environment. The operating assumption is that he is "sick" and hence is not responsible. Physicians, nurses, psychiatrists, aides, and other staff interact with him as if he were sick, and indeed, whatever he does is apt to be interpreted as part of his illness.

Because the numbers involved are large, a premium is placed on the efficient, bureaucratic management of the patient population rather than on treatment aimed toward release. Because of the shortage of high-level professional personnel, effective control over the destiny of patients is in the hands of the ward attendants or aides. Access to the limited rewards available to the patients, getting free time off the ward, job assignments, attention from head nurses or psychiatrists, choice of bed and room, the chance to leave the grounds and go into town, and so on are all controlled by the ward attendants. In the culture of the aides, a good patient does not cause too much trouble, is passive, dependent, and cooperative. The one who begins to be too independent, to assert his rights, to agitate for "privileges" is liable to face the withdrawal of rewards and a considerable arsenal of punishers—recommendation for electroshock "treatment," greater isolation, and so forth.

Faced with this, many patients become extremely apathetic, develop vegetative and childlike behavior patterns (for example, chronic incontinence—wetting and soiling beds and clothes), and other responses which are taken by the staff as further confirmation of sickness. Some patients develop other "sick" strategies of getting along. One way that those who are largely ignored can get attention (perhaps from a high-level nurse or even from the psychiatrist, a potent reward in the hospital) is to behave "psychotically." These "psychotic episodes," which are taken as evidence of sickness by the staff, are better understood as attempts to cope with the system. For those for whom a question is raised about release, the usual superordinate-subordinate relationship between staff and patients (epitomized by the universal practice of addressing patients by first names and staff by some title—Nurse, Doctor) may be changed toward the more equal nature of interaction outside the institution. Given the chance to respond in this way, the patient begins behaving accordingly, and the judgment that he is getting well is confirmed.

The increased use of quick hospitalization and short stays and the community psychiatry movement under way may have already made some (and portend more) changes in this picture. But the tremendous impact of the large institution with a high proportion of long-term patients in creating and maintaining the symptoms and structuring support for the role of the mentally ill has been well documented (Goffman 1961; Belknap 1956; Dunham and Weinberg 1960; Caudill 1958; Ullmann and Krasner 1969:387–98; Bandura 1969:261–62).

Token Economies

The most systematic evidence for the shaping of psychotic behavior by rewards and punishments is that provided by the growing number of controlled experimental treatment programs known as *token economies*. The idea behind the token economy approach is that if the informal system of the hospital already is organized to dispense rewards for behaving in certain ways, it should be possible to set up a system in a more formal and even more effective way by using learning principles. The difference would be that "well" behavior needed for adjustment to normal life on the outside, not behavior needed only to adjust to the ward system of the institution, would be rewarded. Adult, responsible behavior—caring for and providing for oneself, performing remunerative tasks and using the proceeds in a discretionary fashion—would be reinforced; psychotic symptoms—institutional dependency and so forth—would not be rewarded (Ayllon and Azrin 1968: 1–15; Ullmann and Krasner 1969:408–9). This is accomplished not by setting up reinforcement schedules separately for each individual; rather, it involves "social organizational applications of reinforcement contingencies," to use Bandura's phrase (1969:261). An entire population of a ward is organized and placed under a system for the distribution of rewards based on the patients' behavior.

A set of *desirable* target *behavior* is defined: working successfully at a job, maintaining personal hygiene, keeping one's quarters clean, making beds, engaging in vocational or educational training, and maintaining appropriate social behavior and interaction with others. Satisfactory performance of each activity is paid for with *tokens* (chips, disks, or points), which serve as a medium of exchange (hence, *token* economy) for *rewards* (back-up reinforcers), which consist of commissary commodities, time off the ward, the chance to see a nurse or psychiatrist, town leave, opportunity to engage in whatever nondisruptive activity the patient finds enjoyable, assignment to a preferred room, or a radio in the room. The dispensing of tokens may also be accompanied by direct social reinforcement from the staff. In short, the patient is able to obtain rewards, usually mediated by the attendants and staff, but he receives them on the same basis as others on the ward and has equal opportunity to earn them. Acting sick does not bring him any tokens, it interferes with activity that would earn tokens, and it is studiously ignored (and therefore nonrewarded) by the staff.

Although the populations have been composed of "back-ward" psychotics, many of whom had spent decades in the hospital and had been given up as hopeless cases, participation in the token economies produced dramatic changes in behavior. When the token economy is in force on the ward, there is a significant increase in the rewarded behavior. Bizarre and disturbing behavior virtually disappears. The general tone of listless inactivity and docile compliance, punctuated with "psychotic outbursts," is changed to one of activity, interest, and sociability. Patients are responsible for earning their keep and enough to buy the things they want; they must select among alternatives, plan ahead, and manage a medium of exchange. When the token economy is removed, the performance level almost immediately deteriorates; when reinstated, the performance level takes a quick upswing (Ayllon and Azrin 1965; 1968; Atthowe and Krasner 1968; Lloyd and Abel 1970; Bandura 1969:261–78). As Allyon and Azrin, reporting on the first and still best known token economy experiment with mental patients, summarize:

> In each experiment, the performance fell to near zero level when the established response-reinforcement relation was discontinued. . . . The standard procedure for reinforcement had been to provide tokens . . . [for desired behavior, which were exchanged for reinforcers]. Performance decreased when this response-reinforcement relation was disrupted. . . . Furthermore, the effectiveness of the reinforcement procedure did not appear to be limited to an all-or-none basis. Patients selected and performed the assignment that provided the larger number of tokens when reinforcement was available for more than one assignment (Allyon and Azrin 1965: 381).

The difficulty with the token economies, in spite of their impressive success in manipulating behavior in the hospital, is that they have not yet come as close as desirable to the kind of schedules of social reinforcement the patients are apt to meet upon release. People ordinarily do not receive direct, consistent, nonintermittent monetary reward on an egalitarian, noncompetitive basis. They do not get paid for making their own beds. However, the later experiments have come closer to naturalistic social systems, and the next step will probably be to move the system out of the hospital altogether, for there is an irreducible element of coercion and artificiality inherent in any setting within the mental institution (Bandura 1969:275). The token economy programs do provide emphatic demonstration that behavior labeled mental illness grows out of the individual's relationship to his social environment.

Summary

Mental illness is explained as learned adaptations to one's social environment. Behaving in ways that are unusual or different enough to be called mental illness may lead to the person's being formally labeled and taking on the social role of mentally ill. Being assigned to the mental illness role may effect enough change in his interpersonal relations that the reinforcement sustaining the behavior is changed and the behavioral problem is solved. But for some, being formally labeled mentally ill only continues the existing actions and adds other contingencies which sustain the behavior, and they become stabilized into the deviant role. The evidence supporting this learning approach comes from case studies and experiments in which mental illness "symptoms" have successfully been modified, from sociological studies in the community and in mental hospitals, and from experiments with "token economies," in which changed social environments have produced normal behavior among hospitalized mental patients.

Glossary

Addiction (drug): The habitual use of a drug, when such use includes some degree of physiological need for the drug to maintain normal body function. Opiates such as heroin and codeine are addictive drugs.

Alcoholism: Excessive drinking to the extent that it interferes with the drinker's health and/or social relationships.

Anomie: A disorganized or confused condition brought about either by conflicting norms or by the lack of norms. Anomie may refer to a personal feeling or a diffuse state of social disintegration.

Aspiration: A goal which a person hopes to achieve in life, as opposed to expectation (a goal he more realistically believes is possible for him). This concept is part of the (anomie) strain theory of deviant behavior.

Aversion therapy: A method to reduce or change a person's behavior by conditioning certain behavior with aversive (painful or unpleasant) stimuli. It is sometimes used in the treatment of alcoholism and homosexuality.

Behavior modification (behavior therapy): A method of changing a person's behavior by manipulating the consequences of his acts in order to reinforce a specifically desired behavior.

Behavior theory: See *operant conditioning theory*.

Big con: A confidence game devised to trick the victim into relinquishing all the money he has in savings and property. (Compare with *short con.*)

Biofeedback: A technique which allows the individual to see (through electronic monitoring) what effects his actions have on brain waves, heartbeat, etc. so that he can come to exert some voluntary control over these normally involuntary functions.

Booster: A shoplifter.

Boxman: A safecracker.

Classical conditioning: Eliciting a certain response by pairing a new stimulus over time with another stimulus which already elicits that response.

Compulsive crime: A term applied to a crime committed by a criminal whose motives appear irrational or are unknown.

Conditioned stimulus: See *stimulus.*

Confidence game: A swindle in which the criminal (con man) gains the confidence of the victim and then tricks him into giving him money.

Conflict model: A theoretical approach to deviant behavior based on the idea that the diversity of modern society leads to conflicting beliefs and attitudes, because the pursuit of an interest by one group may interfere with the interests of other groups, and behavior deemed deviant by one group may be conforming behavior in another group.

Consensus model: A theoretical approach to deviant behavior based on the idea of a society-wide agreement about right and wrong behavior. This approach implies that these widespread values serve the best interests of all.

Containment theory: Proposes that an individual can be "pushed" toward deviant acts by internal drives and "pulled" in that direction by an unsatisfactory social environment. Individual and social controls, called inner and outer containment, act as counterforces to discourage deviance.

Counterculture (contraculture): A subculture in conflict with, or alternative to, the dominant culture. The term was coined to describe hippies or political radicals.

Cross-cultural studies: Studies comparing some aspect of two or more distinct cultures.

Delinquent: A person, usually a youth, who engages in disapproved behavior which may or may not be criminal.

Deviant behavior: Action departing from or conflicting with standards of behavior or belief generally accepted within a social group. Some examples of deviant behavior are criminal acts, misuse of drugs, alcoholism, and prostitution.

Differential association: The exposure or contacts (varying in frequency, duration, priority, and intensity) a person has with different groups and individuals, from which he learns definitions conducive or counter to deviant behavior.

Differential association theory: Proposes that a person engages in criminal acts because he sees the law as something to violate more than as something to obey. This attitude about crime is learned through communication within intimate groups.

Differential reinforcement: See *reinforcement.*

Discriminative stimuli: Signal a person as to whether his behavior is appropriate, and whether it is likely to be rewarded or punished.

Drug abuse: The misuse of legal drugs or the use of illegal drugs.

Empiricism: The testing of theory by accumulating verifiable data.

Escape-avoidance behavior: Behavior, conditioned by negative reinforcement, to avoid unpleasant or painful stimuli.

Fix: The bribery of a law-enforcement official to avoid arrest and imprisonment.

Function (societal): The purpose or consequence of any social structure.

Gender identification: Part of the process of socialization in which a person learns expected sex-role behavior.
Grifter: A small-time thief who engages in confidence games.

Hallucinogens: A class of drugs, including marihuana, hashish, and LSD.
Homosexual behavior: Direct sexual relations between persons of the same sex.

Ideology: A systematic scheme of ideas about life, held either by an individual or a group.
Imitation: A person's execution of an act as a direct response to his observation of another person performing the act.
Instrumental conditioning: See *operant conditioning*.
Interest (pressure) group: Any group whose members are bound together by shared goals and values and who attempt to influence public policy in favor of their own goals. Interest groups generally operate in the political sphere.

Junkie: A slang term for a drug addict.

Labeling perspective: A theoretical approach which emphasizes that deviance is not created by a person's acts, but by a group's reaction to those acts. Applying a stigmatizing label to a person tends to start or continue his deviant career.
Lesbian behavior: Homosexual relations between females.
Loan shark: A person usually connected with organized crime who makes illegal loans and charges interest in great excess of the legal limit.

Mark: The victim of a crime, particularly of a confidence game.
Mental illness: A term applied to bizarre, irrational, or inappropriate behavior when it is generally believed to indicate a disease, sickness, or disorder of the mind or brain.
Methadone: A legal synthetic opiate used in treating addiction to heroin or other opiates, either through gradual withdrawal or maintenance. It is itself addictive.
Mores (folkways): Folkways are people's shared customs or norms. Mores are folkways deemed serious enough to justify the use of organized sanctions (laws) against a violator.

Narcotics: A nonspecific term referring to any "hard" drug which relieves pain and is physically addictive.
Negative definitions: See *social definitions*.
Negative reinforcement: See *reinforcement*.
Negative stimulus: See *stimulus*.

Neutralization: Social definitions to justify behavior or to deflect social and self-disapproval.
Neutralizing definitions: See *social definitions.*

Occupational crime: See *white-collar crime.*
Operant behavior: Voluntary behavior mediated by the central nervous system.
Operant conditioning theory: Explains behavior by reference to overt behavior and its conditioning by external stimuli—mainly the reinforcing or punishing consequences of the behavior. Also referred to as *Skinnerian* or *behavior theory.*
Operant (instrumental) conditioning: The rewarding or punishing of behavior by its outcomes or consequences.
Organized crime: Any crime committed by a person associated with a group of others whose purpose is criminal activity, when such a group is characterized by an established division of labor. This group includes positions for a corruptor of law-enforcement officials, a corrupted official, and for an enforcer of the group's wishes. The Mafia is the best-known example of organized crime.

Peer-group: A group of homogeneous age composition.
Penny weighter: A jewel thief.
Positive definitions: See *social definitions.*
Positive reinforcement. See *reinforcement.*
Positive stimulus. See *stimulus.*
Power: The possession of controlling influence over others, whether personal, social, or political.
Power-elite: The ruling class of society which controls the legal, political, and economic systems of that society to promote its own ends.
Pressure group: See *interest group.*
Prestige: The respect or high opinion enjoyed by an individual or a group.
Primary group: A small group of people who associate extensively together face-to-face in unspecialized ways and with relative intimacy, and whose personal relations are taken as ends in themselves.
Processual theory of deviant behavior: Any theory which explains the process by which individuals come to engage in deviant behavior.
Professional crime: Crime (usually theft) carried on as a way of life and a means of livelihood, employing complex and highly-developed skills. Involves some connection with legitimate institutions and carries with it a certain prestige.
Prostitution: Nonmarital sexual relations for pay. Call girls are the most expensive female prostitutes and are usually contacted by phone. Streetwalkers, usually picked up on the street, are the least expensive female prostitutes. The term usually refers to prostitution by females, but can also refer to prostitution (primarily homosexual) by males.

Psychedelic: This term, meaning "consciousness-expanding," is used to describe drugs or drug-related experiences. It is usually associated with hallucinogenic drugs and is positive in connotation.

Public policy: The course of action (or intended course of action) pursued to serve the common goals of all or a majority of people in a political unit. Generally refers to government action, but may include supportive action in the private sector.

Punishment: The weakening of an operant behavior so that the probability of future occurrence is decreased. Positive punishment is painful or unpleasant stimuli. Negative punishment is the withholding of a reward.

Race: A group of people with certain common inherited physical characteristics.

Racketeering: The extortion of money from an unwilling victim through intimidation or physical force. For example, a protection racket forces the victim to pay to avoid damage to his person or property.

Radical non-intervention: Recommends that it is better not to punish many offenders (especially young ones) and that it is better to tolerate deviant behavior. A proposed solution to the problem of the imprisonment of criminals, but it often increases their criminal behavior instead of decreasing it.

Reference group: A social group with which an individual identifies and from which he derives his norms, attitudes, and values.

Reinforcement: Strengthening or increasing the probability of the future occurrence of an *operant behavior.* An individual receives *positive reinforcement* when some aspect of his behavior is rewarded. *Negative reinforcement* results when an individual's behavior allows him to avoid an unpleasant stimulus. A person receives *vicarious reinforcement* results when he observes another person's behavior rewarded. *Differential reinforcement* results when an individual comes to prefer one behavior over another because it has been more highly rewarded or less punished.

Respondent behavior: Reflex or involuntary behavior, such as withdrawing one's hand from a flame.

Role-playing: An individual's performance of a sequence of learned actions in order to fulfill a certain social position.

Schedules of reinforcement: The timing of reinforcement, either as a consistent routine or on some intermittent basis.

Secondary deviance: A person's deviant behavior caused by social reaction to his initial deviant acts.

Self-concept: A person's view and evaluation of himself.

Short con: A confidence game in which the victim is tricked into parting with the money he has in his possession at the time. (Compare with *big con.*)

Skinnerian theory: See *operant conditioning theory.*

Social bonding: The ties holding an individual to conventional groups, formed through attachment to others, conventional pursuits, and a moral belief in the group's norms.

Social change: An observed difference from preceding states of the social structure, institutions, and customs of a society.

Social control: The formal and informal limitations placed on a person's behavior by his social group in order to keep him conforming to the norms.

Social definitions: The judgment of a behavior as right or wrong. *Positive definitions* are approving. *Negative definitions* are disapproving. *Neutralizing definitions* justify or excuse a normally undesirable action.

Social disorganization: A weakening or disruption of the patterns of social life, implying a relative decline of social control.

Social interaction: People or groups communicating with one another.

Socialization: The process by which an individual learns socially approved behavior.

Social learning theory: Proposes that a person will participate in deviant behavior to the extent that it has been differentially reinforced over conforming behavior and defined as more desirable or justified than conforming alternatives.

Social norm: A standard of behavior or definition of right and wrong shared by members of a social group, to which each member is expected to conform.

Social organization: A social system characterized by internal agreement about norms and values, orderly patterns of social interaction, and strong ties among its members.

Social sanctions: Rewards or punishments (i.e., positive or negative sanctions) intended to enforce conformity to generally accepted standards of behavior. A mechanism of social control.

Social system: The structure and pattern of interaction of many people who are oriented to one another.

Speed freak: Slang term for a compulsive user of Methedrine or other amphetamines.

Status: A position in a social system with respect to the distribution of prestige, and sometimes the distribution of rights, obligations, power, and authority.

Stimulus: Any event or condition which elicits a response. *Unconditioned stimulus* automatically elicits a given response. *Conditioned stimulus* comes to elicit a given response after being paired with a stimulus which already elicits that response. *Positive stimulus* is pleasant. *Negative stimulus* is unpleasant.

Strain theory: Proposes that deviant behavior results from the faulty integration of cultural ends and societal means. An individual engages in deviant behavior when he has insufficient opportunity to achieve common goals through legitimate means.

Structural theory of deviant behavior: Emphasizes group variations in the rate of deviance along parameters of class, age, sex, race, religion, or ethnic status.

Structure (societal): The arrangement of specialized and mutually dependent institutions in a social system.

Subculture: The values, norms, and beliefs of a subgroup in society.

Suicide: The deliberate taking of one's own life.

Symbolic interaction: The exchange of meanings in face-to-face communication through verbal and gestural symbols.

Taboo: The strict prohibition of certain acts by tradition or social convention.

Tautology: A proposition which is either true by definition or is impossible to test because of the way it is stated.

Therapeutic community: Any group living together for the purpose of mutual rehabilitation; or any residential treatment program in which the entire milieu is considered curative.

Token economy: A behavior modification program in which members of a group are assigned points or given tokens for certain behavior, which can then be exchanged for other rewards.

Unconditioned stimulus: See *stimulus.*

Vicarious reinforcement: See *reinforcement.*

White-collar (occupational) crime: The violation of laws governing business, occupations, or the professions by a person in that business, occupation, or profession.

Whiz mob: A pickpocket gang.

References

*Part One: Central Problems
and Perspectives in the Sociology
of Deviance (Chapters 1, 2, 3, 4, and 5)*

Adams, Reed.
    1973   Differential association and learning principles revisited. *Social Problems* 20 (Spring):447–58.

Akers, Ronald L.
    1964   Socio-economic status and delinquent behavior: a re-test. *Journal of Research in Crime and Delinquency* 1 (January):38–46.
    1968a   Problems in the sociology of deviance: social definitions and behavior. *Social Forces* 46 (June):455–65.
    1968b   The professional association and the legal regulation of practice. *Law and Society Review* 2 (May):463–582.

Akers, Ronald L., and Hawkins, Richard, eds.
    1975   *Law and control in society.* Englewood Cliffs, N.J.: Prentice-Hall.

Alksne, Harold; Lieberman, Lois; and Brill, Leon.
    1967   A conceptual model of the life cycle of addiction. *International Journal of the Addictions* 2 (Fall):221–40.

Anderson, Linda S.
    1973   The impact of formal and informal sanctions on marijuana use: a test of social learning and deterrence. Unpublished M.A. thesis, Florida State University.

Arnold, David O., ed.
    1970   *The sociology of subcultures.* Berkeley, Calif.: Glendessary Press.

Ball, Harry V., and Simpson, George O.
    1962   Law and social change: Sumner reconsidered. *American Journal of Sociology* 67 (March):532–40.

Ball, John C.
    1957   Delinquent and non-delinquent attitudes toward the prevalence of stealing. *Journal of Criminal Law, Criminology, and Police Science* 48 (September–October):259–74.

Ball, Richard A.
    1968   An empirical exploration of neutralization theory. In *Approaches to deviance*, ed. Mark Lefton, James K. Skipper, and Charles H. McCaghy, pp. 255–65. New York: Appleton-Century-Crofts.

Bandura, Albert.
    1969   *Principles of behavior modification.* New York: Holt, Rinehart, and Winston.

Bandura, Albert, and Walters, Richard H.
    1963   *Social learning and personality development.* New York: Holt, Rinehart, and Winston.

Becker, Howard S.
    1953   Becoming a marihuana user. *American Journal of Sociology* 49 (November):235–42.
    1960   Notes on the concept of commitment. *American Journal of Sociology* 66 (July):32–40.
    1963   *Outsiders.* New York: Free Press.

Bijou, Sidney W., and Baer, Donald M.
    1961   *Child development I.* New York: Appleton-Century-Crofts.

Bordua, David J.
    1967   Recent trends: deviant behavior and social control. *Annals* 369 (January):149–63.

Briar, Scott, and Piliavin, Irving.
    1965   Delinquency, situational inducements, and commitment to conformity. *Social Problems* 13 (Summer):35–45.

Burgess, Robert L., and Akers, Ronald L.
    1966a   Are operant principles tautological? *Psychological Record* 16 (July):305–12.
    1966b   A differential association-reinforcement theory of criminal behavior. *Social Problems* 14 (Fall):128–47.

Burgess, Robert L.; Burgess, Judy M.; and Esveldt, Karen C.
    1970   An analysis of generalized imitation. *Journal of Applied Behavior Analysis* 3 (Spring):39–46.

Burgess, Robert, and Bushell, Don, eds.
    1969   *Behavioral sociology.* New York: Columbia University Press.

Burkett, Steven, and Jensen, Eric L.
  1975   Conventional ties, peer influence, and the fear of apprehension: a
            study of adolescent marijuana use. *Sociological Quarterly* 16 (Autumn):
            522–33.

Carey, James T.
  1968   *The college drug scene.* Englewood Cliffs, N.J.: Prentice-Hall.

Chambliss, William J., ed.
  1969   *Crime and the legal process.* New York: McGraw-Hill.

Chambliss, William J., and Seidman, Robert B.
  1971   *Law, order, and power.* Reading, Mass.: Addison-Wesley.

Chiricos, Theodore G., and Waldo, Gordon P.
  1975   Socioeconomic status and criminal sentencing: an empirical assess-
            ment of a conflict proposition. *American Sociological Review* 40 (De-
            cember):753–72.

Clinard, Marshall B., ed.
  1964   *Anomie and deviant behavior.* New York: Free Press.

Cloward, Richard, and Ohlin, Lloyd.
  1959   Illegitimate means, anomie, and deviant behavior. *American Socio-
            logical Review* 24 (April):164–77.
  1961   *Delinquency and opportunity.* Glencoe, Ill.: Free Press.

Cohen, Albert K.
  1955   *Delinquent boys.* Glencoe, Ill.: Free Press.
  1959   The study of social disorganization and deviant behavior. In *Sociology
            today,* ed. Robert K. Merton, Leonard Broom, and Leonard S. Cottrell,
            pp. 461–84. New York: Basic Books.
  1965   The sociology of the deviant act: anomie theory and beyond. *American
            Sociological Review* 30 (February):9–14.
  1966   *Deviance and control.* Englewood Cliffs, N.J.: Prentice-Hall.

Cohen, Lawrence E., and Stark, Rodney.
  1974   Discriminatory labeling and the five finger discount: an empirical
            analysis of differential shoplifting dispositions. *Journal of Research in
            Crime and Delinquency* 11 (January):25–39.

Conger, Rand.
  1976   Social control and social learning models of delinquency: a synthesis.
            Criminology 14 (May):17–40.

Connor, Walter D.
  1972   The manufacture of deviance: the case of the soviet purge, 1936–1938.
            American Sociological Review 37 (August):403–13.

Cooley, Charles Horton.
    1902   *Human nature and the social order.* New York: Scribner's.

Coser, Lewis.
    1956   *The functions of social conflict.* New York: Free Press.

Cressey, Donald.
    1953   *Other people's money.* Glencoe, Ill.: Free Press.
    1960   Epidemiology and individual conduct: a case from criminology. *Pacific Sociological Review* 3 (Fall):47–58.

Currie, Elliot P.
    1968   Crimes without criminals: witchcraft and its control in Renaissance Europe. *Law and Society Review* 3 (August):7–32.

Datesman, Susan K.; Scarpitti, Frank R.; and Stephenson, Richard M.
    1975   Female delinquency: an application of self and opportunity theory. *Journal of Research in Crime and Delinquency* 12 (July):107–23.

Davis, Kingsley.
    1966   Sexual behavior. In Robert K. Merton and Robert A. Nisbet, eds., pp. 322–408.

Davis, Nanette J.
    1972   Labeling theory in deviance research: a critique and reconsideration. *Sociological Quarterly* 13 (Fall):447–74.

DeFleur, Melvin, and Quinney, Richard.
    1966   A reformulation of Sutherland's differential association theory and a strategy for empirical verification. *Journal of Research in Crime and Delinquency* 3 (January):1–22.

Dinitz, Simon; Scarpitti, Frank R.; and Reckless, Walter C.
    1962   Delinquency vulnerability: a cross-group and longitudinal analysis. *American Sociological Review* 27 (August):515–17.

Downes, David.
    1966   *The delinquent solution.* New York: Free Press.

Dynes, Russell R.; Clarke, Alfred D.; Dinitz, Simon; and Ishino, Iwao.
    1964   *Social problems: dissensus and deviation in an industrial society.* New York: Oxford University Press.

Edgerton, Robert B.
    1976   *Deviance: a cross-cultural perspective.* Menlo Park, Calif.: Cummings.

Ehrlich, Eugene.
1936 *Fundamental principles of the sociology of law.* Trans. Walter L. Moll. Cambridge, Mass.: Harvard University Press.

Elliott, Delbert S.
1966 Delinquency, school attendance, and dropouts. *Social Problems* 13 (Winter):307–14.

Elliott, Mabel A., and Merrill, Francis E.
1961 *Social disorganization.* 4th ed. New York: Harper and Row.

Empey, LaMar T., and Lubeck, Steven G.
1971 *The silverlake experiment: testing theory and community intervention.* Chicago: Aldine.

Erikson, Kai T.
1964 Notes on the sociology of deviance. In *The other side*, ed. Howard S. Becker, pp. 9–23. New York: Free Press of Glencoe.
1966 *Wayward puritans.* New York: Wiley.

Eysenck, H. J., ed.
1964 *Experiments in behavior therapy.* New York: Macmillan.

Faris, Robert E. L.
1955 *Social disorganization.* Rev. ed. New York: Ronald Press.

Fox, Vernon.
1976 *Introduction to criminology.* Englewood Cliffs, N.J.: Prentice-Hall.

Geis, Gilbert, ed.
1968 *White-collar criminal.* New York: Atherton Press.

Gibbons, Don C.
1976 *Delinquent behavior.* 2d ed. Englewood Cliffs, N.J.: Prentice-Hall.

Gibbons, Don C., and Jones, Joseph F.
1975 *The study of deviance: perspectives and problems.* Englewood Cliffs, N.J.: Prentice-Hall.

Gibbs, Jack P.
1966 Conceptions of deviant behavior: the old and the new. *Pacific Sociological Review* 9 (Spring):9–14.

Glaser, Daniel.
1956 Criminality theories and behavioral images. *American Journal of Sociology* 61 (March):433–44.

Goffman, Erving.
    1963   *Stigma*. Englewood Cliffs, N.J.: Prentice-Hall.

Goode, Erich.
    1975   On behalf of labeling theory. *Social Problems* 22 (June):570–83.

Gouldner, Alvin W.
    1968   The sociologist as partisan: sociology and the welfare state. *American Sociologist* 3 (May):103–16.
    1973   Foreword to Ian Taylor, Paul Walton, and Jock Young.

Gove, Walter, ed.
    1975   *The labelling of deviance: evaluating a perspective*. New York: Halsted Press.

Haber, Lawrence D., and Smith, Richard T.
    1971   Disability and deviance: normative adaptations of role behavior. *American Sociological Review* 36 (February):87–97.

Hagan, John.
    1973   Labelling and deviance: a case study in the "sociology of the interesting." *Social Problems* 20 (Spring):447–58.
    1974   "Extra-legal attributes in criminal sentencing: an assessment of a sociological viewpoint. *Law and Society Review* 8 (Spring):357–83.

Hall, Edwin L., and Simkus, Albert A.
    1975   Inequality in the types of sentences received by native Americans and whites. *Criminology* 13 (August):199–222.

Hawkins, Richard, and Tiedeman, Gary.
    1975   *The creation of deviance: interpersonal and organizational determinants*. Columbus, Ohio: Charles E. Merrill.

Hewitt, John P., and Stokes, Randall.
    1975   Disclaimers. *American Sociological Review* 40 (February):1–11.

Hill, Winfred F.
    1963   *Learning: a survey of psychological interpretations*. San Francisco: Chandler.

Hills, Stuart L.
    1971   *Crime, power, and morality*. Scranton, Penn.: Chandler.

Hindelang, Michael J.
    1969   Equality under the law. *Journal of Criminal Law, Criminology, and Police Science* 60 (September):306–13.

1970 The commitment of delinquents to their misdeeds: do delinquents drift? *Social Problems* 17 (Spring):502–9.

1973 Causes of delinquency: a partial replication and extension. *Social Problems* 20 (Spring):471–87.

1974a Decisions of shoplifting victims to invoke the criminal justice process. *Social Problems* 21 (April):580–93.

1974b Moral evaluations of illegal behavior. *Social Problems* 21 (3):370–84.

Hirschi, Travis.

1969 *Causes of delinquency.* Berkeley and Los Angeles: University of California Press.

1973 Procedural rules and the study of deviant behavior. *Social Problems* 21 (Fall):159–73.

Hirschi, Travis, and Stark, Rodney.

1969 Hellfire and delinquency. *Social Problems* 17 (Fall):202–13.

Homans, George C.

1961 *Social behavior: its elementary forms.* New York: Harcourt Brace Jovanovich.

1969 The sociological relevance of behaviorism. In Burgess and Bushell, eds., pp. 1–26.

Honig, Werner K., ed.

1966 *Operant behavior: areas of research and application.* New York: Appleton-Century-Crofts.

Jeffery, C. Ray.

1965 Criminal behavior and learning theory. *Journal of Criminal Law, Criminology, and Police Science* 56 (September):294–300.

Jensen, Gary F.

1969 "Crime doesn't pay": correlates of a shared misunderstanding. *Social Problems* 17 (Fall):189–201.

1970 Containment and delinquency: analysis of a theory. *University of Washington Journal of Sociology* 2 (November):1–14.

1972 Parents, peers, and delinquent action: a test of the differential association perspective. *American Journal of Sociology* 78 (November):63–72.

Johnston, Lloyd.

1975 News release on "monitoring the future" study. Ann Arbor, Mich.: Institute for Social Research.

Kitsuse, John I.

1964 Societal reaction to deviant behavior: problems of theory and method. In *The other side,* ed. Howard S. Becker, pp. 87–102. New York: Free Press of Glencoe.

1972   Deviance, deviant behavior, and deviants: some conceptual issues. In *An introduction to deviance,* ed. William Filstead, pp. 233–43. Chicago: Markham.

Kobrin, Solomon.
1951   The conflict of values in delinquency areas. *American Sociological Review* 16 (October):653–61.

Krohn, Marvin D.
1974   An investigation of the effect of parental and peer associations on marijuana use: an empirical test of differential association theory. In *Crime and delinquency: dimensions of deviance,* ed. Marc Riedel and Terence P. Thornberry, pp. 75–89. New York: Praeger.

Kunkel, John H.
1975   *Behavior, social problems, and change.* Englewood Cliffs, N.J.: Prentice-Hall.

Lander, Bernard.
1954   *Towards an understanding of juvenile delinquency.* New York: Columbia University Press.

Lemert, Edwin M.
1953   An isolation and closure theory of naive check forgery. *Journal of Criminal Law, Criminology, and Police Science* 44 (September-October): 296–307.
1967   *Human deviance, social problems, and social control.* Englewood Cliffs, N.J.: Prentice-Hall.
1972   *Human deviance, social problems, and social control.* 2d ed. Englewood Cliffs, N.J.: Prentice-Hall.
1974   Beyond Mead: the societal reaction to deviance. *Social Problems* 21 (April):457–68.

Levitin, Teresa E.
1975   Deviants as active participants in the labeling process: the visibly handicapped. *Social Problems* 22 (April):548–57.

Liazo, Alexander.
1972   The poverty of the sociology of deviance: nuts, sluts, and perverts. *Social Problems* 20 (Summer):103–20.

Linden, Eric, and Hackler, James C.
1973   Affective ties and delinquency. *Pacific Sociological Review* 16 (January): 27–46.

Lindesmith, Alfred R.
1947   *Opiate addiction.* Bloomington, Ind.: Principia Press.

Lofland, John.
   1969   *Deviance and identity*. Englewood Cliffs, N.J.: Prentice-Hall.

Lyman, Stanford M., and Scott, Marvin B.
   1970   *A sociology of the absurd*. New York: Appleton-Century-Crofts.

McGee, Reece.
   1962   *Social disorganization in America*. San Francisco: Chandler.

McGinnies, Elliott, and C. B. Ferster, eds.
   1971   *The reinforcement of social behavior*. New York: Houghton Mifflin.

McLaughlin, Barry.
   1971   *Learning and social behavior*. New York: Free Press.

Mahoney, Ann Rankin.
   1974   The effect of labeling upon youths in the juvenile justice system: a
             review of the evidence. *Law and Society Review 8* (Summer):583–614.

Matthews, Victor M.
   1968   Differential identification: an empirical note. *Social Problems* 14
             (Winter):376–83.

Matza, David.
   1964   *Delinquency and drift*. New York: Wiley.
   1969   *Becoming deviant*. Englewood Cliffs, N.J.: Prentice-Hall.

Mauss, Armand L.
   1975   *Social problems as social movements*. Philadelphia: J. B. Lippincott.

Mead, George Herbert.
   1934   *Mind, self, and society*. Chicago: University of Chicago Press.

Merton, Robert K.
   1938   Social structure and anomie. *American Sociological Review* 3 (October):
             672–82.
   1957   *Social theory and social structure*. Glencoe, Ill.: Free Press.

Merton, Robert K., and Nisbet, Robert A., eds.
   1966   *Contemporary social problems*. 2d ed. New York: Harcourt Brace
             Jovanovich.

Miller, Walter B.
   1958   Lower class culture as a generating milieu of gang delinquency.
             Journal of Social Issues 14:5–19.

Mills, C. Wright.
    1940   Situated action and the vocabulary of motives. *American Sociological Review* 6 (December):904–13.

Mintz, Beth; Freitag, Peter; Hendricks, Carol; and Schwartz, Michael.
    1976   Problems of proof in elite research. *Social Problems* 23 (February): 358–68.

Morris, Norval, and Hawkins, Gordon.
    1969   *The honest politician's guide to crime control.* Chicago: University of Chicago Press.

Newman, Graeme R.
    1974   Criminalization and decriminalization of deviant behavior: a cross national opinion survey. Paper presented to American Society of Criminology, Chicago.

Nuehring, Elane, and Markle, Gerald E.
    1974   Nicotine and norms: the re-emergence of a deviant behavior. *Social Problems* 21 (April):513–26.

Nye, F. Ivan.
    1958   *Family relationships and delinquent behavior.* New York: Wiley.

Orcutt, James D.
    1975   Deviance as a situated phenomenon: variations in the social interpretation of marijuana and alcohol use. *Social Problems* 22 (February): 346–56.

Parton, David.
    1974   Theories of imitation. Department of Sociology, University of Iowa Working Papers.

Pease, Kenneth; Ireson, Judith; and Thorpe, Jennifer.
    1975   Modified crime indices for eight countries. *Journal of Criminal Law and Criminology* 66 (June):209–14.

Petersen, David M., and Friday, Paul C.
    1975   Early release from incarceration: race as a factor in the use of "shock probation." *Journal of Criminal Law and Criminology* 66 (January): 79–87.

Pound, Roscoe.
    1942   *Social control through law.* New Haven, Conn.: Yale University Press.

Quinney, Richard.
1970   *The social reality of crime.* Boston: Little, Brown.
1974a   *Critique of the legal order: crime control in capitalist society.* Boston: Little, Brown.
1975   *Criminology.* Boston: Little, Brown.

Quinney, Richard, ed.
1969   *Crime and justice in society.* Boston: Little, Brown.
1974b   *Criminal justice in America: a critical understanding.* Boston: Little, Brown.

Rachman, Stanley, and Teasdale, John.
1970   *Aversion therapy and behavior disorders: an analysis.* Coral Gables, Fla.: University of Miami Press.

Reasons, Charles E.
1975   Social thought and social structure: competing paradigms in criminology. *Criminology* 13 (November):332–65.

Reckless, Walter.
1961   A new theory of delinquency and crime. *Federal Probation* 25 (December):42–46.
1967   *The crime problem.* 4th ed. New York: Appleton-Century-Crofts.
1970   Containment theory. In *The sociology of crime and delinquency,* 2d ed., ed. Marvin Wolfgang, Leonard Savitz, and Norman Johnston, pp. 401–5. New York: Wiley.

Reckless, Walter C.; Dinitz, Simon; and Murray, Ellen.
1956   Self-concept as an insulator against delinquency. *American Sociological Review* 21 (December):744–46.
1957   The "good boy" in a high delinquency area. *Journal of Criminal Law, Criminology, and Police Science* 48 (August):18–26.

Reiss, Albert J.
1951   Delinquency as the failure of personal and social control. *American Sociological Review* 16 (April):196–207.

Reiss, Albert J., Jr., and Rhodes, A. Lewis.
1963   Status deprivation and delinquent behavior. *Sociological Quarterly* 4 (Spring):135–49.
1964   An empirical test of differential association theory. *Journal of Research in Crime and Delinquency* 1 (January):5–18.

Rogers, Joseph W., and Buffalo, M. D.
1974   Fighting back: nine modes of adaptation to a deviant label. *Social Problems* 22 (October):101–18.

Rooney, Elizabeth A., and Gibbons, Don C.
    1966   Social reactions to "crimes without victims." *Social Problems* 13 (Spring):400–10.

Rose, Arnold.
    1954   *Theory and method in the social sciences.* Minneapolis: University of Minnesota Press.
    1967   *The power structure.* New York: Oxford University Press.

Ross, Edward Alsworth.
    1901   *Social control.* New York: Macmillan.

Rossi, Peter H.; Waite, Emily; Bose, Christine E.; and Berk, Richard E.
    1974   The seriousness of crimes: normative structure and individual differences. *American Sociological Review* 39 (April):224–37.

Rotter, Julian.
    1954   *Social learning and clinical psychology.* Englewood Cliffs, N.J.: Prentice-Hall.

Sagarin, Edward.
    1975   *Deviants and deviance.* New York: Praeger.

Scarpitti, Frank R.; Murray, Ellen; Dinitz, Simon; and Reckless, Walter C.
    1960   The "good boy" in a high delinquency area: four years later. *American Sociological Review* 25 (August):555–58.

Scheff, Thomas J.
    1966   *Being mentally ill.* Chicago: Aldine.

Schur, Edwin M.
    1965   *Crimes without victims.* Englewood Cliffs, N.J.: Prentice-Hall.
    1971   *Labeling deviant behavior: its sociological implications.* New York: Harper and Row.
    1973   *Radical nonintervention: rethinking the delinquency problem.* Englewood Cliffs, N.J.: Prentice-Hall.

Sellin, Thorsten.
    1938   *Culture conflict and crime.* New York: Social Science Research Council.

Shaw, Clifford, and McKay, Henry D.
    1942   *Juvenile delinquency and urban areas.* Chicago: University of Chicago Press.

Short, James F.
    1957   Differential association and delinquency. *Social Problems* 4 (January): 233–39.

1958   Differential association with delinquent friends and delinquent be-
            havior. *Pacific Sociological Review* 1 (Spring):20–25.
1960   Differential association as a hypothesis: problems of empirical testing.
            Social Problems 8 (Summer):14–25.

Short, James F., and Strodtbeck, Fred L.
1965   *Group process and gang delinquency.* Chicago: University of Chicago
            Press.

Silberman, Matthew.
1976   Toward a theory of criminal deterrence. *American Sociological Review*
            41 (June):442–61.

Simmons, J. L.
1965   Public stereotypes of deviants. *Social Problems* 13 (Fall):223–32.

Skinner, B. F.
1953   *Science and human behavior.* New York: Macmillan.
1959   *Cumulative record.* New York: Appleton-Century-Crofts.

Spergel, Irving.
1964   *Racketville, slumtown, haulburg.* Chicago: University of Chicago Press.

Spitzer, Steven.
1975   Toward a Marxian theory of deviance. *Social Problems* 22 (June):638–
            51.

Staats, Arthur.
1964   *Human learning.* New York: Holt, Rinehart, and Winston.
1975   *Social behaviorism.* Homewood, Ill.: Dorsey Press.

Stinchcombe, Arthur L.
1964   *Rebellion in a high school.* Chicago: Quadrangle Books.

Sumner, William Graham.
1906   *Folkways.* Boston: Ginn.

Sutherland, Edwin H.
1939   *Principles of criminology.* 3d ed. Philadelphia: J. B. Lippincott.
1947   *Principles of criminology.* 4th ed. Philadelphia: J. B. Lippincott.
1949   *White collar crime.* New York: Holt, Rinehart, and Winston. (Paper-
            back edition 1961.)

Sutherland, Edwin H., and Cressey, Donald R.
1970   *Criminology.* 8th ed. Philadelphia: J. B. Lippincott.
1974   *Criminology.* 9th ed. Philadelphia: J. B. Lippincott.

Sykes, Gresham M., and Matza, David.
    1957   Techniques of neutralization: a theory of delinquency. *American Journal of Sociology* 22 (December):664–70.

Tangri, Sandra S., and Schwartz, Michael.
    1967   Delinquency research and the self-concept variable. *Journal of Criminal Law, Criminology, and Police Science* 58 (June):182–90.

Tannenbaum, Frank.
    1938   *Crime and the community.* Boston: Ginn.

Taylor, Ian; Walton, Paul; and Young, Jock.
    1973   *The new criminology: for a social theory of deviance.* New York: Harper and Row, Harper Torchbooks.

Thomas, Charles W.; Cage, Robin J.; and Foster, Samuel C.
    1976   Public opinion on criminal law and legal sanctions: an examination of two conceptual models. *Journal of Criminal Law and Criminology* 67 (January):110–16.

Thorsell, Bernard A., and Klemke, Lloyd W.
    1972   The labeling process: reinforcement or deterrent? *Law and Society Review* 6 (February):393–403.

Tittle, Charles R.
    1975   Deterrents or labeling? *Social Forces* 53 (March):399–410.

Tittle, Charles R., and Logan, Charles H.
    1973   Sanctions and deviance: evidence and remaining questions. *Law and Society Review* 7 (Spring):371–92.

Tittle, Charles R., and Rowe, Alan R.
    1973   Moral appeal, sanction threat, and deviance: an experimental test. *Social Problems* 20 (Spring):488–98.

Toby, Jackson.
    1957   Social disorganization and stakes in conformity: complementary factors in the predatory behavior of hoodlums. *Journal of Criminal Law, Criminology, and Police Science* 48 (May-June):12–17.
    1974   The socialization and control of deviant motivation. In *Handbook of criminology,* ed. Daniel Glaser, pp. 85–100. Chicago: Rand McNally.

Turk, Austin.
    1966   Conflict and criminology. *American Sociological Review* 31 (June): 338–52.
    1969   *Criminality and legal order.* Chicago: Rand McNally.

Turner, Ralph.
 1954 Value-conflict in social disorganization. *Sociology and Social Research* 38 (May-June):301-8.

Ullmann, Leonard P., and Krasner, Leonard.
 1964 *Case studies in behavior modification.* New York: Holt, Rinehart, and Winston.
 1969 *A psychological approach to abnormal behavior.* Englewood Cliffs, N.J.: Prentice-Hall.

Ulrich, Roger; Stachnik, Thomas; and Mabry, John, eds.
 1970 *Control of human behavior.* Glenview, Ill.: Scott, Foresman.

Vaz, Edmund W., ed.
 1967 *Middle-class juvenile delinquency.* New York: Harper and Row.

Vold, George B.
 1958 *Theoretical criminology.* New York: Oxford University Press.

Voss, Harwin.
 1964 Differential association and reported delinquent behavior: a replication. *Social Problems* 12 (Summer):78-85.
 1969 Differential association and containment theory: a theoretical convergence: *Social Forces* 47 (June):381-91.

Waldo, Gordon, and Chiricos, Theodore G.
 1972 Perceived penal sanction and self-reported criminality: a neglected approach to deterrence research. *Social Problems* 19 (Spring):522-40.

Watson, J. B.
 1930 *Behaviorism.* 2d ed. Chicago: University of Chicago Press.

Wellford, Charles.
 1975 Labelling theory and criminology: an assessment. *Social Problems* 22 (February):313-32.

Whaley, Donald L., and Malott, Richard W.
 1969 *Elementary principles of behavior.* Kalamazoo, Mich.: Behaviordelia.

Wolfe, Alan.
 1973 *The seamy side of democracy: repression in America.* New York: David McKay.

Part Two: Deviant Drug Use
(Chapters 6, 7, 8, and 9)

Akers, Ronald L.
 1970 Teenage drinking and drug use. In *Adolescents*, ed. Ellis Evans, pp. 266–88. Hinsdale, Ill.: Dryden.

Akers, Ronald L.; Burgess, Robert L.; and Johnson, Weldon.
 1968 Opiate use, addiction, and relapse. *Social Problems* 15 (Spring):459–69.

Alksne, Harold; Lieberman, Louis; and Brill, Leon.
 1967 A conceptual model of the life cycle of addiction. *International Journal of the Addictions* 2 (Fall):221–40.

Anderson, Linda S.
 1973 The impact of formal and informal sanctions on marihuana use: a test of social learning and deterrence. Unpublished M.A. thesis, Florida State University.

Ausubel, D. P.
 1958 *Drug addiction: physiological, psychological, and sociological aspects.* New York: Random House.
 1960 "Controversial issues in the management of drug addiction: legalization, ambulatory treatment, and the British system. *Mental Hygiene* 44 (October):535–44.

Ayllon, T., and Azrin, H.
 1966 Punishment as a discriminative stimulus and conditioned reinforcer for humans. *Journal of Experimental Analysis of Behavior* 9 (July):411–19.

Ball, John C.
 1965 Two patterns of narcotic drug addiction in the United States. *Journal of Criminal Law, Criminology, and Police Science* 56 (June):203–11.
 1967 Marijuana smoking and the onset of heroin use. *British Journal of Criminology* (October):408–13.

Ball, John C., and Chambers, Carl D., eds.
 1970 *The epidemiology of opiate addiction in the United States.* Springfield, Ill.: Charles C. Thomas.

Ball, John C., and Cottrell, Emily S.
 1965 Admissions of narcotic drug addicts to public health service hospitals, 1935–63. *Public Health Reports* 80 (June):471–75.

Ball, John C.; Chambers, Carl D.; and Ball, Marion J.
  1968   The association of marijuana smoking with opiate addiction in the
            United States. *Journal of Criminal Law, Criminology, and Police Science*
            59 (June):171–82.

Barron, Frank; Jarvik, Murray E.; and Bunnell, Sterling, Jr.
  1964   The hallucinogenic drugs. Reprint 483, *Scientific American*, April.

Bates, William M.
  1966   Narcotics, Negroes, and the South. *Social Forces* 45 (September):61–67.

Bean, Philip.
  1971   Social aspects of drug abuse: a study of London drug offenders. *Journal
            of Criminal Law, Criminology, and Police Science* 62 (October):80–86.

Becker, Howard S.
  1963   *Outsiders: studies in the sociology of deviance.* New York: Free Press.
  1967   History, culture, and subjective experience: an exploration of the social
            bases of drug induced experiences. *Journal of Health and Social Behavior*
            8 (September):163–76.

Bettinger, Lewis A.
  1972   Nervous system. In *Drugs, society, and human behavior,* ed. Oakley
            S. Ray, pp. 36–48. St. Louis, Mo.: Mosby Co.

Blum, Richard.
  1967a   Mind-altering drugs and dangerous behavior: narcotics. In *Task force
            report: narcotics and drug abuse,* The President's Commission on Law
            Enforcement and Administration of Justice, pp. 40–61. Washington,
            D.C.: U.S. Government Printing Office.
  1967b   Mind-altering drugs and dangerous behavior: dangerous drugs. In
            Task force report: narcotics and drug abuse, The President's Commission
            on Law Enforcement and Administration of Justice, pp. 21–37. Wash-
            ington, D.C.: U.S. Government Printing Office.

Blum, Richard H., and associates.
  1964   *Utopiates: the use of and users of LSD-25.* New York: Atherton Press.
  1970a   *Society and drugs: drugs I.* San Francisco: Jossey-Bass.
  1970b   *Students and drugs: drugs II.* San Francisco: Jossey-Bass.

Brantingham, Paul Jeffrey.
  1973   The legal administration of drug abuse control in Britain and the role
            of the British police. *Journal of Drug Issues* 3 (Spring):135–43.

Brecher, Edward M., and the editors of *Consumer Reports.*
  1975   Marijuana: the health questions. *Consumer Reports* (March):143–49.

Brown, James W.; Glaser, Daniel; Waxer, Elaine; and Geis, Gilbert.
    1974   Turning off: cessation of marijuana use after college. *Social Problems* 21 (April):527–38.

Burkett, Steven, and Jensen, Eric L.
    1975   Conventional ties, peer influence, and the fear of apprehension: a study of adolescent marijuana use. *Sociological Quarterly* 16 (Autumn): 522–33.

Burnham, David, and Burnham, Sophy.
    1970   El Barrio's worst block is not all bad. In *Crime in the city*, ed. Daniel Glaser, pp. 154–61. New York: Harper and Row.

Burroughs, William.
    1961   Disposition: testimony concerning a sickness. In David Elbin, ed., pp. 209–14.
    1963   Feeding the monkey. In *The addict*, ed. Dan Wakefield, pp. 80–97. New York: Fawcett.

Carey, James T.
    1968   *The college drug scene.* Englewood Cliffs, N.J.: Prentice-Hall.

Chambers, Carl.
    1974   Some epidemiological considerations of opiate use in the United States. In Josephson and Carroll, eds., pp. 65–82.

Chambers, Carl D.; Bridge, Peter; Petersen, David M.; and Ellinwood, Everett H.
    1974   Methaqualone: another "safe" sedative? *Journal of Drug Issues* (Spring): 126–29.

Chein, Isidor; Gerard, Donald L.; Lee, Robert S.; and Rosenfeld, Eva.
    1964   *The road to H: narcotics, delinquency, and social policy.* New York: Basic Books.

Clausen, John A.
    1966   Drug addiction. In *Contemporary social problems*, 2d ed., ed. Robert K. Merton and Robert A. Nisbet, pp. 193–235. New York: Harcourt Brace Jovanovich.

Clinard, Marshall B.
    1968   *Sociology of deviant behavior.* 3d ed. New York: Holt, Rinehart, and Winston.

Cloward, Richard, and Ohlin, Lloyd.
    1960   *Delinquency and opportunity.* New York: Free Press.

Cohen, Sidney.
1969   *The drug dilemma.* New York: McGraw-Hill.

DeFleur, Lois B., and Garrett, Gerald R.
1970   Dimensions of marijuana usage in a land-grant university. *Journal of Counseling Psychology* 17:468–76.

DeFleur, Lois B.; Ball, John C.; and Snarr, Richard W.
1969   The long-term social correlates of opiate addiction. *Social Problems* 17 (Fall): 225–33.

DeRopp, Robert S.
1961   *Drugs and the mind.* New York: Grove Press.

Dickson, Donald T.
1968   Bureaucracy and morality: an organizational perspective on a moral crusade. *Social Problems* 16 (Fall):143–56.

Dishotsky, Norman I.; Loughman, William D.; Mogar, Robert E.; and Lipscomb, Wendell R.
1971   LSD and genetic damage: is LSD chromosome damaging, carcinogenic, mutagenic, or teratogenic? *Science* 172 (April):431–40.

Elbin, David, ed.
1961   *The drug experience.* New York: Grove Press.

Eldridge, William B.
1962   *Narcotics and the law.* New York: American Bar Foundation.

Epstein, Edward Jay.
1974   Methadone: the forlorn hope. *The Public Interest* 36 (Summer):3–24.

Feldman, Harvey W.
1970   Ideological supports to becoming and remaining a heroin addict. In *Youth and drugs*, ed. John H. McGrath and Frank R. Scarpitti, pp. 87–95. Glenview, Ill.: Scott, Foresman.

Finestone, Harold.
1957   Narcotics and criminality. *Law and Contemporary Problems* 22 (Winter): 69–85.
1964   Cats, kicks, and color. In *The other side*, ed. Howard S. Becker, pp. 281–97. New York: Free Press.

Gearing, F. R.
   1970   Evaluation of methadone maintenance treatment programs. *International Journal of the Addictions* 5 (3):517–43.

Girdano, Dorothy D., and Girdano, Daniel A.
   1973   *Drugs—a factual account.* Reading, Mass.: Addison-Wesley, pp. 22–33.

Glasscote, Raymond; Sussex, James N.; Jaffe, Jerome H.; Ball, John; and Brill, Leon.
   1972   *The treatment of drug abuse: programs, problems, and prospects.* Washington, D.C.: American Psychiatric Association.

Goode, Erich.
   1969   Multiple drug use among marijuana smokers. *Social Problems* 17 (Summer):48–64.
   1970   *The marijuana smokers.* New York: Basic Books.

Gould, Leroy.
   1974   Crime and the addict: beyond common sense. In *Drugs and the criminal justice system,* ed. James A. Inciardi and Carl D. Chambers, pp. 57–76. Beverly Hills, Calif.: Sage Publications.

Grinspoon, Lester.
   1969   Marijuana. *Scientific American* 221 (December):17–25.

Grupp, Stanley E.
   1971   Prior criminal record and adult marihuana arrest dispositions. *Journal of Criminal Law, Criminology, and Police Science* 62:74–79.

Grupp, Stanley E., and Lucas, Warren C.
   1970   The "marihuana muddle" as reflected in California arrest statistics and dispositions. *Law and Society Review* 5 (November):251–69.

Hawks, David.
   1974   The epidemiology of narcotic addiction in the United Kingdom. In Eric Josephson and Eleanor E. Carroll, eds., pp. 45–63.

Henley, James R., and Adams, Larry D.
   1973   Marijuana use in post-collegiate cohorts: correlates of use, prevalence patterns, and factors associated with cessation. *Social Problems* 20 (Spring):514–20.

Hollister, Leo E.
   1971   Marihuana in man: three years later. *Science* 172 (April):21–28.

Hughes, Helen M.
   1961   *The fantastic lodge.* Boston: Houghton Mifflin.

Hunt, Leon Gibson.
1974   *Recent spread of heroin use in the United States: unanswered questions.*
            Washington, D.C.: The Drug Abuse Council.

Isbell, Harris.
1963   Historical development of attitudes toward opiate addiction in the
            United States. In *Conflict and creativity,* ed. Seymour Farber and Robert
            H. L. Wilson, pp. 154–70. New York: McGraw-Hill.

Johnston, Lloyd.
1973   *Drugs and American youth.* Ann Arbor, Mich.: Institute for Social Re-
            search.

Josephson, Eric.
1974   Trends in adolescent marijuana use. In Eric Josephson and Eleanor E.
            Carroll, eds., pp. 177–206.

Josephson, Eric, and Carroll, Eleanor E., eds.
1974   *Drug use: epidemiological and sociological approaches.*   New York:
            Halsted Press.

Judson, Horace Freeland.
1974   *Heroin addiction: what America can learn from the British experience.*
            New York: Vintage Books.

Kandel, Denise.
1974   Interpersonal influences on adolescent illegal drug use. In Eric Joseph-
            son and Eleanor E. Carroll, eds., pp. 207–40.

Kaplan, John.
1971   *Marijuana: the new prohibition.* New York: Pocket Books.

King, Rufus.
1974   The American system: legal sanctions to repress drug abuse. In *Drugs
            and the criminal justice system,* ed. James A. Inciardi and Carl D.
            Chambers, pp. 17–38. Beverly Hills, Calif.: Sage Publications.

Klein, Julius, and Phillips, Derek L.
1968   From hard to soft drugs: temporal and substantive changes in drug
            usage among gangs in a working class community. *Journal of Health
            and Social Behavior* 9 (June):139–45.

Kobrin, Solomon, and Finestone, Harold.
1968   Drug addiction among young persons in Chicago. In *Gang delinquency
            and delinquent subcultures,* ed. James F. Short, Jr., pp. 110–30. New York:
            Harper and Row.

Kolb, Lawrence.
    1958   Factors that have influenced the management and treatment of drug
            addicts. In *Narcotic drug addiction problems*, ed. Robert Livingston,
            pp. 23–33. Washington, D.C.: U.S. Government Printing Office.

Krohn, Marvin D.
    1974   An investigation of the effect of parental and peer associations on
            marijuana use: an empirical test of differential association theory. In
            Crime and delinquency: dimensions of deviance, ed. Marc Riedel and
            Terence P. Thornberry, pp. 75–87. New York: Praeger.

LaGuardia Committee.
    1966   The marihuana problem in the city of New York. In David Solomon,
            ed., pp. 227–410.

Larner, Jeremy, and Tefferteller, Ralph.
    1964   *The addict in the street*. New York: Grove Press.

Lauie, Peter.
    1967   *Drugs*. Baltimore: Penguin.

Lennard, Henry L.; Epstein, Leon J.; and Rosenthal, Mitchell S.
    1972   The methadone illusion. *Science* 176 (May):881–84.

Lindesmith, Alfred R.
    1938   A sociological theory of drug addiction. *American Journal of Sociology*
            43 (January):593–613.
    1967   *The addict and the law*. New York: Vintage Books.
    1968   *Addiction and opiates*. Chicago: Aldine.

Lindesmith, Alfred R., and Gagnon, John.
    1964   Anomie and drug addiction. In *Anomie and deviant behavior*, ed. Mar-
            shall B. Clinard, pp. 158–88. New York: Free Press.

Lukoff, Irving F.
    1974   Issues in the evaluation of heroin treatment. In Eric Josephson and
            Eleanor E. Carroll, eds., pp. 129–57.

McAuliffe, William E., and Gordon, Robert A.
    1974   A test of Lindesmith's theory of addiction: the frequency of euphoria
            among long-term addicts. *American Journal of Sociology* 79 (January):
            795–840.

Mauss, Armand L.
    1969   Anticipatory socialization toward college as a factor in adolescent
            marijuana use. *Social Problems* 16 (Winter):357–64.

Merton, Robert K.
    1957   *Social structure and social theory*. New York: Free Press.

Modlin, H. C., and Montes, A.
    1964   Narcotic addiction in physicians. *American Journal of Psychiatry* 121:
                358–65.

National Commission on Marihuana and Drug Use.
    1972   *Marihuana: a signal of misunderstanding*. New York: New American
                Library.

Nichols, John R.
    1965   How opiates change behavior. *Scientific American* 212 (February):
                80–88.

Nichols, John R., and Davis, W. M.
    1959   Drug addiction II: variation of addiction. *Journal of the American
                Pharmaceutical Association* (scientific edition) 48 (May):259–62.

Nichols, John R.; Headless, C. P.; and Coppock, H. W.
    1956   Drug addiction I: addiction by escape training. *Journal of the American
                Pharmaceutical Association* (scientific edition) 45 (December):788–91.

Nyswander, Marie.
    1963   History of a nightmare. In *The addict*, ed. Dan Wakefield, pp. 20–32.
                New York: Fawcett.

O'Donnell, John A.
    1964   A follow-up of narcotic addicts: mortality, relapse, and assistance.
                American Journal of Orthopsychiatry 34 (October):948–54.
    1965   The relapse in narcotic addiction: a critique of follow-up studies. In
                Narcotics, ed. Daniel Wilner and Gene Kassebaum, pp. 226–46. New
                York: McGraw-Hill.
    1966   Narcotic addiction and crime. *Social Problems* 13 (Spring):374–85.
    1967   The rise and decline of a subculture. *Social Problems* 15 (Summer):
                73–84.
    1969   *Narcotic addicts in Kentucky*. Public Health Service Publication no.
                1881. Washington, D.C.: U.S. Government Printing Office.

O'Donnell, John A., and Ball, John C., eds.
    1966   *Narcotic addiction*. New York: Harper and Row.

O'Donnell, John A.; Voss, Harwin L.; Clayton, Richard R.; Slatin, Gerald T.; and
Room, Robin G. S.
    1976   Young men and drugs: a nationwide survey. *Research monograph 5
                of the National Institute on Drug Abuse*. Springfield, Va.: National
                Technical Information Service.

Pescor, Michael J.
    1966   Physician drug addicts. In John O'Donnell and John Ball, eds., pp. 164–67.

Pet, Donald D., and Ball, John C.
    1968   Marihuana smoking in the United States. *Federal Probation* 32 (September):8–15.

Petersen, David M.
    1974   Some reflections on compulsory treatment of addiction. In *Drugs and the criminal justice system,* ed. James A. Inciardi and Carl D. Chambers, pp. 143–69. Beverly Hills, Calif.: Sage Publications.

Putnam, P., and Ellinwood, E.
    1966   Narcotic addiction among physicians: a ten-year follow-up. *American Journal of Psychiatry* 122:745–47.

Rand, Martin E.; Hammond, J. David; and Moscou, Patricia J.
    1970   Survey of drug use at Ithaca College. In *Introductory sociology: selected readings for the college scene,* ed. Fuad Baali and Clifton D. Bryant, pp. 438–53. Chicago: Rand McNally.

Ray, Marsh.
    1964   The cycle of abstinence and relapse among heroin addicts. In *The other side,* ed. Howard S. Becker, pp. 163–78. New York: Free Press.

Richman, Alex.
    1974   Is the onset of narcotic addiction among treated patients in the United States really declining? In Eric Josephson and Eleanor E. Carroll, eds., pp. 83–88.

Robbins, Lee N.
    1973   *A follow-up of Vietnam drug users.* Washington, D.C.: Special Action Office for Drug Abuse Prevention.

Schur, Edwin M.
    1965   *Crimes without victims.* Englewood Cliffs, N.J.: Prentice-Hall, Spectrum Books.

Secretary of Health, Education, and Welfare.
    1972   *Marihuana and health: second annual report to Congress.* Washington, D.C.: U.S. Government Printing Office.
    1975   *Marihuana and health: fifth annual report to Congress.* Washington, D.C.: U.S. Government Printing Office.

Simrell, Earle V.
  1970   History of legal and medical roles in narcotic abuse in the United
            States. In John C. Ball and Carl D. Chambers, eds., pp. 22–35.

Solomon, David, ed.
  1966   *The marihuana papers*. New York: Signet.

Sonnedecker, Glen.
  1958   Emergence and concept of the problem of addiction. In *Narcotic drug
            addiction problems*, ed. Robert S. Livingston, pp. 14–33. Washington,
            D.C.: U.S. Government Printing Office.

Spergel, Irving.
  1966   An exploratory research in delinquent subcultures. In *Juvenile de-
            linquency*, ed. Rose Giallombardo, pp. 233–46. New York: Wiley.

Stephens, Richard C., and Ellis, Rosalind D.
  1975   Narcotic addicts and crime: analysis of recent trends. *Criminology* 12
            (February):474–88.

Suchman, Edward A.
  1968   The hang-loose ethic and the spirit of drug use. *Journal of Health
            and Social Behavior* 9 (June):146–55.

Sutter, Alan G.
  1969   Worlds of drug use on the street scene. In *Delinquency crime and social
            process*, ed. Donald R. Cressey and David A. Ward, pp 802–29. New
            York: Harper and Row.
  1970   A hierarchy of drug users. In *The sociology of crime and delinquency*, 2d
            ed., ed. Marvin Wolfgang, Leonard Savitz, and Norman Johnston, pp.
            666–76. New York: Wiley.

Taylor, Norman.
  1966   The pleasant assassin. In David Solomon, ed., pp. 31–47.

Tec, Nechama.
  1974   *Grass is green in suburbia: a sociological study of adolescent usage of il-
            licit drugs*. New York: Libra.

Thomas, Charles W.; Petersen, David M.; and Zingraff, Matthew T.
  1975   Student drug use: a re-examination of the "hang-loose ethic" hy-
            pothesis. *Journal of Health and Social Behavior* 16 (March):63–73.

Time-Life editors.
  1965   *The drug takers*. Special Time-Life Book Reports. New York: Time.

Verhave, Thom.
  1966   *The experimental analysis of behavior.* New York: Appleton-Century-
            Crofts.

Waldo, Gordon, and Chiricos, Theodore G.
  1972   Perceived penal sanction and self-reported criminality: a neglected
            approach to deterrence research. *Social Problems* 19 (Spring):422–40.

Waldorf, Dan.
  1970   Life without heroin: social adjustment during long-term periods of
            voluntary abstention. *Social Problems* 18 (Fall):228–43.
  1973   *Careers in dope.* Englewood Cliffs, N.J.: Prentice-Hall, Spectrum Books.

Weeks, James R.
  1964   Experimental narcotic addiction. Reprint 178, *Scientific American,*
            March.

Weil, Andrew T.; Zinberg, Norman; and Nelsen, Judith M.
  1968   Clinical and psychological effects of marihuana in man. *Science* 162
            (December):1234–42.

Wikler, Abraham.
  1965   Conditioning factors in opiate addiction and relapse. In Daniel Wilner
            and Gene Kassebaum, eds., pp. 85–100.

Winick, Charles.
  1959   The use of drugs by jazz musicians. *Social Problems* 7:240–54.
  1964   Physician narcotic addicts. *The other side,* ed. Howard S. Becker,
            pp. 261–80. New York: Free Press.
  1965   Epidemiology of narcotics use. In *Narcotics,* ed. Daniel Wilner and
            Gene Kassebaum, pp. 3–18. New York: McGraw-Hill.

Yablonsky, Lewis.
  1965   *The tunnel back: Synanon.* New York: Macmillan.

Part Three: Drinking and Alcohol Behavior
(Chapters 10, 11, and 12)

Akers, Ronald L.
 1968 Teenage drinking: a survey of action programs and research. *Journal of Alcohol Education* 13 (Spring):1–10.
 1970 Teenage drinking and drug use. In *Adolescents*, ed. Ellis Evans, pp. 267–88. Hinsdale, Ill.: Dryden Press.

Akers, Ronald L. (with John L. King).
 1967 *Teenage drinking: a survey of action programs.* Seattle, Wash.: Unigard Insurance Group.

Alexander, C. Norman, Jr.
 1967 Alcohol and adolescent rebellion. *Social Forces* 46 (June):542–50.

Armstrong, John D.
 1958 The search for the alcoholic personality. *Annals* 315 (January):40–47.

Ashem, Beatrice, and Donner, Lawrence.
 1968 Covert sensitization with alcoholics: a controlled replication. *Behavior Research and Therapy* 6 (February):7–12.

Bahr, Howard M.
 1969a Lifetime affiliation patterns of early-and-late-onset heavy drinkers on skid row. *Quarterly Journal of Studies on Alcohol* 30 (September):645–56.
 1969b Institutional life, drinking, and disaffiliation. *Social Problems* 16 (Winter):365–75.

Bailey, Margaret B.; Haberman, Paul W.; and Alksne, Harold.
 1965 The epidemiology of alcoholism in an urban residential area. *Quarterly Journal of Studies on Alcohol* 26 (March):19–40.

Bales, Robert F.
 1949 Cultural differences in rates of alcoholism. *Quarterly Journal of Studies on Alcohol* 6 (March):480–99.

Bandura, Albert.
 1969 *Principles of behavior modification.* New York: Holt, Rinehart, and Winston.

Baur, E. Jackson, and McCluggage, Marston.
    1958   Drinking patterns of Kansas high school students. *Social Problems* 5 (Spring):347–56.

Bittner, Egon.
    1967   The police in skid-row: a study of peace keeping. *American Sociological Review* 32 (October):701–6.

Blum, Eva, and Blum, Richard H.
    1967   *Alcoholism: modern psychological approaches to treatment.* San Francisco: Jossey-Bass.

Cahalan, Don.
    1970   *Problem drinkers: a national survey.* San Francisco: Jossey-Bass.

Cahalan, Don; Cisin, Ira H.; and Crossley, Helen M.
    1967   *American drinking practices.* Social Research Group Report no. 3. Washington, D.C.: George Washington University.

Chapman, Robert F.; Garlington, Warren K.; and Lloyd, Kenneth E.
    1969   A critical review of learning based treatments of alcoholism. Paper presented to State of Washington Alcohol Research Group, Seattle, Washington.

Chappell, Matthew N., et al.
    1953   *Use of alcoholic beverages among high school students.* New York: Sheppard Foundation.

Clay, Margaret L.
    1964a   Conditions affecting voluntary alcohol consumption in rats. *Quarterly Journal of Studies on Alcohol* 25 (March):36–55.
    1964b   Macomb County tackles alcohol education. *Michigan Alcohol Educational Journal* 1 (October):25–33.

Clinard, Marshall B.
    1968   *Sociology of deviant behavior.* 3d ed. New York: Holt, Rinehart, and Winston.

Conger, John J.
    1956   Reinforcement theory and the dynamics of alcoholism. *Quarterly Journal of Studies on Alcohol* 17 (June):296–305.
    1958   Perception, learning, and emotion: the role of alcohol. *Annals* 315 (January):31–39.

Demone, H. W.
    1966   Attitudes and drinking practices of male adolescents. Doctoral dissertation, Brandeis University.

Forslund, Morris A., and Gustafson, Thomas J.
  1970   Influence of peers and parents and sex differences in drinking by high
            school students. *Quarterly Journal of Studies on Alcohol* 31 (December):
            868–75.

Franks, Cyril M.
  1963   Behavior therapy: the principles of conditioning and the treatment
            of the alcoholic. *Quarterly Journal of Studies on Alcohol* 24 (September):
            511–29.

Fry, Lincoln J., and Miller, Jon.
  1975   Responding to skid row alcoholism: self-defeating arrangements in
            an innovative treatment program. *Social Problems* 22 (June):674–88.

Globetti, Gerald.
  1967   A comparative study of white and Negro teenage drinking in two
            Mississippi communities. *Phylon* 28 (Second Quarter):131–38.
  1969   The use of alcohol among high school students in an abstinence set-
            ting. *Pacific Sociological Review* 12 (Fall):105–8.

Globetti, Gerald, and Windham, Gerald O.
  1967   The social adjustment of high school students and the use of beverage
            alcohol. *Sociology and Social Research* 51 (January):148–57.

Greenberg, Leon.
  1958   Intoxication and alcoholism: physiological factors. *Annals* 315 (Jan-
            uary):22–30.

Haer, John L.
  1955   Drinking patterns and the influence of friends and family. *Quarterly
            Journal of Studies on Alcohol* 16:178–85.

Hamburg, Sam.
  1975   Behavior therapy in alcoholism. *Journal of Studies on Alcohol* 36 (Jan-
            uary):69–87.

Holzinger, R.; Mortimer, R.; and Van Dusen, W.
  1967   Aversion conditioning treatment of alcoholism. *American Journal of
            Psychiatry* 124:246–47.

Jellinek, E. M.
  1960   *The disease concept of alcoholism.* New Haven, Conn.: Hillhouse Press.

Jessor, Richard.
  1968   Toward a social psychology of excessive alcohol use: a preliminary
            report from the tri-ethnic project. In *Approaches to deviance,* ed. Mark
            Lefton, James K. Skipper, and Charles H. McCaghy, pp. 233–54. New
            York: Appleton-Century-Crofts.

Jessor, Richard, and Jessor, Shirley L.
    1975   Adolescent development and the onset of drinking. *Journal of Studies on Alcohol* 36 (January):27–51.

Johnston, Lloyd.
    1973   *Drugs and American youth*. Ann Arbor, Mich.: Institute for Social Research.
    1975   News release on "monitoring the future" study. Ann Arbor, Mich.: Institute for Social Research.

Keehn, J. D.
    1969   Consumption of alcohol by rats. *Quarterly Journal of Studies on Alcohol* 30 (June):320–29.

Keller, Mark.
    1958   Alcoholism: nature and extent of the problem. *Annals* 315 (January):1–11.

Kendis, Joseph B.
    1967   The human body and alcohol. In *Alcoholism*, ed. David J. Pittman, pp. 23–30. New York: Harper and Row.

Kepner, Elaine.
    1964   Application of learning theory to the etiology and treatment of alcoholism. *Quarterly Journal of Studies on Alcohol* 25 (June):279–91.

Kingham, R. J.
    1958   Alcoholism and the reinforcement theory of learning. *Quarterly Journal of Studies on Alcohol* 19 (June):320–30.

Knupfer, Genevieve.
    1967   The epidemiology of problem drinking. *American Journal of Public Health* 57 (June):973–86.

Knupfer, Genevieve, and Room, Robin.
    1964   Age, sex, and social class as factors in amount of drinking in a metropolitan community. *Social Problems* 12 (Fall):224–40.

Larsen, Donald E., and Abu-Laban, Baha.
    1968   Norm qualities and deviant drinking behavior. *Social Problems* 15 (Spring):441–49.

Lawrence, Joseph J., and Maxwell, Milton A.
    1962   Drinking and socioeconomic status. In *Society, culture, and drinking patterns*, ed. David Pittman and Charles Snyder, pp. 141–45. New York: Wiley.

Lemert, Edwin.
    1967   Forms and pathology of drinking in three Polynesian societies. In *Human deviance, social problems, and social control*, ed. Edwin Lemert, pp. 174–86. Englewood Cliffs, N.J.: Frentice-Hall.

MacAndrew, Craig, and Edgerton, Robert B.
    1969   *Drunken comportment: a social explanation.* Chicago: Aldine.

McCarthy, Raymond G.
    1964a   Drinking patterns in the United States. In *Alcohol education for class-room and community*, ed. Raymond G. McCarthy, pp. 125–31. New York: McGraw-Hill.
    1964b   Consumption rates and trends from 1850 to 1962 in the U.S. and other countries. In *Alcohol education for classroom and community*, ed. Raymond G. McCarthy. New York: McGraw-Hill.

McCarthy, Raymond G., ed.
    1959   *Drinking and intoxication.* New Haven, Conn.: College and University Press.

MacKay, James R., and Clarke, Donna W.
    1967   Teenage drinking in New Hampshire. *New Hampshire Bulletin on Alcoholism* 3 (January):1–11.

Maddox, George L.
    1958   Drinking in high school: an interpretative summary. *Newsletter of the Association for the Advancement of Instruction about Alcohol and Narcotics* 4 (December):3–14.
    1962   Teenage drinking in the United States. In *Society, culture, and drinking patterns*, ed. David Pittman and Charles R. Snyder, pp. 230–45. New York: Wiley.
    1964   High school student drinking behavior: incidental information from two national surveys. *Quarterly Journal of Studies on Alcohol* 25 (June): 339–47.

Maddox, George L., and Berinski, Ernest.
    1964   Drinking behavior of Negro collegians. *Quarterly Journal of Studies on Alcohol* 25 (December):651–58.

Maddox, George L., and McCall, Bevode C.
    1964   *Drinking among teenagers: a sociological interpretation of alcohol use by high-school students.* New Brunswick, N.J.: Rutgers Center of Alcohol Studies.

Madsen, William, and Madsen, Claudia.
    1969   The cultural structure of Mexican drinking behavior. *Quarterly Journal of Studies on Alcohol* 30 (September) 701–18.

Maxwell, Milton A.
     1952   Drinking behavior in the state of Washington. *Quarterly Journal of Studies on Alcohol* 13 (June):219–39.

Miller, John L., and Wahl, J. Richard.
     1956   *Attitudes of high school students toward alcoholic beverages.* New York: Sheppard Foundation.

Mizruchi, Ephraim H., and Perruci, Robert.
     1962   Norm qualities and differential effects of deviant behavior. *American Sociological Review 27* (June):391–99.

Mulford, Harold A.
     1964   Drinking and deviant drinking USA, 1963. *Quarterly Journal of Studies on Alcohol* 25 (September):634–50.

Mulford, Harold A., and Miller, Donald E.
     1959   Drinking in Iowa, I: socio-cultural distribution of drinkers. *Quarterly Journal of Studies on Alcohol* 20 (December):704–26.
     1960   Drinking in Iowa, V: drinking and alcoholic drinking. *Quarterly Journal of Studies on Alcohol* 21 (September):483–99.
     1963   The prevalence and extent of drinking in Iowa, 1961: a replication and evaluation of methods. *Quarterly Journal of Studies on Alcohol* 24 (March):39–53.

National Clearinghouse for Alcohol Information.
     1974   *Second report on alcohol and health.* Rockville, Md.: NCAI.

Nelson, Dale O.
     1968   A comparison of drinking and understanding of alcohol and alcoholism between students in selected high schools of Utah and in the Utah State Industrial School. *Journal of Alcohol Education* 13 (Spring): 17–25.

O'Donnell, John A.; Voss, Harwin L.; Clayton, Richard R.; Slatin, Gerald T.; and Room, Robin G. S.
     1976   · Young men and drugs: a nationwide survey. *Research monograph 5 of the national institute on drug abuse.* Springfield, Va.: National Technical Information Service.

Pittman, David J.
     1967   International overview: social and cultural factors in drinking patterns, pathological and nonpathological. In *Alcoholism*, ed. David J. Pittman, pp. 3–20. New York: Harper and Row.

Pittman, David J., and Gillespie, Duff G.
    1967   Social policy as deviancy reinforcement: the case of the public intoxication offender. In *Alcoholism*, ed. David J. Pittman, pp. 106–23. New York: Harper and Row.

Pittman, David J., and Gordon, C. Wayne.
    1958   *Revolving door: a study of chronic police case inebriate.* New Haven, Conn.: Yale Center of Alcohol Studies.

Plaut, Thomas F. A. (Cooperative Commission on the Study of Alcoholism).
    1967   *Alcohol problems: a report to the nation.* New York: Oxford University Press.

Quinney, Richard.
    1970   *The social reality of crime.* Boston: Little, Brown.

Rachman, Stanley, and Teasdale, John.
    1970   *Aversion therapy and behavior disorders: an analysis.* Coral Gables, Fla.: University of Miami Press.

Riley, John W.; Marden, Charles F.; and Lifshitz, Marcia.
    1959   The motivational pattern of drinking. Raymond G. McCarthy, ed., pp. 231–39.

Robins, Lee N.; Murphy, G. E.; and Breckenridge, M. B.
    1968   Drinking behavior of young urban Negro men. *Quarterly Journal of Studies on Alcohol* 29 (September):657–84.

Rooney, J. F.
    1961   Group processes among skid row winos: a reevaluation of the undersocialization hypothesis. *Quarterly Journal of Studies on Alcohol* 22 (June):444–60.

Rubington, Earl.
    1968   Variations in bottle gang controls. In *Deviance,* ed. Earl Rubington and Martins Weinberg, pp. 308–16. New York: Macmillan.

Rushing, William A.
    1969   Role conflict and alcoholism. In *Deviance and social process,* ed. W. A. Rushing, pp. 292–300. Chicago: Rand McNally.

Sanderson, R. E.; Campbell, Dugal; and Laverty, S. G.
    1963   An investigation of a new aversive conditioning treatment for alcoholism. *Quarterly Journal of Studies on Alcohol* 24 (June):261–75.

Sebald, Hans.
　　1968　　*Adolescence: a sociological analysis.* New York: Appleton-Century-Crofts.

Skolnick, Jerome.
　　1958　　Religious affiliation and drinking behavior. *Quarterly Journal of Studies on Alcohol* 19 (September):452–70.

Slater, A. D.
　　1952　　A study of use of alcoholic beverages among high school students in Utah. *Quarterly Journal of Studies on Alcohol* 13 (March):78–86.

Smart, Reginald G.
　　1965　　Effects of alcohol on conflict and avoidance behavior. *Quarterly Journal of Studies on Alcohol* 26 (June):187–205.

Snyder, Charles R.
　　1964　　Inebriety, alcoholism and anomie. In *Anomie and deviant behavior,* ed. Marshall B. Clinard, pp. 189–213. New York: Free Press.

Spradley, James P.
　　1970　　*You owe yourself a drunk: an ethnography of urban nomads.* Boston: Little, Brown.

Sterne, Muriel W.
　　1967　　Drinking patterns and alcoholism among American Negroes. In *Alcoholism,* ed. David J. Pittman, pp. 66–99. New York: Harper and Row.

Straus, Robert.
　　1966　　Alcohol. In *Contemporary social problems,* 2d ed., ed. Robert Merton and Robert Nisbet, pp. 236–80. New York: Harcourt Brace Jovanovich.

Straus, Robert, and Bacon, Seldon.
　　1953　　*Drinking in college.* New Haven, Conn.: Yale University Press.

Symes, Leonard.
　　1957　　Personality characteristics and the alcoholic: a critique of current studies. *Quarterly Journal of Studies on Alcohol* 18 (June):288–302.

Trice, Harrison.
　　1966　　*Alcoholism in America.* New York: McGraw-Hill.

Ullman, Albert D.
　　1958　　Sociocultural backgrounds of alcoholism. *Annals* 315 (January):48–54.

Wallace, Samuel E.
    1968   The road to skid row. *Social Problems* 16 (Summer):92–105.

Whitehead, Paul C.
    1975   The prevention of alcoholism: divergences and convergences of two
                approaches. *Addictive Diseases: An International Journal* 1 (4):431–43.

Windham, Gerald O.; Preston, James D.; and Armstrong, Harold B.
    1967   The high school student in Mississippi and beverage alcohol. *Journal
                of Alcohol Education* 13 (Spring):1–12.

Wiseman, Jacqueline P.
    1970   *Stations of the lost: the treatment of skid row alcoholics.* Englewood Cliffs,
                N.J.: Prentice-Hall.

Part Four: Sexual Deviance
(Chapters 13, 14, 15, 16, and 17)

Adler, P.
    1953   *A house is not a home.* New York: Popular Library.

Anonymous.
    1960   *Streetwalker.* New York: Viking Press.

Anthanasiou, Robert; Shaver, Phillip; and Travis, Carol.
    1970   Sex. *Psychology Today* 4 (July):39–52.

Bagley, Christopher.
    1969   Incest behavior and incest taboo. *Social Problems* 16 (Spring):505–19.

Bandura, Albert.
    1969   *Principles of behavior modification.* New York: Holt, Rinehart, and
                Winston.

Bandura, Albert, and Walters, Richard H.
    1963   *Social learning and personality development.* New York: Holt, Rinehart,
                and Winston.

Barlow, David H., and Agras, W. Stewart.
    1973   Fading to increase heterosexual responsiveness in homosexuals. *Journal of Applied Behavior Analysis* 6 (Fall):355–66.

Beach, Frank, ed.
    1965   *Sex and behavior.* New York: Wiley.

Blakemore, C. B.
    1964   The application of behavior therapy to a sexual disorder. In H. J. Eysenck, ed., *Experiments in behavior therapy,* pp. 165–75.

Blakemore, C. B.; Thorpe, J. G.; Barker, J. C.; Conway, C. G.; and Lavin, N. I.
    1963   The application of faradic aversion conditioning in the case of transvestism. *Behavior Research and Therapy* 1 (May):29–34.

Blumstein, Philip W., and Schwartz, Pepper.
    1976a   Bisexuality in women. *Archives of Sexual Behavior* 5 (2):171–81.
    1976b   Bisexuality. Unpublished technical report, Department of Sociology, University of Washington.

Bond, Ian K., and Hutchinson, Harry C.
    1964   Application of reciprocal inhibition therapy to exhibitionism. In H. J. Eysenck, ed., *Experiments in behavior therapy,* pp. 80–86.

Bryan, J. H.
    1965   Apprenticeships in prostitution. *Social Problems* 12 (Winter):287–97.
    1966   Occupational ideologies and individual attitudes of call girls. *Social Problems* 13 (Spring):441–50.

Cappon, Daniel.
    1965   *Toward an understanding of homosexuality.* Englewood Cliffs, N.J.: Prentice-Hall.

Caprio, Frank S.
    1962   *Female homosexuality.* New York: Grove Press.

Commission on Obscenity and Pornography.
    1970   *The report of the commission on obscenity and pornography.* New York: Bantam Books.

Cuber, John F., and Harroff, Peggy B.
    1966   *Sex and the significant Americans.* Baltimore: Penguin Books.

Dank, Barry.
   1971   Coming out in the gay community. *Psychiatry* 34 (May):180–97.

Davenport, William.
   1965   Sexual patterns and their regulation in a society of the southwest
             Pacific. In Frank A. Beach, ed., pp. 164–207.

Davis, Alan J.
   1970   Sexual assaults in the Philadelphia prison system. In John Gagnon and
             William Simon, eds., *The sexual scene*, pp. 107–24.

Davis, Kingsley.
   1966   Sexual behavior. In *Contemporary social problems*, ed. Robert K. Merton
             and Robert A. Nisbet, pp. 322–408. New York: Harcourt Brace Jovano-
             vich.

Davis, Nanette J.
   1971   The prostitute: developing a deviant identity. In *Studies in the sociology
             of sex*, ed. James Henslin, pp. 297–322. New York: Appleton-Century-
             Crofts.

Ellis, Albert.
   1961   *The folklore of sex*. New York: Grove Press.

Eysenck, H. J., ed.
   1964   *Experiments in behavior therapy*. Elmsford, N.Y.: Pergamon.

Feigelman, William.
   c. 1968   Voyeurism as a social process among construction workers: some
             implications for the theory of deviance. Unpublished manuscript,
             Washington University, St. Louis, Mo.

Feldman, M. P., and MacCulloch, M. J.
   1964   A systematic approach to the treatment of homosexuality by condi-
             tioned aversion. *American Journal of Psychiatry* 121:167–71.
   1965   The application of anticipatory avoidance learning to the treatment
             of homosexuality. *Behavior Research and Therapy* 2 (January):165–85.

Ford, Clellan, and Beach, Frank A.
   1951   *Patterns of sexual behavior*. New York: Harper and Row.

Fox, J. R.
   1962   Sibling incest. *British Journal of Sociology* 13 (June):128–50.

Freund, K.
1960   Some problems in the treatment of homosexuality. In H. J. Eysenck, ed., *Behavior therapy and the neuroses*, pp. 312–25.

Gagnon, John H.
1967   Sexuality and sexual learning in the child. In John Gagnon and William Simon, eds., *Sexual deviance*, pp. 15–42.

Gagnon, John H., and Simon, William, eds.
1967   *Sexual deviance*. New York: Harper and Row.
1970   *The sexual scene*. Chicago: Aldine.

Gebhard, Paul H.
1971   Definitions. In Donald S. Marshall and Robert C. Suggs, eds., pp. 251–60.

Gebhard, Paul H.; Gagnon, John H.; Pomeroy, Wardell B.; and Christenson, Cornelia V.
1965   *Sex offenders: an analysis of types*. New York: Harper and Row.

Geis, Gilbert.
1972   *Not the law's business? An examination of homosexuality, abortion, prostitution, narcotics, and gambling in the United States*. Washington, D.C.: (NIMH Center for Studies of Crime and Delinquency) U.S. Government Printing Office.

Giallombardo, Rose.
1966   *Society of women: a study of a women's prison*. New York: Wiley.

Glynn, J. D., and Harper, P.
1964   Behavior therapy in transvestism. In H. J. Eysenck, ed., *Experiments in behavior therapy*, pp. 164ff.

Gold, S., and Neufeld, I. L.
1965   A learning approach to the treatment of homosexuality. *Behavior Research and Therapy* 2 (January):201–5.

Gray, Diana.
1973   Turning-out: a study of teenage prostitution. *Urban Life and Culture* 4 (January):401–24.

Gusfield, Joseph R.
1967   Moral passage: the symbolic process in public designations of deviance. *Social Problems* 15 (Fall):175–88.

Hampson, John L.
  1965   Determinants of psychosexual orientation. In Frank A. Beach, ed., pp. 108–32.

Harlow, Harry F.
  1965   Sexual behavior in the rhesus monkey. In Frank A. Beach, ed., pp. 242–55.

Harlow, Harry F., and Harlow, M. K.
  1962   Social deprivation in monkeys. *Scientific American* 207 (December): 137–46.

Helmer, William J.
  1963   New York's "middle-class" homosexuals. *Harper's*, March, pp. 85–92.

Henriques, Ferdinand.
  1963   *Prostitution and society.* New York: Citadel Press.

Herman, Steven H.; Barlow, David H.; and Agras, W. Stewart.
  1974   An experimental analysis of exposure to "explicit" heterosexual stimuli as an effective variable in changing arousal patterns of homosexuals. *Behavior Research and Therapy* 12:335–45.

Hilton, Diana.
  1971   Turning out: a study of teenage prostitution. M.A. thesis, University of Washington.

Hirschi, Travis.
  1962   The professional prostitute. *Berkeley Journal of Sociology* 7:37–48.

Homberg, David A., and Lunde, Donald T.
  1966   Sex hormones in the development of sex differences in human behavior. In Eleanor E. Maccoby, ed., pp. 1–24.

Hooker, Evelyn.
  1956   A preliminary analysis of group behavior of homosexuals. *Journal of Psychology* 42:217–25.
  1967   The homosexual community. In John Gagnon and William Simon, eds., *Sexual deviance*, pp. 167–84.

Humphreys, Laud.
  1970   *Tearoom trade.* Chicago: Aldine.
  1972   *Out of the closets: the sociology of homosexual liberation.* Englewood Cliffs, N.J.: Prentice-Hall.

Hunt, Morton.
  1974   *Sexual behavior in the 1970s.* Chicago: Playboy Press.

Jackman, Norman; O'Toole, Richard; and Geis, Gilbert.
  1963   The self-image of the prostitute. *Sociological Quarterly* 4 (Spring):
            150–60.

James, Basil.
  1964   Case of homosexuality treated by aversion therapy. In H. J. Eysenck,
            ed., *Experiments in behavior therapy,* pp. 159–63.

James, Basil, and Early, Donal F.
  1963   Aversion therapy for homosexuality. *British Medical Journal* 1 (Feb-
            ruary):538.

Kinsey, Alfred C.; Pomeroy, Wardell B.; and Martin, Clyde C.
  1948   *Sexual behavior in the human male.* Philadelphia: W. B. Saunders.

Kinsey, Alfred C.; Pomeroy, Wardell B.; Martin, Clyde C.; and Gebhard, Paul.
  1953   *Sexual behavior in the human female.* Philadelphia: W. B. Saunders.

Kushner, Malcolm.
  1965   The reduction of a long-standing fetish by means of aversive con-
            ditioning. In L. Ullmann and L. Krasner, eds., pp. 239–42.

Lazarus, Arnold A.
  1965   The treatment of a sexually inadequate man. In L. Ullmann and L.
            Krasner, eds., pp. 243–45.

Leznoff, Maurice, and Westley, William A.
  1956   The homosexual community. *Social Problems* 3 (April):257–63.

McCaghy, Charles H.
  1968   Drinking and deviance disavowal: the case of child molesters. *Social
            Problems* 16 (Summer):43–49.

McCaghy, Charles H., and Skipper, James K.
  1969   Lesbian behavior as an adaptation to the occupation of stripping.
            Social Problems 17 (Fall):262–70.

Maccoby, Eleanor, ed.
  1966   *The development of sex differences.* Stanford: Stanford University Press.

McConaghy, Nathaniel.
   1971   Aversive therapy of homosexuality: measures of efficiency. *American Journal of Psychiatry* 127 (March):1221–24.

McGuire, R. J.; Carlisle, J. M.; and Young, R. J.
   1965   Sexual deviations as conditioned behavior: a hypothesis. *Behavior Research and Therapy* 2 (January):185–90.

McIntosh, Mary.
   1968   The homosexual role. *Social Problems* 16 (Fall):182–92.

Mantegazza, Paolo.
   1935   *The sexual relations of mankind.* New York: Eugenics.

Marshall, Donald S.
   1971   Sexual behavior on Mangaia. In Donald S. Marshall and Robert C. Suggs, eds., pp. 103–62.

Marshall, Donald S., and Suggs, Robert C., eds.
   1971   *Human sexual behavior.* New York: Basic Books.

Maurer, D. W.
   1939   Prostitutes and criminal argots. *American Journal of Sociology* 44 (January):546–50.

Messenger, John C.
   1971   Sex and repression in an Irish folk community. In Donald S. Marshall and Robert C. Suggs, eds., pp. 3–37.

Miller, Patricia Y., and Simon, William.
   1974   Adolescent sexual behavior: context and change. *Social Problems* 22 (October):58–76.

Mischel, Walter.
   1966   A social learning view of sex differences in behavior. In Eleanor E. Maccoby, ed., pp. 56–81.

Murtagh, John M., and Harris, Sara.
   1957   *Cast the first stone.* New York: McGraw-Hill.

Oliver, B. J.
   1967   *Sexual deviation in American society.* New Haven, Conn.: College and University Press.

Quinney, Richard.
    1970   *The social reality of crime.* Boston: Little, Brown.

Rachman, Stanley.
    1966   Sexual fetishism: an experimental analogue. *Psychological Record* 16
                (July):293–96.

Rachman, Stanley, and Teasdale, John.
    1970   *Aversion therapy and behavior disorders: an analysis.* Coral Gables, Fla.:
                University of Miami Press.

Ramsay, R. W., and Van Velzen, V.
    1968   Behavior therapy for sexual perversions. *Behavior Research and Therapy*
                6 (May):233.

Raymond, M. J.
    1960   Case of fetishism treated by aversion therapy. In H. J. Eysenck, ed.,
                Behavior therapy and the neuroses, pp. 303–11.

Reiss, Albert J., Jr.
    1964   The social integration of queers and peers. In *The other side,* ed.
                Howard S. Becker, pp. 181–210. New York: Free Press.

Reiss, Ira L.
    1967   *The social context of premarital sexual permissiveness.* New York: Holt,
                Rinehart, and Winston.
    1970   Premarital sex as deviant behavior: an application of current ap-
                proaches to deviance. *American Sociological Review* 35 (February):78–
                87.

Riess, Bernard F.; Safer, Jeanne; and Yotive, William.
    1974   Psychological test data on female homosexuality: a review of the
                literature. *Journal of Homosexuality* 1 (Fall):71–78.

Roby, Pamela A.
    1969   Politics and criminal law: revision of the New York State penal law
                on prostitution. *Social Problems* 17 (Summer):83–109.

Sagarin, Edward.
    1969   *Odd man in.* Chicago: Quadrangle Books.
    1971   Sex research and sociology: retrospective and prospective. In *Studies
                in the sociology of sex,* ed. James M. Henslin, pp. 377–408. New York:
                Appleton-Century-Crofts.
    1973   The good guys, bad guys, and the gay guys. *Contemporary Sociology* 2
                (January):3–13.

Schofield, Michael.
    1965   *Sociological aspects of homosexuality.* Boston: Little, Brown.

Schur, Edwin M.
    1965   *Crimes without victims: deviant behavior and public policy.* Englewood Cliffs, N.J.: Prentice-Hall.

Sears, Robert R.
    1965   Development of gender role. In Frank A. Beach, ed., pp. 133–63.

Serber, Michael, and Keith, Claudia G.
    1974   The Atascadero project: model of a sexual retraining program for incarcerated homosexual pedophiles. *Journal of Homosexuality* 1 (Fall):87–97.

Simon, William, and Gagnon, John H.
    1967a   The lesbians: a preliminary overview. In John Gagnon and William Simon, eds., *Sexual deviance,* pp. 247–81.
    1967b   Femininity in the lesbian community. *Social Problems* 15 (Fall):212–21.

Solyom, L., and Miller, S.
    1965   A differential conditioning procedure as the initial phase of the behavior therapy of homosexuality. *Behavior Research and Therapy* 3 (January):147–60.

Steele, Marion F.
    1967   A social psychological theory of homosexuality. Paper presented to the meeting of the Pacific Sociological Association, Long Beach, Calif.

Stephenson, Richard M.
    1973   "Involvement in deviance: an example and some theoretical implications. *Social Problems* 21 (Fall):173–89.

Stevenson, I., and Wolpe, J.
    1960   Recovery from sexual deviations through overcoming nonsexual neurotic responses. *American Journal of Psychiatry* 116:737–42.

Stoller, Robert J.
    1968   *Sex and gender.* New York: Science House.

Thorpe, J. G.; Schmidt, E.; and Castell, D.
    1964   A comparison of positive and negative (aversion) conditioning in the treatment of homosexuality. *Behavior Research and Therapy* 1 (March):357–62.

Tinbergen, N.
  1965   Some recent studies of the evolution of sexual behavior. In Frank A.
            Beach, ed., pp. 1–3.

Ullmann, L., and Krasner, L., eds.
  1965   *Case studies in behavior modification*. New York: Holt, Rinehart, and
            Winston.

Ward, D. A., and Kassebaum, G. G.
  1965   *Women's prison: color sex and social structure*. Chicago: Aldine.

Warren, Carol A.
  1974   *Identity and commitment in the gay world*. New York: Wiley.

Weinberg, George.
  1972   *Society and the healthy homosexual*. New York: St. Martin's Press.

Weinberg, Martin S., and Williams, Colin J.
  1974   *Male homosexuals*. New York: Oxford University Press.
  1975   Gay baths and the social organization of impersonal sex. *Social Prob-
            lems* 23 (December):124–36.

West, Donald J.
  1967   *Homosexuality*. Chicago: Aldine.

Williams, Colin J., and Weinberg, Martin S.
  1970   Being discovered: a study of homosexuals in the military. *Social
            Problems* 18 (Fall):217–29.

Winick, Charles, and Kinsie, Paul M.
  1971   *The lively commerce: prostitution in the United States*. New York: Signet.

Wolfe, Roger W., and Marino, Dominic R.
  1975   A program of behavior treatment for incarcerated pedophiles. *Ameri-
            can Criminal Law Review* 13 (Summer):69–83.

Young, Wayland.
  1967   Prostitution. In John Gagnon and William Simon, eds., *Sexual devi-
            ance*, pp. 105–32.

Zagel, James B.
  1973   Supreme Court review, 1973. *Journal of Criminal Law and Criminology*
            64 (December):379–463.

Zurcher, Louis A.; Kirkpatrick, R. George; Cushing, Robert G.; and Bowman, Charles K.
1971   The anti-pornography campaign: a symbolic crusade. *Social Problems* 19 (Fall):217–38.

Part Five: Some Types of Criminal Behavior (Chapters 18, 19, 20, and 21)

Albini, Joseph L.
1971   *The American Mafia: genesis of a legend.* New York: Appleton-Century-Crofts.

Amir, Menachem.
1967a   Patterns of forcible rape. In Marshall B. Clinard and Richard Quinney, eds., pp. 60–74.
1967b   Forcible rape. *Federal Probation* 31 (March):51–58.

Anderson, Robert T.
1967   From Mafia to Cosa Nostra. In Marshall B. Clinard and Richard Quinney, eds., pp. 419–27.

Arnold, David O., ed.
1970   *The sociology of subcultures.* Berkeley, Calif.: Glendessary Press.

Aubert, Wilhelm.
1952   White collar crime and social structure. *American Journal of Sociology* 58 (November):263–71.

Ball-Rokeach, Sandra J.
1973   Values and violence: a test of the subcultural violence thesis. *American Sociological Review* 38 (December):736–49.

Bandura, Albert.
1973   *Aggression: a social learning analysis.* Englewood Cliffs, N.J.: Prentice-Hall.

Bell, Daniel.
1962   Crime as an American way of life. In Marvin E. Wolfgang, Leonard Savitz, and Norman Johnson, eds., pp. 213–25.

Bernstein, Carl, and Woodward, Bob.
       1974   *All the president's men.* New York: Warner Paperback.

Bloch, Herbert A.
       1967   The gambling business: an American paradox. In Marshall B. Clinard
                     and Richard Quinney, eds., pp. 411–18.

Bloch, Herbert A., and Geis, Gilbert.
       1962   *Man, crime, and society.* New York: Random House.
       1970   *Man, crime, and society.* 2d ed. New York: Random House.

Blumenthal, Monica D.; Kahn, Robert L.; Andrews, Frank M.; and Head, Kendra B.
       1972   *Justifying violence: attitudes of American men.* Ann Arbor, Mich.: In-
                     stitute for Social Research.

Bohannan, Paul, ed.
       1960   *African homicide and suicide.* Princeton, N.J.: Princeton University
                     Press.

Burgess, E. W.
       1950   Comment on Hartung and concluding comment. *American Journal of
                     Sociology* 56 (July):33–34.

Caldwell, Robert G.
       1958   A re-examination of the concept of white collar crime. *Federal Proba-
                     tion* 22 (March):30–36.

Cameron, Mary Owen.
       1964   *The booster and the snitch: department store shoplifting.* Glencoe, Ill.:
                     Free Press.

Clinard, Marshall B.
       1952   *The black market.* New York: Holt, Rinehart, and Winston.

Clinard, Marshall B., and Quinney, Richard, eds.
       1967   *Criminal behavior systems: a typology.* New York: Holt, Rinehart, and
                     Winston.

Cloward, Richard H., and Ohlin, Lloyd E.
       1960   *Delinquency and opportunity.* Glencoe, Ill.: Free Press.

Cohen, Albert; Lindesmith, Alfred; and Schuessler, Karl, eds.
       1956   *The Sutherland papers.* Social Science Series No. 15. Bloomington, Ind.:
                     Indiana University Publications.

Conklin, John E.
1972   *Robbery and the criminal justice system.* Philadelphia: J. B. Lippincott.

Cressey, Donald.
1953   *Other people's money.* Glencoe, Ill.: Free Press.
1954   The differential association theory and compulsive crimes. *Journal of Criminal Law, Criminology, and Police Science* 45 (June):29–40.
1961   Foreword to 1961 edition of Edwin H. Sutherland, *White collar crime.* New York: Holt, Rinehart, and Winston.
1962   Role theory, differential association and compulsive crimes. In *Human behavior and social processes,* ed. Arnold Rose, pp. 447–67. Boston: Houghton Mifflin.
1969a   *Theft of the nation.* New York: Harper and Row.
1969b   Role theory, differential association, and compulsive crimes. In *Delinquency, crime and social process,* ed. Donald R. Cressey and David Ward, pp. 1114–28. New York: Harper and Row.
1972   *Criminal organization.* New York: Harper and Row, Harper Torchbooks.

Curvant, Bernard A., and Waldrop, Francis N.
1967   The murderer in the mental institution. In Marvin E. Wolfgang, ed., pp. 156–69.

Dershowitz, Allan M.
1968   Increasing community control over corporate crime. In Gilbert Geis, ed., pp. 136–54.

Doerner, William G.
1975   A regional analysis of homicide rates in the United States. *Criminology* 13 (May):90–101.

Einstadter, Werner J.
1969   The social organization of armed robbery. *Social Problems* 17 (Summer): 64–83.

Erlanger, Howard S.
1974   The empirical status of the subculture of violence thesis. *Social Problems* 22 (December):280–91.

Farberman, Harvey A.
1975   A criminogenic market structure: the automobile industry. *Sociology Quarterly* 16 (Autumn):438–57.

Fuller, Jon G.
1962   *The gentlemen conspirators.* New York: Grove Press.

Gardiner, John A.
1970   *The politics of corruption: organized crime in an American city.* New York: Russell Sage Foundation.

Gastil, Raymond D.
    1971   Homicide: and a regional culture of violence. *American Sociological Review* 36 (June):412–26.

Geis, Gilbert.
    1962   Toward a delineation of white collar offenses. *Sociological Inquiry* 32 (Spring):160–71.
    1966   Violence and organized crime. *Annals* 364 (March):86–95.
    1967   White collar crime: the heavy electrical equipment antitrust cases of 1961. In Marshall B. Clinard and Richard Quinney, eds., pp. 139–50.

Geis, Gilbert, ed.
    1968   *White-collar criminal.* New York: Atherton Press.

Gibbons, Don C.
    1965   *Changing the lawbreaker.* Englewood Cliffs, N.J.: Prentice-Hall.
    1968   *Society, crime, and criminal careers.* Englewood Cliffs, N.J.: Prentice-Hall.

Gold, Martin.
    1958   Suicide, homicide, and the socialization of aggression. *American Journal of Sociology* 43 (May):651–61.

Hall, Jerome.
    1952   *Theft law and society.* 2d ed. Indianapolis, Ind.: Bobbs-Merrill.

Hartung, Frank.
    1953   White collar crime: its significance for theory and practice. *Federal Probation* 17 (June):31–36.
    1965   *Crime, law, and society.* Detroit, Mich.: Wayne State University Press.

Homer, Frederic D.
    1974   *Guns and garlic: myths and realities of organized crime.* West Lafayette, Ind.: Purdue Research Foundation.

Horning, Donald.
    1970   Blue collar crime. In *Crimes against bureaucracy,* ed. Erwin O. Smigel and H. Laurence Ross, pp. 46–64. New York: Von Nostrand.

Ianni, Francis A. J.
    1975   *Black mafia: ethnic succession in organized crime.* New York: Pocket Books.

Inciardi, James A.
    1975   *Careers in crime.* Chicago: Rand McNally.

Jaspan, Norman.
  1960   *The thief in the white collar.* Philadelphia: J. B. Lippincott.

King, Harry (as told to and edited by Bill Chambliss).
  1972   *Box man: a professional thief's journey.* New York: Harper and Row, Harper Torchbooks.

Lane, Robert.
  1953   Why businessmen violate the law. *Journal of Criminal Law, Criminology, and Police Science* 44 (July):151–65.

Lemert, Edwin M.
  1953   An isolation and closure theory of naive check forgery. *Journal of Criminal Law, Criminology, and Police Science* 44 (September–October): 296–307.
  1958   The behavior of the systematic check forger. *Social Problems* 6 (Fall): 141–49.

Leonard, William N., and Weber, Marvin G.
  1970   Automakers and dealers: a study of criminogenic market forces. *Law and Society Review* 4 (February):407–24.

Letkemann, Peter.
  1973   *Crime as work.* Englewood Cliffs, N.J.: Prentice-Hall, Spectrum Books.

Maurer, David W.
  1962   *The big con.* Rev. ed. New York: Signet.
  1964   *Whiz mob: a correlation of the technical argot of pickpockets with their behavior pattern.* New Haven, Conn.: College and University Press.

Minor, W. William.
  1975   Political crime, political justice, and political prisoners. *Criminology* 12 (February):385–98.

Morris, Albert.
  1968   Criminals of the upperworld. In Gilbert Geis, ed., pp. 34–39. (Originally published in 1935.)

Morris, Norval, and Hawkins, Gordon.
  1970   *The honest politician's guide to crime control.* Chicago: University of Chicago Press.

Newman, Donald.
  1958   White collar crime. *Law and Contemporary Problems* 23:735–53.

New York Times.
    1974   *The end of a presidency.* New York: Bantam.

Pittman, David J., and Handy, William.
    1964   Patterns in criminal aggravated assault. *Journal of Criminal Law, Criminology, and Police Science* 55 (December):462–70.

Polsky, Ned.
    1967   *Hustlers, beats, and others.* Chicago: Aldine.

Presidential Transcripts.
    1974   *The presidential transcripts.* New York: Dell Books, in conjunction with the staff of the *Washington Post.*

President's Commission on Law Enforcement and Administration of Justice.
    1967   *Task force report: crime and its impact: an assessment.* Washington, D.C.: U.S. Government Printing Office.
    1968   *The challenge of crime in a free society.* New York: Avon.

Quinney, Earl R.
    1963   Occupational structure and criminal behavior: prescription violations by retail pharmacists. *Social Problems* 11 (Fall):179–85.
    1964   The study of white collar crime: toward a reorientation in theory and research. *Journal of Criminal Law, Criminology, and Police Science* 55 (June):208–14.

Quinney, Richard.
    1970   *The social reality of crime.* Boston: Little, Brown.

Reckless, Walter.
    1967   *The crime problem.* 4th ed. New York: Appleton-Century-Crofts.

Robin, Gerald D.
    1969   Employees as offenders. *Journal of Research in Crime and Delinquency* 6 (January):17–33.

Roebuck, Julian B., and Cadwallader, Mervyn L.
    1961   The Negro armed robber as a criminal type: the construction and application of a typology. *Pacific Sociological Review* 4 (Spring):21–26.

Ross, Edward H.
    1968   The criminaloid. In Gilbert Geis, ed., pp. 25–33. (Originally published in 1907.)

Schelling, Thomas C.
    1967   Economics and criminal enterprise. *Public Interest* 7 (Spring):61–78.

Sellin, Thorsten.
    1967   Organized crime: a business enterprise. In Marshall B. Clinard and Richard Quinney, eds., pp. 405–11.

Shover, Neal.
    1973   The social organization of burglary. *Social Problems* 20 (Spring):499–514.

Smith, Dwight C.
    1976   Mafia: the prototypical alien conspiracy. *Annals* 423 (January):75–88.

Smith, Richard A.
    1962   The incredible electrical conspiracy. In Marvin E. Wolfgang, Leonard Savitz, and Norman Johnson, eds., pp. 357–72.

Spencer, John C.
    1968   A study of incarcerated white-collar offenders. In Gilbert Geis, ed., pp. 335–46.

Spergel, Irving.
    1964   *Racketville, slumtown, and haulburg.* Chicago: University of Chicago Press.

Sutherland, Edwin H.
    1937   *The professional thief.* Chicago: University of Chicago Press.
    1940   White collar criminality. *American Sociological Review* 5 (February):1–12.
    1949   *White collar crime.* New York: Holt, Rinehart, and Winston.
    1956   White collar criminality. In Albert Cohen et al., eds., pp. 46–61.
    1973   *Edwin H. Sutherland on analyzing crime,* ed. Karl Schuessler. Chicago: University of Chicago Press.

Sutherland, Edwin H., and Cressey, Donald R.
    1974   *Criminology.* 9th ed. Philadelphia: J. B. Lippincott.

Tappan, Paul W.
    1947a   Crime and the criminal. *Federal Probation* 11 (1947):41–44.
    1947b   Who is the criminal? *American Sociological Review* 12 (February):96–102.
    1960   *Crime, justice and correction.* New York: McGraw-Hill.

Tyler, Gus, ed.
    1962   *Organized crime in America.* Ann Arbor, Mich.: University of Michigan Press.

Vold, George B.
    1958   *Theoretical criminology.* New York: Oxford University Press.

Voss, Harwin L., and Hepburn, John R.
    1968   Patterns in criminal homicide in Chicago. *Journal of Criminal Law,
                Criminology, and Police Science* 59 (December):499–508.

White, Theodore H.
    1975   *Breach of faith.* New York: Atheneum.

Williamson, Henry.
    1965   *Hustler.* New York: Doubleday.

Wolfgang, Marvin E.
    1957   Victim-precipitated criminal homicide. *Journal of Criminal Law,
                Criminology, and Police Science* 48 (May–June):1–11.
    1958   *Patterns in criminal homicide.* Philadelphia: University of Pennsylvania
                Press.
    1961   A sociological analysis of criminal homicide. *Federal Probation* 23
                (March):48–55.
    1967   Criminal homicide and the subculture of violence. In *Studies in
                homicide,* ed. Marvin E. Wolfgang, pp. 3–12. New York: Harper and
                Row.

Wolfgang, Marvin E., and Ferracuti, Franco.
    1967   *The subculture of violence.* London: Ravistock Publications.

Wolfgang, Marvin E.; Savitz, Leonard; and Johnson, Norman, eds.
    1962   *The sociology of crime and delinquency.* New York: Wiley.
    1970   *The sociology of crime and delinquency.* 2d ed. New York: Wiley.

---

*Part Six: Suicide
(Chapters 22, 23, and 24)*

Akers, Ronald L.
    1971   On the prevalence of persons who have attempted suicide in Los
                Angeles. *Bulletin of Suicidology* 8 (Fall):7–8.

Azrin, N. H.; Gottlieb, L.; Hughart, L.; Wesolowski, M. D.; and Rahn, T.
  1975   Eliminating self-injurious behavior by educative procedures. *Behavior Research and Therapy* 13:101–11.

Beall, Lynnette.
  1968   The dynamics of suicide: a review of the literature 1897–1965. *Bulletin of Suicidology* 5 (March):2–15.

Bijou, Sidney W.
  1965   Experimental studies of child behavior, normal and deviant. In *Research in behavior modifications*, ed. Leonard Krasner and Leonard Ullmann, pp. 56–81. New York: Holt, Rinehart, and Winston.

Blachly, P. A.; Disher, W.; and Roduner, G.
  1968   Suicide by physicians. *Bulletin of Suicidology* 5 (December):1–18.

Bohannan, Paul, ed.
  1960   *African homicide and suicide*. Princeton, N.J.: Princeton University Press.

Breed, Warren.
  1963   Occupational mobility and suicide among white males. *American Sociological Review* 28 (April):179–88.
  1967   Suicide and loss in social interaction. In Edwin S. Schneidman, ed., pp. 188–201.
  1970   The Negro and fatalistic suicide. *Pacific Sociological Review* 13 (Summer):156–62.

Cavan, Ruth S.
  1928   *Suicide*. Chicago: University of Chicago Press.

Chambliss, William J., and Steele, Marion F.
  1966   Status integration and suicide: an assessment. *American Sociological Review* 31 (August):524–32.

Douglas, Jack.
  1967   *The social meanings of suicide*. Princeton, N.J.: Princeton University Press.

Dublin, Louis.
  1963   *Suicide: a sociological and statistical study*. New York: Ronald Press.

Durkheim, Emile.
  1951   *Suicide: a study in sociology*. Trans. John A. Spaulding and George Simpson. Glencoe, Ill.: Free Press.

Fallers, L. A., and Fallers, M. C.
    1960   Homicide and suicide in Busoga. In Paul Bohannan, ed., pp. 65–93.

Farber, Maurice L.
    1968   *Theory of suicide.* New York: Funk and Wagnalls.

Farberow, Norman L., and Schneidman, Edwin S., eds.
    1961   *The cry for help.* New York: McGraw-Hill.

Gibbs, Jack P.
    1966   Suicide. In *Contemporary social problems,* ed. Robert K. Merton and
                Robert Nisbet, pp. 281–321. New York: Harcourt Brace Jovanovich.
    1969   Marital status and suicide in the United States: a special test of the
                status integration theory. *American Journal of Sociology* 74 (March):
                521–33.

Gibbs, Jack P., ed.
    1968   *Suicide.* New York: Harper and Row.

Gibbs, Jack P., and Martin, Walter T.
    1958   A theory of status integration and its relationship to suicide. *American
                Sociological Review* 23 (April):140–47.
    1964   *Status integration and suicide.* Eugene, Ore.: University of Oregon Press.
    1966   On assessing the theory of status integration and suicide. *American
                Sociological Review* 31 (August):533–41.
    1968   Communication to the editor: on status integration and suicide. *Social
                Problems* 15 (Spring):510–12.

Gold, Martin.
    1969   Suicide, homicide and the socialization of aggression. In *Deviant
                behavior and social process,* ed. William A. Rushing, pp. 241–50. Chi-
                cago: Rand McNally.

Hagedorn, Robert, and Labovitz, Sanford.
    1966   Note on status, integration and suicide. *Social Problems* 14 (Summer):
                79–84.

Hendin, Herbert.
    1964   *Suicide and Scandinavia.* Garden City, N.Y.: Doubleday.

Henry, Andrew F., and Short, James F.
    1954   *Suicide and homicide.* New York: Free Press.

Jacobs, Jerry.
    1967   Phenomenological study of suicide notes. *Social Problems* 15 (Summer):
                60–72.
    1971   *Adolescent suicide.* New York: Wiley-Interscience.

Johnson, Barclay D.
1965   Durkheim's one cause of suicide. *American Sociological Review* 30 (December):875–86.

Kalish, Richard.
1968   Suicide: an ethnic comparison in Hawaii. *Bulletin of Suicidology* 5 (December):37–43.

Kilpatrick, Elizabeth.
1968   A psychoanalytic understanding of suicide. In Jack P. Gibbs, ed., pp. 151–69.

Kobler, Arthur L., and Stotland, Ezra.
1964   *The end of hope.* New York: Free Press.

Labovitz, Sanford.
1968   Variation in suicide rates. In Jack P. Gibbs, ed., pp. 57–73.

La Fontaine, Jean.
1960   Homicide and suicide among the Gizu. In Paul Bohannan, ed., pp. 94–129.

Lester, Gene, and Lester, David.
1971   *Suicide: the gamble with death* Englewood Cliffs, N.J.: Prentice-Hall, Spectrum Books.

Lovaas, Ivar O., and Simmons, James Q.
1969   Manipulation of self-destruction in three retarded children. *Journal of Applied Behavior Analysis* 2 (Fall):143–57.

Lovaas, I. O.; Freitag, G.; Gold, Vivian; and Kassorla, Ilene.
1968   Experimental studies in childhood schizophrenia, I: analysis of self-destructive behavior. *Journal of Experimental Child Psychology* 2:67–84.

Maguire, Daniel C.
1975   *Death by choice.* New York: Schocken Books.

Maris, Ronald W.
1969a   *Social forces in urban suicide.* Homewood, Ill.: Dorsey Press.
1969b   The sociology of suicide prevention: policy implications of differences between suicidal patients and completed suicides. *Social Problems* 17 (Summer):132–49.

Martin, Walter T.
1968   Theories and research findings: theories of variation in the suicide rate. In Jack P. Gibbs, ed., p. 74.

Menninger, Karl.
    1938   *Man against himself.* New York: Harcourt Brace Jovanovich.

Mintz, Ronald S.
    1970   Prevalence of persons in the city of Los Angeles who have attempted
                suicide. *Bulletin of Suicidology* 7 (Fall):9–16.

Palmer, Stuart.
    1968   Murder and suicide in forty non-literate societies. In Jack P. Gibbs,
                ed., pp. 246–54.

Phillips, David P.
    1974   The influence of suggestion on suicide: substantive and theoretical
                implications of the Werther effect. *American Sociological Review* 39
                (June):340–54.

Pokorny, Alex D.
    1968   Human violence: a comparison of homicide, aggravated assault, sui-
                cide, and attempted suicide. In Jack P. Gibbs, ed., pp. 227–45.

Powell, Elwin H.
    1958   Occupation, status, and suicide: toward a redefinition of anomie.
                American Sociological Review 23 (April):131–39.

Quinney, Richard.
    1965   Suicide, homicide, and economic development. *Social Forces* 43
                (March):401–6.

Schaefer, Halmuth H.
    1967   Can a mouse commit suicide? In Edwin S. Schneidman, ed.

Schmid, Calvin F.
    1928   *Suicides in Seattle, 1914–1925.* Seattle, Wash.: University of Washington
                Publications in the Social Sciences.

Schmid, Calvin, and Van Arsdol, Maurice D.
    1955   Completed and attempted suicides: a comparative analysis. *American
                Sociological Review* 20 (June):273–83.

Schneidman, Edwin S., ed.
    1967   *Essays in self-destruction.* New York: Science House.

Schneidman, Edwin S., and Farberow, Norman L.
    1957   Clues to suicide. In N. Farberow and E. Schneidman, eds., pp. 3–10.
    1961   Statistical comparisons between attempted and committed suicides.
                In N. Farberow and E. Schneidman, eds., pp. 19–47.

Seiden, R. H.
    1967   Suicide capital? a study of the San Francisco suicide rate. *Bulletin of Suicidology* (December):1–10.

Simpson, George.
    1951   The etiology of suicide. Editor's introduction to Emile Durkheim, *Suicide*, pp. 13–31. Glencoe, Ill.: Free Press.

Stengel, Erwin.
    1964   *Suicide and attempted suicide.* London, Great Britain: C. Nicholls, Penguin Books.
    1967   The complexity of motivations to suicide attempts. *Bulletin of Suicidology* 4 (December):35–40.

Tanner, Barry A., and Zeiler, Marlene.
    1975   Punishment of self-injurious behavior using aromatic ammonia as the aversive stimulus. *Journal of Applied Behavior Analysis* 8 (Spring): 53–57.

Tate, B. G., and Baroff, G. S.
    1966   Aversive control of self-injurious behavior in a psychotic boy. *Behavior Research and Therapy* 4:281–87.

Teele, J. E.
    1965   Suicidal behavior, assaultiveness and socialization principles. *Social Forces* 43 (May):510–18.

West, D. J.
    1966   *Murder followed by suicide.* Cambridge, Mass.: Harvard University Press.

Wilkins, James.
    1967   Suicidal behavior. *American Sociological Review* 32 (April):286–98.

Wood, A. L.
    1961   A socio-structural analysis of murder, suicide and economic crime in Ceylon. *American Sociological Review* 26 (October):744–53.

Part Seven: Mental Illness
(Chapters 25, 26, and 27)

Adams, Henry.
    1969   "Mental illness" or interpersonal behavior? In Ohmer Milton and
                Robert G. Wahler, eds., pp. 44–56.

Atthowe, J., and Krasner, L.
    1968   Preliminary report on the application of contingent reinforcement
                procedures (token economy) on a chronic psychiatric ward. *Journal of
                Abnormal Psychology* 73:37–43.

Ausubel, David P.
    1961   Personality disorder is disease. *American Psychologist* 16 (January):
                69–74.

Ayllon, T., and Azrin, N.
    1965   The measurement and reinforcement of behavior of psychotics.
                Journal of the Experimental Analysis of Behavior 8 (November):357–83.
    1968   *The token economy: a motivational system for therapy and rehabilitation.*
                New York: Appleton-Century-Crofts.

Bandura, Albert.
    1965   Behavioral modification through modeling procedures. In Leonard
                Krasner and Leonard Ullmann, eds., pp. 310–40.
    1969   *Principles of behavior modification.* New York: Holt, Rinehart, and
                Winston.

Belknap, Ivan.
    1956   *Human problems of a state mental hospital.* New York: McGraw-Hill.

Brill, Norman Q., and Storrow, Hugh A.
    1964   Social class and psychiatric treatment. In *Mental health of the poor*, ed.
                Frank Riessman et al., pp. 68–74. New York: Free Press.

Cameron, Norman.
    1943   The paranoid pseudo-community. *American Journal of Sociology* 9
                (July):33–38.

Caudill, William.
    1958   *The psychiatric hospital as a small society.* Cambridge, Mass.: Harvard
                University Press.

Clausen, John A.
    1966   Mental disorders. In *Contemporary social problems*, 2d ed., ed. Robert
                K. Merton and Robert A. Nisbet, pp. 26–83. New York: Harcourt Brace
                Jovanovich.

Davis, James A.; Freeman, Howard E.; and Simmons, Ozzie G.
    1957   Rehospitalization and performance level among former mental pa-
                tients. *Social Problems* 5 (July):37–44.

Davis, Kingsley.
    1938   Mental hygiene and the class structure. *Psychiatry* 1 (February):55–65.

Dinitz, Simon; Lefton, Mark; Angrist, Shirley; and Pasamanick, Benjamin.
    1961   Psychiatric and social attributes as predictors of case outcome in
                mental hospitalization. *Social Problems* 8 (Spring):322–28.

Dunham, H. Warren.
    1965   *Community and schizophrenia: an epidemiological analysis*. Detroit,
                Mich.: Wayne State University Press.

Dunham, H. Warren, and Weinberg, S. Kirson.
    1960   *The culture of the state mental hospital*. Detroit, Mich.: Wayne State
                University Press.

Eysenck, H. J., ed.
    1960   *Behavior therapy and the neuroses*. Glasgow: Pergamon Press.
    1964   *Experiments in behavior therapy: readings in modern methods of treatment
                of mental disorders derived from learning theory*. New York: Macmillan,
                Pergamon Press.

Faris, Robert E. L., and Dunham, H. Warren.
    1939   *Mental disorders in urban areas*. Chicago: University of Chicago Press.

Fein, Sara, and Miller, Kent S.
    1972   Legal processes and adjudication in mental incompetency proceed-
                ings. *Social Problems* 20 (Summer):57–64.

Freeman, Howard E., and Simmons, Ozzie G.
    1959   Social class and posthospital performance levels. *American Sociological
                Review* 24 (June):345–51.

Goffman, Erving.
    1961   *Asylums*. Garden City, N.Y.: Doubleday.

Gove, Walter R.
  1970   Societal reaction as an explanation of mental illness: an evaluation. *American Sociological Review* 35 (October):873–84.
  1975a   The labelling theory of mental illness: a reply to Scheff. *American Sociological Review* 40 (April):242–48.
  1975b   Labelling and mental illness: a critique. In *The labelling of deviance: evaluating a perspective*, ed. Walter R. Gove, pp. 35–81. New York: Halsted Press.

Gove, Walter R., and Fain, Terry.
  1975   The length of psychiatric hospitalization. *Social Problems* 22 (February): 407–19.

Gove, Walter R., and Howell, Patrick.
  1974   Individual resources and mental hospitalization: a comparison and evaluation of the societal reaction and psychiatric perspectives. *American Sociological Review* 39 (February):86–100.

Greenly, James R.
  1972a   The psychiatric patient's family and length of hospitalization. *Journal of Health and Social Behavior* 13 (March):25–37.
  1972b   Alternative views of the psychiatrist's role. *Social Problems* 20 (Fall): 252–62.

Gursslin, Orville; Hunt, Raymond G.; and Roach, Jack L.
  1964   Social class and the mental health movement. In *Mental health of the poor*, ed. Frank Riessman et al., pp. 57–67. New York: Free Press.

Hardt, Robert H., and Feinhandler, Sherwin J.
  1959   Class and mental hospitalization prognosis. *American Sociological Review* 24 (December):815–21.

Hollingshead, August B., and Redlich, Frederick C.
  1958   *Social class and mental illness.* New York: Wiley.

Hollingshead, A. B.; Ellis, R. A.; and Kirby, E. C.
  1967   Social mobility and mental illness. In S. K. Weinberg, ed., pp. 48–53.

Jaco, E. Gartly.
  1960   *The social epidemiology of mental disorders.* New York: Russell Sage Foundation.

Kaplan, Bert; Reed, Robert B.; and Richardson, Wyman.
  1968   A comparison of the incidence of hospitalized and non-hospitalized cases of psychosis in two communities. In Stephan P. Spitzer and Norman K. Denzin, eds., pp. 111–21.

Kleiner, Robert J., and Parker, Seymour.
    1967   Goal-striving, social status, and mental disorders: a research review. In S. K. Weinberg, ed., pp. 55–66.

Krasner, Leonard, and Ullmann, Leonard, eds.
    1965   *Research in behavior modification.* New York: Holt, Rinehart, and Winston.

Laing, R. D., and Esterson, A.
    1967   The Abbotts. In Thomas J. Scheff, ed., pp. 130–48.

Langner, Thomas S., and Michael, Stanley T.
    1963   *Life stress and mental health.* New York: Free Press.

Lemert, Edwin M.
    1967   Paranoia and the dynamics of exclusion. In *Human deviance, social problems, and social control*, E. Lemert, pp. 197–211. Englewood Cliffs, N.J.: Prentice-Hall.

Levy, Leo, and Rowitz, Louis.
    1973   *The ecology of mental disorder.* New York: Behavioral Publications.

Lloyd, K. E., and Abel, L.
    1970   Performance on a token economy psychiatry ward: a two-year summary. *Behavior Research and Therapy* 8 (February):1–9.

Lu, Yi-Chuang.
    1967   Contradictory parental expectations in schizophrenia: dependence and responsibilities. In S. K. Weinberg, ed., pp. 91–102.

Lyman, Stanford M., and Scott, Marvin B.
    1970   *A sociology of the absurd.* New York: Appleton-Century-Crofts.

Maisel, Robert.
    1967   The ex-mental patient and rehospitalization: some research findings. *Social Problems* 15 (Summer):18–24.

Manis, Jerome G.
    1968   The sociology of knowledge and community mental health research. *Social Problems* 15 (Spring):488–501.

Mechanic, David.
    1967   Some factors in identifying and defining mental illness. In Thomas J. Scheff, ed., pp. 23–32.

Miller, Dorothy, and Schwartz, Michael.
    1966   County lunacy commission hearings: some observations of commit-
                ments to a state mental hospital. *Social Problems* 14 (Summer):26–35.

Miller, S. M., and Mishler, Elliot G.
    1964   Social class, mental illness, and American psychiatry: an expository
                review. In *Mental health of the poor*, ed. Frank Riessman et al., pp.
                16–36.

Milton, Ohmer, and Wahler, Robert G., eds.
    1969   *Behavior disorders: perspective and trends.* 2d ed. Philadelphia: J. B.
                Lippincott.

Mosher, Leon R.; Feinsilver, David; Katz, Martin M.; and Wienchowski, Louis A.
    1970   *Special report on schizophrenia.* Washington, D.C.: National Institute of
                Mental Health.

Murphy, H. B. M.; Wittkower, E. D.; Fried, J.; and Ellenberger, H.
    1968   A cross-cultural survey of schizophrenic symptomatology. In Stephan
                P. Spitzer and Norman K. Denzin, eds., pp. 164–77.

Nunnally, Jim C.
    1967   An overview of the public conception of mental health. In S. K. Wein-
                berg, ed., pp. 178–81.

Pasamanick, Benjamin; Roberts, Dean W.; Lemkau, Paul W.; and Krueger, Dean B.
    1964   A survey of mental disease in an urban population: prevalence by
                race and income. In *Mental health of the poor*, ed. Frank Riessman et al.,
                pp. 39–48.

Phillips, Derek L.
    1963   Rejection: a possible consequence of seeking help for mental disorders.
                American Sociological Review 28 (December):963–72.

Phillips, Derek L., and Segal, Bernard E.
    1969   Sexual status and psychiatric symptoms. *American Sociological Review*
                34 (February):58–72.

Rachman, Stanley, and Teasdale, John.
    1970   *Aversion therapy and behavior disorders: an analysis.* Coral Gables, Fla.:
                University of Miami Press.

Reyna, L. J.
    1964   Conditioning therapies, learning theory, and research. In Joseph
                Wolpe et al., eds., pp. 169–79.

Rinehart, James W.
  1968   Mobility aspiration-achievement discrepancies and mental illness. *Social Problems* 15 (Spring):478–88.

Roberts, Bertram H., and Myers, Jerome K.
  1968   Religion, national origin, immigration, and mental illness. In Stephan P. Spitzer and Norman K. Denzin, eds., pp. 139–47.

Rosenhan, D. L.
  1973   On being sane in insane places. *Science* 179 (January):250–58.

Rotter, Julian.
  1954   *Social learning and clinical psychology*. Englewood Cliffs, N.J.: Prentice-Hall.

Rushing, William A.
  1971   Individual resources, societal reaction, and hospital commitment. *American Journal of Sociology* 77 (November):511–26.

Rushing, William A., and Esco, Jack.
  1975   The status resource hypothesis and length of mental hospitalization. In *Deviant behavior and social process*, ed. William A. Rushing, pp. 445–55. Chicago: Rand McNally.

Sampson, Harold; Messinger, Sheldon L.; and Towne, Robert D.
  1968   Family processes and becoming a mental patient. In Stephan P. Spitzer and Norman K. Denzin, eds., pp. 203–13.

Scheff, Thomas J.
  1966   *Being mentally ill: a sociological theory*. Chicago: Aldine.
  1974   The labelling theory of mental illness. *American Sociology Review* 39 (June):444–52.
  1975   Reply to Chauncey and Gove. *American Sociological Review* 40 (April): 252–57.

Scheff, Thomas J., ed.
  1967   *Mental illness and social process*. New York: Harper and Row.

Silverstein, Harry, ed.
  1968   *The social control of mental illness*. New York: Crowell.

Spitzer, Stephan P., and Denzin, Norman K., eds.
  1968   *The mental patients: studies in the sociology of deviance*. New York: McGraw-Hill.

Srole, Leo, and Langner, Thomas.
    1967   Socioeconomic status groups: their mental health composition. In
            S. K. Weinberg, ed., pp. 33–47.

Srole, Leo; Langner, Thomas S.; Michael, Stanley T.; Opler, Marvin K.; and Rennie,
Thomas A. C.
    1968   Mental health in the metropolis. In Harry Silverstein, ed., pp. 68–123.

Steadman, Henry J.
    1972   The psychiatrist as a conservative agent of social control. *Social Prob-
            lems* 20 (Fall):263–71.

Szasz, Thomas S.
    1961   *The myth of mental illness.* New York: Hoeber-Harper.
    1967   The myth of mental illness. In Thomas J. Scheff, ed., pp. 242–54.

Taber, Merlin; Quay, Herbert C.; Mark, Harold; and Nealey, Vicki.
    1969   Disease ideology and mental health research. *Social Problems* 16
            (Winter):349–57.

Ullmann, Leonard.
    1967   *Institution and outcome: a comparative study of psychiatric hospitals.*
            New York: Pergamon Press.

Ullmann, Leonard P., and Krasner, Leonard.
    1969   *A psychological approach to abnormal behavior.* Englewood Cliffs, N.J.:
            Prentice-Hall.

Ullmann, Leonard P., and Krasner, Leonard, eds.
    1965   *Case studies in behavior modification.* New York: Holt, Rinehart, and
            Winston.

Wanklin, J. M.; Fleming, D. F.; Buck, C. S.; and Hobbs, G. E.
    1968   Factors influencing the rate of first admission to mental hospital. In
            Stephan P. Spitzer and Norman K. Denzin, eds., pp. 121–39.

Weinberg, S. K., ed.
    1967a   *The sociology of mental disorders: analyses and readings in psychiatric
            sociology.* Chicago: Aldine.

Weinberg, S. K.
    1967b   Psychiatric sociology: the sociology of mental disorders. In S. K.
            Weinberg, ed., pp. 3–7.

Wolpe, Joseph.
    1964   The comparative clinical status of conditioning therapies and psychoanalysis. In Joseph Wolpe et al., eds., pp. 5–15.

Wolpe, Joseph A.; Salter, Andrew; and Reyna, L. J., eds.
    1964   *The conditioning therapies.* New York: Holt, Rinehart, and Winston.

Wyatt, Richard J.; Termini, Benedict A.; and Davis, John.
    1971   Biochemical and sleep studies of schizophrenia: a review of the literature — 1960–1970. Part 1: biochemical studies. *Schizophrenia Bulletin* 4 (Fall): 10–44.

Yarrow, Marian K.; Schwartz, Charlotte G.; Murphy, Harriet S.; and Deasy, Leila C.
    1968   The psychological meaning of mental illness in the family. In *Deviance*, ed. Rubington and Weinberg, pp. 31–41. New York: Macmillan.

Zinberg, Norman.
    1970   The mirage of mental health. *British Journal of Sociology* 21 (September): 262–72.

Author Index

Subject Index